T0235368

Communications in Computer and Information Science 518

Commenced Publication in 2007
Founding and Former Series Editors:
Alfredo Cuzzocrea, Dominik Ślęzak, and Xiaokang Yang

More information about this series at http://www.springer.com/series/7899

Pavel Klinov · Dmitry Mouromtsev (Eds.)

Knowledge Engineering and Semantic Web

6th International Conference, KESW 2015
Moscow, Russia, September 30 – October 2, 2015
Proceedings

 Springer

Editors
Pavel Klinov
Complexible Inc.
Washington, DC
USA

Dmitry Mouromtsev
ITMO University
St. Petersburg
Russia

ISSN 1865-0929   ISSN 1865-0937 (electronic)
Communications in Computer and Information Science
ISBN 978-3-319-24542-3   ISBN 978-3-319-24543-0 (eBook)
DOI 10.1007/978-3-319-24543-0

Library of Congress Control Number: 2015949463

Springer Cham Heidelberg New York Dordrecht London

Printed on acid-free paper

Springer International Publishing AG Switzerland is part of Springer Science+Business Media
(www.springer.com)

Preface

These proceedings contain the papers accepted for full oral presentation at the 6th International Conference on Knowledge Engineering and Semantic Web (KESW 2015). The conference was held in Moscow, Russia, on September 30 – October 2, 2015.

The principal mission of the KESW conference series is to provide a discussion forum for the community of researchers currently underrepresented at the major International Semantic Web Conference (ISWC) and Extended Semantic Web Conference (ESWC). This mostly includes researchers from Eastern and Northern Europe, Russia, and former Soviet republics.

As in previous years, KESW 2015 aimed at helping the community to get used to the common international standards for academic conferences in computer science. To this end, KESW featured a peer reviewing process in which every paper was reviewed in a rigorous but constructive way by at least three members of the Program Committee. As before, the PC was very international, representing a range of EU countries, the USA, the Ukraine, and Russia.

The strict reviewing policies resulted in the acceptance of only 17 full research papers for publication in these proceedings. Additionally, we accepted 6 system description papers, which discuss practical issues of using and implementing technologies relevant to the Semantic Web. The overall acceptance rate is 58%. The authors represent several EU countries, among which Germany is the top contributor, and various parts of Russia.

KESW 2015 continued the tradition of inviting established researchers for keynote presentations. We are grateful to Yuliya Tikhokhod (Yandex, Russia), Erik Wilde (Siemens Berkeley, USA), and Markus Stocker (University of Eastern Finland, Finland) for their insightful talks. The program also included posters and position paper presentations to help attendees, especially younger researchers, discuss preliminary ideas and promising PhD topics. In addition, this year we introduced a special session on Open Data and Open Science for discussing general issues of availability of research data sets and reproducibility of research results.

Finally, we must acknowledge all the people who helped KESW 2015 take place. Besides the hardworking PC, these include Irina Radchenko and Maxim Kolchin (both ITMO University), Natalya Smelkova (RVC), and Yulia Krasilnikova (MISA University). We are also extremely grateful to the St. Petersburg State University of Information Technologies, Mechanics and Optics (ITMO) for their continuing support, the Moscow Institute of Steel and Alloys University (MISA) for providing the venue, and STI International for their sponsorship.

July 2015

Pavel Klinov
Dmitry Mouromtsev

Organization

Organizing Committee

General Chair
Dmitry Mouromtsev   ITMO University, Russia

Program Chair
Pavel Klinov   Complexible Inc., USA

Open Science and Education Chair
Irina Radchenko   ITMO University, Russia

Publicity Chair
Maxim Kolchin   ITMO University, Russia

Local Organizers
Yulia Krasilnikova   Moscow Institute of Steel and Alloys, Russia

Program Committee

Alessandro Adamou	Knowledge Media Institute, The Open University, UK
Sören Auer	University of Bonn and Fraunhofer IAIS, Germany
Samantha Bail	Flatiron Health, USA
Long Cheng	Technical University of Dresden, Germany
Chiara Del Vescovo	British Broadcasting Corporation, UK
Elena Demidova	L3S Research Center, Germany
Ivan Ermilov	University of Leipzig, Germany
Courtney Falk	Purdue University, USA
Ujwal Gadiraju	L3S Research Center, Germany
Martin Homola	Comenius University, Bratislava, Slovakia
Matthew Horridge	Stanford University, USA
Konrad Höffner	University of Leipzig, Germany
Dmitry Ignatov	National Research University Higher School of Economics, Russia
Vladimir Ivanov	Kazan Federal University, Russia
Valentina Ivanova	Linköping University, Sweden
Natalya Keberle	Zaporizhzhya National University, Ukraine
Evgeny Kharlamov	University of Oxford, UK
Jakub Klimek	Czech Technical University in Prague, Czech Republic

Pavel Klinov	University of Ulm, Germany
Boris Konev	University of Liverpool, UK
Roman Kontchakov	Birkbeck College, University of London, UK
Liubov Kovriguina	SPbNRU ITMO, Russia
Dmitry Kudryavtsev	St. Petersburg State University, and St. Petersburg State Polytechnic University, Russia
Yue Ma	LRI-CNRS, Université Paris Sud, France
Nicolas Matentzoglu	University of Manchester, UK
Dmitry Mouromtsev	SPbNRU ITMO, Russia
Elena Mozzherina	Saint Petersburg State University, Russia
Rafael Peñaloza	Free University of Bozen-Bolzano, Italy
Denis Ponomaryov	Institute of Informatics Systems, Russian Academy of Sciences, Russia
Svetlana Popova	St. Petersburg State University, and St. Petersburg State Polytechnic University, Russia
Héctor Pérez-Urbina	Google, USA
Irina Radchenko	SPbNRU ITMO, Russia
Mariano Rodriguez Muro	IBM Research, USA
Yuliya Rubtsova	Institute of Informatics Systems, Russian Academy of Sciences, Russia
Marvin Schiller	University of Ulm, Germany
Daria Stepanova	Technical University of Vienna, Austria
Lauren Stuart	Purdue University, USA
Anna Szkudlarek	Grenoble Graduate School of Business, France
Darya Tarasowa	University of Bonn, Germany
Julia Taylor	Purdue University, USA
Ioan Toma	STI Innsbruck, Austria
Trung-Kien Tran	University of Ulm, Germany
Dmitry Tsarkov	University of Manchester, UK
Jörg Unbehauen	University of Leipzig, Germany
Dmitry Ustalov	N.N. Krasovskii Institute of Mathematics and Mechanics, Ural Branch of the RAS, Russia
Amrapali Zaveri	University of Leipzig, Germany
Dmitriy Zheleznyakov	University of Oxford, UK
Nikita Zhiltsov	Kazan Federal University and Textocat, Russia

Additional Reviewers

Fayzrakhmanov, Ruslan	Saleem, Muhammad
Galkin, Mikhail	Savenkov, Vadim
Gossen, Gerhard	Shekarpour, Saeedeh
Kirillovich, Alexander	Thost, Veronika
Marx, Edgard	

Sponsors

ITMO University   STI Innsbruck

Contents

Research Track Papers

Subtopic Segmentation of Scientific Texts: Parameter Optimisation 3
Natalia Avdeeva, Galina Artemova, Kirill Boyarsky, Natalia Gusarova,
Natalia Dobrenko, and Eugeny Kanevsky

UIMA2LOD: Integrating UIMA Text Annotations into the Linked Open
Data Cloud. 16
Claudia Bretschneider, Heiner Oberkampf, and Sonja Zillner

An Advanced Query and Result Rewriting Mechanism for Information
Retrieval Purposes from RDF Datasources 32
Efthymios Chondrogiannis, Vassiliki Andronikou,
Efstathios Karanastasis, and Theodora Varvarigou

Identifying Web Tables: Supporting a Neglected Type of Content
on the Web 48
Mikhail Galkin, Dmitry Mouromtsev, and Sören Auer

Feature Selection for Language Independent Text Forum Summarization 63
Vladislav A. Grozin, Natalia F. Gusarova, and Natalia V. Dobrenko

A Provenance Assisted Roadmap for Life Sciences Linked Open Data
Cloud 72
Ali Hasnain, Qaiser Mehmood, Syeda Sana e Zainab, and Stefan Decker

Scholarly Communication in a Semantically Enrichable Research
Information System with Embedded Taxonomy of Scientific Relationships. . . 87
M.R. Kogalovsky and S.I. Parinov

Ontologies for Web of Things: A Pragmatic Review 102
Maxim Kolchin, Nikolay Klimov, Alexey Andreev, Ivan Shilin,
Daniil Garayzuev, Dmitry Mouromtsev, and Danil Zakoldaev

Ontology-Based Approach and Implementation of ADAS System
for Mobile Device Use While Driving 117
Igor Lashkov, Alexander Smirnov, Alexey Kashevnik,
and Vladimir Parfenov

Object-UOBM: An Ontological Benchmark for Object-Oriented Access 132
Martin Ledvinka and Petr Křemen

Semantically Enrichable Research Information System SocioNet   147
Sergey Parinov, Victor Lyapunov, Roman Puzyrev,
and Mikhail Kogalovsky

Aspect Extraction from Reviews Using Conditional Random Fields   158
Yuliya Rubtsova and Sergey Koshelnikov

A Low Effort Approach to Quantitative Content Analysis   168
Maria Saburova and Archil Maysuradze

Semantic Clustering of Website Based on its Hypertext Structure   182
Vladimir Salin, Maria Slastihina, Ivan Ermilov, René Speck, Sören Auer,
and Sergey Papshev

Interactive Coding of Responses to Open-Ended Questions in Russian   195
Nikita Senderovich and Archil Maysuradze

Measuring the Quality of Relational-to-RDF Mappings   210
Darya Tarasowa, Christoph Lange, and Sören Auer

Pattern Mining and Machine Learning for Demographic Sequences   225
Dmitry I. Ignatov, Ekaterina Mitrofanova, Anna Muratova,
and Danil Gizdatullin

System Description Papers

Extracting Metadata from Multimedia Content on Facebook as Media
Annotations   243
Miguel B. Alves, Carlos Viegas Damásio, and Nuno Correia

SPARQL Commands in Jena Rules   253
M.B. Alves, C.V. Damásio, and N. Correia

Gathering Photos from Social Networks Using Semantic Technologies   263
M.B. Alves, C.V. Damásio, and N. Correia

Ontology-Based Approach to Scheduling of Jobs Processed by
Applications Running in Virtual Environments   273
Maksim Khegai, Dmitrii Zubok, and Alexandr Maiatin

Aigents: Adaptive Personal Agents for Social Intelligence   283
Anton Kolonin

Distributed Knowledge Engineering and Evidence-Based Knowledge
Representation in Multi-agent Systems   291
Anton Kolonin

Author Index   301

Research Track Papers

Subtopic Segmentation of Scientific Texts: Parameter Optimisation

Natalia Avdeeva[1], Galina Artemova[2], Kirill Boyarsky[2], Natalia Gusarova[2(✉)],
Natalia Dobrenko[2], and Eugeny Kanevsky[1]

[1] Saint Petersburg Institute for Economics and Mathematics,
Russian Academy of Sciences, Saint Petersburg, Russia
[2] Saint Petersburg National Research University of Information Technologies,
Mechanics and Optics (ITMO University), Saint Petersburg, Russia
natfed@list.ru

Abstract. Information research within a scientific text needs to deal
with the problem of automatic document partition on subtopics by taking text specifics and user purposes into account. This task is important
for primary source selection, for working with texts in foreign languages
or for getting acquainted with research problems. This paper is focused
on the application of subtopic segmentation algorithms to real-life scientific texts. For studying this we use monographs on the same subject
written in three languages. The corpus includes several original and pro-
fessionally trasnlated fragments. The research is based on the TextTiling
algorithm that analyses how tightly adjoining parts of the text cohere.
We examine how some parameters (the cutoff rate, the size of moving window and of the shift from one block to the next one) influence
the segmentation quality and define the optimal combinations of these
parameters for several languages. The studies on Russian suggest that
external lexical resources notably improve the segmentation quality.

Keywords: Text tiling · Classification · Parsing · Segmentation

1 Introduction

The coverage of relevant information sources substantially predetermines the
efficiency in research work, particularly in data intensive fields. The sources in
general include scientific texts, such as monographs, textbooks, scientific articles
etc. As a rule, all of them are large information-rich documents in the original
with a typical structure [17, 19].

All over the world, the scientists take measures to share primary scientific
sources via the Internet. However, the efficiency of the information retrieval in
this corpus is still of poor quality. Their structures cannot always be presented by
search attributes, which are traditional for the Web (meta tags, keywords etc.).
As a result, a user can get either a full document where he has to find information
manually by himself or a detached extract with the greatest keyword frequency
rate. In the latter case, it is hard to form a clear picture of a document topic.

© Springer International Publishing Switzerland 2015
P. Klinov and D. Mouromtsev (Eds.): KESW 2015, CCIS 518, pp. 3–15, 2015.
DOI: 10.1007/978-3-319-24543-0_1

Thus, it is necessary to organize information research within a scientific text. It needs in turn to solve a problem of automation document partition on subtopics taking into account text specifics and the purposes of the users. This task is important for primary source selection, for working with texts in foreign languages or for quick acquaintance with research problems.

Many approaches to topic segmentation of the text have already been described. You can see their brief review in Sec. 2. As a rule, they are quite effective with composed texts like concatenated separate sentences or short reports from newspapers or Internet sources ([3,5,10]) or with large text corpora ([4,8,23]). Meanwhile, results of applying these methods to real scientific texts are rather scantly and contradictory ([5,10,12]).

This paper is focused on application of topic segmentation algorithms to real scientific texts. For studying this we used monographs on the same subject written in three languages. The experimental set includes several fragments both in the original language and in professional translation. During our research, we varied lexical units for analysis, the cutoff rate, the size of moving window and of the shift from one block to the next one. We examined how these parameters, text language, inclusion/exclusion of external lexical resources (classifiers, stoplists etc.) influence the quality of segmentation.

2   Related Work

Almost all topic segmentation methods are based on text cohesion. According to work [25], the most dominated types of subtopic cohesion are lexical (repetition, synonymy and reference) and grammatical types (parallelism):

1. repetition is a usage of the same terms in adjacent sentences of the same subtopic;
2. synonymy refers to the doublets (terms that are close in meaning);
3. reference is the use of an expression (pronoun or a demonstrative pronoun) the meaning of which depends on the previous or next expression;
4. parallelism appears in revealing the thesis by sentences with parallel structure and the same form of their predicates.

Most of the existing methods are based on examining repetition. These methods can be divided in two groups. The ones of the first group use data of cohesion between adjacent parts. One of the most well-known techniques is TextTiling [12,13], that includes the following steps:

(a) text is lemmatized and stop words are removed. Hence the text is regarded as a sequence of N tokens;
(b) sequences of W tokens combine in pseudosentences. The k pseudosentences join in blocks, which then are used as sliding window with the step of s pseudosentences. In a standard technique $s = 1$. Hence, firstly a group of tokens from 0 to $(W \times k)$ is compared with the ones of tokens from W to $W \times (k+1)$. Then the latter group is compared with the ones of tokens from $(W \times 2)$ to $(W \times (k + 2))$. It repeats until the second border is reached.

(c) lexical similarity of adjoining blocks is computed as the cosine of angle φ between $(W \times k)$-dimensional vectors:

$$\cos \varphi_i = \frac{\sum_n w_{n,i-1} w_{n,i}}{\sqrt{\sum_n w_{n,i-1}^2} \sqrt{\sum_n w_{n,i}^2}}, \qquad 0 \leq \cos \varphi \leq 1 \qquad (1)$$

where $w_{n,i}$ is a weight of nth token in i^{th} block.

(d) local minima of (1) are regarded as the boundaries of the segments (rounded to the nearest sentence or paragraph).

The methods of the second group analyse the distribution of tokens repeated throughout the text. Thus, DotPlotting technique [22] examines text cohesion with the use of two-dimensional graph (named dotplot). The positions of tokens in the text are plotted on its X and Y. If a particular token appears in the positions x and y of the text then dots $(x, x), (y, y), (x, y)$ and (y, x) are plotted in the graph. At that, cohesive text segments visually correlate to squares with a high dot density along the diagonal. The resulting distribution is examined for extrema with the help of one of following strategies. You can either minimize dot density on the boundaries or maximize it within the segment. This idea was developed into C99 technique [4]. There the measure of lexical cohesion between tokens of adjacent segments is visualized in the same way and then maximum density areas of this measure are found by means of the dynamic programming.

A number of modifications to the standard techniques (see [5,7,9,15,20]) allows to analyze other types of cohesion besides repetition. For example, a type 2 can be found with the help of external vocabularies (WordNet) or by modifying the cosine measure with a coefficient reflecting word frequency in external document set (Internet) [5]. It is offered to combine the DotPlotting measures of lexical cohesion within the segment and between two segments to take type 4 into account [30].

Hence, now we can list obstacles to implementing discussed techniques into real search engines. First, most of these methods are developed for the English language. Topic segmentation task is less studied for other language groups [3,29]. Secondly, there are no open profound dictionaries of synonyms or other net resources for many languages including Russian. Thirdly, the efficiency of all these methods strongly depends on text cohesion argument, which is initially unknown.

The methods of text hierarchical segmentation have been developed in recent years [8,16,23]. Most of them are based on word cohesion model presented as a multidimensional word distribution by topics. At that, the occurrence of every word connects with one of several topics that are discussed in the text. The mathematical foundation of this approach is Latent Dirichlet Allocation (LDA) [1] widely used in the machine learning. For example, [8] presents a hierarchical Bayes algorithm revealing two levels of linear text segmentation. TopicTiling [23] as TextTiling is based on cosine cohesion measure of two adjacent segments.

However, it uses frequency of topic identifiers calculated for every word by LDA instead of word frequency.

The larger training set and the closer its statistical distributions to the text, the higher effectiveness these approaches show. Ideally, both training set and the analyzed text should be of the same domain [23]. It is hard to reach it while processing real scientific text: its value depends mainly on its uniqueness.

Here we examined which segmentation parameters are important for the purpose of developing topic segmentation of scientific texts. Our key method combines a linear segmentation and cosine cohesion measure between two segments.

3 Experiments

3.1 Text Selection and Pre-Processing

Texts were extracted from monographs on the same technical topics written in three languages (Russian, English and French). See Table 1 for details of sources.

Table 1. Features of text sources

Source label	Source bibliographical entry	Source language	Fragment's size (in printed chars)
1. Romme	Romme N. Ch. :L' Art de la Marine, u Principes t Préceptes Generaux d l'Art de Construire, d'Armer , de Manuvrer et de Conduire ds Vasseaux, par . Re/ ed. : P.-L. Chauvet. La Rochelle, 1787. Chapitres VII, VIII.	French	110261
2.Romme Rus	Romm N. Ch.: The Navy Art, or Principles and Basic Rules of the Shipbuilding, Equipment and Ship Handling by Romm/ A. Shishkov. Saint-Petersburg, 1793. (in Russian) Chapters 7, 8.	Russian	161152
3. U-boat	Williamson G., Johnson L.: U-Boat crew 1914-45/, ed. Osprey Publishing, Great Britain, 1995.	English	60563
4.U-boat Rus	Williamson G.: German Submarine Fleet. 19141945 / M.A. Maltseva, AST, Moscow, Russia, 2003. (in Russian)	Russian	60560
5. News	Concatenated news sources (the Internet)	Russian	23800

The corpus includes several fragments both in the original (lines 1, 3) and in professional translation (lines 2, 4). This approach solves a domain identification problem and allows studying language features of segmentation in pure form. Part-of-speech tagging of English and French texts was fulfilled by the means of net service OpenXerox[1]. The Russian texts were tagged using parser SemSin [14].

---

[1] Xeros Linguistic Tools: Part of Speech Tagging: http://xerox.bz/1HYXX1Q

Stop-lists for every text were formed manually with the help of frequency analysis. Besides we compiled 20 pieces of political news extracted from the Web in a random way (line 5 in Table 1). Sometimes we used a classifier [28] described in Sec. 4.5. See the methods of text pre-processing in Table 2.

Table 2. Pre-processing types

Abbreviation	Description
L	lemmatization
L+SL	lemmatization + stop words removing
L+N	lemmatization + POS tagging + noun selection
L+N+Adj+V	lemmatization + POS tagging + noun, adjective and verb selection
L+POS+Class	lemmatization + POS tagging + the use of external classifier [28]

3.2 Text Processing Method

We applied TestTiling as a basic processing technique because it allows to analyse cohesion of the texts and cosine similarity transparently. See above the processing steps and parameters abbreviation (p. 2). The next parameters were varied during the research: size of blocks [tokens] $W \times k$; overlapping size between blocks [tokens] $s \times k$. Besides, in some experiments we worked with blocks of variable length, which is equal to the paragraph length.

3.3 Segmentation Evaluation Metrics

A range of metrics (including precision-recall ratio [13], edit distance [21], $P\mu$ and Pk measure [6], WindowDiff) is proposed to estimate the quality of text segmentation. Each of them has specific limitations.

For example, WindowDiff compares the positions of segment boundaries, which were set according to the baseline, and of ones, determined by the algorithm, within a sliding window. Then the number of windows that were set as boundaries by mistake is normalized to a total number of windows. However, the subsequent studies [11,18,24] revealed limits of WindowDiff metrics. It equally evaluates false (false positive, FP) and missed (false negative, FN) boundaries, which should have different importance depending on the specific segmentation task. Besides, Window Diff ignores the rate of missed boundaries and emphasizes mistakes at the beginning and end of the text. Thus, modifications of Window Diff were proposed [24].

Here we used balanced F-score [2] to estimate the segmentations quality:

$$F = \frac{2 \times P \times R}{P + R} \qquad (2)$$

where $P = \frac{TP}{H}$ is precision, $R = \frac{TP}{TP+FN}$ means recall, FP means a number of false boundaries, FN a number of missed boundaries and H a total number of found boundaries.

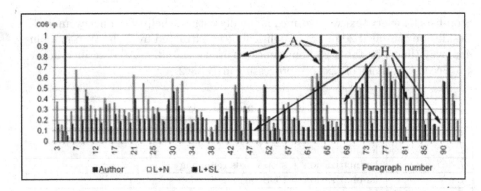

Fig. 1. Author segmentation (A) and automatically detected segment boundaries (H) of two pre-processing types for Romme

We used topic shift boundaries set by the author (A) as baselines (see Fig.1).

Selection of segmentation parameters carried out as follows. The cosine measure (1) was analyzed according to the cutoff rate z, which is on the ordinate axis (Fig. 1). The values of $\cos\varphi$ less than or equal to z, were considered as topic shift, i.e. a boundary between segments (H). Then the sequences A and H were compared. The local minima (valleys) for the same or adjacent segments of these sequences were labeled as true matching (TP). Such rounding is reasonable because, as shown by a detailed analysis, often in the first paragraph of a new topic the author tries to gradually change the subject, and in fact, the transition occurs only in the following paragraph. The other valleys H were marked as false ones (FP) while valleys A were labeled as missed ones. So our task was to determine the optimal cutoff rate z, on which we can easy divide a text into segments. To find the best value of F-score the cutoff rate z ranged from 0 to 1 with step of 0.05.

Note that the above metrics evaluate the segmentation quality only post factum and do not allow to fine-tune the parameters of the segmentation algorithm, while different tasks require different precision and recall ratio, which is especially important for scientific texts. This was one more reason for using F-score (2). It can be regarded as the optimization criterion with its maximum as the best P and R ratio. Moreover, it can be easily adjusted to the users needs by weighting P and R components.

4   Experimental Results and Discussion

4.1   The Influence of the Size of Overlaps Between Blocks

In standard TextTiling scheme [12] it is recommended to choose a sliding window of the size ($W \times k$) tokens, where k is a number of pseudosentences with the size of W tokens, and overlapping blocks $s = \frac{W \times k}{2}$. But according to our experiments on combining different values of s, W and k, any overlap lowers contrast range and valleys that indicate semantic boundaries practically disappear.

A typical example is shown in Fig. 2. On the plot the result of analyzing texts without overlaps is represented by the curve a. Due to the wide data spread there, semantic boundaries can be defined automatically. On the contrary, the curve b is to smooth to find the boundaries as it shows the result of analyzing texts with overlaps. Note that this result agrees with the conclusion reached in the pilot study [5]. Thus, we did not use overlaps in our researches.

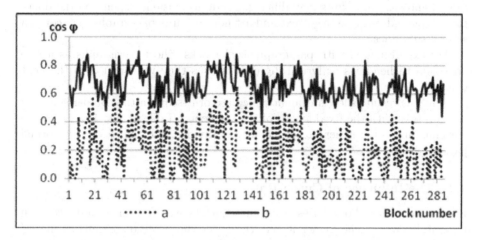

Fig. 2. Cosine measure for U-boat text with $L+N$ pre-processing type: the curve a: $(W \times k) = 10, s = 0$; the curve b: $(W \times k) = 20, s = \frac{W \times k}{2}$.

4.2 The Influence of Block Size

As noted above, the basic algorithm TextTiling [12,13] uses windows of fixed length as the analysis unit, while a resulting boundary position is extended to the nearest sentence or paragraph. Our experiments have shown that in this case the analysis quality does not meet the requirements of actual scientific text (see Table 3). In the case of short window size (10 nouns), word random changes lead to a large number of "false alarms" reducing the precision. However the larger a window size is (e.g. 40 nouns) the higher the probability is that the window overlaps a real boundary, resulting to recall decrease. See sample results for "U-boat" with $L+N$ pre-processing type in Table 3, var. 1-3.

Table 3. The influence of blocks size

Variants	1	2	3	4
Size of blocks [tokens]	10	25	40	paragraph
F-score	0.06	0.04	0.03	0.17

In our work, we examined the assumption that semantic borders should be placed at the boundaries of paragraphs. It should be noted that contradictory opinions on this matter could be found in the literature. For example, [27] suggests that: "...we can say that a paragraph in the scientific text is independent, graphically highlighted text unit containing a particular idea or its fragment". On the other hand, according to [26], the text division by formal components (paragraphs or sections) does not allow to identify subtopics. The boundaries of formal and semantic units may differ; paragraph divisions depend on the document type and purpose (e.g., text and art news). Large paragraphs may contain several subtopics.

We experimented with paragraph-sized blocks. Short paragraphs as a rule are equal to headings or lyrical digressions thus they were joined to the next one.

Analysis results show a dramatic increase of F-score in the comparison with ones on text with the fixed length of the segments (Table 3, var. 4).

Thus in our further experiments we divided all the texts by formal paragraphs.

4.3   The Influence of Cutoff Rate

In our researches, boundaries between segments were set in accordance with the cutoff rate z. The higher it gets the lower the precision P falls as missed boundaries appear; meanwhile the recall R increases as more and more true boundaries can be discovered. Thus, our task is to set the optimum cutoff rate in respect to F-score (Fig. 2). According to our experiments, the optimum cutoff rate z depends on the pre-processing type. Maximum F-score is achieved at $z = 0.1 \ldots 0.15$ for all types except $L+POS+Class$ pre-processing (Table 2). In the latter case examined in Section 4.5 F-score gets its maximum at higher cutoff rate (Fig. 3).

We examined if pre-processing type correlates with the source language. The preprocessing type is obviously determines what words should be selected to analyse texts on different languages. Thus, it may depend on type of cohesion. In particular, we can find repetitions reference in $L+S$ and $L+SL$ (excluding the most frequent words). $L+N+Adj+V$, where the stop list was formed only from function words, indicates both repetitions and parallelism.

In given texts we excluded both standard stop words and the most frequent informative words: boat (лодка) and Germany (Германия) in Russian texts, U-boat, jacket, war (in English ones), voile (sail), poulie (block), mat (mast), fig (Figure), vergue (yard) in French texts.

See how different pre-processing types change the maximum F-scores for given texts in Table 4.

We can easily explain these results using charts of cosine cohesion measurements between adjoining paragraphs in "Romme" (Fig. 1).

Full vertical line graphs indicate the text division into subsections according to headings (author segmentation). According to the chart, the cosine measure is lower when stop words are excluded. Nevertheless, the "valleys" are on the

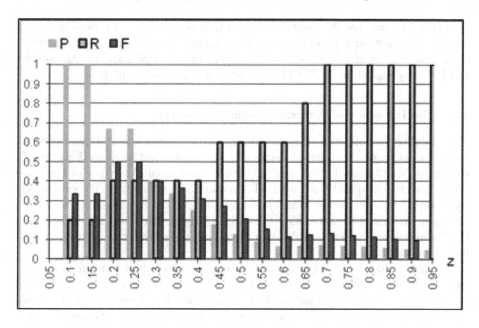

Fig. 3. The dependence of P, R and F-score on the cutoff rate z.

Table 4. F-scores for different pre-processing types

Source	F-score		
	$L+N+Adj+V$	$L+N$	$L+SL$
"U-boat Rus"	0.19	0.21	0.11
"U-boat"	0.24	0.17	0.19
"Romme"	0.46		0.53

same place. Thus, the segmentation quality does not change much. Compare the best F-scores for all nouns, including and excluding stop words: 0.46 at $z = 0.15$ and 0.53 at $z = 0.1$ correspondingly.

Thus, it is preferable to apply $L+N$ type to Russian texts. In English texts, analysis of adjectives and verbs considerably improves the segmentation quality. In French texts analysis without stop words improves it a little.

See maximum F-scores of texts analyzed by words" (i.e. for all pre-processing options except $L+POS+Class$) at optimum cutoff rate in Table 5. Note that these values correlate with the ones in studies [3], [5].

Table 5. Maximum F-scores

Source	U-boat Rus	U-boat	Romme Rus	Romme	News
F-score	0.21	0.17	0.22	0.46	0.60

Table 5 shows that in scientific texts author segmentation on headings and subtitles does not correspond to vocabulary changes. The analyzer poorly detects them. The text is of a low contrast in respect to its vocabulary. On the other hand, the segmentation quality of news texts is considerably higher.

4.4   The Influence of External Lexical Resources

The stability (robustness) of segmentation with external lexical resources is known to increase. As external resources, we can use not only dictionaries of synonyms [5] but lexical databases [23]. There is no open dictionary of Russian synonyms of high quality, so we used a semantic classifier [28]. We suggested that words belonging to the same class would be marked as the same ones. The examples are vessel (судно), ship (корабль), frigate (фрегат) from "Romme Rus" and helmet (каска), service cap (фуражка), peakless cap (бескозырка) from U-boats Rus.

Let us consider a typical example and compare two sentences from adjoining parts of "U-boat Rus":

Ribbons of peakless caps for the Kaiserliche Marine had gilt and silver thread block lettering (for sea-going personnel and for administrative personnel respectively).

Ленточки бескозырок матросов кайзеровского флота имели надпись прописными печатными буквами, вышитыми золотой или серебряной канителью.

and

The field cap was cut from fine-quality navy blue cloth wool, usually with a black or dark blue cotton or artificial silk lining.

Пилотка кроилась из темно-синего плотного сукна, обычно с черной или темно-синей подкладкой из искусственного шелка.

These sentences in spite of belonging to the same subtopic have no lexical repetitions. Thus, its cosine measure computed "by words" is zero. However, words peakless cap (бескозырка), field cap (пилотка), lining (подкладка) are of the class Clothes and ribbon (ленточка), gild or silver thread (канитель), cloth wool (сукно), silk (шелк) belong to the class Fabrics. Hence, analyzing only nouns by classes we get $\cos \varphi = 0.71$.

Fig. 4 shows the functions of F-score from cutoff rate on the example of analyzing "Romme Rus" by words and by classes (the $L+POS+Class$ $type$).

As one can see, F-score of pre-processing "by classes" increases more than twice. The accuracy level can range to reach the best result. For example, head-dresses can be regarded as a separate class or a part of "Clothes". You can compare the best F-scores given in Table 6.

Thus, the results by classes are much higher than the one by words. It is notable that news texts are divided equally at $z = 0.5$ in any way. This means that $FN = FP$.

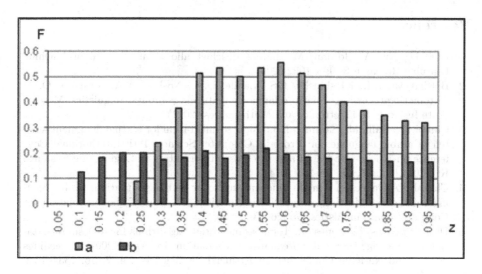

Fig. 4. The comparison of analysis "by classes" and "by words".

Table 6. *F*-score of Analysis "by words" and "by classes"

Text	U-boat Rus	Romme Rus	News
By words	0.21	0.22	0.60
By classes	0.50	0.7	0.78

Thus, to get the best results of automatic segmentation it is necessary to evaluate the similarities and differences between text fragments by packaged vocabulary and not by separate words. This allows to use all types of cohesion more efficient.

5   Conclusion

We studied the specifics of applying subtopic segmentation methods on real scientific texts on the same subject in three languages. The corpus includes several fragments both in the original language and in professional translation. The research is based on the TextTiling algorithm that analyses how tightly adjoining parts of a text cohere. We examined how some parameters (the cutoff rate, the size of moving window and of the shift from one block to the next one) influence the segmentation quality. The optimum combinations of these parameters are defined for several languages. The studies on Russian language suggest that external lexical resources notably improve the quality of segmentation.

References

1. Blei, D., Ng, A., Jordan, M.: Latent dirichlet allocation. Journal of Machine Learning Research **3**, 993–1022 (2003)
2. Bolshakova, E.I., Klyshinsky, E.S., Lande, D.V., Noskov, A.A., Peskova, O.V.: Automatic processing of natural language texts and computer linguistics. Moscow State Institute of Electronics and Mathematics (2011)
3. Chaibi, A., Naili, M., Sammoud, S.: Topic segmentation for textual document written in arabic language. In: Procedia Computer Science: 18th International Conference on Knowledge-Based and Intelligent Information & Engineering Systems, KES2014, vol. 35, pp. 26–33 (2014)
4. Choi, F.: Advances in domain independent linear text segmentation. In: Proceedings of the 1st Meeting of the North American Chapter of the Association for Computational Linguistics, pp. 26–33 (2000)
5. Dias, G., Alves, E., Lopes, J.: Topic segmentation algorithms for text summarization and passage retrieval: an exhaustive evaluation. In: AAAI 2007 Proceedings of the 22nd National Conference on Artificial Intelligence, vol. 2, pp. 1334–1339 (2007)
6. Douglas, B., Berger, A., Lafferty, J.: Statistical models of text segmentation. Machine Learning **34**(1–3) (1999)
7. Du, L., Buntine, W., Johnson, M.: Topic segmentation with a structured topic model. In: Proceedings of the 2013 Conference of the North American Chapter of the Association for Computational Linguistics: Human Language Technologies, pp. 190–200 (2013)
8. Eisenstein, J.: Hierarchical text segmentation from multi-scale lexical cohesion. In: NAACL 2009 Proceedings of Human Language Technologies: The 2009 Annual Conference of the North American Chapter of the Association for Computational Linguistics, pp. 353–361 (2009)
9. Eisenstein, J., Barzilay, R.: Bayesian unsupervised topic segmentation. In: Proceedings of the 2008 Conference on Empirical Methods in Natural Language Processing, pp. 334–343 (2008)
10. Flejter, D., Wieloch, K., Abramowicz, W.: Unsupervised methods of topical text segmentation for polish. In: Balto-Slavonic Natural Language Processing 2007, pp. 51–58 (2007)
11. Georgescu, M., Clark, A., Armstrong, S.: An analysis of quantitative aspects in the evaluation of thematic segmentation algorithms. In: SigDIAL 2006 Proceedings of the 7th SIGdial Workshop on Discourse and Dialogue (2009)
12. Hearst, M.: Texttiling: Segmenting text into multi-paragraph subtopic passages. Computational Linguistics **23**(1), 33–64 (1997)
13. Hearst, M., Plaunt, C.: Subtopic structuring for full-length document access. In: SIGIR 1993: Proceedings of the 16th Annual International ACM SIGIR Conference on Research and Development in Information Retrieval, pp. 59–68 (1993)
14. Kanevsky, E.A., Boyarsky, K.: Semantics and sintactics parser semsin. In: Dialog-2012: International Conference on Computational Linguistics (2012). http://www.dialog-21.ru/digests/dialog2012/materials/pdf/Kanevsky.pdf (date of access June 29, 2015)
15. Kazantseva, A., Szpakowicz, S.: Linear text segmentation using affinity propagation. In: Proceedings of the 2011 Conference on Empirical Methods in Natural Language Processing, pp. 284–293 (2011)

16. Kazantseva, A., Szpakowicz, S.: Hierarchical topical segmentation with affinity propagation. In: Proceedings of COLING 2014, The 25th International Conference on Computational Linguistics: Technical Papers, pp. 37–47 (2014)

17. Kotyurova, M.P.: Scietific style of speech. Akademiya (2010)

18. Lamprier, S., Amghar, T., Levrat, B.: On evaluation methodologies for text segmentation algorithms. In: Proceedings of the 19th IEEE International Conference on Tools with Artificial Intelligence, vol. 2, pp. 11–18 (2007)

19. Lee, D.: Genres, registers, text types, domains, and styles: Clarifying the concepts and navigating a path through the bnc jungle. Language Learning & Technology **5**(3), 37–72 (2001)

20. Misra, H., Yvon, F., Cappe, O., Jose, J.: Text segmentation: A topic modeling perspective. Information Processing and Management **47**(4), 528–544 (2011)

21. Ponte, J.M., Croft, W.B.: Text segmentation by topic. In: Peters, C., Thanos, C. (eds.) ECDL 1997. LNCS, vol. 1324, pp. 113–125. Springer, Heidelberg (1997)

22. Reynar, J.: An automatic method of finding topic boundaries. In: Proceedings of the 32nd Annual Meeting on Association for Computational Linguistics, pp. 331–333 (1994)

23. Riedl, M., Biemann, C.: Text segmentation with topic models. JLCL **27**(1), 47–69 (2012)

24. Scaiano, M., Inkpen, D.: Getting more from segmentation evaluation. In: Conference of the North American Chapter of the Association for Computational Linguistics: Human Language Technologies, pp. 362–366 (2012)

25. Smolyanina, E.A.: Cohesion types in the scientific text (based on english article by m. black "metaphor"). Vestnik of Perm State University: Russian and Foreign Philology **4**(24), 140–150 (2004)

26. Stark, H.: What do paragraph markings do? Discourse Processes **11**, 275–303 (1988)

27. Trofimova, G.K.: Russian language ant the culture of speech: lectures. Flinta, Nauka (2004)

28. Tuzov, V.A.: Computer semantics of the Russian language. Saint-Petersburg University Press (2004)

29. Wan, X.: On the effectiveness of subwords for lexical cohesion based story segmentation of chinese broadcast news. Information Sciences **177**, 3718–3730 (2007)

30. Ye, N., Zhu, J., Wang, H., Ma, M., Zhang, B.: An improved model of dotplotting for text segmentation. Journal of Chinese Language and Computing **17**(1), 27–40 (2007)

UIMA2LOD: Integrating UIMA Text Annotations into the Linked Open Data Cloud

Claudia Bretschneider[1,2]([⊠]), Heiner Oberkampf[2], and Sonja Zillner[2,3]

[1] Center for Information and Language Processing, University Munich,
Munich, Germany
claudia.bretschneider.ext@siemens.com
[2] Siemens AG, Corporate Technology, Munich, Germany
[3] School of International Business and Entrepreneurship, Steinbeis University,
Berlin, Germany

Abstract. The LOD cloud is becoming the de-facto standard for sharing
and connecting pieces of data, information and knowledge on the Web.
As of today, means for the seamless integration of structured data into
the LOD cloud are available. However, algorithms for integrating information enclosed in unstructured text sources are missing. In order to
foster the (re)use of the high percentage of unstructured text, automatic
means for the integration of their content are needed. We address this
issue by proposing an approach for conceptual representation of textual
annotations which distinguishes linguistic from semantic annotations and
their integration. Additionally, we implement a generic UIMA pipeline
that automatically creates a LOD graph from texts that (1) implements
the proposed conceptual representation, (2) extracts semantically classified entities, (3) links to existing LOD datasets and (4) generates RDF
graphs from the extracted information. We show the application and
benefits of the approach in a case study on a medical corpus.

1 Semantic Web and Unstructured Data Sources

The LOD (Linked Open Data) cloud is a resource that uses Semantic Web
technology to gather and interconnect all kinds of useful publicly available web
information from any domain. In particular, the LOD cloud is a very valuable
knowledge resource for reuse in any kind of data-based applications, such as
analytics, search, etc. However, as of today, the integration of text content as
triples into the LOD clouds often relies on human interaction. The integration
of data from previously already structured sources can be realized by means of
schema transformation, but the content enclosed in texts cannot be automatically integrated into the LOD cloud, thus, remains concealed in string objects.

Therefore, in this work we propose an approach that automatically extracts
semantically classified entities and relations between them from unstructured
text and subsequently creates a LOD graph (as illustrated in Figure 1). This
resulting graph contains the triplified representation of information enclosed in
the processed text, which is already linked to existing LOD resources. Compared

© Springer International Publishing Switzerland 2015
P. Klinov and D. Mouromtsev (Eds.): KESW 2015, CCIS 518, pp. 16–31, 2015.
DOI: 10.1007/978-3-319-24543-0_2

to so far chosen representations of text in LOD datasets as string objects, which conceal the text content, we are now able to reference the structured text content by URIs and include it into the LOD cloud.

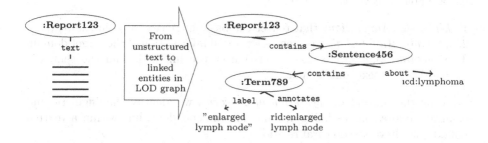

Fig. 1. Simplified illustration of target transformation from unstructured text to LOD graph of linked entities

There are several scenarios that can benefit from the resulting extended LOD cloud: For instance, a mechanism that allows the seamless integration of unstructured content into the LOD cloud drives its growth and enriches this knowledge resource. Furthermore, by enhancing information extraction algorithms with domain knowledge from the LOD cloud, a more holistic semantic understanding, and thus, interpretation of text documents becomes possible.

A first attempt to satisfy the request for structured representation of unstructured text is done by text analytics frameworks such as UIMA, whose usage became a de-facto standard and which already deliver modules for the triplification of their proprietary annotation structures. However, in most cases, their approaches only deliver incomplete solutions that fail to integrate the resulting annotations in the LOD cloud. For UIMA, the currently existing solution operates with data loss and needs intensive refactoring for correct and full creation of RDF graphs, hence, is currently not valuable for the integration task.

Therefore, the contribution of this paper is threefold: First, in Section 2 we introduce our approach for conceptual representation based on three dimensions of the textual annotations. Second, in Section 3 we describe which components with corresponding features have to be implemented in a UIMA pipeline to extract the relevant entities and relations and to create the LOD graph. Third, we evaluate the benefits of this approach in a study on extraction of a LOD dataset from medical texts (see Section 4), which is finally integrated into a semantic model for further data analytics.

2   Conceptual Representation of Text Annotations

2.1   Distinction of Three Dimensions of Annotation Types

We propose a general approach for the creation of new LOD datasets from unstructured text sources. This includes both a pipeline to fulfill the requirements posed to the creation of RDF triples and an approach to represent the annotations created as metadata from the textual content. The conceptual representation acts as common vocabulary and agreed standard. Analyzing the results from text analytics pipelines, we identify three dimensions of annotations that are able to cover the variety:

1. *Linguistic Annotations* that reflect the basic linguistic units in the texts
2. *Semantic Annotations* that represent useful information of the target domain
3. *Structural Annotations* that interconnect the linguistic and the semantic world of the text annotations

Following the concept of *separation of concerns*, we identify the linguistic and semantic annotations as being semantically independent, but within a textual context they have a structural relation.

2.2   Representation of Linguistic Annotations Employing the NIF Ontology

For representation of the linguistic annotations and their relations, we draw on the NLP Interchange Format (NIF) ontology, which was created as core component in the context of the NIF project [4], [11] We only reuse a subset of classes and properties from the NIF ontology to represent the linguistic units in texts (see Figure 2), which is relevant for representing the semantic annotations. The

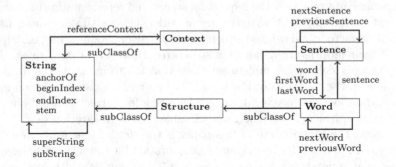

Fig. 2. (Partial) NIF ontology for representation of linguistic annotations.

main class of the model is `nif:String`, which is "the class of all words over the alphabet of Unicode characters" [4]. We model textual reports as `nif:Context`, which hold all other linguistic units via `nif:referenceContext`. `nif:Sentence` and `nif:Word` are used to model the sentence structure and its containing tokens. We also use the `nif:Word` class to model subtokens of compound terms.

We use the NIF ontology, since it satisfies our requirement for distinct representation of the linguistic information in a given text. Other models such as lemon[1] already leverage Semantic Web concepts, but rather target to model the

---

[1] http://lemon-model.net/lemon#

linguistic representation of lexicons or dictionaries from LOD resources than the content in (domain-specific) texts.

2.3 Representation of Semantic Annotations

We describe the annotations resulting from the semantic analysis of the text (Section 3) using the term *Semantic Annotations*. We subsume two types of annotations under this term:

1. In the original sense of the term, we include *annotations that are built based on ontology vocabulary*. The details of this step are described within the named entity recognition pipeline step (Section 3.2.3). There is no dedicated representation model for ontology-based semantic annotations necessary; we employ the concepts included in the Open Annotation (OA) data model. (Details are outlined in Section 2.4)
2. We also use the term Semantic Annotation to reference *annotations that are specific to the use case* tackled. An example of an application-specific annotation is a measurement annotation (shown in Figure 3 in triplified format), which is a metadatum annotated to any sequence of strings that is semantically interpreted as measurement.

```
@prefix ex: <http://example.org/stuff/1.0/> .
@prefix xsd: <http://www.w3.org/2001/XMLSchema/> .

<http://example.org/stuff/1.0/MeasurementAnnotation124112>
            ex:begin    20;   ex:end    26;
            ex:text     "1.5 cm"^^xsd:string;
            ex:measures 1.5;
            ex:unit     "cm"^^xsd:string .
```

Fig. 3. Example RDF resource for application-specific annotation type `MeasurementAnnotation`

2.4 Representation of Structural Annotations Employing the Open Annotation (OA) Ontology

We claim, the interconnection of linguistic and semantic annotations has to be explicitly modeled to show how the semantics is mapped to the linguistic entities and to support the backtracking of the sources of semantic information in the text. We employ the Open Annotation (OA) ontology [3] for modeling this structural relationship. The basic elements *body*, *target* and *annotation* of the ontology enable a generic content annotation approach.

We use the *target* to represent the linguistic entity of the text. The *body* is the part to represent the semantic annotations. The *annotation* is the part that connects the body and target, thus, holds the semantics of which linguistic part in the text is annotated by which semantic concept. For illustrating the semantic annotation of linguistic elements in text, we identify two (OA) annotation types: On the one hand, we model the case that a single target is annotated as *simple annotation* model as illustrated in Figure 4. On the other hand, we also model annotations that associate a sequence of multiple consecutive tokens (a *phrase*) with a *multi-target annotation*. As illustrated in Figure 5, we use the composite element of the OA ontology to model the multitude of tokens, because the order of the tokens is not of importance. As seen in the example, no matter whether the text sequence is `axillary lymph node` or `lymph node axillary`, it is annotated using the same body (`radlex:RID1517`).

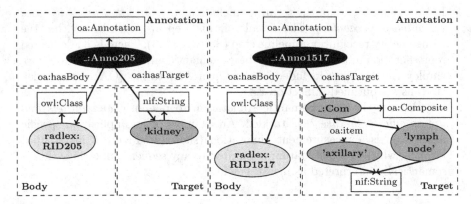

Fig. 4. Simple Annotation Model based on OA ontology. [2]

Fig. 5. Multi-target Annotation Model based on OA ontology. Multiplicity of targets is illustrated with `oa:Composite` element. [2]

3   UIMA-Based Implementation for Automated Creation of LOD Datasets from Unstructured Data Sources

Besides the high-level conceptual modeling of the target LOD dataset, we also present an end-to-end UIMA pipeline that includes all kinds of modules required to (1) extract recognized information pieces and their relations, (2) support our conceptual representation of text annotations and (3) create a serialization in RDF format. At the same time, the pipeline fulfills all requirements posed to new LOD datasets. The pipeline is configurable, so that texts of any domain can be used as input and the pipeline outputs a RDF graph that is at the same time already a LOD dataset that can be published as a part of the LOD cloud.

3.1   The UIMA Framework and Fundamental Components

For implementation of an end-to-end pipeline we build on the Unstructured Information Management Architecture (UIMA) framework, which handles unstructured resources, such as text, and facilitates their annotation and

---

[2] Undefined edges denote `rdf:type` relations. For reasons of simplicity, the ellipses representing linguistic resources are referenced by their labels.

extraction of structured information. The core components of the framework are *analysis engines* (or *annotators*) that extract defined entity types from the input texts as annotations. The framework includes an internal UIMA annotation index, the *Common Analysis Structure (CAS)*, that stores the annotation instances created. In the UIMA framework, the structure of annotations is defined in *type systems*, where each type of annotation gets assigned a list of features, whose values can be specified using three different data types:

1. Features with primitive data types (such as numeric and alphanumeric), for which an `owl:DataProperty` is created during triplification.
2. Features with complex data types that reference other annotation types, thus enable the relation between annotation instances, and for which an `owl:ObjectProperty` is created during triplification.
3. Features with arrays of primitive or complex data types, which can hold multiple instances (which are <u>not</u> created as `owl:FunctionalProperty` unlike the other feature types).

Within the UIMA framework, the architectural component that is responsible for integration of resulting annotations to external resources is defined as *consumer*. It extracts the annotation information from the CAS and persists selected information to resources such as search engine indexes, relational databases, or (as in our case) triple stores.

3.2 Description of the UIMA Pipeline's Modules

In order to fulfill the requirements towards correct conceptual and structural representation of the resulting RDF graph, our pipeline requires five functional processing steps: (1) *Linguistic Preprocessing* (2) *Information Extraction* (3) *Named Entity Recognition* (4) *Open Annotation (OA) Creation* and (5) *Triplification*. The correlating functionalities are implemented in one or more UIMA annotators. The steps of the pipeline are designed in a way so that the resulting RDF graph will be already a valid LOD dataset, which can be integrated into the cloud without further postprocessing. Thus, all pipeline's modules fulfill the four requirements imposed by the fundamental Linked Data principles formulated by Tim Berners-Lee[2] (marked in boldface):

1. **Use URIs as names for things**
2. **Use HTTP URIs so that people can look up those names**
   During the *Triplification* step each annotation instance gets assigned a unique ID represented as HTTP URI, so that the first two requirements are fulfilled.
3. **When someone looks up a URI, provide useful information, using the standards (RDF, SPARQL)**
   For extraction of useful information we included a number of steps (*Linguistic Preprocessing, Information Extraction, Open Annotation (OA) Creation*), which at the same time support the envisioned conceptual representation. Again here, for the correct structural representation of the resulting triples, the *Triplification* step is implemented to use the defined standards.

4. **Include links to other URIs, so that they can discover more things.**
   Finally, to enhance the LOD cloud with additional information entities that
   are also interconnected with existing datasets, we included the *Named Entity
   Recognition* step.

3.2.1 Linguistic Preprocessing

As first step in the pipeline, we conduct the basic linguistic analyses, such as sentence splitting and tokenization. In addition, we conduct a compound splitting
step (to instantiate the object properties `nif:subString` and `nif:superString`)
and add three annotators in order to resolve the object properties representing
the linguistic relations (e.g. `nif:word` and `nif:sentence`). We describe details
on the sentence splitting and semantic compound splitting in [7]. The underlying
UIMA type system adapts the subset of NIF concepts as shown in Figure 2 and
the annotation types are organized analogous to the `rdfs:subClassOf` hierarchy
of the NIF ontology. We map the ontology classes to UIMA annotation types to
have the implementation independent from the ontology, and thus, are able to
support the adaptation of *existing* UIMA annotators for the respective task –
not only annotators designed specifically for this task.

3.2.2 Information Extraction

The information extraction step targets the annotation of *domain-specific
semantic annotations*. The information pieces resulting from this step are
descibed by Berners-Lee as useful information. However, what useful information is and how it is modeled depends on the context of the application or the
domain addressed. Therefore, the domain respectively the use case defines the
annotators necessary. Depending on the type of information to be extracted,
the implemented annotators make use of the multitude of NLP algorithms to
identify and annotate the respective information in the text.

One example annotator implemented for the case study is an annotator that
recognizes strings interpreted as measurements (`MeasurementAnnotator`) with
the attributes illustrated in Figure 3. The underlying algorithm is based on pre-
compiled regular expressions or list of entities (for the measurement units) and
are also able to recognize other medical semantic types, such as diseases (based on
typical suffixes), dates (regular expressions), abbreviations and negations (lists).

3.2.3 Named Entity Recognition (NER)

The second type of semantic annotations – *ontology-based semantic annotations*
– are created during this processing step. Hence, this step satisfies two purposes:
First, it serves the need for identification of domain-specific semantically classified concepts in the text and subsequently interconnect the knowledge in the
ontology to the textual information. Second, this step satisfies the requirement
to link to other, existing LOD datasets, since the resulting LOD dataset needs
to link to existing entities (LOD principle #4). Thus, this implies that at least
one of the employed ontologies for NER has to be published as resource in the
LOD cloud.

The realization of ontology-based semantic annotations is based on the UIMA Concept Mapper[3]. To recognize ontology concepts it employs a previously created XML dictionary that contains the vocabulary to match and the metadata to annotate. For our case study, we transform the RadLex vocabulary into a dictionary that is Concept Mapper-compatible. Each ontology concept is transformed into a UIMA token (example shown in Figure 6) with its URI and preferred name as attributes. Additionally, each synonym and non-English variants are added as UIMA variants, which are used during the annotation process. The Concept Mapper creates annotations by mapping the stemmed UIMA variants from the XML dictionary to the text's tokens. If matches are found, an annotation is created that encloses the URI of the matching ontology concept. The Concept Mapper creates annotations for phrases if each of the tokens in a dictionary phrase can be mapped to a token within a sentence. The URI is the only information necessary to be annotated, since its semantics is already defined in the source ontology.

```
<token RID="RID1301" URI="http://www.owl-ontologies.com/Ontology1392225293.owl#RID1301"
       pn="lung" semanticClass="anatomical">
       <variant base="lung"/>
       <variant base="Lunge"/>
       <variant base="pulmo"/>
</token>
```

Fig. 6. Sample entry from UIMA Concept Mapper-compatible dictionary

3.2.4   Creating Open Annotations (OA)

The final step to reach the targeted conceptual representation model of the annotations is this transformation step to create the OA annotations shown in Figures 4 and 5. Simple annotations are created if single tokens in a sentence are annotated. Multi-target annotations are created if a semantic annotation needs to reference multiple linguistic entities for full semantic coverage. Within the created OA annotations, the respective linguistic and semantic annotations are just referenced by their URIs, since they already have been created in the proceeding steps.

3.2.5   Triplification

The main objective of this step is the correct representation of the annotations created in the steps before. Analyzing the data structure-wise, how existing modules triplify text annotations and where their shortcomings lie, we found five aspects to consider when creating RDF triples from text annotations. We conducted the analysis with strong influence from the existing UIMA RDF consumer[4] from the UIMA framework. As a result from this analysis, we developed

---

[3] https://uima.apache.org/downloads/sandbox/ConceptMapperAnnotator
   UserGuide/ConceptMapperAnnotatorUserGuide.html

[4] UIMA CAS2RDF consumer http://uima.apache.org/downloads/sandbox/RDF_CC/
   RDFCASConsumerUserGuide.html

a module to transform the CAS into a RDF graph, which is intended to work for any kind of annotation types. It builds on the existing RDF consumer, but addresses the following limitations. This is the most important component for translating the structural requirements for LOD datasets into technical implementation.

1. **Declarative modeling of data properties (primitive data type features).** In the graph that the existing RDF consumer produces, each annotation feature that is triplified to `owl:DataProperty` is assigned a resource with two literals representing the feature name and feature value, so that each feature needs three triples for being represented. For us, this representation is not intuitive and not easy to process subsequently. Since this is more convenient and intuitive, we prefer a representation where the feature value corresponds to the literal's lexical form and the feature name corresponds to the edge label, which also avoids unnecessarily large numbers of triples.

2. **Typed literals instead of plain piterals.** The problem with triples, whose objects are defined as plain literals, is that they cannot be interpreted with their correct data type but rather have per default a string type assigned. This hinders the automated analysis of the data. As each feature is defined with a distinct data type in the UIMA type system, it is easy to access this information and reuse it for triplification of the annotations. Therefore, we define each literal as typed literal, which has a lexical form and an additional data type URI.

3. **Resolution of ambiguities with unique IDs.** In the RDF graph, each resource is identified by its URI. However, if the ID is not unique, because the calculation of the URI is not correct, this ambiguity leads to wrong representation of the annotations created. As a resolution, we calculate a hashcode for each text annotation that combines all available (primitive) feature names and values of each annotation instance in order to resolve this ambiguity and deliver a unique numeric identifier. This hashcode is combined with the annotation type name and an application-defined HTTP path to the final URI of a resource (example shown in Figure 3). A (desired) side effect of this calculation is that there is only a single instance of an annotation created, which subsequently can be referenced multiple times.

4. **Triplification of object properties (references between annotations).** The serialization of `owl:ObjectProperty` from features with complex data types requires a more sophisticated handling. The existing consumer does not resolve the objects attached to object properties, but rather triplifies the referenced annotation to its full string representation. This representation loses the link between the annotation instances. To prevent this loss, we implement a mechanism that considers the complex data type of the feature, triplifies the object property (if not already done) and maintains the reference.

5. **Triplification of non-functional properties (multi-value annotation features).** Per default all annotation features are defined as functional properties. If a feature allows multiple instances (for which the cardinal-

ity restriction of functional properties do not apply), each value needs to be triplified separately. This applies for feature values that are triplified to `owl:DataProperties` and `owl:ObjectProperties`, respectively. The existing consumer loses this information, since it represents the whole set using the string '`FSArray`'.

If the aspects just mentioned are not considered, this causes the effects of data loss, which leads to misinterpretation of the annotation values. Therefore, our implementation of a UIMA2LOD UIMA consumer builds upon the existing consumer functionality, but resolves the listed issues and now integrates more information – and even shows a more intuitive and leaner representation. At the same time, the resulting graph already represents a valid LOD dataset that can be published as part of the LOD cloud without any further postprocessing.

4   Case Study on Integrating RDF Annotations into the Model for Clinical Information (MCI)

4.1   General Goal and How the Approach Fits

Using our approach on representing and triplifying textual annotations, we want to show how structured information can be extracted from an example text and how it can be subsequently transformed into a LOD dataset. Also, we want to demonstrate how the graph can be used in Semantic Web applications for reasoning on the information enclosed in the texts. Therefore, we use a medical corpus and show how the pipeline operates and which output it produces. In a further step, this output is integrated in a semantic Model for Clinical Information (MCI) that integrates clinical information in a patient-centric way.

4.2   Resources Used in the Case Study

Corpus of Medical Reports. One of the core resources applied in our case study is a medical corpus containing 2,713 German radiology reports that describe the health status of lymphoma patients. The texts are provided by our clinical partner, the University Hospital Erlangen.

RadLex Ontology. To satisfy the requirements for creating links to existing LOD datasets and since the its vocabulary matches the vocabulary of the corpus, we employ the RadLex ontology [9]. RadLex is a medical ontology for the radiology domain and aims to unify the domain's vocabulary for the purpose of organization, indexing and retrieval of radiology resources, such as textual radiology reports. The current version of Radlex 3.12 (11/2014) contains 74,875 terms. RadLex is also published as LOD dataset `bioportal-rid`.

Model for Clinical Information (MCI). The MCI [8] provides the basis for data integration and knowledge exploration . It defines the most important structural concepts (classes and relations) for the representation of clinical data. This is, in the first place structured data about the patient like diagnoses and findings, as well as provided examinations, procedures and therapies. The MCI is based on selected upper- and midlevel ontologies from the OBO library and reuses established schemas like the Dublin Core. It is used in combination with large reference terminologies such as RadLex or the Foundational Model of Anatomy (FMA) to represent clinical findings from unstructured data resources.

4.3   Creation of Text Annotations and the RDF Graph

For illustrating the outcome of the process and how it can be used for further processing, we use the sentence `Axillary lymph node with diameter 1.5 cm.`, which is representative for the corpus given. Following the process steps and iterating the UIMA pipeline, several annotations are created (see Figure 7).

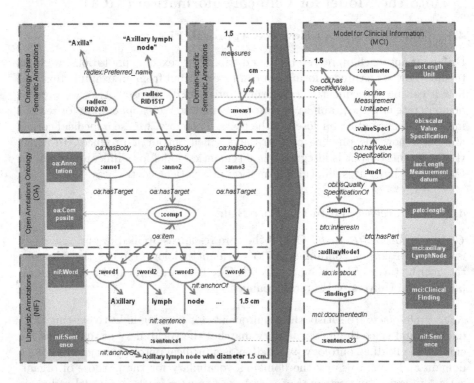

Fig. 7. Example illustrating a subset of annotations created from the sentence `Axillary lymph node with diameter 1.5 cm.` (left-hand side) and their transformation into the clinical model MCI (right-hand side).[5]

---

[5] Undefined edges denote `rdf:type` relations.

The linguistic annotators produce one sentence annotation, six token annotations and the respective relations defined in NIF schema. As domain-specific annotation type a measurement annotation with measure 1.5 and unit cm is identified. As results from the RadLex-based NER step, two possible anatomical entities are annotated in the sentence: axilla and axillary lymph node. Finally, the structural relations between the linguistic and the semantic annotations are generated as OA annotations. After being processed by the pipeline the semantic text content triplified to RDF and can be used for further analysis.

4.4 Transformation of Text Annotation RDF Graph into MCI

In general, the annotations from radiology reports represent clinical information, such as the observations made and the findings discovered. However, in the context of medical information, the textual information from examination reports are just one single piece to the holistic information describing the current and past health status of a patient. For clinical decision making this data however needs to be linked and interpreted to gain a holistic view on the patient data. In order to gain such a holistic representation, we employ the MCI. The process to transform the structured annotation data to the schema and semantics of MCI requires several steps:

Transformation of RDF Graph into the MCI Schema. Since the annotations are already represented in RDF format, we can simply use SPARQL queries to facilitate the required schema transformation. Once established, the transformation of the RDF graph to the MCI schema can be conducted automatically.

Transformation and Normalization of Measurement Annotations. The provided piece of measurement information is directly transformed to a size finding. Therefore, an instance of a length measurement datum, which describes a length quality, is created. We map the unit (represented in the annotation as a string) to an entity of the Units Ontology (UO) and normalize the value to centimeters (if necessary) to obtain a representation as shown in Figure 7.

Disambiguation of Anatomical Entities. Finally the correct relation to the described anatomical entity has to be created. We use the disambiguation algorithm described in [7] to determine the correct anatomical entity from the annotated ones (axilla and axillary lymph node), which is the latter.

Inference. Now, the MCI is combined with RadLex to link findings about same or similar anatomical entities from consecutive examinations, e.g. for treatment evaluation. Additionally, formalized medical knowledge about normal size specifications is used to infer that the finding represents an *abnormally enlarged* axillary lymph node, since normal size lymph nodes typically measure up to 1 cm. In a further diagnostic process this finding can be interpreted in the context of diseases: An enlarged lymph node is an abnormality caused by the immune system and related to specific types of cancer, such as lymphoma.

Finally, we point out that this information can be only inferred, because two information resources are combined: text and LOD knowledge. Since this clinical information is only reported as text, it requires our textual annotation and transformation process to link the enclosed information with clinical LOD knowledge.

4.5   Evaluation

4.5.1   Quantitative Comparison of UIMA2LOD Consumer

For a quantitative evaluation of the strength of the proposed approach, we compare the RDF graphs resulting from the triplification substep using a UIMA pipeline that integrates either the CAS2RDF consumer or our new triplification component UIMA2LOD but with the same annotator components (c.f. Table 1).

Table 1. Qualitative comparison of the RDF graph from annotation pipelines integrating either the CAS2RDF or the UIMA2LOD consumer

	CAS2RDF	UIMA2LOD
# NIF Annotations	1,506,029	
# Semantic Annotations	416,251	
# OA Annotations	486,425	
# Triples	144,215,917	47,700,368
# Triples with wrong serialization of		
Non-Functional Properties	681,745	–
Object Properties	8,302,645	–
Runtime of Annotation Pipeline	24h	9 min
	for 180 docs	for all 2713 docs

indent Given the medical corpus with 2,713 texts as input, 2,408,705 text annotations are created. The graph resulting from the UIMA2LOD consumer only needs a third of the triples compared to the graph resulting from the CAS2RDF consumer. The difference is due to the simplified representation of annotation features with name and values. However, a more detailed analysis of the delta is not possible because the numbers are blurred by the wrong serialization of non-functional and object properties by the CAS2RDF consumer. This irregular triplification leads to data loss which can not be corrected by post processing either. Also, the existing process is highly resource intense. It leads to an extrapolated time of 2 weeks for the serialization of the whole corpus. (We stopped the process after 24h with 180 reports triplified.) The reason is the attempt to serialize object properties (and all of their subsequent object properties) as string representations. Because of this limitation, we only recommend the usage of the CAS2RDF module for creating RDF representation of un-linked text annotations. Whereas, the usage of the UIMA2LOD component, which addresses those limitations, is recommended for highly linked graphs, which are intented to be integrated into the LOD cloud as datasets. Finally, only our pipeline is able to automatically create a valid LOD dataset from unstructured text, in a reasonable time. The CAS2RDF consumer does not create a valid LOD dataset, because it fails to comply to two core requirements: First, it does not create URIs as unique IDs, but rather IDs in an own format. Second, it fails to create links to existing datasets, thus does not add to the creation of a larger linked data cloud.

4.5.2   Comparison with Other Text2Semantic Web Systems

Only in the recent years the question of how to integrate results from NLP pipelines and the Semantic Web has become of importance. However, numerous information extraction pipelines for unstructured text can be found that take the first step to transform their outcomes into RDF triples. While taking a further step, they also succeed in extracting entities from the text that are part of LOD resources, such as MeSH for biomedical texts [10], plant information [5] or general information from DBpedia [1]. Thus, while their primary goal in terms of information extraction is the identification of *existing* entities, they focus on supporting the discovery of so far undiscovered relations between these entities.

Another field of research is the population of existing ontologies. Kawamura et al. [5] extract newly explored plant information from text. The resulting RDF representation is a requirement for their integration. Just recently, Augenstein et al. [1] propose a domain-independent approach for information that transforms the results into RDF without predefined schema. The main limitation from these existing systems is their lack in the ability to support the creation of new LOD datasets, either because of the missing link of the RDF graphs to existing LOD datasets or because they fail to generate new information from the given textual resource, while they just recognize existing LOD instances.

4.6   Future Work

We plan to fully integrate the UIMA pipeline into the Semantic Web context by automating the initial step of transforming a semantic model into the UIMA type system, which we currently conduct manually. First such attempts have been made by Lui [6] and Verspoor [12]. They also show how the resulting graph can be used within reasoning applications. Further, we regard the applied medical corpus as medium-size. We aim to extract information from corpora of Big Data size (which is text from about 10,000 patient from examinations over up to 30 years time). Additionally, we will evaluate the individual steps of the pipeline, in particular the quality of the information extraction and NER steps.

5   Conclusion

In this work we present an automatic approach for creating LOD datasets from entities and relations extracted from unstructured texts, whose content has been concealed so far. On the one hand, we propose an approach to conceptual representation that separates linguistic, semantic and integrating annotation. On the other hand, we introduce a (reusable) UIMA pipeline, that extracts and serializes the structured annotation information from the input text. Compared to existing annotation systems our pipeline is advantageous, because we are able to create new LOD datasets from unstructured data sources in an automated manner. Our pipeline creates a full representation of text annotations without data loss and reuses URIs from existing LOD resources for seamless integration. The resulting RDF graph can be published as-is as a LOD dataset, since it fulfills all necessary requirements imposed. This results in the availability of semantic information from so far unexplored data sources for a subsequent data analysis. At the same time, also existing LOD datasets can benefit from this integration effort, since it is also applicable for unstructured text enclosed. In a case study we show the advantages of our approach: We decrease the number of triples necessary to a third, while preventing data loss from wrong serialization of object and non-functional properties. The subsequent data analysis reveals so far undiscovered knowledge, because the content in unstructured texts can now be integrated with LOD resources.

Acknowledgments. This research has been supported by the KDI project funded by the German Federal Ministry of Economics and Technology under grant number 01MT14001 and by the EU FP7 Diachron project (GA 601043).

References

1. Augenstein, I., Padó, S., Rudolph, S.: LODifier: generating linked data from unstructured text. In: Simperl, E., Cimiano, P., Polleres, A., Corcho, O., Presutti, V. (eds.) ESWC 2012. LNCS, vol. 7295, pp. 210–224. Springer, Heidelberg (2012). http://dblp.uni-trier.de/db/conf/esws/eswc2012.html#AugensteinPR12
2. Berners-Lee, T.: Linked Data - Design Issues, July 2006. http://www.w3.org/DesignIssues/LinkedData.html
3. Ciccarese, P., Ocana, M., Garcia-Castro, L.J., Das, S., Clark, T.: An open annotation ontology for science on web 3.0. J. Biomedical Semantics 2(S–2), S4 (2011). http://dblp.uni-trier.de/db/journals/biomedsem/biomedsem2S.html#Ciccarese OGDC11
4. Hellmann, S., Lehmann, J., Auer, S., Brümmer, M.: Integrating NLP using linked data. In: Alani, H., et al. (eds.) ISWC 2013, Part II. LNCS, vol. 8219, pp. 98–113. Springer, Heidelberg (2013). http://svn.aksw.org/papers/2013/ISWC_NIF/public.pdf
5. Kawamura, T., Ohsuga, A.: Toward an ecosystem of LOD in the field: LOD content generation and its consuming service. In: Cudré-Mauroux, P., et al. (eds.) ISWC 2012, Part II. LNCS, vol. 7650, pp. 98–113. Springer, Heidelberg (2012). http://dblp.uni-trier.de/db/conf/semweb/iswc2012-2.html#KawamuraO12
6. Liu, H., Wu, S.T.I., Tao, C., Chute, C.G.: Modeling UIMA type system using web ontology language - towards interoperability among UIMA-based NLP tools. In: Proceedings of Workshop on Managing Interoperability and compleXity in Health Systems (MIX-HS), pp. 31–36 (2012). http://dblp.uni-trier.de/db/conf/cikm/mixhs2012.html#LiuWTC12

7. Oberkampf, H., Bretschneider, C., Zillner, S., Bauer, B., Hammon, M.: Knowledge-based extraction of measurement-entity relations from german radiology reports. In: IEEE International Conference on Healthcare Informatics (ICHI) (2013)
8. Oberkampf, H., Zillner, S., Bauer, B., Hammon, M.: An OGMS-based model for clinical information (MCI). In: Proceedings of International Conference on Biomedical Ontology, pp. 97–100 (2013). http://www2.unb.ca/csas/data/ws/icbo2013/papers/ec/icbo2013_submission_56.pdf
9. Radiological Society of North America: Radlex (2012). http://rsna.org/RadLex.aspx
10. Ramakrishnan, C., Kochut, K.J., Sheth, A.P.: A framework for schema-driven relationship discovery from unstructured text. In: Cruz, I., Decker, S., Allemang, D., Preist, C., Schwabe, D., Mika, P., Uschold, M., Aroyo, L.M. (eds.) ISWC 2006. LNCS, vol. 4273, pp. 583–596. Springer, Heidelberg (2006). http://dx.doi.org/10.1007/11926078_42
11. Rizzo, G., Troncy, R., Hellmann, S., Brümmer, M.: In: Workshop on Linked Data on the Web (LDOW), Lyon, France
12. Verspoor, K., Baumgartner Jr., W., Roeder, C., Hunter, L.: Abstracting the types away from a UIMA type system. From Form to Meaning: Processing Texts Automatically, 249–256 (2009)

An Advanced Query and Result Rewriting Mechanism for Information Retrieval Purposes from RDF Datasources

Efthymios Chondrogiannis[✉], Vassiliki Andronikou, Efstathios Karanastasis, and Theodora Varvarigou

National Technical University of Athens, 9 Heroon Politechniou Str, 15773 Athens, Greece
{chondrog,vandro,ekaranas}@mail.ntua.gr, dora@telecom.ntua.gr

Abstract. The volume and variety of data published on the Semantic Web is constantly increasing with a growing number of entities and stakeholders expressing their data in the form of OWL and/or RDFS ontologies. However, a large amount of data is still maintained in relational databases. The recent developments in SPARQL endpoints, such as D2R server, constitute an important step towards the introduction of relational databases in the Semantic Web. However, the underlying models are tightly linked with the data structure and controlled terminologies employed, and hence, they pose a serious barrier to accessing the data by using different languages. In our previous work, we presented an Ontology Alignment Tool for bridging the gap among the terms of two ontologies based on the instantiation of one or more Ontology Patterns. In this paper, we analytically describe a novel approach and an accordingly designed system for enabling users to access data residing in relational databases by using different models and vocabularies than the ones supported by the SPARQL endpoint. The approach is based on the specification and consumption of correspondences with particular focus on SPARQL query and RDF data rewriting mechanisms, which are responsible for making the necessary changes in the queries and optionally results retrieved from the SPARQL endpoint taking into account the models and vocabularies used in each side.

Keywords: Semantic web · Query answering · Ontology alignment · D2R server · Relational databases

1 Introduction

Ontologies have a distinctive role in the Semantic Web. They enable users to formally describe a domain of knowledge while they can also share their data with the other members of the Semantic Web community in the form of OWL [1] and RDFS [2] documents. However, due to their independent design and the different purposes they serve, they are often highly heterogeneous which in turn prevents their seamless integration and use by relevant systems. Additionally, when their size increases significantly, they need a large amount of computing resources, while typical operations, such as searching and updating datasources, require a considerable amount of time for their execution.

P. Klinov and D. Mouromtsev (Eds.): KESW 2015, CCIS 518, pp. 32–47, 2015.
DOI: 10.1007/978-3-319-24543-0_3

Relational Database Management Systems provide a stable solution for data storage purposes, while they can efficiently handle the data, even when they have to deal with billions of user records. Consequently, quite often, the information captured about the entities of a domain, is stored in a relational database. The recent achievements in the Semantic Web community and especially the development of SPARQL endpoints, such as the D2R server [3], have made an important step for accessing relational databases using Semantic Web technologies. However, the underlying models and controlled vocabularies supported by the SPARQL endpoint are close to the data structure and terminologies used while they often lack a formal description.

The design of another ontology which provides a real conceptualisation of the domain a datasource covers with adequate description of their terms from a user point of view, can facilitate the interaction with the end users [4]. However, mapping among the two ontologies' terms is necessary for accessing their data. Also, in many cases in which it is desired to access the information captured by one or more overlapping datasources using a "common language", mapping among the terms of the "global" ontology and the ones supported by the corresponding SPARQL endpoints is necessary as well as mapping among the terms of the controlled Vocabularies used in each side. In such cases, a variety of heterogeneity issues is expected to be encountered especially when patients' data is concerned, as has already been presented in our previous work [5].

Ontology alignment has been extensively studied in related work and various algorithms and tools have been proposed for correspondence detection and specification purposes. However, the way the specified mapping rules are used for query answering purposes is still a real challenge. In this paper we analytically describe the approach followed and the mechanisms used in the background for rewriting both SPARQL queries [6] and the data retrieved from the SPARQL endpoint, whenever required.

The document is structured as follows. In section 2 the related work is presented. In section 3 the overall approach followed as well as the Tools and Components developed are presented. In section 4 the SPARQL query and RDF data rewriting mechanisms are analytically described, while in section 5 a relevant example is given. In section 6 a discussion follows, and, in the last section, the main points of this work are summarised.

2   Related Work

Correspondence specification among the terms of two ontologies as well as application of the specified mapping rules (aka correspondence consumption) for the implementation of relevant tasks (e.g., ontology integration, SPARQL query and/or RDF data rewriting) are two complementary processes. However, for enabling direct usage of the specified mapping rules without the need for any human intervention, both correspondence specification and consumption systems should share the same mapping language.

For specifying the correspondences among two or more ontologies, a variety of systems and tools exists, such as AgreementMaker [7], OPTIMA [8] and COMA 3.0

[9]. However, the existing mapping tools focus on discovering 1:1 alignments, while many of them either provide a simple interface for specifying 1:1 correspondences or are not equipped with a graphical user interface at all [10]. Taking into account the variety of mismatches among the ontologies, especially the ones used for the formal description of the information captured by the underlying datasources, a novel tool is needed which provides a highly interactive, user friendly environment for specifying n:m correspondences, while in the background a very expressive mapping language, which satisfies a series of requirements [11], is being used for their formal description.

The Correspondence Patterns (CPs) [12] and especially the Ontology Patterns (OPs) [13] satisfy the majority of these requirements while they provide to the end user a rather expressive mapping language for ontologies alignment purposes. In fact, the OPs overcome the limitations of the CPs enabling users to independently determine the entities participating in the left and right side of a Mapping Rule (MR) while they can be also combined in order to formulate more complex ones.

The algorithms implemented by relevant systems for the consumption of the MRs specified are tightly linked with the mapping language used. When only "semantic mismatches" (e.g., equivalent terms) must be dealt with, the corresponding mechanisms are quite simple, as e.g. the one presented in the work [14]. In order to properly handle more complicated mismatches a much more challenging approach is required. For this purpose, some authors ([15] and [16]) have specified the mapping between the ontologies in the form of triple patterns (TPs), which can be directly used for SPARQL query answering purposes. However in such cases, the MRs specified are closely associated with the specific task they serve, and hence, they cannot support the implementation of relevant tasks, such as ontologies integrations. Also, the authors of paper [17] have used CONSTRUCT SPARQL queries for RDF [18] data rewriting purposes. However in this context, the introduction of user defined functions is necessary, which practically means that an extension of the SPARQL language be used, which in turn may not already be supported by the SPARQL endpoint.

Concerning the application of MRs specified for query answering purposes, we have presented in our previous work an innovative query (and optionally results) rewriting mechanism [5], which is responsible for making the necessary interventions in the SPARQL query and/or RDF data based on the specific CPs used. An important parameter in the aforementioned process is the fact that the mapping language is totally based on a limited number of CPs, while each of the elements participating in the left and right side of the MR has been precisely determined. In the current work, since a much more expressive mapping language is used for ontology alignment purposes, which enables users to dynamically combine the appropriate OPs for specifying the entities participating in the left and right side of a MR, a completely different approach is required.

3   Approach Followed and Components Developed

For enabling end users or systems to access information residing in a relational data-base by using a SPARQL endpoint, a mapping among the terms of the corresponding models and controlled vocabularies is necessary (step 1). Then, the users are able to access the datasource using their own models and controlled vocabularies, based on the correspondences specified (step 2). The overall approach followed and the internal tools and components developed are presented in Fig 1.

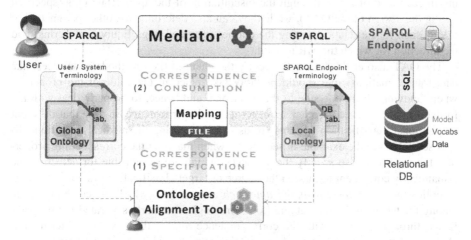

Fig. 1. The Overall Approach Followed and Tools/Components Developed.

In this work, the models (Global and Local ontologies) and vocabularies used (User and DB vocabularies) are taken for granted. Additionally, it is assumed that the vocabularies used in both sides are either the same or come from international classi-fications systems, and hence, the correspondence among their terms is already avail-able on the web.

3.1   Correspondence Specification Using Ontology Patterns

Taking into account the variety of mismatches that can take place among the terms of the Global and Local ontologies, the whole ontology alignment approach is based on OPs. An OP precisely determines an entity of a mapping rule and may refer to a) an existing element (e.g., an existing class), b) a "new" one implied by the restriction of the meaning and/or usage of an existing element (e.g., restricting the domain of a property within a specific class) or c) generally any combination of ontological ele-ments (e.g., union of classes). Hence, by using (aka instantiating) the appropriate OP the users can specify the entities participating in the left and right side of a MR.

The real power of the OPs lies in their combination. For instance, the Property Domain Restriction OP specifies a property on condition that it is applied to the enti-ties coming from a specific class. The OPs have been specified in such way that their internal elements (i.e., property and domain-class) are also OPs, which can be simple elements (such as an existing property and class) or more complicated ones, described by another OP. For example, a property may be the path that should be followed to reach its value(s) (i.e., an Object Property followed by a Datatype Property) and a class may be the intersection of two or more OWL classes provided.

The Ontology Alignment Tool (OAT) [19] that we developed enables users to specify the correspondence among the terms of two Ontologies through a semi-automatic process by accepting/rejecting the suggested MRs or by manually specifying those missing. In the latter case, the users can easily define the entities participating in each side of a MR through the instantiation of the appropriate OPs (specified during the design of the OAT), while they can also determine the other parameters of a MR, such as the relation among the entities provided (e.g., Equivalent Terms) and the direction for which the MR is valid.

The OAT also enables users to specify the changes (i.e., methods or services, aka data transformations) that should possibly take place in the value of the properties when "moving" from one side to the other one, and hence, to properly deal with the format of data or the controlled set of terms used. For instance, in case that different international classification systems are used for capturing the medical conditions diagnosed (also see the example in section 5), when mapping the corresponding properties, the users can also specify the service(s) which are responsible for detecting the semantically equivalent term(s) in the source or target classification system.

Following a *two-level mapping approach* according to which the correspondence among the terms of the Global and Local ontologies is clearly separated but properly linked through services with the correspondence among the Vocabulary terms, enables users to easily integrate and use existing services, while it also enables the independent specification of the corresponding alignments, if not already provided (e.g., when international codes are mapped with the specific local codes used in a relational database).

3.2 Correspondence Consumption for SPARQL Queries Answering

When the mapping among the terms of the Global and Local ontologies has been specified (including mappings among the corresponding vocabularies), the end users are able to access the data stored in the underlying datasource based on their own language. More precisely, they can express the appropriate SPARQL query using the terms of the Global ontology and the controlled Vocabularies used, while the results retrieved will be also expressed using the aforementioned terms.

The system (Mediator) used in the background is responsible for a) rewriting the provided SPARQL queries to the corresponding new ones, using the SPARQL endpoint terms, b) executing them, and c) making any changes required in the retrieved RDF data (for CONSTRUCT SPARQL queries). Both the SPARQL query and RDF data rewriting processes are totally based on the MRs specified and will be analytically described in the next section.

It should be noted that the system has been designed to support two types of SPARQL queries: a) The SELECT SPARQL queries, which are ideal for retrieving statistics, such as the total number of entities that satisfy a set of conditions provided or data that do not need any further processing, such as the IDs of the eligible entities; b) The CONSTRUCT SPARQL queries (both the production and restriction clauses are compatible with user terminology), which are ideal for retrieving one or more parameters about the eligible data, which are expressed in a different language (and especially vocabulary) than the one used by the end user.

4   Background Mechanisms

The OPs are the basic elements for specifying the correspondence among the terms of the provided ontologies. Taking into account the fact that the OPs used in each side of a MR are not known in advance, along with the fact that the OPs can be combined to form more complex ones, the changes that should take place in the SPARQL query or RDF data are decided upon dynamically, based on the specific OPs that are used in the entities 1 and 2 of the MR along with the other parameters provided (e.g., data transformation, when necessary).

For enabling the automatic construction of the corresponding Transformation Rules (TRs) which precisely determine the changes to be applied in the SPARQL query or RDF data, the Basic Graph Patterns (BGPs) for some "primitive" OPs were specified, in an abstract manner, during the design phase of the system, while the process to be followed for synthesizing the BGPs based on the internal OPs was also established. Based on the concrete OPs used within each MR, the system then automatically generates the corresponding TRs which are accordingly used for both SPARQL query and RDF data rewriting purposes. A conceptual view of the followed approach is presented in Fig. 2.

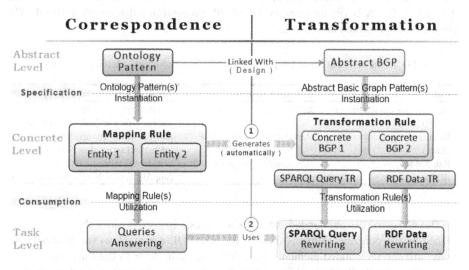

Fig. 2. Ontology Patterns and Transformation Rules for SPARQL Query Answering.

4.1   Abstract Level: Ontological Elements and Abstract Basic Graph Patterns

The Abstract Basic Graph Pattern (A-BGP) provides a formal triple-based representation of an OP. The A-BGPs for some "simple" ontology patterns, which precisely determine an existing ontological element by providing its URI, are shown in Table 1. The string enclosed within curly brackets denotes an *unspecified ontological element* and is to be replaced with the concrete elements used in the MRs during the instantiation process. The string enclosed within square brackets denotes an *unbounded entity* and is to be replaced with the specific elements used in the SPARQL query or RDF graph when applying the TRs generated for achieving a specific goal (e.g., SPARQL query rewriting).

Table 1. The Abstract Basic Graph Patterns for the "simple" Ontology Patterns.

Ontology Pattern	Abbrev.	Internal Element	Abstract Basic Graph Pattern
Simple Class Pattern	SCP	Class URI	[subject] rdf:type {class-uri}
Simple Relation Pattern	SRP	Object Property URI	[subject] {property-uri} [object]
Simple Property Pattern	SPP	Datatype Property URI	[subject] {property-uri} [object]

In general, an A-BGP consists of a finite set of Abstract Triple Patterns (A-TPs). An A-TP is a triple $(s, p, o) \in (U \cup A \cup I \cup L) \times (U \cup A \cup I) \times (U \cup A \cup I \cup L)$, where U is the set of unbounded entities, A is the set of unspecified ontological elements, I is the set of URIs and L is the set of Literals. The A-BGP that corresponds to the "complex" OPs (i.e., the OPs which internally use one or more OPs) is automatically constructed by taking into account the A-BGP of the internal OPs as well as their roles. The A-BGPs for some complex OPs on condition that simple internal OPs are used, are presented in Table 2.

Table 2. The Abstract Basic Graph Patterns for some "complex" Ontology Patterns.

Ontology Pattern	Internal Elements	Abstract Basic Graph Pattern
Relation Domain Restriction (RDR)	Relation: SRP, Domain: SCP	[subject] {property-uri} [object] . [subject] rdf:type {subject-class-uri}
Relation Range Restriction (RRR)	Relation: SRP, Range: SCP	[subject] {property-uri} [object] . [object] rdf:type {object-class-uri}
Relation Property Path (RPP)	Relation: SRP, Property: SPP	[subjectA] {relation-uri} [tmpAB] . [tmpAB] {property-uri} [objectB]

The names of the unbounded elements are not so important since they will be replaced by the concrete elements used in the SPARQL query. However, it should be noted that the unbounded elements with the same name refer to the same entity. For instance, in the RDR OP the "subject" of the property should belong to the specified class.

4.2   Concrete Level: Mapping and Transformation Rules

The construction of the TRs is driven by the MRs specified. More precisely, based on the entities specified within each MR (i.e., OP instance) the corresponding concrete BGP is produced (C-BGP aka A-BGP instance) by replacing the unspecified onto-logical elements in the A-BGP of entities 1 and 2 with the concrete ones. Conse-quently, a C-BGP consists of a finite set of concrete TPs (C-TPs aka A-TP instances). Then, the necessary interventions are made in the unbound entities present in the C-BGP of entities 1 and 2 so that the corresponding unbounded elements refer to the same entities. For example, the classes should share the same subject while the sub-ject and object of the properties specified in each side should be the same. The inverse relations comprise a special case according to which the subject and object of the first one should be the same with the object and subject of the second one as presented in the following expression.

$$[subject] \text{ associated-With } [object] \leftrightarrow [object] \text{ belongs-To } [subject] \tag{1}$$

A TR may be accompanied by one or more conditions depending on the OPs used within entities 1 and 2, while it may also contain a data transformation. The condi-tions and data transformations were implemented as services (uniquely determined by their URI) associated with a specific unbounded entity, which are accordingly used for locating the corresponding values in the SPARQL query or RDF graph. The "con-dition" services receive as input a value and return true or false, depending on whether the condition is satisfied or not. On the other hand, the "data transformation" services receive as input a value and return a new one as a response.

Formally, a TR is defined recursively as follows: (1) If C-BGP$_1$ and C-BGP$_2$ are the C-BGPs for the entities 1 and 2 of a MR, then the expression (C-BGP$_1$ $\leftrightarrow$ C-BGP$_2$) is a TR, on condition that the set unb(C-BGP$_1$) $\cap$ unb(C-BGP$_2$) $\neq \emptyset$, where "unb" is the function that provides the set of unbounded entities used in the C-BGP provided. (2) If T is a TR and CP is a tuple (u, s) that belongs to U × I$_C$, where I$_C$ is the set of URIs from known (i.e., publicly available or internally specified) "condi-tion" services, then the (T & CP) is a TR. (3) If T is a TR and DTP is a tuple (u, s) that belongs to U × I$_{DT}$, where I$_{DT}$ is the set of URIs from known "data transforma-tion" services, then the (T & Direct: DTP) and (T & Inverse: DTP) are also TRs on conditions that the direct or inverse data transformations have not previously been specified.

The SPARQL queries and RDF data TRs were also implemented as services which receive as input the aforementioned parameters of a TR and accordingly update the SPARQL query or RDF data. In a nutshell, the SPARQL query TR (SPAR-TR) makes the necessary changes in the SPARQL query, replacing the corresponding TPs with the new ones, while it also makes the necessary changes in the value often pre-sented within a FILTER clause. On the other hand, the RDF data TR (RDF-TR) re-places the corresponding triples with the new ones, while it also makes the necessary changes in the retrieved data so that they are expressed using the model and vocabu-laries supported by the end user.

4.3   Tasks Level: SPARQL Query and RDF Data Rewriting

SPARQL Query Rewriting. The SPARQL query rewriting process is based on a set of automatically produced SPAR-TRs according to the MRs specified. In overall, the first step is to determine which of the available SPAR-TRs can be fired accordingly (if necessary) to specify the order in which they should be executed and finally to apply the corresponding TRs. A SPAR-TR can be fired on condition that the C-BGP present in the left side of the TR matches with the Triple Patterns (TPs) of the provided SPARQL query, and that simultaneously all the other conditions specified (if any) are satisfied.

A C-TP that belongs to a C-BGP matches with a TP specified in the BGP of a SPARQL query on condition that the corresponding elements are either the same (for URIs and Literals) or a mapping (aka binding) can take place among the unbounded entities used and the elements specified in the TP. We define a binding b as a partial function $b : U \rightarrow (I \cup L \cup V)$ which links an unbounded element (u) specified within a C-TP of a C-BGP with the specific entity used in the TP of the BGP. Since the range of function b includes elements from different types including URIs, Literals and Variables, the values are the same if they belong to the same type and consist of the same sequence of characters. Two bindings b1 and b2 are compatible when for all the unbounded entities that belong to $dom(b_1)$ AND $dom(b_2)$, $b_1(u) = b_2(u)$, where $dom(b)$ is a subset of U for which the function b is defined.

A C-BGP matches with the TPs specified in the BGP of a SPARQL query on condition that a) all the internal C-TPs match and b) all the bindings that took place for the internal C-TPs are compatible with each other. For satisfying both conditions, any binding that took place in the previously examined C-TPs of a C-BGP is taken for granted when checking the presence of the remaining C-TPs. It should be mentioned that a C-BGP may be present in the same BGP more than once, while the corresponding elements (especially the value of properties) may also participate in one or more FILTER clauses. In case that a condition is specified, the corresponding unbounded entity (which will have been replaced either by the specific element or a variable after the C-BGP matching process) is used to locate the appropriate value in either TPs or FILTER clauses and accordingly the condition that should be satisfy is examined.

A TR can be fired if both the C-BGP matches and all the conditions (if any) are satisfied. A TR can be fired more than once, as mentioned before, depending on the number of times the (left) C-BGP of a TR matches. In each case, the corresponding TPs can be replaced with the new one while a transformation in the corresponding value(s) may be necessary, depending on whether a "direct" data transformation has been specified or not. It should be noted that the bindings taking place in the left C-BGP of a MR are also valid for the unbound entities existing in the right side, on condition that they have the same name. Moreover, the unbounded entities existing in the right side of a MR (i.e., the ones with a different name from the unbounded entities existing in the left side) should be replaced by a new variable with a unique name. Finally, in case a data transformation is necessary, the corresponding value or values in the TPs or FILTER clauses of the SPARQL query are found using the appropriate entity, and they are replaced with the new ones using the specific service provided (i.e., a function which provides the corresponding value/values taking into account the model and vocabularies supported by the SPARQL endpoint).

The order in which the TRs will be executed is not so important on condition that there is no overlap among their C-BGPs. When an overlap takes place, the corresponding TPs in the SPARQL query will be removed on condition that they do not participate in any of the TRs that have not been executed yet. Also, priority is given to those TRs which contain a condition, while the more complex TRs (practically the ones which contain the most C-TPs) are considered to be more specific from the other ones and are executed at the beginning. After the application of all possible SPAR-TRs, the initial SPARQL query will have been rewritten using the terminology supported by the SPARQL endpoint. However, the TPs that could not be rewritten, due to absence of the corresponding information from the datasource, should be removed.

RDF Data Rewriting. Rewriting of RDF Data is based on the RDF-TRs produced. However, in this case, a slightly different approach is followed. For each of the RDF-TRs, the corresponding CONSTRUCT SPARQL query is automatically generated, which is accordingly used for rewriting the corresponding triples (expressed using the SPARQL endpoint terminology) to the new ones and, then it is examined if the corresponding conditions (if any, in the right side of the TR) are satisfied or not. The production part of the SPARQL query is based on the Left side of the TR whereas the restriction part on the Right side of the TR. During this process, all the unbounded entities present in the WHERE clause are replaced by the corresponding variables, while the unbounded elements present in the CONSTRUCT clause (that do not exist in the where clause, if any) are replaced by a blank node. In case that the outcome of the CONSTRUCT SPARQL query is not empty, the corresponding data are examined whether they satisfy the conditions specified (if any). In case that the outcome is not empty and the corresponding conditions are satisfied the RDF-TR can be fired. In such cases, the corresponding triples will be replaced by the new ones. Also the necessary changes in the values are made, if being necessary. However, during this process, the "inverse" data transformation is used, which provides the corresponding data based on the model and vocabularies supported by the end user.

The order in which the RDF-TRs will be applied is not important on condition that there is no overlap among the C-BGP present in the Right side of the TRs. Otherwise, an approach is followed which is similar with the one used in the SPARQL query rewriting process for specifying their order. The rewritten RDF graph is produced after the application of all possible RDF-TRs. The triples that were not rewritten, if any, should be removed.

5   Example: Patients Recruitment for Clinical Research Purposes

In this section, an example is presented, which shows the retrieval of the eligible patients from a Healthcare Entity (assuming that all legal and ethical issues are satisfied) by using a different model than the one supported by the available SPARQL endpoint. It should be noted that within our model, we capture the Medical Conditions associated with each person, while for each of them its ICD-10 code (i.e., a code from the 10th version of ICD [20]) and its date of diagnosis are recorded, among others. On the Healthcare entity side ICD-9 codes are used for the same purpose, while the date on which each condition was recorded is also available. The aforementioned models, as well as the specified MRs (M1 to M6) along with the OPs used and the data transformation services needed are presented in Fig 3.

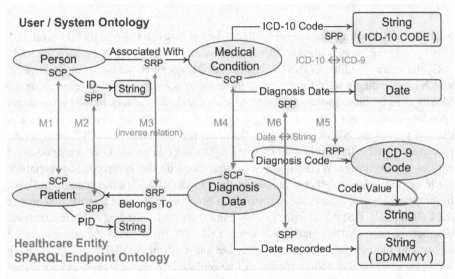

Fig. 3. Mapping Rules specified among the terms of the User and the Healthcare Entity models.

The specified MRs are valid for both directions while the specified correspondences are considered to be equivalent, with adequate explanations provided wherever required. For instance, when searching for the eligible "Persons" the "Patients" should be sought for in the corresponding datasource, despite the fact that the aforementioned terms are not generally equivalent. Also, when moving from one model to the other, in the MRs M5 and M6 a data transformation is necessary. The first transformation provides the corresponding ICD code, whereas the second one provides the date in the appropriate format. The automatically generated TRs are presented in Table 3. Both SPARQL query and RDF data TRs are derived from this one, through a straightforward process, as already mentioned.

Table 3. The automatically generated concrete Transformation Rules (TRs).

ID	MR	TR: Left Side	TR: Right Side	TR: Data Trans.
TR1	M1	[sth] rdf:type usr:Person	[sth] rdf:type db:Patient	-
TR2	M2	[sth1] usr:ID [sth2]	[sth1] db:PID [sth2]	-
TR3	M3	[sth1] usr:associatedWith [sth2]	[sth2] db:belongsTo [sth1]	-
TR4	M4	[sth] rdf:type usr:MedicalCondition	[sth] rdf:type db:DiagnosisData	-
TR5	M5	[sth1] user:icd10code [sth2]	[sth1] db:diagnosisCode [tmp] . [tmp] db:codeValue [sth2]	[sth2]:ICD-10 to/from ICD-9
TR6	M6	[sth1] user:diagnosisDate [sth2]	[sth1] user:dateRecorded [sth2]	[sth2]:Date to/from String

Taking into account the specified MRs and especially the automatically generated TRs, the SPARQL query for retrieving the patients diagnosed with Acute Myocardial Infarction (ICD-10 code: I21) along with the date each diagnosis took place is rewritten as shown in Fig. 4. It should be noted that the order in which the TRs are fired is not important since there is no overlap among them. Also, some TRs are fired more than once (e.g., TR1).

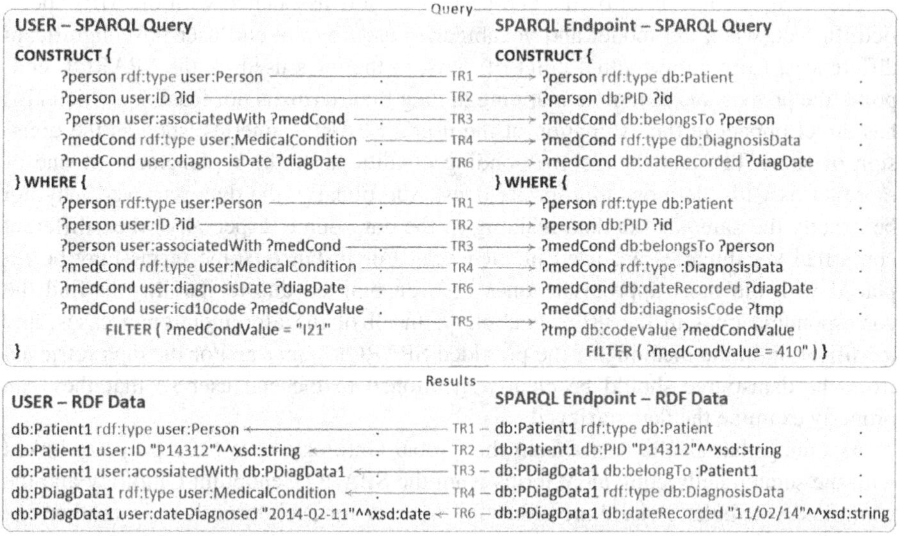

Fig. 4. The initial and rewritten SPARQL queries and RDF data along with the TRs used - The definitions of prefixes in both SPARQL queries and RDF data have been deliberately omitted.

Since both the construct and where clauses of the SPARQL query have been rewritten, the results retrieved from the SPARQL endpoint are compatible with the model and vocabularies used by the SPARQL endpoint. For example, the date in which each diagnosis took place is a String with the format "DD/MM/YY". Consequently, further processing of the retrieved data is necessary, so that the results are finally expressed according to the model and vocabularies used by the end user. In Fig. 4, the triples retrieved from the SPARQL endpoint are also presented (but only for one patient, due to space limitations) in the Turtle format [21], as well as the re-written ones. It should be noted that in TR6 the "inverse" data transformation is used, which produces the date based on the sequence of characters retrieved.

6   Discussion

In this work, CONSTRUCT SPARQL queries have been deliberately used for infor-mation retrieval purposes, since their outcome is an RDF graph which provides a model-based description of the eligible data, and hence, it is amenable to any further processing. However, it should be noted that the same information can be also re-trieved by using SELECT SPARQL queries, but in order to properly handle the retrieved data the SPARQL query provided must be also taken into account. More precisely, the WHERE clause of the SPARQL query must be further processed for detecting the meaning of the variables existing in the SELECT clause. Then the se-quence of retrieved characters should be examined and probably some changes be made on them (i.e., the data existing in each column) taking into account the meaning of the corresponding column fields.

The "terminology" used by the end users is closely associated with the MRs speci-fied. In fact, when the model and vocabularies used by the end user pose significant differences, from a conceptual point of view, to the ones used by the SPARQL end-point, the precise and complete mapping among their terms is not feasible, which also has direct impact in the evaluation of the user's SPARQL queries, such as the omis-sion of some TPs and their corresponding conditions or the replacement of one or more terms with the most appropriate ones. Additionally, the data retrieved may not be exactly the same as the data residing in the datasource, especially when different controlled vocabularies are used in each side. For instance, some terms may be re-placed with the most appropriate ones or even omitted due to inability to find the corresponding ones in the user vocabulary. In all of the aforementioned cases, any modification in the meaning of the provided SPARQL query and/or the data retrieved from the datasource should be clearly mentioned to the end user so that they can properly examine the data retrieved.

Assuming that all the terms from the Global Ontology have been properly linked with the semantically equivalent terms from the SPARQL endpoint Ontology and the controlled vocabularies used are either the same or for each term there is another one in the DB with exactly the same meaning, then the *semantics* of the SPARQL query [22] do not change after the application of the TRs. The SPARQL query preserves its meaning since its overall structure is not changed (every change takes place in the TPs of a BGP) while both TPs and the corresponding terms specified within the FILTER clauses (if necessary) are being replaced with their semantically equivalent TPs and terms respectively.

In case the *controlled vocabularies* used in each side are different, in general, there may not be a one-to-one correspondence among their terms. For example, one term may be the same as the union or intersection of two or more terms from another vocabulary or vice versa. During the SPARQL query rewriting process the aforementioned cases can be efficiently handled by introducing the appropriate conditions using AND/OR operators within a FILTER clause. In order for the retrieved data to be translatable in case they also come from the aforementioned vocabularies, the Global Ontology should be carefully designed so that the values of the properties are either a coded element (i.e., a vocabulary term) or an expression formed by the intersection or union of the corresponding terms.

Concerning the SPARQL query rewriting mechanism, in our work focus was given on such MRs which do not change the *structure* of the SPARQL query. However, in some cases, it may be necessary to introduce (or remove) an OPTIONAL or UNION clause, which should be examined more thoroughly in our future work. Also, in case that a data transformation is necessary the conditions specified in the FILTER clause should be carefully examined, since some operators used may not be valid any more, especially when the type of data changes (e.g., from string to integer or vice versa). Consequently the whole condition(s) should be replaced with their semantic equivalents rather than their values. Additionally, in some cases, the value of a property depends on the value of two or more properties. For instance, the date of birth (specified in one of the global or local ontologies) depends on the age of a person and the date recorded (specified in the other ontology) and hence the values of both properties should be taken into account when applying the necessary changes in the FILTER clause.

The *cardinality restriction* of the specified properties is a very important parameter, especially when one of the entities participating in the left and/or right side of a mapping rule is not an existing property, but a new one implied by the path formed by a relation and a property. In the MR M5 presented in Section 5, the cardinality of both properties is the same and more precisely, each entity from the corresponding classes has exactly one instance of the corresponding properties. However, the cardinality restriction may be different (e.g. one-to-many) and hence both the specified MRs as well as the TPs they are specified in should be properly handled in a SPARQL query.

7   Conclusion

Ontology alignment plays a distinctive role for accessing a SPARQL endpoint using models and controlled vocabularies that are different than the ones supported by the endpoint. OPs, in combination with the appropriate conditions and data transformation services can adequately handle possible mismatches while the OAT enables users to easily determine the corresponding MRs through a semi-automatic process. In this work, particular focus has been given to the utilisation of the specified MRs for query answering purposes. More precisely, the processes followed for rewriting users' SPARQL queries as well as the retrieved data (formally expressed through an RDF graph) have been extensively described. The novel approach presented along with the components implemented take into account a variety of heterogeneity issues at both model and vocabularies used. Hence, they comprise a significant improvement towards facilitating the interaction and linking of semantically enabled systems and software agents with existing SPARQL endpoints or relational databases.

Acknowledgments. This work is being supported by the OpenScienceLink project [23] and has been partially funded by the European Commission's CIP-PSP under contract number 325101. This paper expresses the opinions of the authors and not necessarily those of the European Commission. The European Commission is not liable for any use that may be made of the information contained in this paper.

References

1. W3C - Web Ontology Language (OWL). http://www.w3.org/TR/owl-guide/
2. W3C - RDF Schema (RDFS). http://www.w3.org/TR/rdf-schema/
3. D2R Server. http://d2rq.org/d2r-server
4. Chondrogiannis, E., Andronikou, V., Karanastasis, E., Varvarigou, T.: A novel framework for user-friendly ontology-mediated access to relational databases. In: International Conference on Web and Semantic Technology, vol. 1(3), p. 1100. WASET (2014)
5. Chondrogiannis, E., Andronikou, V., Mourtzoukos, K., Tagaris, A., Varvarigou, T.: A novel query rewriting mechanism for semantically interlinking clinical research with electronic health records. In: 2nd International Conference on Web Intelligence, Mining and Semantics, pp. 48:1–48:12. ACM, New York (2012)
6. W3C - SPARQL Query Language for RDF. http://www.w3.org/TR/rdf-sparql-query/
7. Cruz, I.F., Antonelli, F.P., Stroe, C.: Agreement maker efficient matching for large real-world schemas and ontologies. In: Proceeding of International Conference on Very Large Databases, pp. 1586–1589 (2009)
8. Kolli, R., Doshi, P.: OPTIMA: tool for ontology alignment with application to semantic reconciliation of sensor metadata for publication in SensorMap. In: Proceedings of the 2008 IEEE International Conference on Semantic Computing (ICSC 2008), pp. 484–485. IEEE Computer Society, Washington, DC (2008)
9. Massmann, S., Raunich, S., Aumueller, D., Arnold, P., Rahm, E.: Evolution of the coma match system. In: Proceedings of the 6th International Workshop on Ontology Matching, Bonn, Germany (2011)
10. Shvaiko, P., Euzenat, J.: Ontology Matching: State of the Art and Future Challenges. IEEE Transactions on Knowledge and Data Engineering 25(1), 158–176 (2013)
11. Scharffe, F., de Bruijn, J.: A language to specify mappings between ontologies. In: Proceedings of the Internet Based Systems IEEE Conference (SITIS 2005), Yandoue, Cameroon (2005)
12. Scharffe, F., Fensel, D.: Correspondence patterns for ontology alignment. In: Gangemi, A., Euzenat, J. (eds.) EKAW 2008. LNCS (LNAI), vol. 5268, pp. 83–92. Springer, Heidelberg (2008)
13. Šváb-Zamazal, O., Svátek, V., Scharffe, F., David, J.: Detection and transformation of ontology patterns. In: Fred, A., Dietz, J.L., Liu, K., Filipe, J. (eds.) IC3K 2009. CCIS, vol. 128, pp. 210–223. Springer, Heidelberg (2011)
14. Ghawi, R., Poulain, T., Gomez, G., Cullot N.: OWSCIS: ontology and web service based cooperation of information sources. In: Proceedings of the Third International IEEE Conference on Signal-Image Technologies and Internet-Based Systems (SITIS 2007), pp. 246–253. IEEE Computer Society (2007)
15. W3C - Semantic Web Health Care and Life Sciences (HCLS) Interest Group. http://www.w3.org/blog/hcls/

16. Correndo, G., Salvadores, M., Millard, I., Glaser, H., Shadbolt, N.: SPARQL query rewriting for implementing data integration over linked data. In: Proceedings of the 2010 EDBT/ICDT Workshops (EDBT 2010), pp. 4:1–4:11. ACM, New York (2010)
17. Euzenat, J., Polleres, A., Scharffe, F.: Processing ontology alignments with SPARQL. In: Second International Conference on Complex, Intelligent and Software Intensive Systems (CISIS-2008), pp. 913–917 (2008)
18. W3C - Resource Description Framework (RDF). http://www.w3.org/RDF/
19. Chondrogiannis, E., Andronikou, V., Karanastasis, E., Varvarigou, T.: An intelligent ontology alignment tool dealing with complicated mismatches. In: Proceedings of the 7th International Workshop on Semantic Web Applications and Tools for Life Sciences, Berlin, Germany (2014)
20. World Health Organization (WHO) - International Classification of Diseases (ICD). http://www.who.int/classifications/icd/en/
21. W3C - Turtle - Terse RDF Triple Language. http://www.w3.org/TeamSubmission/turtle/
22. Pérez, J., Arenas, M., Gutierrez, C.: Semantics and complexity of SPARQL. ACM Trans. Database Syst. **34**(3), 1–45 (2009)
23. Karanastasis, E., Andronikou, V., Chondrogiannis, E., Tsatsaronis, G., Eisinger, D., Petrova, A.: The OpenScienceLink architecture for novel services exploiting open access data in the biomedical domain. In: 18th Panhellenic Conference on Informatics, pp. 28:1–28:6 ACM, New York (2014)

Identifying Web Tables: Supporting a Neglected Type of Content on the Web

Mikhail Galkin[1,2], Dmitry Mouromtsev[2](✉), and Sören Auer[1](✉)

[1] University of Bonn, Bonn, Germany
auer@cs.uni-bonn.de
[2] ITMO University, Saint Petersburg, Russia
mouromtsev@mail.ifmo.ru

Abstract. The abundance of the data in the Internet facilitates the improvement of extraction and processing tools. The trend in the open data publishing encourages the adoption of structured formats like CSV and RDF. However, there is still a plethora of unstructured data on the Web which we assume contain semantics. For this reason, we propose an approach to derive semantics from web tables which are still the most popular publishing tool on the Web. The paper also discusses methods and services of unstructured data extraction and processing as well as machine learning techniques to enhance such a workflow. The eventual result is a framework to process, publish and visualize linked open data. The software enables tables extraction from various open data sources in the HTML format and an automatic export to the RDF format making the data linked. The paper also gives the evaluation of machine learning techniques in conjunction with string similarity functions to be applied in a tables recognition task.

Keywords: Machine learning · Linked Data · Semantic Web

1 Introduction

The Web contains various types of content, e.g. text, pictures, video, audio as well as tables. Tables are used everywhere in the Web to represent statistical data, sports results, music data and arbitrary lists of parameters. Recent research [2,3] conducted on the *Common Crawl* census[1] indicated that an average Web page contains at least nine tables. In this research about 12 billion tables were extracted from a billion of HTML pages, which demonstrates the popularity of this type of data representation. Tables are a natural way how people interact with structured data and can provide a comprehensive overview of large amounts and complex information. The prevailing part of structured information on the Web is stored in tables. Nevertheless, we argue that table is still a neglected content type regarding processing, extraction and annotation tools.

---

[1] Web: http://commoncrawl.org/

© Springer International Publishing Switzerland 2015
P. Klinov and D. Mouromtsev (Eds.): KESW 2015, CCIS 518, pp. 48–62, 2015.
DOI: 10.1007/978-3-319-24543-0_4

For example, even though there are billions of tables on the Web search engines are still not able to index them in a way that facilitates data retrieval. The annotation and retrieval of pictures, video and audio data is meanwhile well supported, whereas on of the most widespread content types is still not sufficiently supported. Assumption that an average table contains on average 50 facts it is possible to extract more than 600 billion facts taking into account only the 12 billion sample tables found in the Common Crawl. This is already *six* times more than the whole *Linked Open Data Cloud*[2]. Moreover, despite a shift towards semantic annotation (e.g. via RDFa) there will always be plain tables abundantly available on the Web. With this paper we want turn a spotlight on the importance of tables processing and knowledge extraction from tables on the Web.

The problem of deriving knowledge from tables embedded in an HTML page is a challenging research task. In order to enable machines to understand the meaning of data in a table we have to solve certain problems:

1. Search for relevant Web pages to be processed;
2. Extraction of the information to work with;
3. Determining relevance of the table;
4. Revealing the structure of the found information;
5. Identification of the data range of the table;
6. Mapping the extracted results to existing vocabularies and ontologies.

The difference in recognizing a simple table by a human and a machine is depicted in Fig. 1. Machine are not easily able to derive formal knowledge about the content of the table.

	P1	P2	P3
Obj1	a1	B2	C3
Obj2	D1	E2	F3
Obj3	G1	H2	I3
Obj4	J1	K2	L3
Obj5	MkS	NxA	xyz

```
<style type="text/css">
.tg  {border-collapse:collapse;border-spacing:0;}
.tg td{font-family:Arial, sans-serif;font-size:14px;padding:10px
5px;border-style:solid;border-width:1px;overflow:hidden;word-break:normal;}
.tg th{font-family:Arial, sans-serif;font-size:14px;font-weight:normal;padding:10px
5px;border-style:solid;border-width:1px;overflow:hidden;word-break:normal;}
.tg .tg-s6z2{text-align:center}
</style><table class="tg" style="undefined;table-layout: fixed; width: 208px">
<colgroup><col style="width: 41px"><col style="width: 55px"><col style="width: 51px">
<col style="width: 61px"></colgroup><tr><th class="tg-031e"></th><th class="tg-s6z2">P1</th>
<th class="tg-s6z2">P2</th><th class="tg-s6z2">P3</th></tr><tr><td class="tg-031e">Obj1</td>
<td class="tg-s6z2">a1</td><td class="tg-s6z2">b2</td><td class="tg-s6z2">c3</td></tr><tr>
<td class="tg-031e">Obj2</td><td class="tg-s6z2">d1</td><td class="tg-s6z2">e2</td>
<td class="tg-s6z2">f3</td></tr><tr><td class="tg-031e">Obj3</td><td class="tg-s6z2">g1</td>
<td class="tg-s6z2">h2</td><td class="tg-s6z2">i3</td></tr><tr><td class="tg-031e">Obj4</td>
<td class="tg-s6z2">j1</td><td class="tg-s6z2">k2</td><td class="tg-s6z2">l3</td></tr><tr>
<td class="tg-031e">Obj5</td><td class="tg-s6z2">m1</td><td class="tg-s6z2">op</td>
<td class="tg-s6z2">xyz</td></tr></table>
```

Fig. 1. Different representations of one table.

The paper describes current methodologies and services to tackle some crucial Web table processing challenges and introduces a new approach of table data processing which combines advantages of Semantic Web technologies with robust machine learning algorithms. Our approach allows machines to distinguish certain types of tables (genuine tables), recognize their structure (orientation check) and dynamically link the content with already known sources.

The paper is structured as follows: Section 2 gives an overview of related studies in the field of unstructured data processing. Section 3 presents Web services

[2] Web: http://stats.lod2.eu/

which provide the user with table extraction functions. Section 4 describes the approach and establishes a mathematical ground for a further research. Section 5 presents used machine learning algorithms and string distance functions. Section 6 showcases the evaluation of the approach. Finally, we derive conclusions and share plans for future work.

2   Related Work

The Linked Open Data concept raises the question of automatic tables processing as one of the most crucial. Open Government Data is frequently published in simple HTML tables that are not well structured and lack semantics. Thus, the problems discussed in the paper [11] concern methods of acquiring datasets related to roads repair from the government of Saint Petersburg. There is also a raw approach [9] in information extraction, which is template-based and effective in processing of web sites with unstable markup. The crawler was used to create a LOD dataset of CEUR Workshop[3] proceedings.

Silva et al. in their paper [13] suggest and analyze an algorithm of table research that consists of five steps: location, segmentation, functional analysis, structural analysis and interpretation of the table. The authors provide a comprehensive overview of the existing approaches and designed a method for extracting data from ASCII tables. However, smart tables detection and distinguishing is not considered.

J. Hu et al. introduced in the paper [7] the methods for table detection and recognition. Table detection is based on the idea of edit-distance while table recognition uses random graphs approach. M. Hurst takes into consideration ASCII tables [8] and suggests an approach to derive an abstract geometric model of a table from a physical representation. A graph of constraints between cells was implemented in order to determine position of cells. Nevertheless, the results are rather high which indicates the efficiency of the approach. The authors of the papers achieved significant success in structuring a table, but the question of the table content and its semantic is still opened.

D. Embley et al. tried [4] to solve the table processing problem as an extraction problem with an introduction of machine learning algorithms. However, the test sample was rather small which might have been resulted in overfitting [1].

Y. A. Tijerino et al. introduced in [14] TANGO approach (Table Analysis for Generating Ontologies) which is mostly based on WordNet with a special procedure of ontology generation. The whole algorithm implies 4 actions: table recognition, mini-ontology generation, inter-ontology mappings discovery, merging of mini-ontologies. During the table recognition step search in WordNet support the process of table segmentation su that no machine learning algorithms were applied.

To sum up, there are different approaches to information extraction developed last ten years. In our work we introduce an effective extraction and

---

[3] Web: http://ceur-ws.org/

analyzing framework built on top of those methodologies combining tables recognition techniques, machine learning algorithms and Semantic Web methods.

2.1 Existing Data Processing Services

Automatic data extraction has always been given a lot of attention from the Web community. There are numerous web-services that provide users with sophisticated instruments useful in web scraping, web crawling and tables processing. Some of them are presented below.

ScraperWiki[4] is a powerful tool based on subscription model that is suitable for software engineers and data scientists whose work is connected with processing of large amounts of data. Being a platform for interaction between business, journalists and developers, ScraperWiki allows users to solve extracting and cleaning tasks, helps to visualize acquired information and offers tools to manage retrieved data. Some of the features of the service:

- Dataset subscription makes possible the automatic tracking, update and processing of the specified dataset in the Internet.
- A wide range of data processing instruments. For instance, information extraction from PDF documents

ScraperWiki allows one to parse web tables in CSV format, but processes all the tables on the page even thought they do not contain relevant data, e.g. layout tables. Also the service does not provide any Linked Data functionality.

Scrapy[5] is a fast high-level framework written in Python for web-scraping and data extraction. Scrapy is spread under BSD license and available on Windows, Linux, MacOS and BSD. Merging performance, speed, extensibility and simplicity Scrapy is a popular solution in the industry. A lot of services are based on Scrapy, such as ScraperWiki or PriceWiki[6].

Import.io[7] is am emerging data processing service. Comprehensive visualization and an opportunity to use the service without programming experience tend Import.io to become one of the most wide-spread and user-friendly software. The system offers users three methods of extraction arranged by growing complexity: an extractor, a crawler and a connector. The feature of automatic table extraction is also implemented but supports only CSV format.

3 Concept

In order to achieve the automatic tables processing certain problems have to be solved:

1. HTML tables search and localization from a URL provided by the user;
2. Computing of appropriate heuristics;

---

[4] Web: https://scraperwiki.com/
[5] Web: http://scrapy.org/
[6] Web: http://www.pricewiki.com/blog/
[7] Web: https://import.io/

3. Table genuineness check, in other words, check whether a table contains relevant data;
4. Table orientation check (horizontal or vertical);
5. Transformation of the table data to an RDF model.

The importance of correct tables recognition affects the performance of most of web–services. The growth of the data on the Web facilitates the data- and knowledge bases updates with such a frequency, that does not allow errors, inconsistency or ambiguity. With the help of our methodology we aim to address the challenges of automatic *knowledge extraction* and *knowledge replenishment*.

3.1   Knowledge Retrieval

Knowledge extraction enables the creation of knowledge bases and ontologies using the content of HTML tables. It is also a major step towards five-star open data[8] making the knowledge linked with other datasources and accessible, in addition, in a machine-readable format. Thus, a correct table processing and an ontology generation is a crucial part of the entire workflow. Our framework implements learning algorithms which allow automatic distinguishing between *genuine* and *non-genuine* tables [16], as well as automatic ontology generation.

We call a table *genuine* when it contains consistent data (e.g. the data the user is looking for) and we call a table *non-genuine* when it contains any HTML page layout information or a rather useless content, e.g. a list of hyperlinks to other websites within one row or one column.

3.2   Knowledge Acquisition

Knowledge replenishment raises important questions of data updating and deduplication. A distinctive feature of our approach is a fully automatic update from the datasource. The proposed system implements components of the powerful platform *Information Workbench* [6] which introduces the mechanism of *Data Providers*. Data Providers observe a datasource specified by a user and all its modifications according to a given schedule. Therefore, it enables the replenishment of the same knowledge graph with new entities and facts, which, in turn, facilitates data deduplication.

4   Formal Definitions

The foundation of the formal approach is based on ideas of Ermilov et al. [5]

Definition 1. *A table* $\mathcal{T} = (\mathcal{H}, \mathcal{N})$ *is tuple consisting of a header* $\mathcal{H}$ *and data nodes* $\mathcal{N}$, *where:*

- *the header* $\mathcal{H} = \{h_1, h_2, \ldots, h_n\}$ *is an n-tuple of header elements* h_i. *We also assume that the set of headers might be optional, e.g.* $\exists \mathcal{T} \equiv \mathcal{N}$. *If the set of headers exists, it might be either a row or a column.*

---

[8] Web: http://5stardata.info/

- the data nodes $\mathcal{N} = \begin{pmatrix} c_{1,1} & c_{1,2} & \cdots & c_{1,m} \\ c_{2,1} & c_{2,2} & \cdots & c_{2,m} \\ \vdots & \vdots & \ddots & \vdots \\ c_{n,1} & c_{n,2} & \cdots & c_{n,m} \end{pmatrix}$ are a (n,m) matrix consisting of n rows and m columns.

Definition 2. *The genuineness of the table is a parameter which is computed via the function of grid nodes and headers, so that $G_T(\mathcal{N}, \mathcal{H}) = g_k \in \mathcal{G}, \mathcal{G} = \{true, flase\}$.*

Definition 3. *The orientation of the table is a parameter which values are defined in the set $\mathcal{O} = \{horizontal, vertical\}$ if and only if $G_T(\mathcal{N}, \mathcal{H}) = true$. So that $\exists O_T \iff G_T \equiv true$. The orientation of the table is computed via a function of grid nodes and headers, so that $O_T(\mathcal{N}, \mathcal{H}) = o_k \in \mathcal{O}$. If the orientation is horizontal, then the headers are presented as a row, so that $O_T \equiv horizontal$. If the orientation is vertical, then the headers are presented as a column, so that $O_T \equiv vertical$.*

Table 1. Horizontal orientation

H0	Header 1	Header 2	Header 3	Header 4
Obj 1				
Obj 2				
Obj 3				
Obj 4				

Table 2. Vertical orientation

H0	Obj 1	Obj 2	Obj 3	Obj 4
Header 1				
Header 2				
Header 3				
Header 4				

Definition 4. *A set of heuristics $\mathcal{V}$ is a set of quantitative functions of grid nodes $\mathcal{N}$ and headers $\mathcal{H}$ which is used by machine learning algorithms in order to define genuineness and orientation of the given table $\mathcal{T}$.*

$$G_T(\mathcal{N}, \mathcal{H}) = \begin{cases} true, & V_{g1} \in [v_{g1_{min}}, v_{g1_{max}}], \ldots V_{gm} \\ false, & otherwise. \end{cases} \quad (1)$$

where $V_{g1}, ..., V_{gm} \in \mathcal{V}$, $[v_{g1_{min}}, v_{g1_{max}}]$ is the range of values of V_{g1} necessary for the true value in conjunction with $V_{g2}, ..., V_{gm}$ functions.

$$O_T(\mathcal{N}, \mathcal{H}) = \begin{cases} horizontal, & V_{h1} \in [v_{h1_{min}}, v_{h1_{max}}], ..., V_{hn}. \\ vertical, & V_{v1} \in [v_{v1_{min}}, v_{v1_{max}}], ..., V_{vl}. \end{cases} \quad (2)$$

where $V_{h1}, ..., V_{hn} \in \mathcal{V}$, $V_{v1}, ..., V_{vl} \in \mathcal{V}$, $[v_{h1_{min}}, v_{h1_{max}}]$ is the range of values of V_{h1} necessary for the horizontal value in conjunction with $V_{h2}, ..., V_{hn}$ functions, $[v_{v1_{min}}, v_{v1_{max}}]$ is the range of values of V_{v1} necessary for the vertical value in conjunction with $V_{v2}, ..., V_{vl}$ functions.

Algorithm 1. The workflow of the system

1: **procedure** WORKFLOW
2:      $URI \leftarrow$ specified by the user
3:      tables localization
4:      $n \leftarrow$ found tables
5: *while* $n > 0$:
6:      $n \leftarrow n - 1.$
7:      **if** genuine $= true$ **then**
8:          orientation check.
9:          RDF transformation.
10:     **goto** *while*.

Thus, it becomes obvious, that the *heuristics* are used in order to solve the classification problem [10] $X = \mathbb{R}^n, Y = \{-1, +1\}$ where the data sample is $X^l = (x_i, y_i)_{i=1}^l$ and the goal is to find the parameters $w \in \mathbb{R}^n, w_0 \in \mathbb{R}$ so that:

$$a(x, w) = sign(\langle x, w \rangle - w_o). \tag{3}$$

We describe heuristics and machine learning algorithms in detail in Section 5. From description logics we define the terminological component $TBox_T$ as a set of concepts over the set of headers $\mathcal{H}$. We define the assertion component $ABox_T$ as a set of facts over the set of grid nodes $\mathcal{N}$.

Hypothesis 1. *Tables in unstructured formats contain semantics.*

$$\exists T | \{\mathcal{H}_T \iff TBox_T, \mathcal{N}_T \iff ABox_T\} \tag{4}$$

In other words, there are tables with the relevant content, which could be efficiently extracted as knowledge.

The evaluation of the hypothesis is presented in the Section 7

4.1   Algorithm Description

The algorithm is depicted as Algorithm 1. The valid URL of the website where the data is situated is required from the user.

The next step is a process of search and localization of HTML tables on a specified website. One of the essential points in the process is to handle DOM < *table* > leaf nodes in order to avoid nested tables. Most of the systems described in 2.1 suggest a user with all the extracted tables, whether they are formatting tables or relevant tables. In contrast, our approach envisions full automation with the subsequent ontology generation.

The next step is a computation of heuristics for every extracted table. Using a training set and heuristics a machine learning algorithm classifies the object into a genuine or a non-genuine group. The input of the machine learning module is a *table trace* – a unique multi-dimensional vector of computed values of the heuristics of a particular table. Using a training set the described classifiers decide, whether the vector satisfies the genuineness class requirements or not.

If the vector is decided to be genuine the vector then is explored by classifiers again in attempt to define the orientation of the table.

The correct orientation determination is essential for correct transformation of the table data to semantic formats. Then it becomes possible to divide data and metadata of a table and construct an ontology.

If the table is decided to be a non-genuine then a user receives a message where it is stated that a particular table is not genuine according to the efficiency of a chosen machine learning method. However, the user is allowed to manually mark a table as a genuine which in turn modifies machine learning parameters.

5   Machine Learning Methods

Machine learning algorithms play vital role in the system which workflow is based on appropriate heuristics which in turn are based on string similarity functions. The nature of the problem implies usage of mechanisms that analyze the content of the table and calculate a set of parameters. In our case the most suitable option is implementation of string similarity (or string distance) functions.

5.1   String Metrics

String metric is a metric that measures similarity or dissimilarity between two text strings for approximate string matching or comparison. In the paper three string distance functions are used and compared.

Levenshtein distance is calculated as a minimum number of edit operations (insertions, substitutions, deletions) required to transform one string into another. Characters matches are not counted.

Jaro-Winkler distance is a string similarity metric and improved version of the Jaro distance. It is widely used to search for duplicates in a text or a database. The numerical value of the distance lies between 0 and 1 which means two strings are more similar the closer the value to 1.

Being popular in the industry [18] **n-gram** is a sequence of n items gathered from a text or a speech. In the paper n-grams are substrings of a particular string with the length n.

5.2   Improvements

Due to the mechanism of tables extraction and analysis certain common practices are improved or omitted. Hence particular changes in string similarity functions have been implemented:

- The content type of the cell is more important than the content itself. Thus it is reasonable to equalize all numbers and count them as the same symbol. Nevertheless the order of magnitude of a number is still taken into account. For instance, the developed system recognizes 3.9 and 8.2 as the same symbols, but 223.1 and 46.5 would be different with short distance between these strings.

– Strings longer than three words have fixed similarity depending on a string distance function in spite of previously described priority reasons. Moreover, tables often contain fields like "description" or "details" that might contain a lot of text which eventually might make a mistake during the heuristics calculations. So that the appropriated changes have been implemented into algorithms.

5.3 Heuristics

Relying on the theory above it is now possible to construct a set of primary heuristics. The example table the heuristics mechanisms are explained with is:

Table 3. An example table

Name	City	Phone	e-mail
Ivanov I. I.	Berlin	1112233	ivanov@mail.de
Petrov P.P	Berlin	2223344	petrov@mail.de
Sidorov S. S.	Moscow	3334455	sidorov@ya.ru
Pupkin V.V.	Moscow	4445566	pupkinv@gmail.com

Maximum Horizontal Cell Similarity. The attribute indicates the maximum similarity of a particular pair of cells normalized to all possible pairs in the row found within the whole table under the assumption of horizontal orientation of a table. It means the first row of a table is not taken into account because of a header of a table (see Table 1). Having in mind the example table the strings "Ivanov I.I." and "ivanov@mail.de" are more similar to each other than "Ivanov I.I." and "1112233".

The parameter is calculated under the certain rule:

$$maxSimHor = max_{i=2,n} \frac{\sum_{j_1=1}^{m} \sum_{j_2=1}^{m} dist(c_{i,j_1}, c_{i,j_2})}{m^2} \tag{5}$$

where i – a row, n – number of rows in a table, j – a column, m – number of columns in a table, $dist()$ – a string similarity function, $c_{i,j}$ – a cell of a table.

Maximum Vertical Cell Similarity. The attribute indicates the maximum similarity of a particular pair of cells normalized to all possible pairs in the column found within the whole table under the assumption of vertical orientation of a table. It means the first column of a table is not taken into account because in most cases it contains a header (see Table 2). According to the example table the parameter calculated for this table would be rather high because it contains pairs of cells with the same content (for instance "Berlin" and "Berlin").

Using the same designations the parameter is calculated:

$$maxSimVert = max_{j=2,m} \frac{\sum_{i_1=1}^{n} \sum_{i_2=1}^{n} dist(c_{i_1,j}, c_{i_2,j})}{n^2} \tag{6}$$

It is obvious that the greater the maximum horizontal similarity the greater a chance that a table has vertical orientation. Indeed, if the distance between values in a row is rather low it might mean that those values are instances of a particular attribute. The hypothesis is also applicable to the maximum vertical similarity which indicates possible horizontal orientation.

Average Horizontal Cell Similarity. The parameter indicates average similarity of the content of rows within the table under the assumption of horizontal orientation of a table. Again, the first row is not taken into account. The parameter is calculated under the certain rule:

$$avgSimHor = \frac{1}{n} \sum_{i=2}^{n} \frac{\sum_{j_1=1}^{m} \sum_{j_2=1}^{m} dist(c_{i,j_1}, c_{i,j_2})}{m^2} \tag{7}$$

where i – a row, n – number of rows in a table, j – a column, m – number of columns in a table, $dist()$ – a string similarity function, $c[i,j]$ – a cell of a table.

The main difference between maximum and average parameters is connected with size of a table. Average parameters give reliable results during the analysis of large tables whereas maximum parameters are applicable in case of small tables.

Average Vertical Cell Similarity. The parameter indicates average similarity of the content of columns within the table under the assumption of vertical orientation of a table. The first column is not taken into account.

$$avgSimVert = \frac{1}{m} \sum_{j=2}^{m} \frac{\sum_{i_1=1}^{n} \sum_{i_2=1}^{n} dist(c_{i_1,j}, c_{i_2,j})}{n^2} \tag{8}$$

5.4   Machine Learning Algorithms

With the formalization established we are now ready to build classifiers which use apparatus of machine learning. Four machine learning algorithms are considered in the paper:

Naive Bayes classifier is a simple and popular machine learning algorithm. It is based on Bayes' theorem with naive assumptions regarding independence between parameters presented in a training set. However, this ideal configuration rarely occurs in real datasets so that the result always has a statistical error [10].

A decision tree is a predictive model that is based on tree–like graphs or binary trees [12]. Branches represent a conjunction of features and a leaf represents a particular class. Going down the tree we eventually end up with a leaf (a class) with its own unique configuration of the features and values.

k-nearest neighbours is a simple classifier based on a distance between objects [15]. If an object might be represented in Euclidean space then there is a number of functions that could measure a distance between these objects. If the majority of neighbours of the object belongs to one class than the object would be classified into the same class.

Support Vector Machine is a non–probabilistic binary linear classifier that tries to divide instances of classes presented in a training set by a gap as wide as possible. In other words, SVM builds separating surfaces between categories, which might be linear or non-linear [17].

6   Implementation

The proposed approach was implemented in Java as a plugin for the Information Workbench[9] platform developed by fluidOps. The platform provides numerous helpful APIs responsible for the user interaction, RDF data maintenance, ontology generation, knowledge bases adapters and smart data analysis. The machine learning algorithms are supplied by $WEKA$[10] – a comprehensive data mining Java framework developed by the University of Waikato. The $SimMetrics$[11] library by UK Sheffield University provided string similarity functions. The plugin is available on a public repository[12] both as a deployable artifact for the Information Workbench and in source codes.

7   Evaluation

The main goal of the evaluation is to assess the performance of the proposed methodology in comparison with the existing solutions. By the end of the section we decide whether the hypothesis made in Section 4 is demonstrated or not. The evaluation consists of two subgoals – the evaluation of machine learning algorithms with string similarity functions and the evaluation of the system as a whole.

7.1   Algorithms Evaluation

A training set of 400 tables taken from the corpus[13] as a result of [2] was prepared to test suggested heuristics and machine learning methods. In addition, the efficiency of algorithms modifications was estimated during the tests. Results are presented on the Table 4 and Fig. 2,3. In case of the genuineness check $Precision$, $Recall$ and $F–Measure$ were computed.

Fig. 2 represents the overall fracture of correctly classified genuine and non-genuine tables w.r.t. used machine learning algorithms and string similarity functions. The machine learning algorithm based on kNN in conjunction with Levenshtein distance or n-grams demonstrated the highest efficiency during the genuineness check. A slight increase in efficiency in spite of modifications is observed mostly for kNN. It also could be noted that overall results of classification are generally lower in comparison with orientation classification task. This may indicate a lack of information about the table structure caused by a small amount of heuristics. Development and implementation of more sophisticated numerical parameters is suggested in order to improve the performance of classification. Hence, the way towards improving overall F–Measure is connected with raising Recall of the approach.

---

[9] Web: http://www.fluidops.com/en/portfolio/information_workbench/
[10] Web: http://www.cs.waikato.ac.nz/ml/weka/
[11] Web: http://sourceforge.net/projects/simmetrics/
[12] Web: https://github.com/migalkin/Tables_Provider
[13] WDC – Web Tables. Web: http://webdatacommons.org/webtables/

Table 4. Evaluation of the genuineness check

Method			Precision	Recall	F-Measure
Naive Bayes	Levenshtein	unmodified	0.925	0.62	0.745
		modified	0.93	0.64	0.76
	Jaro-Winkler	unmodified	0.939	0.613	0.742
		modified	0.939	0.617	0.744
	n-grams	unmodified	0.931	0.633	0.754
		modified	0.937	0.643	0.763
Decision Tree	Levenshtein	unmodified	0.928	0.65	0.765
		modified	0.942	0.653	0.76
	Jaro-Winkler	unmodified	0.945	0.637	0.761
		modified	0.946	0.64	0.763
	n-grams	unmodified	0.933	0.603	0.733
		modified	0.945	0.637	0.76
kNN	Levenshtein	unmodified	0.904	0.623	0.74
		modified	0.943	0.667	0.78
	Jaro-Winkler	unmodified	0.928	0.607	0.734
		modified	0.941	0.64	0.762
	n-grams	unmodified	0.948	0.663	0.78
		modified	0.949	0.677	0.79
SVM	Levenshtein	unmodified	0.922	0.597	0.725
		modified	0.93	0.62	0.744
	Jaro-Winkler	unmodified	0.924	0.61	0.735
		modified	0.926	0.623	0.745
	n-grams	unmodified	0.922	0.627	0.746
		modified	0.927	0.637	0.755

Fig. 3 indicates the high efficiency of the orientation check task. Most of the used machine learning methods except Naive Bayes demonstrated close to 100% results. A relatively low result of Naive Bayes regardless of the chosen string similarity function might be explained by a number of assumptions which the method is established on. On the one hand the algorithm has the advantage of simplicity and on the other hand it might overlook important details which affect the classification process because of such simplicity. During the orientation check only genuine tables are considered and assessed. Therefore, the eventual result is Precision.

Having analyzed the efficiency of machine learning methods with string metric mechanisms we decided to apply modified kNN in conjunction with Levenshtein distance during the genuineness check process and modified SVM in conjunction with Levenshtein distance during the orientation check process.

7.2   System Evaluation

The overall performance of the approach is defined as a product of the highest *F–Measure* of the genuineness check and the highest *Precision* of the orientation check, which results in *0.77* or *77%*. It is therefore indicating, that we are able to correctly extract knowledge at least from three of given four arbitrary tables.

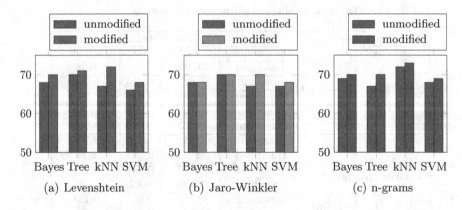

Fig. 2. Genuineness check, correctly classified, %

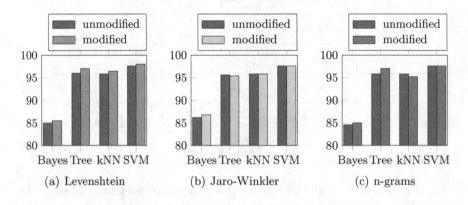

Fig. 3. Orientation check, correctly classified, %

On Fig. 4 the results of tables recognition are presented. All the tables that are marked in HTML code of web–pages as tables are coloured in red and blue. The tables were extracted from the websites of Associated Press[14], Sports.ru[15] and Saint Petersburg Government Portal[16]. According to the theory those tables might be divided in genuine and non-genuine (relevant or irrelevant) groups. It might be easily noted that the tables coloured in red use the tag for formatting reasons and do not contain appropriate table data. In contrast, the tables coloured in blue are relevant tables which data might be parsed and processed. ScraperWiki was able to extract all the red and blue tables. The user therefore should choose relevant tables for a further processing. As a counter to

---

[14] Associated Press. Web: http://www.aptn.com/

[15] Sports.ru. Web: http://www.sports.ru/

[16] Roads repair dataset — Official Website of Government of Saint Petersburg. Web: http://gov.spb.ru/gov/otrasl/tr_infr_kom/tekobjekt/tek_rem/

Fig. 4. Table recognition results

ScraperWiki the developed system was able to extract and process only blue genuine tables using appropriate heuristics and machine learning algorithms.

Taking into account the achieved results we consider the hypothesis suggested in Section 4 demonstrated. Indeed, unstructured data contains semantics. Hence, the next questions are raised. *How much semantics does unstructured data contain? Is there an opportunity to semantically integrate tables with other types of Web content?* Answering the questions will facilitate the shift from neglecting the tables towards close integration of all the Web content.

8   Conclusion and Future Work

Automatic extraction and processing of unstructured data is a fast–evolving topic in science and industry. Suggested machine learning approach is highly effective in table structure analysis tasks and provides the tools for knowledge retrieval and acquisition.

To sum up, the system with the distinctive features was developed:

1. Automatic extraction of HTML tables from the sources specified by a user;
2. Implementation of string metrics and machine learning algorithms to analyze genuineness and structure of a table;
3. Automatic ontology generation and publishing of the extracted dataset;
4. The software takes advantages of Information Workbench API, enabling data visualization, sharing and linking

Future work concerns the question of ontology mapping. The datasets to be extracted might be linked with the already existing ones in the knowledge base dynamically during the main workflow, e.g. discovery of the same entities and relations in different datasets. It will facilitate the development of the envisioned Web of Data as well as wide implementation of Linked Open Data technologies.

Acknowledgments. This work was in part financially supported by Government of Russian Federation, Grant 074-U01.

References

1. Babyak, M.A.: What you see may not be what you get: a brief, nontechnical introduction to overfitting in regression-type models. Psychosomatic Medicine **66**(3), 411–421 (2004)
2. Cafarella, M., Wu, E., Halevy, A., Zhang, Y., Wang, D.: Webtables: exploring the power of tables on the web. In: VLDB 2008 (2008)
3. Crestan, E., Pantel, P.: Web-scale table census and classification. In: ACM WSDM 2011 Proceedings of the Fourth ACM International Conference on Web Search and Data Mining, pp. 545–554 (2011)
4. Embley, D., Tao, C., Liddle, S.: Automating the extraction of data from html tables with unknown structure. Data and Knowledge Engineering **54**, 3–28 (2005). Special issue: ER
5. Ermilov, I., Auer, S., Stadler, C.: User-driven semantic mapping of tabular data. In: Proceedings of the 9th International Conference on Semantic Systems, pp. 105–112. ACM (2013)
6. Haase, P., Schmidt, M., Schwarte, A.: The information workbench as a self-service platform for linked data applications. In: COLD. Citeseer (2011)
7. Hu, J., Kashi, R., Lopresti, D., Wilfong, G.: Evaluating the performance of table processing algorithms. International Journal on Document Analysis and Recognition **4**, 140–153 (2002)
8. Hurst, M.: A constraint-based approach to table structure derivation. In: Proceedings of International Conference on Document Analysis and Recognition (ICDAR 2003), pp. 911–915 (2003)
9. Kolchin, M., Kozlov, F.: A template-based information extraction from web sites with unstable markup. In: Presutti, V., et al. (eds.) SemWebEval 2014. CCIS, vol. 475, pp. 89–94. Springer, Heidelberg (2014)
10. Mitchell, T.: Machine Learning. McGraw-Hill Science/Engineering/Math (1997)
11. Mouromtsev, D., Vlasov, V., Parkhimovich, O., Galkin, M., Knyazev, V.: Development of the st. petersburg's linked open data site using information workbench. In: 14th FRUCT Proceedings, pp. 77–82 (2013)
12. Rokach, L., Maimon, O.: Data mining with decision trees: theory and applications. World Scientific Pub. Co., Inc. (2008)
13. Silva, A., Jorge, A., Torgo, L.: Design of an end-to-end method to extract information from tables. International Journal of Document Analysis and Recognition (IJDAR) **8**, 144–171 (2006)
14. Tijerino, Y., Embley, D., Lonsdale, D., Ding, Y., Nagy, G.: Towards ontology generation from tables. World Wide Web **8**, 261–285 (2005)
15. Tou, J., Gonzalez, R.: Pattern Recognition Principles. University of Southern California (1974)
16. Ukkonen, E.: Approximate string matching with q-grams and maximal matches. Theoretical Computer Science, 191–211 (1992)
17. Vorontsov, K.: Machine learning methods (2009). http://www.machinelearning.ru
18. Wang, Y., Hu, J.: A machine learning based approach for table detection on the web. In: Proceedings of the 11th WWW, pp. 242–250 (2002)

Feature Selection for Language Independent Text Forum Summarization

Vladislav A. Grozin[✉], Natalia F. Gusarova, and Natalia V. Dobrenko

National Research University of Information Technologies, Mechanics and Optics,
Saint-Petersburg 197101, Russia
grozin@my.ifmo.ru

Abstract. Nowadays the need for multilingual information retrieval for searching relevant information is rising steadily. Specialized text-based forums on the Web are a valuable source of such information. However, extraction of informative messages is often hindered by large amount of non-informative posts (the so-called *offtopic* posts) and informal language commonly used on forums.

The paper deals with the task of automatic identification of posts potentially useful for sharing professional experience within text forums irrespective of the forum's language. For our experiments we have selected subsets from various text forums containing different languages. Manual markup was held by native speaking experts. Textual, thread-based, and social graph features were extracted. In order to select satisfactory language-independent forum features we used gradient boosting models, relative influence metric for model analysis, and NDCG metric for measuring selection method quality.

We have formed a satisfactory set of forum features indicating the post's utility which do not demand sophisticated linguistic analysis and is suitable for practical use.

1 Introduction

Nowadays we are facing the rapid growth of non-English documents on the Internet. The need for multilingual information retrieval and language-independent information access for professionals, organizations and businesses is rising steadily. Specialized text forums are a valuable source of knowledge of that kind. Forums contain experience of people who actually used the technology and its features, often expressed in their native language. Forums contain both positive and negative experience—something that is not available from official documentation at all. But they also contain a lot of trivial, repeated and still irrelevant posts. Therefore the expert not knowing forum language should have opportunity to extract useful and informative posts in order to study them in more detail subsequently.

The obvious solution is to use techniques of text summarization. But important information can be provided in different languages, including highly inflected, having complex grammar and rather weak text analysis tools. It is

© Springer International Publishing Switzerland 2015
P. Klinov and D. Mouromtsev (Eds.): KESW 2015, CCIS 518, pp. 63–71, 2015.
DOI: 10.1007/978-3-319-24543-0_5

a challenge for using parsers, part-of-speech taggers, morphological analyzers and full dictionaries for any of the languages. In fact, most application for text processing are monolingual tools or tools covering a few commonly spoken languages. In [17] the lack of linguistic resources is called "one obvious bottleneck for the development of multilingual tools". So, the procedure of text forum summarization has to be simple and language-independent in order to be used in practice.

In this paper, we address the task of automatically identifying posts potentially useful for sharing professional experience within text forums irrespective of forum language. We aim to choose a reasonable set of forum features indicating the post's utility which doesn't demand sophisticated linguistic analysis and is suitable for practical use.

2   Related Work

The task of Web Forum Thread Summarization typically aims to give a brief statement of each thread that involving multiple dynamic topics. Traditional summarization methods are cramped here by some challenges [15]. The first is topic drifting: as the post conversation progresses, the semantic divergence among subtopics will be widened. Besides, most posts are composed of short and elliptical messages, their language is highly informal and noisy, and traditional text representation methods have sufficient limitations here.

According to the survey in [15], the majority of works in the area of forum summarization use extraction-based techniques [16] and single-document approach. A lot of research on automatic dialogue summarization use corpus-based and knowledge-based methods. For example, authors [23] identify clusters in the Internet relay chats and then employ lexical and structural features to summarize each cluster. Authors [15] have proposed a forum summarization algorithm that models the reply structures in a discussion thread. In order to represent information of online forum in a learning environment author [5] uses concept-based summarization: each word in the document is labeled as a part of speech in grammar, and to handle the word sense disambiguation problem similarity measures based on WordNet is used. Statistical methods of dialogue summarization are also of great interest. For example, in [20] unsupervised (TF-IDF and LDA topic modeling) and supervised clustering procedures (using SVMs and MaxEnt) are used in combination for decision summarization for spoken meetings. Authors [4] consider the problem of extracting relevant posts from a discussion thread as a binary classification problem where the task is to classify a given post as either belonging to the summary or not. In general statistical methods are very various, including genetic algorithms [6], hybrid approaches [13,18], an integer linear programming approach [2], and so on.

There is a number of the works devoted to multi-lingual aspects of text summarization. For example, in order to fulfill sentiment analysis of multi-lingual Web resource [12] consider English as basic and use language-specific semantic lexicons of sentiment-carrying words. Contrary to this approach, authors [3] show that the multilingual model consistently outperforms the cross-lingual one. Practical experience of developing natural language processing applications for many languages is described in [17]. The author considers Machine Learning methods as an extremely promising approach to develop highly multilingual systems.

A fast-growing number of studies have shown that the social factor can be useful in text forum summarization. For example, authors [14] apply similar measures as used in blogs to the forums, such as counting the number of common tags and replying or citing the same threads. Authors [22] explain that in an online forum context a central core (strongly connected component) contains users that frequently help each other by following questioner (requester) answerer (expert) links.

Feature categories being used in forum analysis studies mainly depend on specifics of a task. For example, authors [1] are concerned with classifying sentiments in extremist group forums. To do this they use syntactic, semantic, link-based, and stylistic features. In [4] thread-specific features are used for identifying subjectivity orientation of threads. These include structural features, dialog act features, subjectivity lexicon based features and sentiment features. Authors [10] use textual features for detecting the reputation dimension of a post. Authors [8,19] extract contexts and answers of questions from online forums using discourse and lexical features as well as non-textual and structural features. But in general the selected features are highly language-dependent and need complicated techniques for their analysis.

To sum up, we can say that information retrieval within text forums irrespective of its language represents a complex problem, and its decision in an explicit form isn't submitted in literature. Methods of dialogue summarization based on machine learning algorithms showed good prospects, but there is a great need of simple and language-independent techniques.

3   Methods

For our experiments we have selected some forums held in highly inflective languages with complex grammar and rather weak text analysis tools, in particular - German, Russian and Chinese (Mandarin). Also, we selected one forum held in English for comparison. Detailed information about the forums is presented in Table 1. Within each forum we selected thread of interest. Each posts' usefulness was manually marked down by experts (Table 2). We have invited experts of the relevant field who are native speakers in the languages of the forums.

As mentioned above, there is a lot of works proposing different features for text forums, potentially suitable for usefulness evaluation. However, not all of them are suitable for machine learning due to the specifics of our task since we need language-independent features. We have chosen features applicable for multilinguistic approach. The list of the chosen features is presented in Table 3.

We calculated text sentiment value using stemmed sentiment keywords and word parts specific for the forums language as well as stemming technique. The

Table 1. The chosen Internet forums, their language, topics, keywords, and statistics

Forum	Language	Topic	Threads/posts	Keywords
1 gamedev.ru	Russian	Unity	10/410	unity
2 hifi-forum.de	German	Windows vs Linux	13/173	windows, linux
3 forum.modelsworld.ru	Russian	Ship modeling	3/150	ship, model
4 5500.forumactif.org	French	Ship modeling	3/150	ship, model
5 bbs.csdn.net	Chinese	cocos2d-x	11/120	cocos
6 bbs.chinaunix.net	Chinese	Linix for beginners	11/103	linux
7 knittinghelp.com	English	Knitting techniques	43/450	knit

Table 2. Thread's usefulness scale

Value	Comment
0	Offtopic
1	Post is on the chosen topic, but argumentation is incomplete or absent
2	Post is on the chosen topic, and the authors point of view is well-justified with explanations or external links

resulting values were normalized to the range from -1 (strongly negative text) to +1 (strongly positive text).

Also, simple non-semantic text features were extracted: text length in characters, number of links and number of keywords. Keywords were chosen strictly corresponding to the name of the forum topic. A more extensive list of keywords would mean a search for synonyms and equivalents, but it requires semantic analysis.

We represented social structure in the form of a social graph, where the nodes are the users, and edges indicate a link between two users. For the creation of the social graph we have used citation analysis: if person A quotes person B by explicitly mentioning his name in text, there is a guaranteed connection between A and B. We used two methods: a non-sentiment graph (edge weight is always 1) and a sentiment graph (edge weight is related to the posts sentiment value). After the creation of the graph parallel edges weights were summed. Then, the weights of the edges were inverted.

Node centrality is often used to find people who are important members of society. We considered some proven [7, 21] metric to evaluate node centrality: Betweenness centrality - the number of shortest paths between all pairs of nodes that pass through the node; inDegree - the total weight of incoming edges; outDegree - the total weight of the outgoing edges.

Position in thread is calculated as number of post in chronological order (first post has position in thread equal to one, next one is equal to two etc.).

In order to select features indicating post usefulness we need models to capture dependence of usefulness on features. We used gradient boosting models in "gbm v.2.1" package (gbm) with following settings:

Table 3. Selected features

Type	Feature	What this feature means
Posts author graph features	Betweenness, non-sentiment graph	Authors social importance
	inDegree, non-sentiment graph	How many times author was quoted
	outDegree , non-sentiment graph	How many times author quoted someone
	Betweenness, sentiment graph	Authors social importance
	inDegree, sentiment graph	With which sentiment author was quoted
	outDegree, sentiment graph	Authors quotes sentiment
Posts author features	Number of threads author is participating in	Author activity
Thread-based post features	Position in thread	Chance of off-topic
	Times quoted	Posts impact on forum
Text features	Length	Number of arguments and length of explanations
	Links	Number of external sources/images
	Sentiment value (calculated using sentiment keywords)	Posts usefulness
	Number of keywords	Topic conformity

- CV folds: 3
- Shrinkage: 0.005
- Number of trees: 4000

Other parameters were left default. Models were constructed for each language independently.

In order to estimate quality of constructed models to ensure that models constructed from features listed in Table 3 give the same results for each language, i.e. are language-independent. To do this we divided available data into training set (60% of each forum) and test set (40%). Widely used recall/precision metrics are not applicable due to the fact that we have three Utility levels, and those metrics are used for estimating binary classification quality. To estimate quality of our models we follow these steps:

1. Fit model to train set.
2. Apply model to test set; it gives $\widetilde{Utility}$ - some approximation of true $Utility$ values of test set.
3. Sort posts in descending order by $\widetilde{Utility}$, and take N top posts. This gives selection of N best posts according to model.
4. Calculate NDCG metric:

$$NDCG_N = \frac{DCG_N}{IDCG_N}; DCG_N = rel_1 + \sum_{i=2}^{N} \frac{rel_i}{log_2(i)},$$

where N is number of selected posts, $rel(i)$ is quality (i.e. true $Utility$) of i-th selected post, and $IDCG_N$ is normalization coefficient calculated as maximum possible DCG_N for specified dataset and N. This metric lies between 0 and 1 (assuming non-negative $rel(i)$), and is cross-query comparable. It is commonly used for calculating ranking method quality.

In order to ensure stability of solution quality on different input sets we used bootstrap resampling-based method. Training set and test set for each forum were resampled with replacement before fitting model and calculating NDCG. This process was repeated 100 times. In each iteration some records were sampled out, and in fact in every iteration we had different training and test sets, so NDCG changed from iteration to iteration. Then, mean NDCG and 0.01 and 0.99 quantiles were calculated for each "language and N" pair, giving mean with confidence intervals for each language and N. 0.01 and 0.99 quantiles were also calculated for each N (ignoring language) to estimate overall confidence interval.

For baseline our experts formed an extensive list of keywords related to the topic of each chosen forum and their list of synonyms, i.e. semantic core (up to 50 words per forum). Then we applied stemming and lemmatization where possible (R package) to each post and these keywords, and counted amount of keywords and their stems in each post. After that we built linear regression model with this count and semantic value as features and post Utility as target variable. By doing this we emulated operation of a information retrieval system aware of forum language, its syntax and semantics and context of chosen narrow topic.

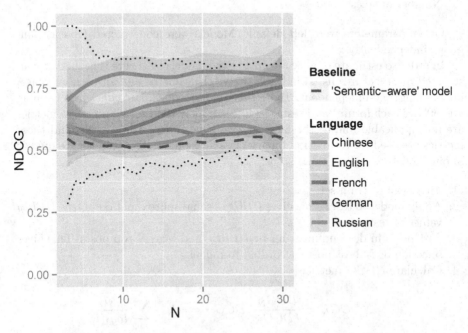

Fig. 1. Dependence of NDCG on language and size of selection

4 Results and Discussion

Fig. 1 shows the dependence of quality of selection (mean NDCG) with confidence intervals (0.01 and 0.99 quantiles) on the language and N. Our shortest forum contains 100 messages (and test set has 40), so we evaluated metrics for N varying from 1 to 30. Dotted lines represent 0.01 and 0.99 quantiles calculated for all available dataset (i.e. language is ignored). Also, simple baseline model performance (red dashed line) is drawn.

The analysis of dependence allows drawing the following conclusions:

- Allocation quality of our methods are generally better than baseline method. Also, baseline model requires knowledge extensive list of synonims and words related to chosen topics, forum language knowledge and complex forum post preprocessing. Our models are simple and stable, and do not require such things. It should be noted that our baseline uses sentiment value as a feature; as explained below, it is one of the most important features, so decent baseline performance is expected. Moreover, amount of semantic core words

Table 4. Features with the highest Relative Influence (RI)

Language	Top features ordered by relative influence
Chinese	Sentiment value
	Text length
	Position in thread
	Number of keywords
	Number of links
Russian	Sentiment value
	Text length
	Author betweenness, non-sentiment graph
	Number of keywords
	Position in thread
German	Text length
	Position in thread
	Sentiment value
	inDegree, non-sentiment graph
	outDegree, sentiment graph
French	Sentiment value
	Text length
	Number of threads the author participates in
	Number of keywords
English	Text length
	Sentiment value
	Author betweenness, non-sentiment graph
	outDegree, sentiment graph
	Number of keywords

in text (another feature in baseline model) is highly corellated with texts length, another important feature in out models.

– for French, German, Chinese and Russian confidence intervals overlap, and lines lie within each others confidence intervals ($NDCG = 0.63\pm0.07$). Better $NDCG$ values were received for English ($NDCG = 0.82\pm0.07$). It is apparently connected with overall simplicity of English language.

We also have to investigate which of selected features were the most important for each language. To do so we used Relative Influence (RI) metric [9] for each model. Top five features with the highest RI are presented in Table 4. Each column represents language, each Nth row is Nth top feature for each language. Features are sorted in descending order by their relative influence. Note that there are recurring top features: "Sentiment value", "Text length", "Position in thread". Therefore it is reasonable to assume that those features are language-independent.

5   Conclusion

In this paper, we have addressed the task of automatically identifying posts potentially useful for sharing professional experience within technical text forums irrespective of forum language. We have shown that it is possible to allocate a reasonable set of forum features indicating the posts utility which doesn't demand sophisticated linguistic analysis and is suitable for practical use. In our future work we plan to design more sophisticated models for feature selection, usage of complex features and considering quality of forum moderation.

References

1. Abbasi, A., Chen, H., Salem, A.: Sentiment Analysis in Multiple Languages: Feature Selection for Opinion Classification in Web Forums. The University of Arizona (2007). http://ai.arizona.edu/intranet/papers/AhmedAbbasi_SentimentTOIS.pdf
2. Alguliev, R.M., Aliguliyev, R.M., Hajirahimova, M.S., Mehdiyev, C.A.: MCMR: Maximum coverage and minimum redundant text summarization model. Expert Systems with Applications **38**, 14514–14522 (2011)
3. Banea, C., Mihalcea, R., Wiebe, J.: Sense-level subjectivity in a multilingual setting. Computer Speech and Language **28**, 7–19 (2014)
4. Biyani, P., Bhati, S., Caragea, C., Mitra, P.: Using non-lexical features for identifying factual and opinionative threads in online forums. Knowledge-Based Systems **69**, 170–178 (2014)
5. Carbonaro, A.: WordNet-based Summarization to Enhance Learning Interaction Tutoring. Peer Reviewed Papers **6**(2) (2010)
6. Chen, J.-S., Hsieh, C.-L., Hsu, F.-C.: A study on Chinese word segmentation: Genetic algorithm approach. Information Management Research **2**(2), 27–44 (2000)
7. Ding, S.L., Cong, G., Lin, C.Y., Zhu, X.Y.: Using conditional random fields to extract contexts and answers of questions from online forums. In: Proceedings of the 46th Annual Meeting of the Association of Computational Linguistics, Columbus, Ohio, pp. 710–718. ACL (2008)

8. Freeman, L.C.: Centrality in social networks: Conceptual clarification. Social Networks **1**, 215–239 (1978)
9. Friedman, J.: Greedy boosting approximation: a gradient boosting machine. Ann. Stat. **29**, 1189–1232 (2001)
10. Garbacea, C., Tsagkias, M., de Rijke, M.: Feature Selection and Data Sampling Methods for Learning Reputation Dimensions. The University of Amsterdam at RepLab 2014 (2014). http://ceur-ws.org/Vol-1180/CLEF2014wn-Rep-Garbacea Et2014.pdf
11. Generalized Boosted Regression Models. http://cran.r-project.org/web/packages/gbm/index.html
12. Hogenboom, A., Heerschop, B., Frasincar, F., Kaymak, U., de Jong, F.: Multilingual support for lexicon-based sentiment analysis guided by semantics. Decision Support Systems **62**, 43–53 (2014)
13. Huang, C.-C.: Automated knowledge transfer for Internet forum. Master thesis, Graduate School of Information Management, I-Shou University, Taiwan, ROC (2003)
14. Li, Y., Liao, T., Lai, C.: A social recommender mechanism for improving knowledge sharing in online forums. Information Processing and Management **48**, 978–994 (2012)
15. Ren, Z., Ma, J., Wang, S., Liu, Y.: Summarizing web forum threads based on a latent topic propagation process. In: CIKM 2011, October 24–28, Glasgow, Scotland, UK (2011)
16. Jones, K.S.: Automatic summarising: the state of the art. Information Processing and Management, Special Issue on Automatic Summarising (2007)
17. Steinberger, R.: Challenges and methods for multilingual text mining. http://citeseerx.ist.psu.edu/viewdoc/summary?doi=10.1.1.167.4724
18. Tao, Y., Liu, S., Lin, C.: Summary of FAQs from a topical forum based on the native composition structure. Expert Systems with Applications **38**, 527–535 (2011)
19. Wang, B., Liu, B., Sun, C., Wang, X., Sun, L.: Thread Segmentation Based Answer Detection in Chinese Online Forums. Acta Automatica Sinica **39**(1) (2013)
20. Wang, L., Cardie, C.: Summarizing decisions in spoken meetings. In: Proceedings of the Workshop on Automatic Summarization for Different Genres, Media, and Languages, Portland, Oregon, June 23, 2011, pp. 16–24. Association for Computational Linguistics (2011)
21. White, D.R., Borgatti, S.P.: Betweenness centrality measures for directed graphs. Social Networks **16**, 335–346 (1994)
22. Yang, S.J.H., Chen, I.Y.L.: A social network-based system for supporting interactive collaboration in knowledge sharing over peer-to-peer network. International Journal of Human Computer Studies **66**(1), 36–40 (2008)
23. Zhou, L., Hovy, E.: Digesting virtual geek culture: the summarization of technical internet relay chats. In: Proceedings of the 43rd Annual Meeting on Association for Computational Linguistics, ACL 2005, Stroudsburg, PA, USA, pp. 298–305. Association for Computational Linguistics (2005)

A Provenance Assisted Roadmap
for Life Sciences Linked Open Data Cloud

Ali Hasnain[(✉)], Qaiser Mehmood, Syeda Sana e Zainab, and Stefan Decker

Insight Center for Data Analytics, National University of Ireland, Galway, Ireland
{ali.hasnain,qaiser.mehmood,syeda.sanaezainab,
stefan.decker}@insight-centre.org

Abstract. A significant portion of Web of Data is composed of multiple datasets that add high value to biomedical research. These datasets have been exposed on the web as a part of the Life Sciences Linked Open Data (LSLOD) Cloud. Different initiatives have been proposed for navigating through these datasets with or without vocabulary reuse. The significance of provenance information regarding life sciences data is great as compared to any other domain. With the provenance information, user becomes aware regarding the source, size, format along with authorization and privilege associated with the data. Previously, we proposed an approach for the creation of an active Linked Life Sciences Data Roadmap, that catalogues and links concepts as well as properties from 137 public SPARQL endpoints. In this work we extend the Roadmap with the provenance information collected directly by querying datasets. We designed a set of queries and the results were catalouged. This extended Roadmap is useful for dynamically assembling queries for retrieving data along with the provenance from multiple SPARQL endpoints. We also demonstrate its use in conjunction with other tools for selective SPARQL querying and the visualization of the LSLOD cloud. We have evaluated the performance of our approach in terms of time taken and success rates of data retrieved.

Keywords: Linked Data (LD) · Provenance · SPARQL · Life Sciences (LS) · Semantic web · Query federation

1 Introduction

A considerable portion of the Linked Open Data cloud is comprised of datasets from Life Sciences Linked Open Data (LSLOD). The significant contributors include the Bio2RDF project[1], Linked Life Data[2], Neurocommons[3], Health care and Life Sciences knowledge base[4]. This deluge of biomedical data in recent years

---

[1] http://bio2rdf.org/ (l.a.: 2014-03-31)
[2] http://linkedlifedata.com/ (l.a.: 2014-07-16)
[3] http://neurocommons.org/page/Main_Page (l.a.: 2014-07-16)
[4] http://www.w3.org/TR/hcls-kb/ (l.a.: 2014-07-16)

© Springer International Publishing Switzerland 2015
P. Klinov and D. Mouromtsev (Eds.): KESW 2015, CCIS 518, pp. 72–86, 2015.
DOI: 10.1007/978-3-319-24543-0_6

is due to the advent of high-throughput gene sequencing technologies, that have been a primary motivation for these efforts. Although publishing datasets as RDF is a necessary step towards unified querying of biological datasets, there is a critical requirement for a single interface to access the Life Sciences (LS) data. It is not sufficient to retrieve information as data being heterogeneously exposed through different public as well as private endpoints [2,17]. As LSLOD data is extremely heterogeneous and dynamic [8,18]; and integrative solutions increasingly rely on federation of queries [4]. Moreover due to the nature of domain, biologists sometimes want to get more information regarding the data including its source, creator, publisher and also statistics with respect to its size. Such information comes under the provenance spectrum and the significance of provenance information regarding life sciences data is great as compared to any other domain. To assemble queries encompassing multiple graphs distributed over different places, we previously introduced the notion of an active Roadmap for LS data – a representation of entities and the links connecting these entities from 137 public SPARQL endpoints[5], an approach described as *"a posteriori integration"*, which makes use of mapping rules that change the topology of remote graphs to match the global schema [12]. In this paper we extend our roadmap that would not only help understand which data exists in each LS SPARQL endpoint, but more importantly enable assembly of multiple source-specific federated SPARQL queries along with the provenance information available at these sources. We call it as a *Provenance Roadmap*. To generate the *Provenance Roadmap*, a set of domain independent SPARQL queries were designed to catalogue provenance information directly from the SPARQL endpoint. Our initial exploratory analysis of several LS endpoints revealed that some endpoints responded well for the designed queries whereas other lack in the direct retrieval of provenance information. Hasnain et al. [10,12] describe the methodology for developing the active Roadmap consisted of two steps: *i)* catalogue development, in which metadata is collected and analyzed, and *ii)* links creation and Roadmap development, which ensures that concepts and properties are properly mapped to a set of Query Elements (Qe) [19]. We assumed in this work that federated queries are assembled within a context that entails the initial identification of a set of Qe, in the context of cancer chemoprevention [19], identified by the domain experts participating in the EU GRANATUM project[6]. The main contribution of this publication is:

1. identification and design of initial set of queries that can contribute to retrive provenance directly from public endpoint.
2. creation of Provenance Roadmap that would lead to the provenance assisted SPARQL queries.
3. proposal of Provenance Assisted Query Engine (PAQE).
4. visual representation of Provenance Roadmap subset.
5. evaluation and analysis based on the *success rates* and *response time* for queries.

---

[5] https://goo.gl/bfh7Qd
[6] http://www.granatum.org(l.a.: 2015-03-05)

It is worth noticing that in this paper we are neither proposing a new provenance model as presented by Lebo et al. [14], nor our defined queries extensively include existing provenance vocabularies due to their limited use in the dataset as mentioned by Buil–Aranda et al. [3]. The rest of this paper is organized as follows: In Section 2, we discuss the related research in line with the subject of this paper. In Section 3, we discuss the methodology and introduce the set of queries designed to collect provenance. In Section 4, we showcase some applications including a provenance assisted query engine which reasons over the Provenance Roadmap to query the LSLOD and show provenance along with the retrived data. We evaluate the results and performance in terms of time taken and query response per endpoint in Section 5.

2   Related Work

We can divide related literature into three sub-categories: SPARQL Endpoints Analysis, SPARQL Data Catalogues and Provenance for SPARQL.

SPARQL Endpoints Analysis: Buil–Aranda et al. [3] analysed 427 public SPARQL endpoints registered on the DataHub web-site [7]. It was found that:

1. VoID descriptions[8] were only available for one-in-three of the registered endpoints.
2. around one-in-six endpoints supported SPARQL 1.1 aggregate features e.g. GROUP BY.
3. there is reported difference between the performance of different endpoints for similar queries.
4. Service Description files for one-in-ten; that only about half the registered endpoints.
5. only one-in-three endpoints are available more than 99% of the time.
6. endpoints mostly implement result-size thresholds (10,000 being the most popular threshold; e.g. in case of virtuoso).

SPARQL Data Catalogues: Paulheim & Hertling [16] discussed the method to find a SPARQL endpoint containing content regarding any particular Linked Data URI using VoID descriptions and also uses the DataHub catalogue. Hasnain et. al [10], [12] described the process of cataloguing and linking data from LOD for Life Science domain. The proposed methodology uses catalogues that facilitate query federation. Our provenance roadmap is also a catalogue contains provenance generated by querying SPARQL endpoints.

Provenance for SPARQL: Zhao et. al [20], proposes the design patterns that represent and query provenance information relating to mapping links between heterogeneous RDF data from sources in the genomics domain. Omitola et al.[15] proposes voidp, a provenance extension for the VoID vocabulary, that allows

---

[7] http://datahub.io/ (l.a.: 2015-05-01)
[8] http://rdfs.org/ns/void#.

data publishers to specify the provenance relationships of their data, while our work is focused towards querying the provenance directly from SPARQL endpoints. Damasio et al. [6] provides an approach capable of providing provenance information for a large fragment of SPARQL 1.1 which is based on the translation of SPARQL into relational queries over annotated relations. This works largely towards finding provenance for SPARQL queries rather than querying dataset for finding provenance. Chris et. al [1] discusses a role for provenance in quality assessment for Linked Sensor Data. Mariangiola et. al [7] proposes a notion of provenance using named graph that helps tracing where the data has been published (source) and who published it (publisher). Olaf Hartig [9] develops an automatic trust assessment approach based on provenance information. Our approach is unique from aforementioned as we focus to collect provenance directly from the data available at publicly SPARQL endpoints.

3 Methodology

Hasnain et. al [10], [12], developed an active Roadmap for navigating the LSLOD cloud and the methodology followed consists of two stages namely i) catalogue generation and ii) link generation. For Roadmap creation, data was retrieved from 137 public SPARQL endpoints[9] and organized in an RDF document - the LSLOD Catalogue. The list of SPARQL endpoints was captured from publicly available Bio2RDF datasets and by searching for datasets in CKAN[10] tagged *"life science"* or *"healthcare"* during the month of May 2014. A semi-automated method was devised to retrieve all classes (concepts) and associated properties (attributes) available through any particular endpoint by probing data instances. For collecting provenance we consider the list of endpoints already available in the Roadmap[12]. However, as noted by Buil–Aranda et al. [3], (i) many endpoints listed in the DataHub catalogue are no longer available. Hence our first step was to remove unresponsive endpoints from experimental consideration. We consider an endpoint available if it is accessible through the HTTP SPARQL protocol [5], it responds to a SPARQL-compliant query, and it returns a response in an appropriate SPARQL format; for this, we use query Q0: SELECT * WHERE { ?s ?p ?o } LIMIT 1. Issuing the query in April 2015, to 137 endpoints, 57 (41.63%)[11] responded to query Q0; we call these endpoints *live* and select them for collecting provenance.

3.1 Adding Provenance to the Catalogue

We designed the set of queries to collect information regarding Dataset and SPARQL endpoint directly by querying the endpoint. We call this information as Provenance. The spectrum of provenance may vary and for this research we collect basic:

---

[9] http://goo.gl/ZLbLzq
[10] http://wiki.ckan.org/Main_Page (l.a.: 2014-05-05)
[11] The list is available at https://goo.gl/89PueC.

Table 1. Dataset-level Queries - VoID statistics

Query
Q1 SELECT (COUNT(*) AS ?count) WHERE { ?s ?p ?o }
Q2 SELECT (COUNT(DISTINCT ?o) AS ?count) WHERE { ?s a ?o }
Q3 SELECT (COUNT(DISTINCT ?p) AS ?count) WHERE { ?s ?p ?o }
Q4 SELECT (COUNT(DISTINCT ?o) AS ?count) WHERE { ?s ?p ?o }

Table 2. Dataset-level Queries - beyond VoID statistics

Query
Q5 SELECT (COUNT(DISTINCT ?s) AS ?count) WHERE { ?s ?p ?o . FILTER(isBlank(?s))}
Q6 SELECT (COUNT(DISTINCT ?o) AS ?count) WHERE { ?s ?p ?o . FILTER(isLiteral(?o))}
Q7 SELECT (COUNT(DISTINCT ?o) AS ?count) WHERE { ?s ?p ?o . FILTER(isBlank(?o))}
Q8 SELECT (COUNT(DISTINCT ?b) AS ?count) WHERE { { ?s ?p ?b } UNION { ?b ?p ?o } FILTER(isBlank(?b)) }

- VoID statistics including totalTriples, totalDistinctClasses, totalDistinct-Properties and totalDistinctObjectNodes.
- statistics beyond VoID including subjectBlankNodes, objectLiteralNodes, objectBlankNodes and totalBlankNodes
- SD information including feature, resultFormat, supportedLanguage. and dataset information including format, license, publisher, rights, retrievedOn.

For VoID statistics each query is formulated to build the equivalent of a VoID description of the dataset. We design queries to ascertain what high-level statistics, the endpoints can return about the dataset they index. We issue four queries, as listed in Table 1, to ascertain the number of triples (Q1), number of distinct classes (Q2), number of distinct properties (Q3), and number of distinct objects (Q4). These queries involve the SPARQL 1.1 features e.g. COUNT.

We further look at queries that yield statistics not supported by VoID as listed in Table 2, query (Q5- (Q8)). In particular, we experiment to see if endpoints can return a subset of statistics from the VoID Extension Vocabulary http://rdfs.org/ns/void-ext, which include counts of different types of unique RDF terms in different positions: subject blank nodes (Q5), object literal nodes (Q6), object blank nodes (Q7), all blank nodes (Q8). According to the Linked Data principles the useage of bank nodes is typically not recommended. But our

Table 3. SD and Dataset Level Provenance Queries

Query
Q9 SELECT distinct * WHERE { ?endpoint a sd:Service ; ?p ?o }
Q10 SELECT distinct * WHERE { ?dataset rdf:type dcterms:Dataset . ?dataset dcat:distribution ?dist . ?dist ?p ?o .} order by ?dataset ?dist ?p ?o

exploration revealed that data publishers are still using them. It is therefore we designed a set of queries to collect information regarding balnk nodes at various positions.

Finally we issue two queries, as listed in Table 3, to ascertain the Service description of the endpoint (Q9), and dataset provenance information (Q10). For each query, we record: (i) *number of endpoints that ran the query*, and (ii) *total execution time*. Results will differ for different endpoints as we are looking at how many SPARQL endpoints responded to the queries rather than comparing performance of different endpoints. Based on the results of the queries Q1-Q10 a catalogue is generated known as Provenance Roadmap - an extract is presented in Listing 1.

3.2   An Extract from Provenance Roadmap

RDFS, SD[12], PAV[13], Dublin Core[14] and VoID[15] vocabularies are used to represent the data in the Provenance Roadmap - a slice of which is presented[16]

Listing 1. An Extract from the LSLOD Catalogue for Drugbank dataset

```
<http://cu.drugbank.bio2rdf.org/sparql> a void:Dataset ;
void:class bio2rdf-drugbank_vocabulary:Drug ;
void:sparqlEndpoint <http://cu.drugbank.bio2rdf.org/sparql> ;
void:classes "141"^^xsd:integer" ;
void:distinctObjects "1939582"^^xsd:integer" ;
void:properties "242"^^xsd:integer" ;
void:triples "4084924"^^xsd:integer" ;
void-ext:distinctBlankNodes "3"^^xsd:integer" ;
void-ext:distinctObjectBlankNodes "3"^^xsd:integer" ;
void-ext:distinctObjectLiteralNodes "1525040"^^xsd:integer" ;
void-ext:distinctSubjectBlankNodes "3"^^xsd:integer" ;
dcterms:Dataset <http://identifiers.org/drugbank/>;
sd:Service <http://drugbank.bio2rdf.org/sparql#endpoint> .

bio2rdf-drugbank_vocabulary:Drug rdfs:label "Drug";
void:exampleResource <http://bio2rdf.org/drugbank:DB00313> ;
void:uriRegexPattern "^http://bio2rdf\\.org/drugbank:.*" ;
void-ext:sourceIdentifier "drugbank" .

bio2rdf-drugbank_vocabulary:patent a rdf:Property ;
rdfs:label "patent" ;
void-ext:domain bio2rdf-drugbank_vocabulary:Drug ;
void-ext:range bio2rdf-drugbank_vocabulary:Patent .

bio2rdf-drugbank_vocabulary:Patent rdfs:label "Patent" ;
void:exampleResource <http://bio2rdf.org/uspto:1338344> ;
void:uriRegexPattern "^http://bio2rdf\\.org/uspto:.*" ;
void-ext:sourceIdentifier "uspatent" .

<http://identifiers.org/drugbank/> dcat:distribution
<http://www.drugbank.ca/system/downloads/current/drugbank.xml.zip> .

<http://www.drugbank.ca/system/downloads/current/drugbank.xml.zip>
```

---

[12] http://www.w3.org/TR/sparql11-service-description/(l.a.: 2015-05-15)

[13] http://pav-ontology.github.io/pav/ (l.a.: 2015-05-15)

[14] http://dublincore.org/documents/dcmi-terms/ (l.a.: 2015-04-12)

[15] http://www.w3.org/TR/void/ (l.a.: 2015-04-12)

[16] In the extract, we omit URI prefixes for brevity. All prefixes can be looked up at http://prefix.cc/ (l.a.: 2015-04-31)

```
rdfs:label "DrugBank (drugbank.xml.zip)" ;
dcterms:format "application/zip" , "application/xml" ;
dcterms:license "http://www.drugbank.ca/about" ;
dcterms:publisher "http://drugbank.ca" ;
dcterms:rights "no-commercial" , "use" , "by-attribution" ;
dcterms:title "DrugBank (drugbank.xml.zip)" ;
pav:retrievedOn "2014-11-12T07:57:03-05:00^^xsd:dateTime" ;
foaf:page "http://drugbank.ca" .

<http://cu.drugbank.bio2rdf.org/sparql#endpoint>
sd:feature sd:UnionDefaultGraph , sd:DereferencesURIs ;
sd:resultFormat formats:Turtle, formats:SPARQL_Results_JSON,
formats:RDF_XML, formats:SPARQL_Results_CSV, formats:N-Triples,
formats:N3, formats:SPARQL_Results_XML , formats:RDFa;
sd:supportedLanguage  sd:SPARQL10Query .
```

Listing 1 is an illustrative example of a portion of the provenance roadmap generated for the Drugbank SPARQL endpoint[17]. VoID is used for describing the dataset: the void#Dataset being described in this entry is "Drugbank" SPARQL endpoint. In cases where SPARQL endpoints were available through mirrors (e.g. most Bio2RDF endpoints are available through Carleton Mirror URLs) or mentioned using alternative URLs (e.g. http://drugbank.bio2rdf.org/sparql), these references were also added as a second value for the void#sparqlEndpoint property. One identified Class(http://bio2rdf-drugbank_vocabulary:Drug), and one property using that class as domain (http://bio2rdf-drugbank_vocabulary:patent) are also included. Classes are linked to datasets using the void#classproperty; the labels were collected usually from parsing the last portion of the URI and probed instances were also recorded (http://bio2rdf.org/drugbank:DB00313)as values for void#exampleResource. Properties (http://bio2rdf-drugbank_vocabulary:patent) were classified as rdfs:property. In regard to the provenance information basic void and void-ext statistics are recorded based on results retrieved from queries listed in Table 1 and 2. This includes:

void:classes"141^^xsd:integer",void:distinctObjects"1939582^^xsd:integer",
void:properties "242^^xsd:integer",void:triples "4084924^^xsd:integer",
void-ext:distinctBlankNodes"3^^xsd:integer",void-ext:distinctObjectBlank
Nodes "3^^xsd:integer",void-ext:distinctObjectLiteralNodes"1525040^^xsd:
integer", void-ext:distinctSubjectBlankNodes "3^^xsd:integer".

Service Description and futher provenance regarding dataset are recorded based on results retrieved from queries listed in Table 3. This includes:

sd:feature sd:UnionDefaultGraph, sd:DereferencesURIs; sd:resultFormat
formats:Turtle,formats:SPARQL_Results_JSON,formats:RDF_XML,formats:N-Tri-
ples,formats:SPARQL_Results_CSV,formats:N3,formats:SPARQL_Results_XML,fo-
rmats:RDFa; sd:supportedLanguage sd:SPARQL10Query in case of service description, whereas rdfs:label "DrugBank (drugbank.xml.zip)";dcterms:format "application/zip","application/xml" ; dcterms:license "http://www.drugbank.ca/about";dcterms:publisher "http://drugbank.ca" ; dcterms:rights "no-commercial","use","by-attribution" ; dcterms:title "DrugBank (drugbank.xml.zip)"; pav:retrievedOn "2014-11-12T07:57:03-05:00^^xsd:dateTime" ; foaf:page "http://drugbank.ca" . in case of dataset description. It is worth notic-

---

[17] http://cu.drugbank.bio2rdf.org/sparql (l.a.: 2015-04-01)

ing that mentioned dataset description belongs to one distribution for one dataset whereas any SPARQL endpoint may have multiple datasets with different distributions.

4   Provenance Roadmap Applications

With the inclusion of provenance (results of the queries (Q1-10)) for the available endpoint to the existing roadmap the new Provenance Roadmap is exposed as a SPARQL endpoint[18] and relevant information is also documented[19]. As of 15th May 2014, the Roadmap consists of 263731 triples representing 1861 distinct classes and 3299 distinct properties catalogued from 137 public SPARQL endpoints. With provenence information added (May 2015), the Provenance Roadmap consists of 280064 triples representing 1861 distinct classes and 3299 distinct properties catalogued from 57 available endpoints out of 137 previously catalouged. This increase in total triple count is due to the addition of provenance information for 57 live endpoints. The remaining 80 endpoints are still part of roadmap and their correspondiing provenance information can be included in future based on their availability.

4.1   Provenance Assisted Query Engine

As an application of Provenance Roadmap, a Provenance Assested Query Engine (PAQE) is designed which is fundamentally a SPARQL query engine that transforms the expressions from one vocabulary into those represented using vocabularies of known SPARQL endpoints and combines those expressions into a single query using SPARQL "SERVICE" calls. The engine executes the resulting statement and returns the results to the user. The catalogued provenance organized as Provenance Roadmap is also available along with the results. DSQE is implemented on top of the Apache Jena query engine and extends it by intercepting and rewriting the SPARQL algebra.

PAQE is essentaily an extension of Domain Specifc Query Engine (DSQE) defined by Hasnain et al. [11,12] that comprises two major components: the SPARQL Algebra rewriter and the Roadmap. The algebra rewriter examines each segment of the Basic Graph Pattern (BGP) triples and attempts to expand the terms based on the vocabulary mapping into the corrosponding terms of the endpoint graphs and stores the result. Major extension to DSQE that makes it PAQE is the inclusion of provenance to the roadmap. An instance of PAQE[20] is available online that can be used to write federated SPARQL queries using drop down menu. The user can query over LSLOD using subset of predefined query elements defined in the context of drug discovery and cancer chemoprevention as mentioned earlier. For a simple query present in Listing 2, PAQE shows provenance as shown in (fig 1).

---

[18] http://srvgal86.deri.ie:8000/graph/Provenance_Roadmap (l.a.: 2015-05-15)

[19] Roadmap Homepage: https://code.google.com/p/life-science-roadmap/

[20] http://srvgal86.deri.ie:8000/graph/Granatum

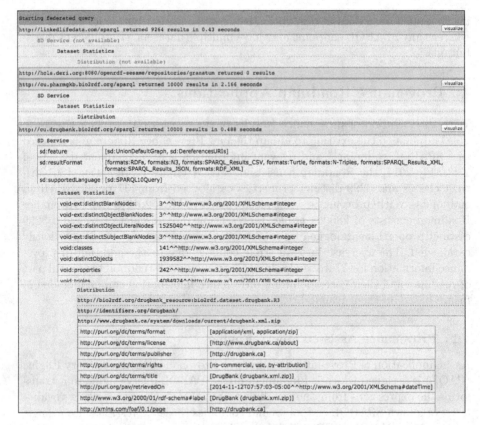

Fig. 1. Provenance for Drugbank Dataset

Listing 2. Sample query using PAQE Interface

```
SELECT * WHERE
{ ?x a <http://chem.deri.ie/granatum/Drug> }
```

Provencance information along with the query result help users and systems to select any particular data source based on the its size (total triple count), type of data (list of classes and properties), data distributions, the information regarding the data creator and how old was the data published. Information regarding service features, formats and supported languages can be helpful for making decisions for data itegration scenarios.

4.2 Provenance Roadmap SPARQL Service

We created Provenance Roadmap public SPARQL endpoints[21] that index the provenance information based on the results retrived for queries. Using this service, a client can query the criteria collected for a specific endpoint, or can query

---

[21] http://srvgal86.deri.ie:8000/graph/Provenance_Roadmap

for endpoints matching criteria such as ordering endpoints according to number of instances of a given class, or finding endpoints that use certain properties in combination with certain classes. We provide a set of sample queries to elaborate the significance of the Provenance Roadmap and the nature of questions that can be answered querying it. For example (i) Query Drugbank SPARQL Endpoint for VoID and beyond VoID statistics (Listing 3), (ii) List of Endpoints and corresponding Classes (Listing 4), (iii) List of Endpoints and corrosponding SD Services (Listing 5) and (iv) Drugbank endpoint with available datasets distribution facts (Listing 6).

Listing 3. Drugbank SPARQL Endpoint- VoID and beyond VoID statistics

```
PREFIX void: <http://rdfs.org/ns/void#>
PREFIX void-ext: <http://rdfs.org/ns/void-ext#>
SELECT distinct *
{ <http://cu.drugbank.bio2rdf.org/sparql> a void:Dataset;
void:triples ?triples;
void:classes ?classes;
void:properties ?properties;
void-ext:distinctObjectBlankNodes ?ObjectBlankNodes;
void-ext:distinctSubjectBlankNodes ?SubjectBlankNodes;
void-ext:distinctBlankNodes ?BlankNodes;
void-ext:distinctObjectLiteralNodes ?ObjectLiteralNodes. }
```

Listing 4. List of Endpoints and corresponding Classes

```
PREFIX void: <http://rdfs.org/ns/void#>
SELECT ?dataset ?class
WHERE { ?dataset void:class ?class }
order by (?dataset)
```

Listing 5. List of Endpoints and SD Services

```
PREFIX sd: <http://www.w3.org/ns/sparql-service-description#>
PREFIX void: <http://rdfs.org/ns/void#>
SELECT distinct ?endpoint ?p ?o
{ ?endpoint a void:Dataset;
sd:Service ?Service.
?Service ?p ?o. }
```

Listing 6. Drugbank endpoint and available datasets distribution facts

```
PREFIX void: <http://rdfs.org/ns/void#>
PREFIX dcterms: <http://purl.org/dc/terms/>
PREFIX dcat: <http://www.w3.org/ns/dcat#>
SELECT distinct ?distr ?p ?o
{ <http://cu.drugbank.bio2rdf.org/sparql> a void:Dataset;
dcterms:Dataset ?dataset.
?dataset dcat:distribution ?distr.
?distr ?p ?o. }
```

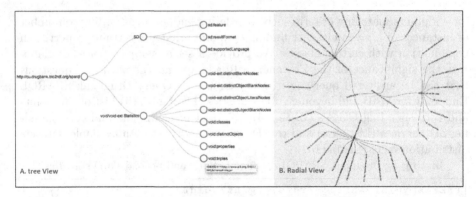

Fig. 2. A subset of Provenance Roadmap. A: Tree View, B: Radial View

4.3   Visualizing the Provenance Roadmap

Earlier the visualization of complete roadmap was displayed as a force-directed concept map representation in [13]. A Visualization of the provenance information is also developed to enable the domain users to visually and intuitively navigate the subset of provenance roadmap retrieved along any query result. The endpoint, its SD represenation, its VoID statistics and dataset information is visually displayed as soon as any query is executed through PAQE and user can visually explore the provenance data. Hovering over any particular node displays its information and provides value associated to that node (fig 2).

5   Results

We previously evaluated the performance of Link Generation methodology [10] by comparing it against the popular linking approaches whereas catalogues generation methodology was evaluated by analyzing the times taken to probe instances through endpoint analysis of 12 different endpoints whose underlying data sources were considered relevant for drug discovery [12]. Since Provenance Roadmap was developed by sending queries directly to the live endpoints, we evaluate and analyze our methodology in terms of comparing the success rate and response time for different queries per endpoint.

5.1   Experimental Setup

As mentioned earlier we collected a list of 137 Life Sciences public SPARQL endpoints catalogued in the roadmap in May 2014 and for collecting provenance directly from these endpoints only 57 responded to Q0, hence considered for further querying Q1 - Q10. System on which all the queries were run has a 2.53 GHz i5 processor, 8GB RAM and 320GB hard disk. For the system with Java implementation, we used Eclipse with default settings, i.e. Java Virtual Machine (JVM) initial memory allocation pool (Xms) size of 128.53MB and the maximum memory allocation pool (Xmx) size of 2057.30MB.

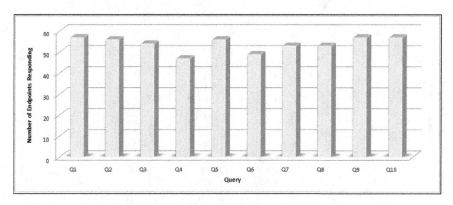

Fig. 3. SPARQL endpoints returning results per query

Success Rates

We focus on the overall success rates for each query, looking at the number of endpoints that return results. The results are illustrated in Figure 3, where the success rates varying from 100% for **Q1**, **Q9**, **Q10** to 82% for **Q4**. It is worth noticing that the queries with the highest success rates require both SPARQL 1.0, SPARQL 1.1 features to run i.e. SD-Service (**Q9**, Dataset Level Provenance **Q10** and total number of triples (**Q1**)).

Response Times

We also focus on runtimes for successfully executed queries, incorporating the total response time for issuing the query and streaming all results. In Figure 4, we present the runtimes for each query across all available endpoints returning non-empty results. The maximum, minimum, average and mean run time per query are ploted in the log scale. We see quite a large variance in runtimes, which is to be expected given that different endpoints host datasets of a variety of sizes and schemata on servers with a variety of computational capacity. **Q6** took the maximun run time in order to retrive the result from `http://linkedlifedata.com/sparql`, whereas **Q10** took minimum time for geting data from `http://pubmed.bio2rdf.org/sparql`. **Q9** appears to be the quickest in terms of retriving the data with lowest average time.

6 Discussion

In this paper we describe the concept and methodology for devising Linked Life Sciences Data Provenance Roadmap. Our methodology relies on systematically issuing queries on various publicly available life sciences SPARQL endpoints and collecting its provenance information. We investigated the extent to which these SPARQL endpoints can be queried to collect necessary provenance information, allowing consumer agents to (e.g.) automatically select endpoints relevant to a

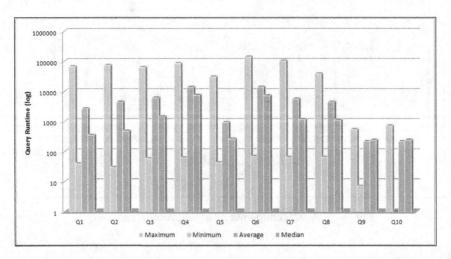

Fig. 4. Runtimes taken by different queries (Max, Min, Avg, Median)

given task. With the advent of SPARQL 1.1, new features such as aggregates allow endpoints to be interrogated for high-level statistics about the underlying dataset itself. However, it is not clear that the resulting queries would be feasible for SPARQL query engines/services to run in practice.

Investigating the issue for collecting the provenance, we proposed a set of queries (extending on existing de facto standards such as VoID, SD, DCTERM) that could be used to automatically extract provenance from a SPARQL endpoint. These queries ranged in complexity and features used. We first determined that most of the live endpoints would answer queries using novel SPARQL 1.1 features. This served as a baseline for the recall of many queries using aggregate and/or sub-query features.

We provided a list of 10 self-descriptive queries that can be issued to a SPARQL endpoints to (in theory) derive basic level of Provenence about its content that covers a large subset of VoID and beyond. The queries interrogate high-level statistics about the dataset, meta-data about its use of classes and properties, as well as information about the creater and creation date of different dataset exposed by different life science SPARQL endpoints. However, we also noted that for queries generating larger result sizes, thresholds and timeouts would likely lead to only partial results being returned.

We noticed that the number of triples per endpoint varied from few thousands to couple of hundred thousand. We also measured the frequency of usage of different URI roots (or namespaces). We found that 99.5% of class namespaces and 91% of properties namespaces are reused. This can be useful for helping LD publishers determine the appropriate vocabulary to use. We faced multiple challenges during the roadmap development which can hinder the applicability of our approach:

- Some endpoints consider unavailable when unable to respond to simple query (`SELECT * WHERE {?s ?p ?o} LIMIT 1`).
- Some endpoints return timeout errors when a simple query (`SELECT * WHERE {?s ?p ?o} LIMIT 1`) is issued.

Nevertheless, we still found the Provenance Roadmap approach highly applicable for collecting, cataloguing and publishing provenance information after extracting directly from the live SPARQL endpoints

As future work, we would like to provide an interface for browsing the catalogue and to create a framework for updating results once a month for each new Life Sciences endpoint registered to DataHub. Though the results will indeed be partial and our evaluation has demonstrated the shortcomings, the responses we have seen for most queries are competitive. Even still, we must conclude that creating a *high quality*, *up-to-date* roadmap with *broad coverage* of all available Life Sciences public SPARQL endpoints seems infeasible: if so, this would be a notable limitation of the SPARQL infrastructure itself.

7   Conclusion

Our Provenance Roadmap is a step towards cataloguing Provenance information for LSLOD SPARQL endpoints by querying those endpoints. We also notice that static descriptions of indexed datasets in formats such as VoID remain a necessity in spite of the novel aggregation features of SPARQL 1.1. We evaluated the proposed Roadmap in terms of response time and success rate of different queries and also showcased a few applications - namely Provenance assisted Query Engine, Provenance Roadmap SPARQL Service and Provenance visualization.

Acknowledgments. This research has been supported in part by Science Foundation Ireland under Grant Number SFI/12/RC/2289 and SFI/08/CE/I1380 (Lion 2).

References

1. Baillie, C., Edwards, P., Pignotti, E.: Quality assessment, provenance, and the web of linked sensor data. In: Groth, P., Frew, J. (eds.) IPAW 2012. LNCS, vol. 7525, pp. 220–222. Springer, Heidelberg (2012)
2. Bechhofer, S., Buchan, I., De Roure, D., Missier, P., et al.: Why linked data is not enough for scientists. Future Generation Computer Systems **29**(2), 599–611 (2013)
3. Buil-Aranda, C., Hogan, A., Umbrich, J., Vandenbussche, P.-Y.: SPARQL web-querying infrastructure: ready for action? In: Alani, H., et al. (eds.) ISWC 2013, Part II. LNCS, vol. 8219, pp. 277–293. Springer, Heidelberg (2013)
4. Cheung, K.H., Frost, H.R., Marshall, M.S., et al.: A journey to semantic web query federation in the life sciences. BMC Bioinformatics **10**(Suppl. 10), S10 (2009)
5. Clark, K.G., Feigenbaum, L., Torres, E.: Sparql protocol for rdf. World Wide Web Consortium (W3C) Recommendation (2008)

6. Damásio, C.V., Analyti, A., Antoniou, G.: Provenance for SPARQL queries. In: Cudré-Mauroux, P., et al. (eds.) ISWC 2012, Part I. LNCS, vol. 7649, pp. 625–640. Springer, Heidelberg (2012)

7. Dezani-Ciancaglini, M., Horne, R., Sassone, V.: Tracing where and who provenance in linked data: a calculus. Theoretical Computer Science **464**, 113–129 (2012)

8. Goble, C., Stevens, R., Hull, D., et al.: Data curation+ process curation= data integration+ science. Briefings in Bioinformatics **9**(6), 506–517 (2008)

9. Hartig, O.: Trustworthiness of data on the web. In: Proceedings of the STI Berlin & CSW PhD Workshop. Citeseer (2008)

10. Hasnain, A., Fox, R., Decker, S., Deus, H.F.: Cataloguing and linking life sciences LOD cloud. In: 1st International Workshop on Ontology Engineering in a Data-driven World Collocated with EKAW 2012 (2012)

11. Hasnain, A., et al.: Linked biomedical dataspace: lessons learned integrating data for drug discovery. In: Mika, P., et al. (eds.) ISWC 2014, Part I. LNCS, vol. 8796, pp. 114–130. Springer, Heidelberg (2014)

12. Hasnain, A., et al.: A roadmap for navigating the life sciences linked open data cloud. In: Supnithi, T., Yamaguchi, T., Pan, J.Z., Wuwongse, V., Buranarach, M. (eds.) JIST 2014. LNCS, vol. 8943, pp. 97–112. Springer, Heidelberg (2015)

13. Kamdar, M.R., Zeginis, D., Hasnain, A., Decker, S., Deus, H.F.: ReVeaLD: A user-driven domain-specific interactive search platform for biomedical research. Journal of Biomedical Informatics **47**, 112–130 (2014)

14. Lebo, T., Sahoo, S., McGuinness, D., Belhajjame, K., Cheney, J., Corsar, D., Garijo, D., Soiland-Reyes, S., Zednik, S., Zhao, J.: Prov-o: The prov ontology. W3C Recommendation, 30th April (2013)

15. Omitola, T., Zuo, L., Gutteridge, C., Millard, I.C., Glaser, H., Gibbins, N., Shadbolt, N.: Tracing the provenance of linked data using void. In: Proceedings of the International Conference on Web Intelligence, Mining and Semantics, p. 17. ACM (2011)

16. Paulheim, H., Hertling, S.: Discoverability of SPARQL endpoints in linked open data. In: ISWC (Posters & Demos), pp. 245–248 (2013)

17. Quackenbush, J.: Standardizing the standards. Molecular Systems Biology **2**(1) (2006)

18. Stein, L.D.: Integrating biological databases. Nature Reviews Genetics **4**(5), 337–345 (2003)

19. Zeginis, D., et al.: A collaborative methodology for developing a semantic model for interlinking Cancer Chemoprevention linked-data sources. Semantic Web (2013)

20. Zhao, J., Miles, A., Klyne, G., Shotton, D.: Linked data and provenance in biological data webs. Briefings in Bioinformatics **10**(2), 139–152 (2009)

Scholarly Communication in a Semantically Enrichable Research Information System with Embedded Taxonomy of Scientific Relationships

M.R. Kogalovsky[1] and S.I. Parinov[2(✉)]

[1] Market Economy Institute of RAS, Moscow, Russia
`kogalovsky@ipr-ras.ru`
[2] The Central Economical and Mathematical Institute of RAS, Moscow, Russia
`sparinov@gmail.com`

Abstract. The paper discusses why and how the semantically enrichable research information system with embedded taxonomy of scientific relationship should support some specific scholarly communication. We illustrate it by examples of some services designed within the research information system SocioNet

Keywords: Semantically enrichable research information system · Scientific relationships taxonomy · Controlled vocabulary · SocioNet system

1 Introduction

Let us consider the research community as a labor division system where each researcher with her/his specific scientific specialization is a node having communication and cooperation with the neighbor nodes. These neighbor nodes, taking into account the global research community, typically are: (a) an author, who published a paper, and (b) researchers, who used some research results from the paper published by the author and cited the paper into their research outputs. If we create a research information system, which initiates and supports scientific communication between researchers who are neighbors in the global scientific cooperation network the community will get a lot of benefits. We are taking up this challenge by developing the semantically enrichable Research Information System (seRIS).

In this paper we discuss why and how seRIS with embedded taxonomy of the scientific relationships should support some specific communications between its users, when and if these users are using this taxonomy for semantic enrichment of its content. The paper continues a series of about 30 publications[1] with outputs of the SocioNet project during the last 15 years. In [6] and [7] we have a general evaluation of the proposed approach, a discussion of the related works and other relevant to this paper background.

---

[1] There are 12 papers in English and other in Russian language at https://socionet.ru/collection.xml?h=repec:rus:mqijxk&l=en

© Springer International Publishing Switzerland 2015
P. Klinov and D. Mouromtsev (Eds.): KESW 2015, CCIS 518, pp. 87–101, 2015.
DOI: 10.1007/978-3-319-24543-0_7

The seRIS SocioNet (https://socionet.ru/) [9] provides a test bed for our experiments. We illustrate the discussion by examples from this system.

At its most general and simple level, we can think of user interface of the seRIS as containing web pages that describe, at least, two kinds of things. These are (1) research outputs (RO), e.g. papers that have been written by authors, and (2) personal profile pages (PP) of these authors. A landscape of a real seRIS of course is much more complicated [9].

To present the discussing research problem let us examine a particular situation. An author makes enrichment of metadata of their research outputs (papers) using the functionality of the seRIS. All results of such enrichment activities are public and freely available for readers on the web pages with metadata of the papers. Other users will see the results and they may have issues with the enriched data. It motivates communication between them.

All semantic linkages produced as a result of enrichment activity will have a source object and a target object where linking direction is "source" $\rightarrow$ "target". The source object will either be a PP or an RO. The target object will always be an RO. We label it as two cases CS1: PP $\rightarrow$ RO and CS2: RO $\rightarrow$ RO.

There are two basic actions for CS1 (PP $\rightarrow$ RO). In the first action, an author annotates the abstract of their RO. In the second, an author specifies their personal roles in preparing a collective RO. We also discuss some additional actions in the next section.

The first action of CS1 gives birth to the first communication case called as "CC1".

CC1: If the target RO (e.g. a paper) has several co-authors and one of them expresses his/her opinion about the paper – be it by annotating the paper's abstract or by specifying their personal role – the other co-authors have to be informed about this action. The enrichment made by this action is public and available for readers of their paper. Therefore, we need to give co-authors an opportunity to inform readers of the paper about their (non)consensus with a content of the enrichment.

CS2 gives birth to three additional communication cases (CC2-CC4). In our application a semantic linkage from some research output (RO1) to another research output (RO2) appears when an author is making any of following three actions:

1. linking his/her RO1 and RO2 to visualize some relationships/dependences between them;
2. providing motivation for citing RO2 from a reference list of RO1;
3. specifying relationship from some their own RO1 to RO2 with an authorship of other researchers.

All results of such enrichment actions are also public and available for readers both RO1 and RO2 papers.

CC2: If the paper RO1 has several co-authors (say set A1), the communication should work in the same way as CC1. All co-authors of RO1 should be informed about the enrichment made by one of them and should be able to show their consensus with his/her action.

CC3: If the paper RO2 has a set of authors (say set A2), and set A2 is a subset of set A1, the system should do nothing since all co-authors already served by the communication case 2 (CC2).

CC4: If the set A2 has a subset A3 of authors that doesn't belong to the authors set A1, the system should notify authors from A3 about the enrichment of their RO2 and provide them with ability to express their reaction. For example, if a researcher's paper was cited with a now-explicit citing motivation the researcher should know about this immediately. The researcher should be able to react on this action. She/he may be interested to help other researchers in improving how they are using his/her research output. Or she/he may be willing to improve her/his research results to provide a better effect for other researchers who are using it.

The notification mentioned in the communication cases 1-4 above is more or less the same for all actions of CS1 and CS2.

These CC1-CC4 provide only a starting point for communication between an author and a user of research outputs. We also need to take authors' reactions on relationships made by users with their research outputs into account. And we need to visualize it properly for readers of papers with these relationships. This secondary communication is highly dependent on the specific action (use case). It also depends on the meaning of the taxonomy value used to classify the scientific relationship.

The cases CS1 and CS2 discussed above are about actions made by the authors of papers. In the next section, we also discuss the case CS3 of papers' reader actions and CS4 with re-actions of researchers on actions made according CS1-CS3.

The next section of this paper presents a set of the controlled semantic vocabularies designed to embed the scientific relationships taxonomy into the research information system. We also discuss some communication features of the system and communication actors who should be served according to specific actions (use cases). In the third section, we present a pilot implementation of the scholarly communication features designed within the research information system SocioNet with embedded taxonomy of scientific relationships. The fourth section concludes the discussion.

2   Taxonomy of Scientific Relationships Embedded into SocioNet System

We designed our taxonomy of scientific relationships using certain modules of the Semantic Publishing and Referencing (SPAR) ontology created by researchers from the Oxford University and University of Bologna [11, 12], SWAN (Semantic Web Applications in Neuromedicine) [10], SKOS (Simple Knowledge Organization System) [13] from W3C, the classification of the diverse roles performed in the work leading to a published research output in the sciences from the CRediT project [1, 2], and other.

The taxonomy embedded into SocioNet has a two-level structure. It is organized as a set of controlled vocabularies. Each single controlled vocabulary corresponds to a certain class of the scientific relationships. The controlled vocabulary values correspond to subclasses of this class. The taxonomy of scientific relationships and its controlled vocabularies are discussed in more detail in [8].

The SocioNet system supports updating already existed controlled vocabularies. It also allows creating new ones. Users can extend taxonomies of semantic linkages by adding subclasses (values) to existing vocabularies and/or by creating new classes/vocabularies under a supervision of the system administrator.

When a user creates a semantic linkage the controlled vocabulary that is suitable to the particular use case appears in the form used to create that type of a link. The user can select its proper value. The selected value adds semantics to the created linkage. The semantic linkage technique and a form that used for creating semantic linkages are presented in [6].

As of the beginning of May 2015, the SocioNet system configuration includes a set of the six controlled vocabularies:

1. Relationships between versions and components of a research output;
2. Relationships of development and complement of between research outputs;
3. Recommendations and comments for authors of research outputs;
4. Researcher's contributions to collaborative research output;
5. Professional opinion and evaluation of research outputs;
6. Researcher's reactions on relationships and on the opinion expressed by other researchers with/for his/her research outputs.

These controlled vocabularies are available for the SocioNet users according to some specific use cases. The vocabularies are also available at SocioNet as ordinary collections[2] for re-using outside our system. When a user is creating a semantic linkage under some use case and with some related controlled vocabulary the result of this action affect different actors. We have summarized this in Table 1.

Table 1. Supported use cases, related controlled vocabularies, and affected actors

Use case: action	Controlled vocabulary	Affected actors
CS1, 1: An author annotates the abstract of his/her research output RO	None	Co-authors of the research output RO, if any
CS1, 2: An author specifies their personal roles in preparing collective paper RO	Researcher's contribution to collaborative research output	Co-authors of the research output RO, if any
CS2, 1: An author semantically links her/his papers RO1 and RO2 to visualize relationships or dependences between them	Relationships between versions and components of a research output Relationships of development and complement between research outputs	Co-authors of the research outputs RO1 and RO2, if any

---

[2] https://socionet.ru/section.xml?h=metrics_interdisciplinary&l=en

Table 1. (*Continued*)

Use case: action	Controlled vocabulary	Affected actors
CS2, 2: An author provides motivations for citing a paper RO2 from a reference list of a paper RO1	Relationships of development and complement of between research outputs	Co-authors of the research outputs RO1 and authors of RO2
CS2, 3: An author specifies relationships from some own paper RO1 to a paper RO2 written by other researchers	Relationships of development and complement of between research outputs Recommendations and comments for authors of papers	Co-authors of the research outputs RO1 and authors of RO2
CS3: A reader annotates the abstract of a research output RO and/or provides an opinion about RO	Professional opinions and evaluations of research outputs	Author(s) of the research output RO
CS4: An author provides his/her reaction on relationships/linkages made with their research output RO by other scientists	Researcher's reaction on relationships and on opinions created with/for his/her research outputs	Author(s) of scientific relationships/linkages with feedback reactions

There are two special cases in Table 1: CS3 and CS4. The case CS3 illustrates a situation when reader's actions can also initiate some kind of the system activity and scholarly communication. The case CS4 allows some kind of feedback reactions on relationships/linkages affected authors of research outputs. We will illustrate CS4 in the third section by examples of the real implementation at SocioNet.

For now in this section we have six tables. They illustrate how the content of research relationships specified by subclasses of the controlled vocabularies can initiate different kind of the system activity and scholarly communication.

The first example is in Table 2. It illustrates that some research relationships concern the scientific inference or the scientific usage dependence between linked research outputs. So the system should notify authors of papers, e.g. if the papers have scientific inference/usage relationships with other papers where some critical errors were found.

Each table in this section below includes subclasses of the controlled vocabulary and related with them alarm events and initiated a system activity or a communication with affected actors.

Table 2. Vocabulary of subclasses of the development and complement relationship between research outputs (CS2, 1-3)

Subclasses	System activity
uses data from	If one found an error or expressed a suspicion in the quality of the used entity, the author of relationship with this value has to be notified and should revise their related research outputs.
uses method from	the same
uses a model from	the same
uses software from	the same
uses statistics from	the same
details idea/method/model from	the same
generalizes idea/method/model from	the same
implements idea/method/model from	the same
develops results from	the same
interprets results from	the same
analyzes results from	none by default, the warning notification can be switch on by the user
illustrates results from	none by default, the warning notification can be switch on by the user
corrects errors in	none by default, the warning notification can be switch on by the user
refines results from	none by default, the warning notification can be switch on by the user
refutes results from	none by default, the warning notification can be switch on by the user

Table 3. Vocabulary of subclasses of the relationship between versions and components of a research output, its parts or components (CS2, 1)

Subclasses	System activity
<ul><li>author's version (manuscript) for</li><li>open access version for</li><li>version with slight changes for</li><li>version with minor changes for</li><li>substantially revised version for</li><li>revised or new version for</li><li>duplicated copy for</li><li>presentation of</li><li>part of</li><li>abstract for</li><li>table of contents for</li><li>foreword for</li><li>bibliography for</li></ul>	There is no a specific activity related with content of this vocabulary

Table 4. Vocabulary of subclasses of the relationship of recommendations and comments for authors of papers (CS2, 3)

Subclasses	System activity
• you can apply software that I used • your results are analyzed in my publication • your idea/method/model/results are itemized in my publication • your data/method/model/results are illustrated in my publication • your results are interpreted in my publication • my data/method/model are better • your idea/method/model/results are generalized in my publication • a similar problem is discussed in my publication • your results are refuted in my publication • I received the same results • your idea/method/model are implemented in my work • your errors are detected and corrected in my publication.	There is no a specific activity related with content of this vocabulary

Table 5. Vocabulary of subclasses of a researcher's contribution to collaborative research output (CS1, 2)

Subclasses	System activity
• manuscript preparation: writing the initial draft • manuscript preparation: visualization/data presentation • manuscript preparation: critical review, commentary or revision • performing the experiments • methodology development • study conception • investigation: data/evidence collection • computation • resources provision • formal analysis • data curation • project administration • supervision • funding acquisition	There is no a specific activity related with content of this vocabulary

Table 6. Vocabulary of subclasses of the professional opinion and evaluation of research outputs (CS3)

Subclasses	System activity
• innovative result • very interesting result • the turning point for the science development • best, most relevant on the subject • responds negatively to • unscientific approach • potentially dangerous effect • result based on confusion • suspected plagiarism	There is no a specific activity related with the positive content of this vocabulary. If someone used the negative content (e.g. "suspected plagiarism") the system should send an alarm to the system administrator.

Table 7. Vocabulary of subclasses of the scientist's reaction on relationships and on opinions created by other scientists with/for his/her research outputs (CS4)

Subclasses	System activity
• agree with this relationship • disagree with this relationship • ready to improve my paper • ready to help with taking better effect from using my paper • propose making a joint paper • propose a joint development of my results • misunderstanding of my paper • protest against	The "agree" and "disagree" subclasses from the content of this vocabulary initiate the system activity described in the next section.

The controlled vocabulary in Table 7 is a very special one. The vocabulary includes direct calls for scientific cooperation ("propose making a joint paper" or "propose a joint development of my results"). It is used to initiate direct communication between an author and a user of a research result and to push them to scientific cooperation.

In the next section, we present some SocioNet seRIS facilities for authors based on using this controlled vocabulary and aimed to support some new scholarly communication.

3   Scholarly Communication Initiated by Enrichment Activity

In [3] and [4] we started a discussion of the scholarly communication within a research information system with authors' facilities to enrich their papers' descriptions.

This section demonstrates how the SocioNet seRIS organizes the scholarly communication initiated by authors' activity to enrich metadata of their research outputs.

The application is publically available for testing and experiments at https://socionet.ru/. Additionally to authors of this paper there are two members of the SocioNet project team. Victor Lyapunov made the user's status monitoring and notification services. Roman Puzyrev made the tool and the online form for semantic linkage creation.

3.1   Notifications

At the introduction section of this paper, we specified the cases CS1 and CS2 when the system has to inform authors of papers that someone linked their papers with other papers by some scientific relationships. Figure 1 provides an example of such notification. It also includes a link to a user's list of currently unconfirmed relationships/linkages. Using the list shown at the Figure 2 the user can check new relationships and she/he can express their opinion (e.g. consensus) about these relationships.

You logged-in as: Krichel Thomas / Крихель Томас [log out]
You have unconfirmed relationships/linkages: 7

Fig. 1. An example of a notification about unconfirmed relationships

Unconfirmed relationships/linkages with publication of the author:
Krichel Thomas // Крихель Томас
total unconfirmed relationships/linkages: 7 on date: 2015-05-15

1	repec:rus:ecoper:parinov_sergey.56054-1 repec:rus:mqijxk:26 отношение не задано (date: 2015-04-17)
	Паринов Сергей
2	repec:rus:ecoper:parinov_sergey.56054-1 repec:rus:mqijxk:26 развитие методологии (date: 2015-04-17)
	Паринов Сергей

Fig. 2. An example of a list of unchecked relationships

The next subsections demonstrate the user interfaces to express her/his opinion and examples of how such user's reaction is visualized on the papers' metadata web pages.

3.2   User Interfaces

If a user creates a scientific relationship in the SocioNet, all necessary data are saved and stored into the system as a semantic linkage [6].

When an authorized user opens a semantic linkage web page the system recognizes the user's status. There are four cases: (1) the user is the author of the browsed linkage; (2) the user is a co-author of the linked papers (see Figure 3); (3) the user is an author of used/cited paper; (4) the user is just a reader, he/she has no relation with the browsed linkage and linked papers.

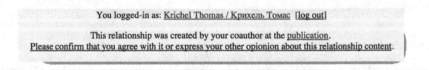

Fig. 3. An example of the system messages about the user status

The system displays the user status at the linkage web. Depending on the user status it provides a hyperlink with following opportunities (Table 8):

1. the co-author of the linked papers can specify "agree" or "disagree" with the relationship made by another co-author of their collective paper;
4. the author of the used/cited paper can specify any of controlled vocabulary values listed in Table 8;
5. the reader can specify only "agree" or "disagree";
6. the author of the browsed linkage can express nothing.

Fig. 4. An example of the form to express opinion about the relationship

When a user clicks on a hyperlink to express their opinion, she/he reaches a form presented on Figure 4. In the field "Comments" the user can enter some explanation to her/his opinion. The drop-down list "Relationship type" uses values from the Table 8 according the user status. All other options of the form can be used by default [9].

Table 8. Types of scientist reactions on professional evaluation of research relationships according to the their user status

taxonomy values	available for co-authors	available for authors of used papers	available for readers
agree with this relationship	√	√	√
disagree with this relationship	√	√	√
ready to improve my paper		√	
ready to help with taking better effect from using my paper		√	
propose making a joint paper		√	
propose a joint development of my results		√	
misunderstanding of my paper		√	
protest against		√	

If you have expressed your opinion on the relationship the system displays that at the linkage web page as a new status. It does not allow users to do it one more time (see Figure 5).

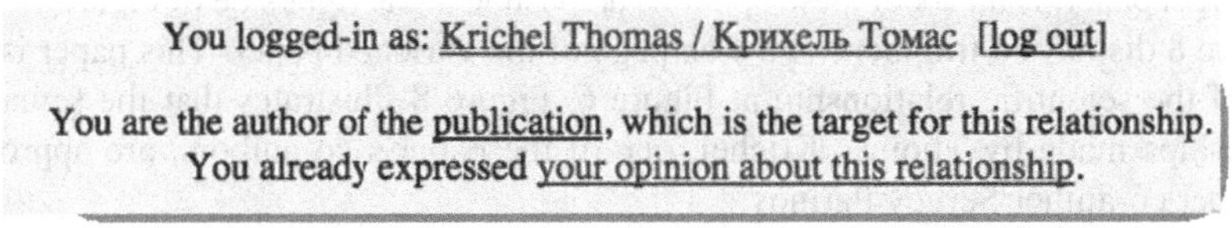

You logged-in as: Krichel Thomas / Крихель Томас [log out]

You are the author of the publication, which is the target for this relationship.
You already expressed your opinion about this relationship.

Fig. 5. An example how the system messages a changed user status

For other technical details on how this system works see [7].

3.3   Data Visualization

Semantic linkages with information about user opinion on the scientific relationship content are public. This data are visible at SocioNet in three places: (1) on the web page of the evaluated scientific relationship it is visualized at the column "Opinions about the relationship" at the right side of the web page (examples at Figures 6 and 7); (2) on the web page of a paper with the scientific relationship, at the beginning of data about this relationship there appears the green ("agree") or pink ("disagree") icons (examples at Figures 8-9); and (3) there is a web page for every created semantic linkage.

Figure 6 displays a fragment of a web page of the scientific relationship created by Thomas Krichel according the use case CS1, 2. The target paper ("linked object" at Figure 6) has two co-authors. The second co-author (Sergey Parinov) expresses his opinion: "agree with this relationship". This information is shown at the right of Figure 6.

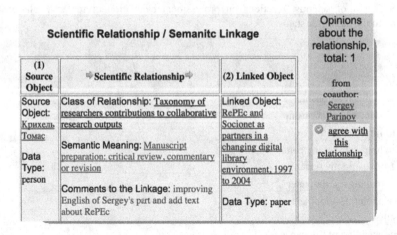

Fig. 6. An example for a visualization of opinions about relationships

Figure 7 illustrates that the scientific relationship according to the use case CS2, 1 created by an author of the source paper (Sergey Parinov) has two opinions from the author of the target paper. Data about these opinions are visible at the right side of Figure 7.

Figure 8 displays a fragment of a web page of the enriched paper. This paper is the target of the scientific relationship at Figure 6. Figure 8 illustrates that the semantic relationships made by Thomas Krichel, one of the paper's co-authors, are approved by another co-author Sergey Parinov.

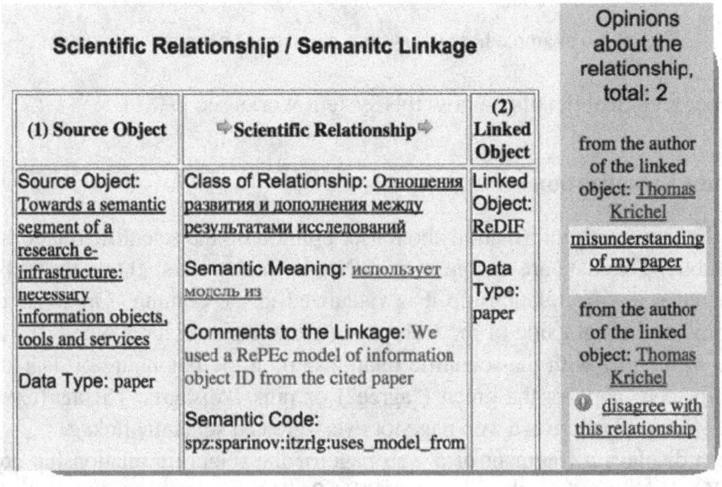

Fig. 7. An example of a visualization of opinions about relationships

claimed author: Sergey Parinov ☀; all claimed publications: 77
claimed author role: -Methodology development -Manuscript preparation: writing the initial draft

claimed author: Thomas Krichel; all claimed publications: 6
claimed author role: ⊘Manuscript preparation: critical review, commentary or revision ⊘Methodology development

1 coauthor approved it

Fig. 8. An example of a visualization of approved relationships

This style of visualization allows readers of the paper see a consensus between paper's co-authors on contents of scientific relationships, even though the co-authors created the relationships independently of each other. The green icon means "agree". The pink icon as at Figure 7 means "disagree". The absence of any icon means that another co-author has not reacted yet.

The Figure 9 illustrates how the system visualizes the data about approved scientific relationships between two research outputs with co-authors, which was made according to the use case CS2, 1.

The author specified related paper(s)

relationship	to a paper
outgoing linkages to versions or components	⊘ substantially revised version for	Thomas Krichel; Паринов Сергей: База данных RePEc и ее российский партнер система Соционет;

Fig. 9. An example for a visualization of approved relationships

There are other research information systems with the social network functionality that provide to some extend similar communication features. Typically it is just users' tools for annotating of or expressing their opinions about papers (e.g. Mendeley). Interesting approach is presented in [5]. It is the nanopublication portal called "nanobrowser", which visualizes relationships between nanopublications (like "same meaning"). It also allows scientists to create meta-nanopublications by expressing their opinions about these relationships and nanopublications itself. See Figure 3 in [5].

4   Conclusion

We presented an approach and facilities to introduce new types of scholarly communication within research information systems. They create additional opportunities for improving global cooperation among authors of research results, as well as between them and users of these results.

As of the beginning of May 2015, the presented semantic enrichment facilities with some services for scholarly communication are available for SocioNet users only during the two months. At this moment, we have not had yet any sufficient statistics about usage of these facilities.

Acknowledgements. We are grateful to Thomas Krichel for his help with preparing of this paper. This project is funded by the Russian Foundation for Basic Research, grant 15-07-01294-a, and the Russian Foundation for Humanities, grant 14-02-12020-v.

References

1. Allen, L., Brand, A., Scott, J., Altman, M., Hlava, M.: Credit where credit is due. Nature International Weekly Journal of Science. Nature **508**(7496), April 2014. http://www.nature.com/polopoly_fs/1.15033!/menu/main/topColumns/topLeftColumn/pdf/508312a.pdf
2. CRediT. An open standard for expressing roles intrinsic to research. Taxonomy. http://credit.casrai.org/proposed-taxonomy/
3. Kogalovsky, M.R., Parinov, S.I.: Social Network Technologies for Semantic Linking of Information Objects in Scientific Digital Library. Programming and Computer Software **40**(6), 313–320 (2014)
4. Kogalovsky, M.R., Parinov, S.I.: Scientific communications in the semantic enrichable digital libraries. Program Engineering **4**, 31–38 (2015). Когаловский М.Р., Паринов С.И. Научные коммуникации в среде семантически обогащаемых электронных библиотек //Программная инженерия. 2015. № 4. С. 31-38
5. Kuhn, T., Barbano, P.E., Nagy, M.L., Krauthammer, M.: Broadening the scope of nanopublications. In: Cimiano, P., Corcho, O., Presutti, V., Hollink, L., Rudolph, S. (eds.) ESWC 2013. LNCS, vol. 7882, pp. 487–501. Springer, Heidelberg (2013). http://arxiv.org/abs/1303.2446
6. Parinov, S.: Towards a semantic segment of a research e-infrastructure: necessary information objects, tools and services. In: Dodero, J.M., Palomo-Duarte, M., Karampiperis, P. (eds.) MTSR 2012. CCIS, vol. 343, pp. 133–145. Springer, Heidelberg (2012). http://socionet.ru/pub.xml?h=RePEc:rus:mqijxk:30
7. Parinov, S.: Semantic enrichment of research outputs metadata: new CRIS facilities for authors. In: Closs, S., Studer, R., Garoufallou, E., Sicilia, M.-A. (eds.) MTSR 2014. CCIS, vol. 478, pp. 206–217. Springer, Heidelberg (2014)
8. Parinov, S., Kogalovsky, M.: Semantic Linkages in Research Information Systems as a New Data Source for Scientometric Studies. Scientometric **98**(2), 927–943 (2014)
9. Parinov, S., Lyapunov V., Puzyrev R., Kogalovsky M.: Semantically enrichable research information system SocioNet. In: Proceedings of the same conference KESW-2015 (2015)

10. Semantic Web Applications in Neuromedicine (SWAN) Ontology. W3C Interest Group Note, October 20, 2009. http://www.w3.org/TR/hcls-swan/
11. Shotton, D.: Open Citations and Related Work. Introduction the Semantic Publishing and Referencing (SPAR) Ontologies. October 14, 2010. http://opencitations.wordpress.com/2010/10/14/introducing-the-semantic-publishing-and-referencing-spar-ontologies/
12. Shotton, D., Peroni, S.: Semantic annotation of publication entities using the SPAR (Semantic Publishing and Referencing) Ontologies/Beyond the PDF Workshop, La Jolla, January 19, 2011. http://speroni.web.cs.unibo.it/publications/shotton-2010-semantic-annotation-publication.pdf
13. SKOS Simple Knowledge Organization System Reference. W3C Recommendation, August 18, 2009. http://www.w3.org/TR/skos-reference/

Ontologies for Web of Things:
A Pragmatic Review

Maxim Kolchin[⊠], Nikolay Klimov, Alexey Andreev, Ivan Shilin,
Daniil Garayzuev, Dmitry Mouromtsev, and Danil Zakoldaev

ITMO University, Saint-Petersburg, Russia
{kolchinmax,nikolay.klimov}@niuitmo.ru,
{a_andreev,shilinivan,garayzuev}@corp.ifmo.ru,
mouromtsev@mail.ifmo.ru, d.zakoldaev@mics.spb.ru

Abstract. Web of Things (WoT) is another area where Semantic Web
technologies provides a foundation for effective data access through a unified data model that in its turn realises interoperability among all components of WoT landscape. There exists significant amount of research
focusing on applying RDF data model, OWL ontologies and Reasoning
in different WoT scenarios, such as home automation, Industry 4.0 and
etc. But so far this approach didn't get wide adoption beyond research
community. In this paper we attempt to answer the question: Are existing ontologies ready to form an ontology framework for annotating real-
world devices? By the example of three real-world devices, we review
existing ontologies which can be used to describe their facilities, location
and etc. And in the end, we present an instrument to generate semantic
descriptions for such devices.

Keywords: OWL · Ontology · Web of things · Knowledge engineering

1 Introduction

Physical *(or virtual)* devices that are able to communicate their states between
each other form a network of connected devices. These devices are sensors and
actuators that can be wearable devices for health monitoring, geospatial and
environmental monitoring sensors and other devices from different fields such as
automation and industrial manufacturing, logistics, intelligent transportation of
people and goods. Technologies transforming ordinary devices to connected ones
and the networks of these devices constitute the concept of Internet of Things
(IoT) which has gathered significant attention from industry and academia [1,
14,20]. The Web of Things was proposed [6] as a next evolutionary step for
Internet of Things concept where the devices "are fully integrated in the Web
by reusing and adapting technologies and patterns commonly used for traditional
Web content"[7].

Data or service providers face several problems when they want to expose
data of the physical devices on the Web. One of them is the heterogeneity of

P. Klinov and D. Mouromtsev (Eds.): KESW 2015, CCIS 518, pp. 102–116, 2015.
DOI: 10.1007/978-3-319-24543-0_8

the devices at the communication and data levels. At the communication level, it can be mitigated by a middleware which has a modular architecture allowing to implement specific modules providing support for particular technologies and protocols. In this paper we don't aim to review existing middleware for WoT, therefore we refer readers to [2] paper which does it and also classifies them based on proposed fundamental functional blocks. At the data level, the heterogeneity is caused by different and sometimes substandard data models and formats supported by various device manufacturers. The same things (observations, observed properties, units of measurement and etc.) can be described in different ways without a possibility for integration. At the data level this problem can be solved using the ontology-based approach which is based on using semantically rich models (ontologies that can be extended for a particular use-case). Several works already have shown how this approach can be applied to easy integration of diverse data sources [11,15]. Ontologies and vocabularies such as the SSN (Semantic Sensor Network) Ontology [4] have been created and adopted in a number of research projects [5,10,13,17,19].

Although in the ontology based approach has got significant adoption in research projects, it still hasn't got similar adoption in industry and among application developers. This situation can be explained by different reasons: (a) lack of standardisation, (b) high complexity of existing ontologies, (c) even with three reasons provided by Lanthaler and Gult for what they call *semaphobia* [12]. Whatever reason it is, in this paper we aim to answer the following question: *Are existing ontologies ready to form an ontology framework to annotate real-world devices?*

To answer the given question we take three examples of real-world devices, based on these examples we define several high-level conceptual groups that include concepts to describe these devices and their measurements or observations, review existing ontologies which can provide concepts that fall down at least in one of the conceptual groups. Also using the reviewed ontologies we define an integrated ontology framework and present a tool that provides a user interface to rapidly build semantic descriptions of WoT devices, making complexity of formal specification transparent to the user. We argue that such tools play a significant role in ricing adoption of the approach, because writing semantic descriptions by hand is time consuming, tedious and a error-prone task.

Limitations. This work has two limitations which are based on the fact that we take in a account only three examples of real-world devices which maybe don't cover all of the concepts of WoT:

- We don't aim to provide a comprehensive review of existing ontologies, but only ones that are related to the given examples of real-world devices,
- We don't aim to outline all possible conceptual groups, but only the ones that are related to the given examples.

For a comprehensive review of existing ontologies and use cases we refer readers to the review done by W3C Semantic Sensor Network Incubator[1] Group and published in their final report [3].

Structure. The remainder of the paper is organised as follows. In Section 2 we introduce three examples of real-world devices. In Section 3, we introduce the conceptual groups that include concepts required to describe the given devices. In Section 4 we review existing ontologies which, from our point of view, provides concepts falling down at least in one of the conceptual groups. Section 5 introduces a tool providing a user interface to rapidly build semantic descriptions for WoT devices. Section 6 describes the current states and issues of the reviewed ontologies. And the last section we conclude the paper.

2   Examples of Real-World Devices

To derive conceptual groups and concepts which constitute these groups, we suggest examples of three real-world devices that will help us later to review existing ontologies. The first devices is an Arduino[2]-based weather station that may seem a toy device, but such devices actually actively used by enthusiasts to create a crowd-sourced weather portals such as *NarodMon Project*[3] where people share air temperature, humidity and other readings of their sensors with the community. The second device is a wall/ceiling mount exhaust bath fan with a humidity sensor that switches on/off the fan if humidity at high or normal levels respectively. The third device is an electric meter which is installed in a residential building and measuring energy consumption by all consumers in this building.

RW1. An Arduino-based Weather Station. The weather station is called "EnvTH-0.0.1", it's a research prototype developed in ITMO University and capable to measure air temperature and humidity. It's equipped with DHT-22[4] sensor which measures air temperature and humidity. Detailed characteristics of the sensor, such operating range, accuracy and etc., listed in Table 1. The station was deployed on the window of room 380 at the main campus of ITMO University. The station publishes its measurements on the Internet through CoAP protocol. A photo of this stations is shown in Figure 1a.

RW2. A Wall/Ceiling Mounted Exhaust Bath Fan. The model of the fan is called "Soler & Palau DECOR-100 CHZ"[5]. It's a commercial product of

---

[1] Cf. http://www.w3.org/2005/Incubator/ssn/

[2] Cf. http://www.arduino.cc

[3] Cf. http://narodmon.ru

[4] Cf. https://www.sparkfun.com/datasheets/Sensors/Temperature/DHT22.pdf

[5] Cf. http://www.solerandpalau.co.uk/
    product.jsp?PRODUCTID=157&CATEGORYID=41

Table 1. Characteristics of an Arduino-based weather station

Measuring property	Air temperature	Humidity
Operating range	0–100% RH	-40–80 C^o
Accuracy	±2% RH	±0.5 C^o
Sensitivity	0.1% RH	0.1 C^o
Measurement range	0–100% RH	-40–80 C^o
Frequency	2s	
Resolution	0.1% RH	0.1 C^o

"Soler & Palau" company and capable to exhaust a room only if the humidity is higher than a threshold and then switch off automatically if the humidity is back to normal. The fan has a humidity sensor and an actuator which allows the user to switch on/off the fan manually. A photo of the fan is shown in Figure 1b.

RW3. An Electric Meter in a Residential Building. The model of the electric meter is called "Mercury 230 ART"[6], it's a three phase electric meter and a commercial product of Incotex, LLC company, see Fig. 1c. The meter was deployed on 29th April 2015 in a residential building at Kotelnikova alley 5/1 (60.013456, 30.288267) and is maintained by WingHouse company. The measurements taken by the meter are transmitted by a gateway (Fig. 1d) to a server in a single packet by a specified interval. The packet contains the following information: (i) serial number, (ii) current date and time, (iii) sampling date and time, (iv) voltage on each phase, (v) amperage on each phase, (vi) total active power on all phases, (vii) total reactive power on all phases.

3   Conceptual Groups

In this section high-level concepts and their relations that describes the devices are presented. They are grouped in several groups which we call *conceptual groups*. Below each of the conceptual groups is explained. In Section 4, we review existing ontologies which provide enough expressiveness in terms of concepts they allow to represent to fall in one of the groups.

---

[6] Cf. http://www.incotexcom.ru/m230art_en.htm

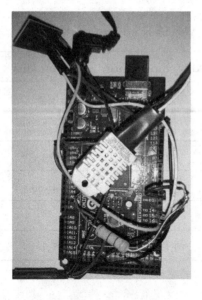

(a) An Arduino-based weather
station

(b) A wall/ceiling mount exhaust
bath fan

(c) An electric meter in a
residential building

(d) A gateway transmitting
measurements from the electric
meter in Fig. 1c

Fig. 1. Photos of devices used in this work as examples of real-world devices

CG1. Actuator, Sensor, System. Each of the example devices is a composite device, consisting of one or more sensors and/or actuators. So it's needed to have an ontology representing a hierarchy of parts of a composite device. In this group we define the following concepts:

- *Sensors* are "physical objects that perform observations, i.e. they transform an incoming stimulus into another, often digital, representation"[8]. They have several characteristics such as measuring capabilities, accuracy, measuring frequency, observed property (e.g. wind, air temperature) and etc.,
- *Actuators* are physical objects that modify (e.g. rotate, switch on/off and etc.) the physical state of another physical object. Actuators characterised by the physical object whose state they change, operating range and etc.
- *Systems* are composite devices consisting of one or several sensors or actuators. A system can be also a subsystem of a large device.

CG2. Global and Local Coordinates. Since the *devices* are often physical objects (e.g. in environmental monitoring, advanced meter management, etc.) their location is important. The location can be *global* represented with the geo-coordinates such as latitude and longitude, and *local* (e.g in a building) represented with the geo-coordinates of the place, relative coordinates within this place and moreover the place may have a number of levels (e.g. floors).

CG3. Communication Endpoint. This conceptual group referes to a fundamental requirement for Web of Things is a notion of physical objects which are able to communicate their states over the Internet by itself or using intermediate gateways. Therefore the applications accessing the sensor data need to know how to communicate with the objects, e.g. which *protocol* and *version* to use.

CG4. Observations, Features of Interest, Units, and Dimensions. The sensor *observation* is another core concept in the field which is a result of a stimulus observed by a sensor. It's characterised by sampling time, feature of interest (e.g. electricity, air, water), observed property (e.g. current strength, air temperature). Also in this group we include *units of measure* and *dimensions*.

CG5. Vendor, Version, Deployment Time. *Sensors* and *actuators* are devices which were manufactured by a *vendor* and usually have the *version* of hardware and software. Also it may be important for some use cases to know the date and time when a particular device was deployed. So this conceptual group focus on the following information:

- about device vendor and manufacturer which may contain the name of the organisation, web site, or some other information that can identify it,
- about device deployment such as time, place (see CG2) and so on,
- about the organisation which responsible for maintenance and support of the device such as the name of the organisation, contact information, responsible person, etc.

4   Ontologies

After we defined the conceptual groups in the previous section, in this section we review existing ontologies which allow to represent concepts falling into another the conceptual groups. Also we take in account the *rating* of the ontologies accroding to [9] rating defined by Janowicz et al. There is an option to found them and count popularity, richness and other properties in Linked Open Vocabularies[7] catalogue. In Table 2 we summarise the ontologies we selected to represent the concept and their relations from the defined groups.

Table 2. Matrix with conceptual groups and corresponding ontologies

Conceptual group	Ontology
CG1 Actuator, sensor, system	Semantic Sensor Network (ssn)[8], DogOnt[9]
CG2 Global and local coordinates	WGS84 Geo Positioning (geo)[10], LIMAP[11], OGC GeoSPARQL[12], DUL[13]
CG3 Communication endpoint	OSGi DAL[14], SAREF[15], FIEMSER[16], FIPA[17]
CG4 Observations, features of interest, units and dimensions	OGC OM[18], QUDT[19], OM[20], MUO[21], AWS[22]
CG5 Vendor, versions, deployment time	MMI Device[23], FOAF[24], linkingyou[25]

---

[7] Cf. http://lov.okfn.org
[8] Cf. http://purl.oclc.org/NET/ssnx/ssn#
[9] Cf. http://lov.okfn.org/dataset/lov/vocabs/dogont
[10] Cf. http://www.w3.org/2003/01/geo/wgs84_pos#
[11] Cf. http://data.uni-muenster.de/php/vocab/limap
[12] Cf. http://www.opengis.net/ont/geosparql#
[13] Cf. http://www.loa-cnr.it/ontologies/DUL.owl#
[14] Cf. https://sites.google.com/site/smartappliancesproject/ontologies/osgi_dal-ontology
[15] Cf. http://ontology.tno.nl/saref
[16] Cf. https://sites.google.com/site/smartappliancesproject/ontologies/fiemser-ontology
[17] Cf. http://sites.google.com/site/smartappliancesproject/ontologies/fipa#
[18] Cf. http://www.opengeospatial.org/standards/om
[19] Cf. http://qudt.org/
[20] Cf. http://www.wurvoc.org/vocabularies/om-1.6/
[21] Cf. http://idi.fundacionctic.org/muo/muo-vocab.html
[22] Cf. http://www.w3.org/2005/Incubator/ssn/ssnx/meteo/aws
[23] Cf. http://mmisw.org/ont/mmi/device
[24] Cf. http://xmlns.com/foaf/spec/
[25] Cf. http://purl.org/linkingyou/

4.1   CG1: Actuator, Sensor, System

There are several ontologies including concepts from this group. One of them is Semantic Sensor Network (SSN) Ontology[4] that was developed by W3C Semantic Sensor Network Incubator Group[26] in 2011. The concept of *Sensors* is represented based on the Stimulus-Sensor-Observation Ontology Design Pattern [8] and also allows to represented an hierarchy of *Systems* using *ssn:hasSubSystem* object property, see Listing 1.1. But the ontology doesn't have representations for the concept of *Actuators*, this fact is mentioned in [18] paper where the authors suggest several extensions to the SSN ontology, but unfortunately the developed ontology is not available any more, so we don't consider it.

Actuators can be represented by another ontology called DogOnt[5] which has class *dogont:Actuator* and several properties such as *dogont:actuatorOf*, *dogont:hasActuator*, *dogont:controlledObject* and etc.

```
: system −0  a  ssn : System  ;
    ssn : hasSubsystem  [
        a  ssn : Sensor  ;
        ssn : observes  : Temperature  .
    ];
    ssn : hasSubsystem  [
        a  ssn : Sensor
        ssn : observes  : Heat  .
    ];
```

Listing 1.1. An example of a *System* with two *Sensors* (temperature and heat)

The concept of *Sensors* more popular in existing ontologies, than *Actuators*. According to the LOV [3] catalogue, 19 ontologies has a class with "sensor" in its name and only 2 ontologies for "actuator". The SSN is a "5 star" ontology which follows all the rating requirements and DogOnt is only a "4 star" ontology, because according to the LOV [7] catalogue it doesn't have incoming links.

4.2   CG2: Global and Local Coordinates

In this group we cover concepts and relations related to the spatial nature of *things*. As stated in CG2, the spatial information can be *global* and *local*.

The global location of the *things* is described with geocoordinates such as latitude and longitude which can be represented by well known WSG84 ontology[6] which has class *geo:Point* and properties *geo:latitude*, *geo:longitude*, *geo:altitude*. By combining these properties with *dul:hasLocation* from DUL[9] ontology is possible to represent the sensor location, see Listing 1.2.

---

[26] Cf. http://www.w3.org/2005/Incubator/ssn/

```
:system-0 a ssn:Sensor ;
    dul:hasLocation [
        a geo:Point ;
        geo:latitude "59.956438" ;
        geo:longitude "30.3095818"
    ] .
```

Listing 1.2. An example of a *Sensor* with geo-coordinates

The *local* coordinates are relative to the *global* and used took locate something in a building, e.g. an electric meter in an apartment. In Listing 1.3, you can find an example of a *System* located in a room at the 4th floor of some building which has global coordinates expressed in geo-coordinates of a polygon. For this example we used LIMAP[7], OGC GeoSPARQL[8], DUL[9] and WSG84[6] ontologies.

```
:system-0 a ssn:System ;
    limap:isOccupantOf [
        a limap:Room ;
        limap:hasLocalCoordinates [
            a limap:LocalCoordinates ;
            geosparql:hasGeometry "POLYGON((
                3.976 0,
                6.765 0,
                6.765 2.273,
                3.976 2.273))"^^geo:wktLiteral .
        ] ;
        limap:isLocated :plan-4 .
    ] .
:plan-4 a limap:EscapePlan ;
    limap:hasSourceImage <...image url...> ;
    limap:isEscapePlanOf [ a limap:Floor ;
        dul:hasLocation [ geo:floor "4"^^xsd:int ] ;
        limap:isFloorIn [ a limap:Building ;
            limap:hasGlobalCoordinates [
                a limap:GlobalCoordinates ;
                geosparql:hasGeometry
                    "POLYGON((
                        -81.587 45.336,
                        -81.148 39.774,
                        -69.964 39.300,
                        -70.403 45.583,
                        -81.587 45.336))"^^geo:wktLitera
            ] .
        ] .
    ] .
```

Listing 1.3. An example of a *Sensor* located in a room of a building

Although the LIMAP ontology provides enough expressiveness, it's mainly focused on people and their locations in buildings, so the ontology requires minor customisation particularly in *limap:isOccupantOf* object property which has *rdfs:domain* referring to a person.

4.3   CG3: Communication Endpoint

The concepts from this group are needed to represent the way to communicate with the *things* which at least are communication *protocol* and its *version*. For that purpose we suggest to look at FIPA[13] and FIEMSER[12] ontologies which comply with our requirements. Listing 1.4 shows an example of using FIPA ontology and the similar example, but using FIEMSER ontology in Listing 1.5.

```
: sensor −0 a ssn : Sensor , fipa : Device ;
     fipa : hasHwProperties  [ a fipa : HwDescription  ;
          fipa : hasConnection  [
               a fipa : ConnectionDescription  ;
               fipa : hasConnectionInfo [
                    a fipa : InfoDescription  ;
                    fipa : hasName  "CoAP"  ;
                    fipa : hasVersion  "1.0"  .
               ]
          ]
     ] .
```

Listing 1.4. An example of sensor description with information about the *protocol* and *version* described with FIPA ontology

```
: sensor −0 a ssn : Sensor , fiemser : CommDevice ;
     fiemser : uses  :CoAP  .

:CoAP a fiemser : NetProtocol  ;
     fiemser : hasName  "CoAP"  ;
     fiemser : hasVersion  "1.0"  .
```

Listing 1.5. An example of sensor description with information about the *protocol* and *version* described with FIEMSER ontology

Both ontologies comply with the requirements, but only FIEMSER ontology has a separate class for the protocol which means it's more unambiguous.

4.4 CG4: Observations, Features of Interest, Units and Dimensions

The concept of *observation* can be represented by the SSN ontology that also covers other related concepts mentioned in CG4. Listing 1.6 shows an example of a temperature observation described with the SSN[4] and QUDT[15] ontologies.

```
:obs-0 a ssn:Observation ;
    ssn:observationResultTime
        "2015-05-18T10:00:00"^^xsd:dateTime ;
    ssn:observedBy :sensor-0 ;
    ssn:observationResult :obs-0-result .

:obs-0-result a ssn:SensorOutput ;
    ssn:isProducedBy :sensor-0 ;
    ssn:hasValue :obs-0-resultvalue .

:obs-0-resultvalue a ssn:ObservationValue ,
                       qud:QuantityValue ;
    qud:numbericValue "15"^^xsd:double ;
    qud:unit qud:DegreeCelsius .
```

Listing 1.6. An *observation* represented using the SSN and QUDT ontologies

The QUDT ontology allows to represent a comprehensive list of quantities, units and dimensions. We refer readers to [16] for a more detailed survey of existing ontologies for quantities, units, and dimensions.

4.5 CG5: Vendor, Version, Deployment Time

Information about *vendor, version* of the device and other information are relevant to many domains, not only to IoT. Therefore there exists a lot of ontologies focusing on this conceptual group. Probably the most popular one is FOAF[20] ontology which allows to represent organisations, people and most of required information such as name, address, web-site and etc. Regardless of whether information is in people's heads, in physical or digital documents, or in the form of factual data, it can be linked. Also there exists other more focused ontologies allowing to describe people and organizations such as:

- Ontology for public services and organizations (OSP)[27]. It is mostly for government organizations and not completely translated into English.
- Linking-you vocabulary[21]. Vocabulary for describing common web pages provided by an organisation. It is possible to describe the type of the web page such as contact page, about page, etc.

---

[27] http://data.lirmm.fr/ontologies/osp

The MMI Device Ontology[19] developed by the Marine Metadata Interoperability Project[28] provides abstractions for representing a *device, manufacturer, model id, owner of a device* and its *serial number* and so on.

5   Tool

Using the ontologies we reviewed in the previous section, we created a tool to generate semantic description of WoT devices. Currently it supports on the concepts and relations suitable for the examples devices described in Section 2, but we plan to extend it further. The tool is called Web of Things Semantic Description Helper and can be found online on https://github.com/semiotproject/wot-semdesc-helper. On Fig. 2, you can find a screenshot of the user interface which is used to constructed the semantic descriptions.

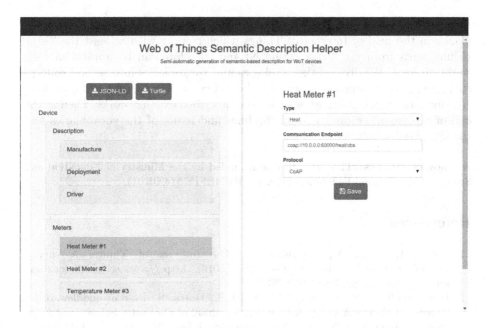

Fig. 2. A screenshot of Web of Things Semantic Description Helper

6   Discussion

There exist a lot of ontologies and vocabularies providing primitives for representation of all the conceptual groups we outlined, but they have different issues which are actually relevant to most of the ontologies in any field:

---

[28] http://marinemetadata.org

– poor documentation and lack of examples of the correct use of the ontology,
– some ontologies are only described in papers and are not implemented.
– lack of modularity so that more time is spent on reasoning than needed.

The ontologies and vocabularies should be improved following the 5-star Linked Data Vocabularies principles [9]. Also, to lower the barrier to start using ontologies, the ontologies for WoT should be standardised by a community, the similar way it was done in Schema.org project. More general concepts and relations are sufficiently covered by existing ontologies, the next step could be ontologies that are very focused on a particular domain such as different kinds of meters, specific sensors and so on. Also instruments providing all needed functionalities for managing the life-cycle of the *devices* representations are needed.

7   Conclusion

In this paper we provided a pragmatic review of existing ontologies and vocabularies in the field of Internet of Things which comply with at least the 2-star requirements from the 5-star rating [9] and therefore can be applied in real-world projects. We divided the ontologies and vocabularies into several conceptual groups which focus on a set of high-level concepts and relations from IoT. And for each such a group we selected and described existing works. Then at the end of the paper we discussed our findings and issues of the vocabularies and suggest possible solutions.

Acknowledgments. This work has been funded by the Ministry of Education and Science of the Russian Federation (Grant #RFMEFI57514X0101).

References

1. Atzori, L., Iera, A., Morabito, G.: The Internet of Things: A survey. Computer Networks **54**(15), 2787–2805 (2010). http://www.sciencedirect.com/science/article/pii/S1389128610001568
2. Bandyopadhyay, S., Sengupta, M., Maiti, S., Dutta, S.: Role of middleware for internet of things: A study. International Journal of Computer Science and Engineering Survey **2**(3), 94–105 (2011). http://dx.doi.org/10.5121/ijcses.2011.2307
3. Barnaghi, P., Compton, M., Corcho, O., Castro, R.G., Graybeal, J., Herzog, A., Janowicz, K., Neuhaus, H., Nikolov, A., Page, K.: Semantic Sensor Network XG Final Report. Tech. rep., The World Wide Web Consortium (W3C), June 2011. http://www.w3.org/2005/Incubator/ssn/XGR-ssn/
4. Compton, M., Barnaghi, P., Bermudez, L., García-Castro, R., Corcho, O., Cox, S., Graybeal, J., Hauswirth, M., Henson, C., Herzog, A., Huang, V., Janowicz, K., Kelsey, W.D., Phuoc, D.L., Lefort, L., Leggieri, M., Neuhaus, H., Nikolov, A., Page, K., Passant, A., Sheth, A., Taylor, K.: The SSN ontology of the W3C semantic sensor network incubator group. Web Semantics: Science, Services and Agents on the World Wide Web **17**, 25–32 (2012). http://www.sciencedirect.com/science/article/pii/S1570826812000571

5. Corcho, O., Calbimonte, J.P., Jeung, H., Aberer, K.: Enabling Query Technologies for the Semantic Sensor Web. Int. J. Semant. Web Inf. Syst. **8**(1), 43–63 (2012). http://dx.doi.org/10.4018/jswis.2012010103
6. Guinard, D., Trifa, V.: Towards the web of things: web mashups for embedded devices. In: Workshop on Mashups, Enterprise Mashups and Lightweight Composition on the Web (MEM 2009), in proceedings of WWW (International World Wide Web Conferences), Madrid, Spain, April 2009
7. Guinard, D., Trifa, V., Mattern, F., Wilde, E.: From the internet of things to the web of things: resource-oriented architecture and best practices. In: Architecting the Internet of Things, pp. 97–129. Springer, Heidelberg (2011). http://dx.doi.org/10.1007/978-3-642-19157-2_5
8. Janowicz, K., Compton, M.: The stimulus-sensor-observation ontology design pattern and its integration into the semantic sensor network ontology. In: Proceedings of the 3d International Workshop on Semantic Sensor Networks (2010). http://ceur-ws.org/Vol-668/paper12.pdf
9. Janowicz, K., Hitzler, P., Adams, B., Kolas, D., Vardeman II, C.: Five stars of Linked Data vocabulary use **5**(3). http://dx.doi.org/10.3233/SW-140135
10. Kolchin, M., Mouromtsev, D., Arustamov, S.: Demonstration: web-based Visualisation and Monitoring of Smart Meters using CQELS. In: Proceedings of the 7th International Workshop on Semantic Sensor Networks (2014). http://knoesis.org/ssn2014/paper_3.pdf
11. Kotis, K., Katasonov, A.: Semantic interoperability on the web of things: the semantic smart gateway framework. In: 2012 Sixth International Conference on Complex, Intelligent and Software Intensive Systems (CISIS), pp. 630–635, July 2012
12. Lanthaler, M., Gutl, C.: A semantic description language for restful data services to combat semaphobia. In: 2011 Proceedings of the 5th IEEE International Conference on Digital Ecosystems and Technologies Conference (DEST), pp. 47–53, May 2011
13. Le-Phuoc, D., Nguyen-Mau, H.Q., Parreira, J.X., Hauswirth, M.: A middleware framework for scalable management of linked streams. Web Semantics: Science, Services and Agents on the World Wide Web **16**, 42–51 (2012). http://www.sciencedirect.com/science/article/pii/S1570826812000728. The Semantic Web Challenge 2011
14. Perera, C., Zaslavsky, A., Christen, P., Georgakopoulos, D.: Context Aware Computing for The Internet of Things: A Survey. IEEE Communications Surveys Tutorials **16**(1), 414–454 (2014)
15. Pfisterer, D., Romer, K., Bimschas, D., Kleine, O., Mietz, R., Truong, C., Hasemann, H., Kröller, A., Pagel, M., Hauswirth, M., Karnstedt, M., Leggieri, M., Passant, A., Richardson, R.: Spitfire: toward a semantic web of things. IEEE Communications Magazine **49**(11), 40–48 (2011)
16. Simons, B., Yu, J., Cox, S.: Defining a water quality vocabulary using QUDT and ChEBI. In: Proceedings of the 20th International Congress on Modelling and Simulation, December 2013. http://www.mssanz.org.au/modsim2013/L6/simons.pdf
17. Taylor, K., Griffith, C., Lefort, L., Gaire, R., Compton, M., Wark, T., Lamb, D., Falzon, G., Trotter, M.: Farming the Web of Things. IEEE Intelligent Systems **28**(6), 12–19 (2013). http://dx.doi.org/10.1109/MIS.2013.102

18. Wang, W., De, S., Toenjes, R., Reetz, E., Moessner, K.: A comprehensive ontology for knowledge representation in the internet of things. In: 2012 IEEE 11th International Conference on Trust, Security and Privacy in Computing and Communications (TrustCom), pp. 1793–1798, June 2012

19. Wetz, P., Trinh, T.D., Do, B.L., Anjomshoaa, A., Kiesling, E., Tjoa, A.M.: Towards an environmental information system for semantic stream data. In: Proceedings of the 28th Conference on Environmental Informatics - Informatics for Environmental Protection, Sustainable Development and Risk Management, pp. 637–644. BIS-Verlag (2014). http://publik.tuwien.ac.at/files/PubDat_230174.pdf

20. Whitmore, A., Agarwal, A., Da Xu, L.: The Internet of Things - A survey of topics and trends. Information Systems Frontiers $17(2)$, 261–274 (2015). http://dx.doi.org/10.1007/s10796-014-9489-2

Ontology-Based Approach and Implementation of ADAS System for Mobile Device Use While Driving

Igor Lashkov[1], Alexander Smirnov[1,2], Alexey Kashevnik[1,2(✉)], and Vladimir Parfenov[1]

[1] ITMO University, 49, Kronverkskiy av., 197101 St. Petersburg, Russian Federation
igor-lashkov@ya.ru, {smir,alexey}@iias.spb.su,
parfenov@mail.ifmo.ru
[2] SPIIRAS, 39, 14th Line, 199178 St. Petersburg, Russian Federation

Abstract. Many people drive while being tired or drowsy and according to experts, many drivers fail to recognize they are in a fatigued state. The paper describes an ontology-based approach and a real-time prototype of a computer vision system for monitoring driver's dangerous behaviour patterns such as distraction, drowsiness and reduced vigilance. Our approach focuses on widely used mobile devices, such as a smartphone or a tablet, which have become an integral part of our daily life. The main components of the system consist of a front-facing camera, gyroscope sensor installed on the smartphone and various computer vision algorithms for simultaneous, real-time and non-intrusive monitoring of various visual bio-behaviours that typically characterize a driver's level of vigilance. The visual behaviours include eyelid movement (PERCLOS percentage of eye closure, eye blink rate), face orientation (face pose), and gaze movement (pupil movement). The two ontological models presented in the paper are a driver model and a vehicle model. Based on these models and the information available from cameras and sensors, the context is created that allows the system to determine dangerous situations using the driver mobile device mounted on the windshield of the vehicle. The system was tested in a simulated environment with subjects of different ethnic backgrounds, genders, ages, with/without glasses, and under different illumination conditions, and it was found very robust, reliable and accurate.

Keywords: Ontology · Context · Mobile device · ADAS systems

1 Introduction

Advanced Driver Assistance Systems (ADAS) are systems aimed to help the driver in the driving process through the making alerts for preventing dangerous situations. When designed with a safe Human-Machine Interface, they offer increased car and road safety. Safety features are designed to avoid collisions and accidents by offering technologies that provide possibilities to recognize dangerous situations beforehand. This work is an extension of [1] that aims at developing mobile assistant for Segway riders.

© Springer International Publishing Switzerland 2015
P. Klinov and D. Mouromtsev (Eds.): KESW 2015, CCIS 518, pp. 117–131, 2015.
DOI: 10.1007/978-3-319-24543-0_9

The EuroFOT consortium [2] published the findings of a four-year study focused on the impact of driver assistance systems in the Europe. The €22-million (US$27.4-million) European Field Operational Test (EuroFOT) project, which began in June 2008 and involved 28 companies and organizations, was led by Aria Etemad from Ford's European Research Centre in Aachen, Germany. Almost 1000 vehicles (cars and trucks) were equipped with ADAS and more than a thousand drivers participated. Data were collected from onboard computer systems, video recordings, driver surveys, and questionnaires submitted to drivers at the start of the FOT, at the end of baseline phase, and at the end of treatment phase. The study [2] shows a decrease of safety risk up to 42% due to timely alert of the driver or an automatic adjustment of speed, and that over 90% of accidents involve driver behavior as a contributing factor.

At the modern market advanced driver assistance systems are divided into two categories: (i) manually installed mobile applications from application stores and (ii) specific hardware and software, integrated into automobiles by manufactures. Despite advanced safety features are equipped on premium and high-end vehicles models, but the majority of drivers still do not have access to these safeguards. But they can manually install such type of application in his/her mobile phone and use it while driving a vehicle.

The paper proposes an approach for mobile application development that assists the driver during the travel by providing visual and tactile feedback if an unsafe situation is predicted. The front camera facing up to the rider allows the application to determine the driver's mental states, whereas the rear camera, GPS, motion and orientation sensors to detect the external environment as well as the dynamical characteristics of the vehicle. The proposed reference model in this paper incorporates different services and algorithms. The reference model is based on the ontological knowledge representation that allows providing for ontology-based information sharing between different services in the developed system. The ontological driver and vehicle models portray them formally in terms of comprehensibility of the information systems and using these descriptions in the assisting processes. For assistive functionalities, the motion related parameters are observed and evaluated simultaneously.

The rest of the paper is structured as follows. Section 2 presents an overview of existing at the moment ADAS solutions. The proposed reference model ADAS system is presented in Section 3. Section 4 and Section 5 present ontological models of the driver and vehicle. Implementation is given in the Section 6. The results are summarized in Conclusion.

2   Related Work

CarSafe [3] is a driver safety application for Android phones that detects and alerts drivers in case of dangerous driving conditions and behavior. It uses computer vision and machine learning algorithms to monitor and detect whether the driver is tired or distracted using the front-facing camera while at the same time tracking road conditions using the rear-facing camera. CarSafe also tries to solve the problem of processing video streams from both the front and rear cameras simultaneously by using a context-aware algorithm. This application has two main disadvantages. The first one is a lack of emotions, gestures and speech recognition. The second one is that it is not available for downloading in any application store (it has been developing for prototyping an approach).

The iOnRoad [4] is an Android- and iOS-based application that provides a range of personal driving assistance functions including augmented driving, collision warning and "black-box" like video recording. The application uses the GPS sensor, gyroscope, and video camera stream of the native mobile device for monitoring the vehicle position on the road. Application makes alerts for drivers with audio and visual cues in case of dangerous situations. The main weakness of this application is that it does not use front-facing camera for tracking driver behavior.

DriveSafe [5] is a driver safety application for iPhone-based devices that detects inattentive driving behaviors and gives corresponding feedback to drivers, scoring their driving and alerting them in case their behaviors are unsafe. It uses computer vision and pattern recognition techniques on the iPhone to assess whether the driver is drowsy or distracted using the rear-camera, the microphone, the inertial sensors and the GPS.

WalkSafe [6] is an Android-based application that aids people that walk and talk, improving the safety of pedestrian mobile phone users. WalkSafe uses the back camera of the mobile phone to detect vehicles approaching the user. It makes alerts for the user of a potentially unsafe situation. The application uses machine-learning algorithms implemented on the mobile phone to detect the front views and back views of moving vehicles. WalkSafe alerts the user of unsafe conditions using mobile phone sound and vibration.

Augmented Driving [7] is an iPhone-based application that uses the phone's built-in camera to view the road ahead. It detects the road obstacles, warning the driver of any potential hazards with voice notifications. This program provides a rather wide range of driving assistance features including vehicle headway, lane departure warning, speeding avoidance, video recording, and sound & voice output.

Driver Guard application [8] is an Android-based ADAS application that avoids accidents. It uses smartphone's camera to monitor the scene in front of the driver, detect preceding cars, estimates the distance to all preceding cars and fires an alarm when driver approaches any car dangerously. This application also shows the driver's current speed using GPS sensor and distance to the nearest car in front of the driver.

One major disadvantage of the considered applications is that they are taking into account only watching by video camera conditions on the road. The research projects CarSafe, Augmented Driving, and iOnRoad are distinguished as they provide more significant safety features for drivers than other mobile applications mentioned above. A detailed comparison of ADAS systems is presented by authors in [9].

3   ADAS System Reference Model

The reference model of the smartphone-based ADAS is presented in Fig. 1. It consists of five main modules: mobile application, cameras, sensors, local database, cloud service, and synchronization service. Information from the device's different sensors collected by Sensor fusion component caters for estimating the various useful quantities such as the speed, the acceleration, and the location. Internal components of the mobile application are context-aware camera switching algorithm, multi-core computation planner and image processing unit. Today's smartphones do not have the capability to process video streams from both of the front and the rear cameras simultaneously. In this respect, we use a context-aware algorithm that switches between the two cameras while processing the data real-time with the goal of minimizing missed events inside.

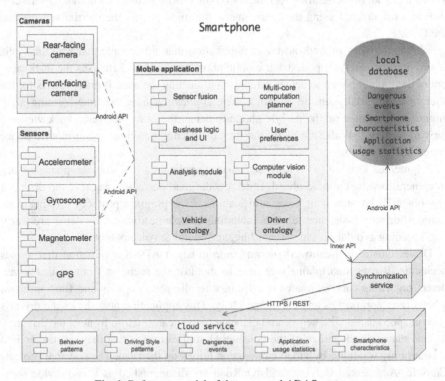

Fig. 1. Reference model of the proposed ADAS system

The image processing unit is responsible for extracting the visual features from the images taken by the rear and front cameras. The computation planner aims to effectively leverage the multi-core architecture of modern smartphones to perform heavy calculations. User preferences module allows saving and retrieving persistent key-value pairs of primitive data types. If the Internet connection is not available, local database is responsible for storing data collected from the smartphone. As soon as the Internet connection becomes available, we are ready to synchronize a local database with the cloud service. Synchronization service is a component of the assistant system responsible for managing the information flows to/from the database located on the smartphone and to/from the cloud.

Such information as smartphone characteristics, application usage statistics, and dangerous events occurred during trip is stored for using in the future. Smartphone characteristics are GPU, sensors (GPS, Accelerometer, Gyroscope, Magnetometer), cameras (front-facing / rear-facing), memory & battery capacity, and version of operation system. In addition, the cloud storage is used for keeping behaviour patterns and driving style patterns. Operations that can be carried out in the cloud storage are:

- Recognition of true and false responses due to occurrence of dangerous events.
- Matching of behavior and driving style patterns.
- Analysis and classification of driver behavior and driving style for further making recommendations for safe driving.

4   Driver Ontology Model

The system is focused on the behavioral and physiological signals acquired from the driver to assess their mental state in real-time. In the presented approach, the driver is considered as a set of mental states. Each of these states has its own particular control behavior and interstate transition probabilities. The canonical example of this type of model would be a bank of standard linear controllers (e.g., Kalman Filters plus a simple control law). Each controller has different dynamics and measurements, sequenced together with a Markov network of probabilistic transitions. The states of the model can be hierarchically organized to describe the short and long-term behaviors.

People in fatigue state exhibit certain types of visual behaviors that can easily be observed from the changes in their facial expressions and features from the eyes, head, and face. The typical visual characteristics observable on a face image of a person are the reduced alertness level that includes slow eyelid movement [10, 11], smaller degree of eye openness (or even closed), frequent nodding [12], yawning, gaze (narrowness in the line of sight), sluggish in facial expression, and sagging posture. The features that can be assessed are given as follows: PERCLOS – PERcentage of CLOSure of eyelid, eye blink time, eye-blinking rate, eye gaze, pupil movement, eyelid movement, postures, and head pose. Visual behaviors observable from the changes in facial features listed above are: eyes are opened or closed, facing to the left, facing to the right, facing forwards, gaze concentration towards the road, gaze concentration not towards the road, dilated pupils, not dilated pupils.

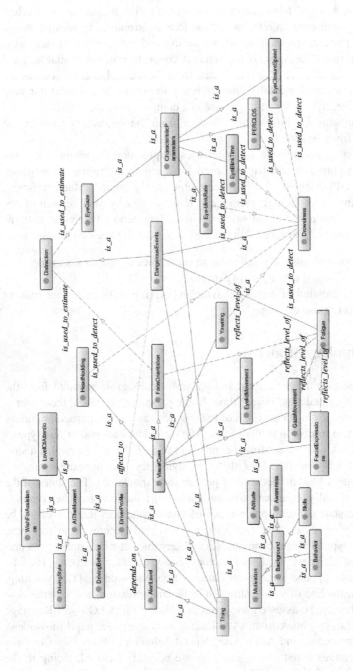

Fig. 2. The Driver ontology model

The developed driver ontology (Fig. 2) includes these visual cues and visual behaviors and determines relationships between them. It consists of the five main top level classes: "AlertLevel" (warning level), "DangerousEvents" (commonly occurring dangerous driving events), "CharacteristicParameters" (visual characteristics observable from the image of a person), "DriverProfile" (a driver profile that reflects the certain personal characteristics) and "VisualCues" (the visual cues on which we focus to detect dangerous events). Each driver has a profile (class "DriverProfile") that reflects personal characteristics. Driver profile consists of background (class "Background") and real-time (class "AtTheMoment") context. Background context in its turn includes five elements that underpin a driver safety culture – behavior (class "Behavior"), attitude (class "Attitude), awareness (class "Awareness"), motivation (class "Motivation") and skills (class "Skills"). These classes are associated with each other with the relationship "is_a". On the other hand we need to consider the real-time data (class "AtTheMoment"). It consists of a wish for assistance (class "WishForAssistance"), driving style (class "DrivingStyle"), level of attention (class "LevelOfAttention") and driving behavior (class "DrivingBehavior"). The relationship between these classes is "is_a". System alert level (class "AlertLevel") depends on driver profile.

Class "AlertLevel" is associated with the class "DriverProfile" with the relationship "depends_on". The basic characteristic parameters (class "CharacteristicParameters") that typically characterize driver's state are PERCLOS (class "PERCLOS"), eye-blink rate (class "Eye-BlinkRate"), eye closure speed (class "EyeClosureSpeed"), eye-blinking time (class "EyBlinkTime"), eye gaze (class "EyeGaze"), pupillary state (class "PupillaryState), yawning (class "Yawning") and nodding level (class "HeadNodding"). The relationship between these classes is "is_a". We infer the dangerous driver behaviours (class "DangerousEvents") such as drowsiness (class "Drowsiness"), distraction (class "Distraction") and fatigue (class "Fatigue"). In the proposed ontology, the corresponding classes ("Drowsiness", "Distraction" and "Fatigue") are associated with the class "DangerousEvents" with the relationship "is_a".At the same time, face orientation and eye gaze are used to detect distraction (classes "FaceOrientation" and "EyeGaze" are associated with the class "Distraction" with the relationship "is_used_to_estimate"). PERCLOS, eye-blink rate, eye closure speed, eye blink time, yawning and nodding level are used to recognize drowsiness. (Classes "PERCLOS", "Eye-blinkRate", "EyeClosureSpeed", "EyeBlinkTime", "Yawning" and "HeadNodding" are associated with the class "Drowsiness" with the relationship "is_used_to_detect"). And finally, eyelid movement, face orientation, gaze movement and facial expressions reflect level of fatigue (classes "EyelidMovement", "FaceOrientation", "GazeMovement" and "FacialExpressions" are associated with the class "Fatigue" with the relationship "reflects_level_of"). Open or closed eyes are a good indicator of fatigue. (Property "EyeState" is associated with the class "Fatigue" with the relationship "is_an_indicator_of").

5   Vehicle Ontology Model

The vehicle drivers are faced with a multitude of road hazards and an increasing number of distractions (e.g. music, phone calls, smartphone texting and browsing, advertising information on the road, and etc.). In the presented approach, the following five of the most commonly occurring dangerous driving events are addressed: drowsy driving, vigilance decrement, inattentive driving, tailgating, ignoring blind spots.

The developed Vehicle ontology model (Fig. 3) consists of five main top level classes: "DangerousEvents" (dangerous events that can occur during driving), "Sensors" (embedded sensors on the phone), "Cameras" (built-in front-facing and rear-facing cameras), "VehicleBehaviorParameters" (vehicle behavior parameters) and "RoadParameters" (parameters that characterize the road the vehicle moves). At the same time, classes "VehicleBehaviorParameters", "Sensors" and "RoadParameters" are used to recognize hazards (class "DangerousEvents"). Classes "Vehicle BehaviorParameters", "Sensors" and "RoadParameters" are associated with the class "DangerousEvents" with the relationship "is_used_to_recognize"). The class "DangerousEvents" is classified as "Tailgating" (driver should maintain a minimum safe distance with the vehicle or moving object ahead) and "IgnoringBlindSpots" (executing lane changes safely also requires a driver to check blind spots before proceeding). In the proposed ontology, the corresponding classes ("Tailgating" and "DangerousEvents") are associated with the class "DangerousEvents" with the relationship "is_a".

Most Android-powered devices have built-in sensors (class "Sensors") such as accelerometer (class "Accelerometer"), gyroscope (class "Gyroscope"), magnetometer (class "Magnetometer") and GPS (class "GPS). Corresponding classes ("Accelerometer", "Magnetometer", "Gyroscope" and "GPS") are associated with the class "Sensors" with the relationship "is_a". But also Android framework includes support of cameras (class "Cameras") and camera features available on device, allowing to capture pictures and videos in applications. We aim to work with front-facing ("FrontFacingCamera") and rear-facing ("RearFacingCamera") cameras. These classes are associated with "Camera" by relationship "is_a". Rear-facing camera pictures help us to recognize behavior parameters such as turn (class "Turn"), vehicle headway (class "VehicleHeadway), trajectory (class "Trajectory") and lane position (class "LanePosition"). These classes are associated with each other with the relationship "is_used_to_recognize". The class "VehicleBehaviorParameters" includes such parameters such as the speed (class "Speed"), acceleration (class "Acceleration"), lane position (class "LanePosition"), trajectory (class "Trajectory), vehicle turns (class "Turn") and vehicle headway (class "VehicleHeadway"). They are associated with the class "VehicleBehaviorParameters" with the relationship "is_a". The GPS sensor (class "GPS") and accelerometer (class "Accelerometer") are used to estimate the position, acceleration (class "Acceleration") and the speed (class "Speed"). The classes "Acceleration" and "Speed" are associated with the classes "GPS" and

"Accelerometer" with the relationship "is_used_to_estimate". Besides, inertial sensors (classes "Acceletometer", "Magnetometer" and "Gyroscope") are used for trajectory detection (class "Trajectory) and these are associated with the relationship "is_used_to_detect". The vehicle turns (class "Turn) are detected by observing the significant changes in the direction from the time-series data of the GPS (class "GPS") positions. The class "GPS" is associated with the class "Turn" with the relationship "is_used_to_detect". The last top level class is "RoadParameters". It contains lane markers (class "LaneMarkers"), road conditions (class "RoadConditions"), obstacles (class "Obstacles") and road signs (class "RoadSigns). Classes "LaneMarkers", "RoadConditions", "Obstacles" and "RoadSigns" are associated with the class "Road" with the relationship "is_a". Finally, the road parameters (class "Road parameters"), sensors (class "Sensors") and the vehicle behaviour parameters ("VehicleBehaviorParameters") are used to recognize dangerous events. These classes are associated with each other with the relationship "are_used_to_recognize".

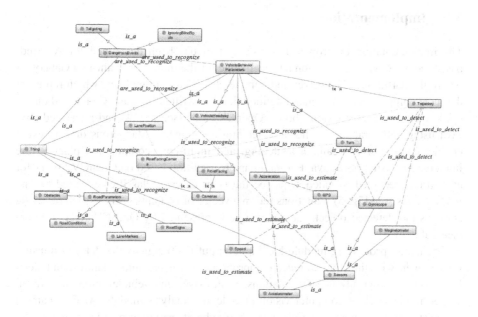

Fig. 3. Vehicle ontology model

The developed ontologies describing the behavior models of driver and vehicle allow the ADAS system to accurately interpret data from multiple sources and verify the mappings between entities as we come to the unsafe factors (driver visual state, road, vehicle parameters) extracted from cameras and embedded sensors on the phone. Dangerous driving events are modeled using vehicle and driver ontologies and we focus on five of the most commonly occurring one:

- Careless lane change;
- Tailgating;

- Drowsy driving;
- Inattentive driving;
- Fatigue.

Each driver has his own skills, motivation, attitude and qualifications that we should consider in monitoring and detecting dangerous events occurring throughout the trip. That is why the driver and vehicle models are rather closely related. For example, executing lane changes safely requires a driver to check blind spots before proceeding. The driver does this by looking in the side and front mirrors of the car to check for unexpected vehicles. The system should be capable of recognising the head position of the driver using the phone's front camera, allowing the app to ensure the appropriate mirror checks are performed before each lane change. Lane changing itself can be detected using the rear camera and inertial sensors, as described above.

6   Implementation

The implementation of proposed ADAS system has been developed for Android-based mobile device. Evaluation has been done for the multi-core Samsung Galaxy S4 Android smartphone. The driver and vehicle classification pipelines, which represent the most computationally demanding modules, are written in C and C++ based on the open source computer vision library (OpenCV) [13] (see Fig. 4) and interfaced with Java using JNI wrappers. Other architectural components (dangerous driving event engine, context-driven camera switching, and multi-core computation planner) are implemented using pure Java. For the image recognition based on OpenCV library for each frame received in video sequence the Haar cascade classifier is called to find faces or eyes (see Fig. 5). Functions return a vector of rectangles where each rectangle contains the detected object. Each rectangle is presented by OpenCV Rect structure (see Table 1).

The image processing module has input/output (I/O) signals that let you transmit image taken with the camera, receive appropriate driver recommendations, and alerts later on to prevent any unsafe situations. Both driver and vehicle ontologies are involved in the work of computer vision module and analysis module. At first, camera image (Bitmap) is scanned to find and identify objects and their position that are relevant to the situation. In the next step, vectors of rectangles that contain the detected objects are passed to the Analysis module for further processing. With the help of predefined types of rules that cover unsafe situations and scenarios, it runs search-match calculation. If the procedure returns true, the system will make an appropriate alert, otherwise this event will be ignored. For example, if the system determines that the driver is likely to enter a dangerous drowsy state, it will make an audible alert for a driver. Quantitative parameters helping to identify dangerous driving events are presented as follows.

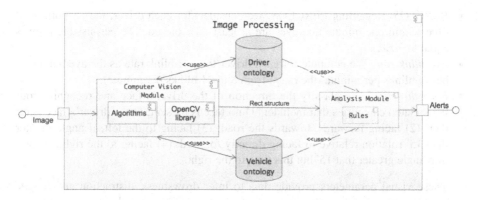

Fig. 4. Image processing module implementation

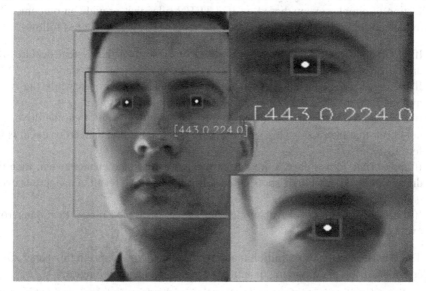

Fig. 5. Example of finding faces and eyes using OpenCV library

Table 1. OpenCV output data for face and eyes recognition

Face				Left eye				Right eye				Time
X	**Y**	**W**	**H**	**X**	**Y**	**W**	**H**	**X**	**Y**	**W**	**H**	
243	108	372	372	429	190	163	124	266	190	163	124	119
243	108	372	372	429	190	163	124	266	190	163	124	60
243	108	372	372	429	190	163	124	266	190	163	124	59

- *PERCLOS.* Regarding PERCLOS, we consider, for each driver, the proportion of time within one minute that eyes are at least 80% closed. The permissible limit is equal to 30%.
- *Eye-blink rate.* We compute for each driver the eye-blink rate as the average number of blinks per minute (the range from 8 to 21 blinks per minute).
- *Face direction.* We classify the direction of the driver's face and recognize four face related categories that include: (1) no face is present; or the driver's face is either; (2) facing forwards, towards the road; (3) facing to the left, if angle greater than 15° rotation relative to facing directly forward; (4) facing to the right, if rotation angle greater that 15° but this time to the right.

These visual parameters provide data to infer drowsiness, distraction and fatigue states. We use a rule-based approach to evaluate our project and to increase the expressiveness of the underlying knowledge. We compose our dangerous events as a collection of simpler events based on IF / THEN rules that provide an outcome. We have defined five rules that provide an output score. They are defined as follows:

- If PECLOS parameter exceeds a threshold of 30%, then the system declares the driver "drowsy".
- If the driver is not facing forward for longer than three seconds while the car is moving forward, then dangerous driving event is inferred.
- If there is no a head turn corresponding to a car turning event, then the driver did not check that the road is clear before turning – as a result, a dangerous event is inferred.
- If appropriate mirror checks are not performed before lane change event, then the driver did not check blinds spots before proceeding – as a result, a dangerous event is inferred.
- If the eye-blink rate of driver misses the above-mentioned range, then dangerous event is signaled.

There exist other rules definition that have not been considered in this paper. Built rules are the result of combining quantitative parameters and ontologies.

Detection Classification. Inferring the direction of the driver's face is divided into two steps: (1) detection classification and (2) direction classification. Images from the front camera are scanned to find the relative position of the driver's face. The overall image is provided to a classifier that determines if a face is present, and if so the face direction is classified.

Facial Features. Facial analysis includes a number of processing steps that attempt to detect or track the face, to locate characteristic of facial regions such as eyes, pupils if speaking more precisely and nose, to extract and follow the movement of facial features, such as characteristic points in these regions or model facial gestures using anatomic information about the face.

Drowsy state. Drowsy driving, a combination of sleepiness and driving, has become a worldwide problem that often leads to tragic accidents and outcomes. The smartphone's front camera should be able to monitor the prolonged and frequent blinks indicative of micro sleep. Existing research findings have shown that the percentage of closure of eyelid (a.k.a PERCLOS) is an effective indicator to evaluate the driver's drowsiness. A measure of drowsiness, PERCLOS, was generated and associated with degradation in driving performance in a simulated roadway environment.

PERCLOS is the proportion of time that the driver's eyes are 80 to 100% closed over a specified interval. Its validity was tested, along with other new technologies, and it was shown to be an accurate drowsiness detector.

Although PERCLOS is considered the best among other indicators in drowsiness detection, the original PERCLOS is not suitable for smart phones, since smart phones could not analyze every frame accurately or effectively. However, in an analogy to PERCLOS, we can detect fatigue by analyzing a series of states of eyes, classified by Neural Network to either open or closed. The states of eyes are necessary to simulate not only PERCLOS, but also the frequency of wink and the time of continuous closing eyes, which are all using in the driver alert mechanism. The faster we can acquire image of eyes and analysis, the less error between simulation and reality of the indicators.

The algorithm focuses on driver's eyes recognition, implemented in OpenCV computer vision library, classified by Neural Network, and then used to discrete-approximate several indicators including PERCLOS, blink time and blink rate to evaluate the fatigue level of the driver.

Distraction state. Maintaining eye contact with the road is fundamental to safe driving. By using the front camera of the phone, the head position of the driver can be used to determine an inattentive driving behavior when the driver is not looking at the road ahead.

Two types of inattentive driving are monitored by our approach. In the first case, the output of the face direction classifier is tracked. If the driver's face is not facing forward for longer than three seconds [14] while the vehicle is moving forward (i.e., while a positive speed is reported by the available smartphone sensors) and not turning as reported by the turn detector (also reported by car classification pipeline) then a dangerous driving event is inferred. However, you should keep in mind, that it's not a constant value and this parameter depends on various factors (e.g. vehicle speed, acceleration). In the second case, we monitor the turn detector. Each time a turn is detected the historical output of the face direction classifier is checked. If there is no a head turn corresponding to a car turning event then the driver did not check that the road is clear before turning – as a result, a dangerous event is inferred.

Persons's gaze. The direction of a person's gaze is determined by two factors: face orientation (face pose) and eye orientation (eye gaze). Face pose determines the global direction of the gaze, while eye gaze determines the local direction of the gaze. Global gaze and local gaze together determine the final gaze of the person. According to these two aspects of gaze information, video-based gaze estimation approaches can be divided into a head-based approach, an ocular-based approach, and a combined head- and eye-based approach.

7   Conclusion

The paper presents an ontology-based approach and its implementation for ADAS system development. Such systems can be used by drivers while driving vehicles using personal mobile devices. The paper contains an overview of existing current ADAS solutions. The proposed reference model ADAS system is based on ontological knowledge representation and cloud computing technology that allows to provide information exchange between drivers and mobile devices and then take this information into account while discovering dangerous events. Implementation is based on open source computer vision library (OpenCV) that allows to detect objects using smartphone camera. The testing of system shows that it is robust, reliable and accurate and provides the driver alerts in case of dangerous situations beforehand.

Acknowledgements. The presented results are part of the research carried out within the project funded by grants # 13-07-00336, 13-07-12095, 13-01-00286 of the Russian Foundation for Basic Research. This work was partially financially supported by Government of Russian Federation, Grant 074-U01.

References

1. Smirnov, A., Kashevnik, A., Lashkov, I., Hashimoto, N., Boyali, A.: Smartphone-based two-wheeled self-balancing vehicles rider assistant. In: 17th Conference of the Open Innovations Association FRUCT, Yaroslavl, Russia, pp. 201–209 (2015)
2. European Field Operational Test on Activity Safety Systems. http://www.eurofot-ip.eu
3. You, C., Lane, N., Chen, F., Wang, R., Chen, Z., Bao, T., Montes-de-Oca, M., Cheng, Y., Lin, M., Torresani, L., Campbell, A.: CarSafe app: alerting drowsy and distracted drivers using dual cameras on smartphones. In: 11th International Conference on Mobile Systems, Applications, and Services, Taipei, Taiwan, pp. 461–462 (2013)
4. iOnRoad official website. http://www.ionroad.com/
5. Bergasa, L., Almería, D., Almazán, J., Yebes, J., Arroyo, R.: DriveSafe: an app for alerting inattentive drivers and scoring driving behaviors. In: IEEE Intelligent Vehicles Symposium, Dearborn, MI, USA (2014)
6. Wang, T., Cardone, G., Corradi, A., Torresani, L., Campbell, A.: WalkSafe: a pedestrian safety app for mobile phone users who walk and talk while crossing roads. In: 14th International Workshop on Mobile Computing Systems and Applications, No. 5 (2012)
7. Augmented Driving website, iOS application. http://www.imaginyze.com/
8. Driver Guard application, Google Play. https://play.google.com/store/apps/details?id=com.badrit.cv.vehicledetect&hl=ru
9. Smirnov, A., Lashkov, I.: State-of-the-art analysis of available advanced driver assistance systems. In: 17th Conference of the Open Innovations Association FRUCT, Yaroslavl, Russia, pp. 345–349 (2015)
10. Wierville, W.: Overview of research on driver drowsiness definition and driver drowsiness detection, ESV, Munich (1994)

11. Dinges, D., Mallis, M., Maislin, G., Powell, J.W.: Evaluation of techniques for ocular measurement as an index of fatigue and the basis for alertness management. Department of Transportation Highway Safety Publication, 808 762 (1998)
12. Anon. Proximity array sensing system: head position monitor/metric. Advanced Safety Concepts, Inc., Sante Fe (1998)
13. OpenCV library. http://opencv.org
14. Breakthrough Research on Real-World Driver Behavior Released. http://www.nhtsa. gov/Driving+Safety/Distracted+Driving+at+Distraction.gov/Breakthrough+Research+on+Real-World+Driver+Behavior+Released

Object-UOBM: An Ontological Benchmark for Object-Oriented Access

Martin Ledvinka[(✉)] and Petr Křemen

Czech Technical University in Prague, Prague, Czech Republic
{martin.ledvinka,petr.kremen}@fel.cvut.cz

Abstract. Although many applications built on top of market-ready ontology storages are generic and lack dependence on the particular application domain, most users prefer applications tailored to their particular task. Such applications are typically built using object-oriented paradigm that accesses data differently than generic applications. In this paper, we define a benchmark consisting of an ontology and ontological queries tailored for testing suitability of ontological storages for object-oriented access. We present results of experiments on several state-of-the-art ontological storages and discuss their suitability for the purpose of object-oriented application access.

Keywords: Ontological storage · Benchmark · Object-oriented applications

1 Introduction

Although many applications built on top of market-ready ontology storages are generic and lack dependence on the particular application domain, most users prefer applications tailored to their particular task. Such applications are typically built using object-oriented paradigm, which sticks to particular entities and their relationships in the domain, see [11].

In order to construct/store an object model expressed in the given application language (e.g. Java), specific types of ontological queries are posed to the underlying storage. Different frameworks for object-oriented access to OWL [17] ontologies use different access techniques to the underlying ontology stores, including custom interface or SPARQL [9] queries. To unify these ontology storage access techniques, OntoDriver was introduced in [14] as a layer for storing object models into ontological storages. OntoDriver defines an API to be used by an application access layer, like the JOPA framework [12], [13]. The API defines optimized ontological methods that are suitable for object-oriented access, allowing CRUD[1] operations, transactional support, multiple contexts, SPARQL queries, as well as integrity constraints checking.

---

[1] Create, Retrieve, Update, Delete.

© Springer International Publishing Switzerland 2015
P. Klinov and D. Mouromtsev (Eds.): KESW 2015, CCIS 518, pp. 132–146, 2015.
DOI: 10.1007/978-3-319-24543-0_10

In this paper, we contribute to this story by comparing the actual performance of various ontological queries tailored for object-oriented access to ontology storages. As a side-effect, we experimentally justify the OntoDriver design. For this purpose we define a benchmark consisting of an ontology and ontological queries. Next we perform experiments on several state-of-the-art storages and discuss their suitability for the purpose of object-oriented application access.

Section 2 shows the relationship of our work to the state-of-art research. Section 3 reviews the JOPA architecture, and the OntoDriver API in particular, together with a running example used in benchmark queries. Section 4 defines the benchmark based on existing datasets. Section 5 presents experiments on existing ontological storages and discusses their suitability for object-oriented applications. The paper is concluded in Section 6.

2 Related Work

Interoperability benchmarking for semantic web is discussed in [5]. More interesting for our purposes are various ontological benchmarks combining expressive power of ontological languages with the medium-to-large dataset size. We consider the following two benchmarks.

LUBM [8] was one of the first OWL [18] benchmarks, featuring support for extensional queries, data scaling and moderate ontology size. It contains fourteen generic queries and a data generator allowing to produce randomly created datasets in the university domain. The generation is parametrized by the requested number of universities, producing around 100k triples for each university. The complexity of the ontological schema is significantly below OWL expressiveness, lacking nominals, number restrictions, or negation.

UOBM [16] is an extension of LUBM aimed at leveraging expressiveness towards OWL-DL by augmenting LUBM schema with the missing constructs (see Section 4.1). The dataset contains around 250k triples for each university.

For SPARQL benchmarking, the Berlin SPARQL benchmark (BSBM) [2] has been defined. This benchmark is purely RDF-oriented, focusing at SPARQL queries without ontological inference.

Neither of these benchmarks, however, is tailored to the scenario of object-oriented access to ontological knowledge.

3 Background

The main motivation for our benchmark is finding out how some of the most advanced ontology storages are suitable for access by object-oriented applications. Such applications often use frameworks providing object-ontological mapping (OOM) to facilitate working with the data. OOM is a technique for mapping ontological classes to classes in object-oriented paradigm, individuals to object instances and properties to instance attributes. Such object representation is arguably easier to use for application programmers. Examples of frameworks providing, among other features, OOM are Empire [7], AliBaba[2] and JOPA.

---

[2] https://bitbucket.org/openrdf/alibaba, accessed 07-14-2015.

3.1 JOPA

JOPA (Java OWL Persistence API) is a Java persistence API and provider for applications working with ontological data. It tries to present API resembling JPA 2 [10], with which Java developers are familiar. In addition to the compiled object model present also in other OOM frameworks, JOPA provides access to properties not mapped by the object model, capturing thus also the dynamic nature of the underlying knowledge [12].

3.2 OntoDriver

In order to provide access to various ontology storages without committing to a vendor-specific API of the storage, we proposed the concept of *OntoDriver* as a software layer which separates the object-ontological mapping performed by JOPA and the actual ontology access [13]. We designed the OntoDriver API to provide a single API for object-oriented access to different storages as well as enough margin for vendor-specific optimizations of the operations performed by OntoDriver. In its nature, OntoDriver is very similar to standard JDBC[3] drivers used for accessing relational databases, although instead of being based on statements written in query and data definition language (SQL in case of JDBC), we defined specialized CRUD operations.

When one examines the operations required by JOPA or any other object-ontological mapping performing framework, it turns out that their set is rather small. Object-ontological mapping does not require any complex queries consisting of joins over multiple properties or selecting data with unbound subject and object variables. On the contrary, typical operations required by JOPA consist of selecting values of beforehand known set of properties of a single individual or retracting and asserting values of such properties.

3.3 Example Object Model

The queries used in our benchmark are based on a relatively simple object model, which we will now describe. The object model, however, exercises a wide range of possible property usage, including single and multi-valued data and object properties, types specification or unmapped properties [13].

Since our benchmark is based on the LUBM and UOBM datasets, the object model is also built upon the university and students domain. A class diagram of the domain model can be seen in Figure 1. Besides simple data properties like name, email and telephone, the model also contains a number of object properties. Most notable of them are

- *hasSameHomeTownWith*, which is a transitive and symmetric property and occurs only in UOBM datasets,
- *isFriendOf*, which is a symmetric property and occurs only in UOBM datasets,

---

[3] Java Database Connectivity.

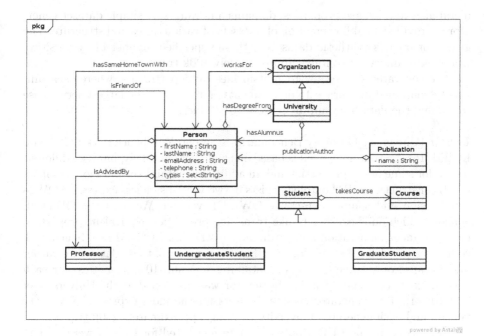

Fig. 1. Object model used as a base for the benchmark queries. The properties are from UOBM, most of them having LUBM equivalents, although sometimes with different names.

- *hasAlumnus*, which is an inverse of *hasDegreeFrom* and is never used explicitly in the datasets, therefore always requiring reasoning to return results,
- *hasDegreeFrom*, which has a number of sub-properties.

4   Benchmark

In this section we describe the benchmark set up, namely the datasets and queries used, storages that we evaluated and the chosen metrics. Let us begin with description of the datasets.

4.1   Datasets

The proposed benchmark reuses parts of existing OWL benchmark datasets – LUBM and UOBM.

LUBM (Lehigh University Benchmark) is an ontology and benchmark developed to evaluate semantic web knowledge base systems [8]. The ontology concerns university domain and contains basic OWL constructs like concept and property hierarchies and inverse properties, domains and ranges. A simple dataset generator is provided, enabling creation of datasets of various sizes and structure. The generator creates synthetic datasets with the specified number of universities, where each university contains approximately 100k triples.

The generated datasets were split in files by departments, where each university contained in average 15 departments. This lead in the largest server case to loading the data from approximately 16 000 files.

UOBM (University Ontology Benchmark) is an ontology benchmark built upon LUBM [16]. The ontology itself is based on the LUBM ontology, but uses different names for some of the properties and, in addition, contains several more complex OWL constructs. UOBM ontology exists in two versions - a less expressive OWL-Lite version and a more expressive OWL-DL version. We used the OWL-DL version, which adds constructs like transitive properties, equivalent properties, class instance enumeration and cardinality restrictions. UOBM as a benchmark contains a pre-defined set of datasets, but the number of these datasets is rather low, because only three datasets (containing 1, 5 and 10 universities) for each version exist. Fortunately, a data generator was developed at the University of Oxford [21]. This generator creates datasets for the more expressive OWL-DL version and each generated university contains approximately 250k triples.

In contrast to the LUBM datasets, data generated for UOBM were split in files by universities.

4.2   Queries

Both of the benchmarks that we decided to utilize contain their own sets of SPARQL queries that are used to evaluate the storage systems. These queries are general-purpose statements containing joins, unbound subjects and/or objects. Such queries are tailored for reasoner benchmarking, trying to capture complex data structure. Most of the time, applications using object model require a rather narrow set of operations used for creating, retrieving, updating and deleting data. These operations are in case of JOPA exposed through the OntoDriver API and are described in greater detail in [14].

For the purpose of evaluating ontology storages in terms of efficiency for object-oriented application access, we have defined a set of eight SPARQL and SPARQL Update [6] queries, which correspond to a major subset of the operations declared in OntoDriver API. Let us now briefly describe each query.

Q_{S1} selects all statements with the given individual as subject. This query corresponds to a retrieve operation, which loads an entity instance from the storage. In this case the entity attributes either cover most of the individual's properties so that it is more efficient to ask for them in a single query instead of asking for each property separately (see query Q_{S2}), or the entity contains a field which holds all the unmapped property values (see [14]). A single query with bound subject and unbound property and object is also used to load entities in Empire.

Q_{S2} is similar to query Q_{S1}, it represents the same entity retrieval operation. However, in this instance the required properties are enumerated and the whole query is thus a union of triple patterns with bound subject and predicate. Such a query would be used in case the entity contained several attributes, but the ontological individual had multiple other properties connected to it. As in case of Q_{S1}, it is the responsibility of the OOM provider to map the returned values to entity attributes.

Q_{S2OPT} is a variation of Q_{S2}, only in this case using SPARQL's *OPTIONAL* operator instead of *UNION*. Although the properties of Q_{S2OPT} do not seem to be very suitable for the OOM case (it returns the result as a cartesian product of the matching values for multiple variables), we keep it in the comparison for the sake of completeness of our study.

Q_{S3} represents a *find all* operation – it returns attributes of all individuals of the specified class. This operation is actually not defined in the OntoDriver API, but retrieval of all instances of a certain type is a very common operation in object-oriented applications. Therefore, we decided to add such a query into the benchmark. In addition, given the structure of the datasets, this query returns a large amount of results (hundreds of thousands for larger datasets), so we also used it to see how the evaluated storages were able to handle such situations.

Q_{S4} retrieves values of a single property for the given individual. This query can be viewed as an attempt to load values of a single attribute and in JOPA such operation is used to provide lazily loaded attributes[4] for entity instances. Moreover, this query requires reasoning to take place to return any results, because it looks for values of the *hasAlumnus* property, which is never explicitly used in the dataset. This type of query is also used by AliBaba, which loads entities by querying attributes one by one.

Q_{U5} removes values of several properties of the given individual and then inserts new values for those properties. Thus it corresponds to an entity attribute update. In the general case of ontological storages, this cannot be achieved by updating the values in-place, but the old values have to removed and new inserted.

Q_{I6} inserts assertion about individual's type(s) and property values into the ontology. Such query represents a *persist* operation, when new entity instance is saved into the storage.

Q_{D7} deletes property assertions about the given individual. JOPA performs *epistemic remove* [14], in which only values of properties known to the object model are removed. Thus the query deletes statements by specifying triple patterns with bound subject and property, instead of simply removing everything concerning the removed individual.

The queries themselves are written in full in our technical report [15], appendix A. The aforementioned queries represent the core operations defined in the OntoDriver API and used by JOPA. Other methods defined in the API,

---

[4] Attributes loaded only when actually accessed.

e.g. *getTypes*, *updateTypes*, are simply variations of the core methods. The key difference between our queries and the queries in LUBM and UOBM is that our queries do not require any joins and most of them use bound subject. LUBM and UOBM queries, on the other hand, always have variable in the subject position. In addition, neither LUBM nor UOBM contain SPARQL Update queries, which are crucial for application access.

It is worth mentioning that the current experimental prototype of OntoDriver uses dedicated methods of the storage access framework (Sesame API [3] in this case) instead of relying on generation of SPARQL queries. However, the OntoDriver implementations are not restricted to either approach. Also, we are using SPARQL queries in our benchmark because the same queries can be used over various storages without any modifications.

4.3 Storages

Following our theoretical study of OntoDriver operations complexity for storages GraphDB and Stardog in [14], we decided to experimentally verify our conclusions. Another reason for choosing GraphDB and Stardog is that they represent two complementing approaches to reasoning – the former performing total materialization using forward chaining, the latter executing inference at real time without any materialization.

GraphDB. GraphDB, formerly known as OWLIM [1], is a storage implementing Sesame's storage and inference layer (SAIL) paradigm. Thus, it can be accessed through the Sesame API in the same way as any other SAIL-compliant storage.

GraphDB performs reasoning by materializing all possible inferred knowledge on insertion. This theoretically leads to very fast query answering, but slower updates. Especially statement retraction can have detrimental effect on performance, since GraphDB employs a combination of forward and backward chaining in order to identify inferred knowledge that is no longer backed by any explicit statement.

GraphDB's inference engine is rule-based. Therefore, besides pre-defined rule-sets for various OWL and OWL 2 profiles, it provides the possibility to define user's own inference rules. The rule-based inference, however, represents a restriction on expressiveness, since some OWL constructs, e.g. full logical negation, cannot be expressed using rules.

Stardog. Stardog[5] is an RDF database with its own proprietary API, but providing bridges for Jena [4] and Sesame API as well. Stardog does no materialization. Instead, it performs real time model checking, inferring knowledge at query time. This has obviously impact on query performance, however it also results in smaller repository size and theoretically faster updates.

---

[5] http://www.stardog.com, accessed 05-14-2015.

Stardog uses Pellet [20] as its reasoner and thus supports full OWL 2 DL reasoning over TBox. Queries involving ABox can use reasoning in profiles OWL 2 EL, OWL 2 QL, OWL 2 RL [18] and a combination of them (called in Stardog's documentation SL).

4.4   Benchmark Metrics

To thoroughly evaluate performance of tested storages, we have used the following metrics:

- **Dataset load time** – first task when running the benchmark was always loading the dataset. We measured how long it took the storages to fully load the data,
- **Repository size** – we measured the size of the resulting repository (in statements) to determine what effect has materialization on space consumption,
- **Query execution time** – the most obvious criterion, which tells us how fast can the storage perform a query and return results for it. For easier interpretation, we express the results in a more read-friendly *queries per second* measure,
- **Query completeness and soundness** – since reasoning was involved in some of the queries, we also verified soundness and completeness of the results.

Benchmark Application. We developed a small application which served as benchmark runner. Its task was to load the queries, run them against a given SPARQL endpoint, collect results and measure the execution time of the queries. The application itself was written in Java and is very similar to the benchmark application used by BSBM [2].

5   Experiments

In this section we present results we obtained by running the benchmark against both GraphDB and Stardog.

5.1   Experiment Setup

The following versions of the storages were used in the benchmark:

- GraphDB-SE 6.1 SP1,
- Stardog 3.0.

Both storages were evaluated in two modes, one with no reasoning and the other with maximum supported expressiveness, in case of Stardog, we thus used the *SL* reasoning level. In case of GraphDB, we used the *OWL-Max* rule set, which corresponds to the maximum subset of OWL that can be captured using rules.

Table 1. Parameters of machines that were used to run the benchmark.

PC	Server
• Linux Mint 17 64-bit	• Linux Debian 3.2.65 64-bit
• CPU Intel i5 2.67 GHz (4 cores)	• CPU Intel Xeon E3-1271 3.60 GHz (8 cores)
• 8 GB RAM	• 32 GB RAM
• 500 GB SATA HDD	• 100 GB SSD HDD
• Java 8u40, -Xms6g -Xmx6g	• Java 8u40, -Xms20g -Xmx20g
• Apache Tomcat 8.20	• Apache Tomcat 8.20

The experiments were run by our benchmark application in two batches, the first containing all the *select* queries, the second containing the *update* queries. The queries were run in rounds in which all the queries were executed sequentially. We ran 20 warm-up rounds without measuring anything and then 500 rounds, from which the results were computed.

The experiments were run in two environments, one being a regular PC with a SATA hard drive, the other a server with an SSD drive. Setup of the machines can be seen in Table 1.

We used datasets of varying size, starting with one university up to 100 universities for the PC, amounting to approximately 13 million statements in case of the UOBM dataset, and 600 universities for the server (around 153 million statements for the UOBM dataset).

Please note that due to space restrictions, we present here only some of the results we measured. Tables with all recorded data can be found in the technical report [15], appendices B, C, D, E and F.

5.2 Dataset Loading

Dataset loading was conducted using bulk loaders provided by both storages. In case of Stardog, this meant specifying files to load on repository creation.

Bulk loading on GraphDB was a more complicated matter, because since GraphDB does materialization on insertion, it is necessary to specify inference level (ruleset) before creating the repository. In addition, to perform better, GraphDB asks the user to specify the expected size of the storage, including the inferred statements. Therefore, we first had to load the datasets without measuring the performance and feed the resulting repository size to the configuration of the actual benchmark repository.

Stardog is in all cases able to load the datasets significantly faster than GraphDB. We expected Stardog to outperform GraphDB with the OWL-Max ruleset, because of the inference taking place in GraphDB during insertion. However, even for an empty ruleset, where no materialization occurs, Stardog performed much better than GraphDB. It is also interesting to note that in case of the more expressive UOBM datasets, the size of the GraphDB storage with inferred statements is more than twice the size of the loaded data.

Figure 2 shows a chart of dataset loading times on the server. It is clear that GraphDB, performing materialization, is significantly slower than Stardog.

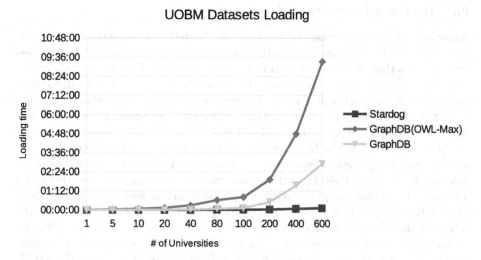

Fig. 2. Loading times for the UOBM datasets, executed on the server.

For the largest dataset the loading time in GraphDB almost reaches 9 hours and 30 minutes, while Stardog loads it in 7 minutes and 10 seconds.

Table 2 shows the loading times in numbers plus resulting sizes of the datasets. Notice that for the largest dataset and the OWL-Max ruleset, we were unable to determine repository size, because GraphDB kept failing with exceptions for any queries we issued to the storage through its SPARQL endpoint. Therefore, we cannot even be certain that the storage was able to load the whole dataset and perform all materialization.

Table 2. Loading of the UOBM datasets on the server. $\#U$ is the number of universities in dataset, T is the loading time, S is the size of the resulting repository in triples. * *It is not certain that the dataset was fully loaded, because the storage failed to process all queries.*

$\#U$	$T_{Stardog}$	$T_{GraphDB}^{OWL-Max}$	$T_{GraphDB}$	$S_{Stardog}$	$S_{GraphDB}^{OWL-Max}$	$S_{GraphDB}$
1	1 s	22 s	2 s	258 370	542 312	258 370
5	3 s	121 s	8 s	1 355 941	2 832 003	1 355 941
10	4 s	229 s	15 s	2 509 169	5 242 259	2 509 169
20	10 s	493 s	32 s	5 183 092	10 829 617	5 183 092
40	20 s	970 s	93 s	10 212 049	21 339 224	10 212 049
80	42 s	2212 s	280 s	20 286 983	42 390 542	20 286 983
100	53 s	2892 s	419 s	25 478 086	53 239 768	25 478 086
200	124 s	6770 s	1854 s	51 110 402	106 795 361	51 110 402
400	293 s	17 371 s	5760 s	102 224 372	-	102 224 372
600	430 s	30 758 s*	10 414 s	153 178 000	-	153 178 000

5.3   Benchmark Results for PC

Experiments undertaken on the PC confirm theoretical expectations in case of select queries. Indeed, GraphDB with materialized inference provides faster execution times than Stardog with reasoning at query time. The difference is actually very significant, as can be seen for example in Figure 3. The difference between GraphDB with and without inference can be easily explained by the fact that in case of storage with inference, the repository size is more than twice the size of the repository without inference.

More surprising is the fact that GraphDB actually performs better even in case of update queries. Theoretical expectations in this case favour Stardog, because it does not have to perform any inference during updates. However, Figure 4 shows that GraphDB not only performs better without inference, but even with inference it is able to execute more queries per second than Stardog. The fact that Stardog shows virtually the same performance with and without reasoning is no surprise, because in fact for these update queries no reasoning occurs. The situation is radically different only in case of Q_{D7}, where GraphDB with enabled inference performs by far worst, most likely due to the fact that a combination of forward and backward chaining occurs in order to find out which inferred statements should be removed as well [1].

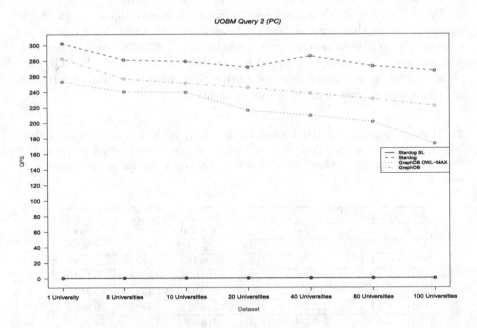

Fig. 3. Plot of storage performance for Q_{S2} on UOBM datasets. QPS represents the number of queries executed per second, higher is better. While Stardog without reasoning performs the best, it clearly looses when inference is required.

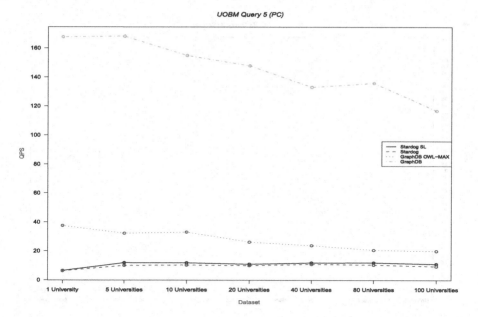

Fig. 4. Plot of storage performance for Q_{U5} on UOBM datasets. GraphDB outperforms Stardog even in update operation, although the difference for repository with inference is not so large.

5.4   Benchmark Results for Server

Evaluation on the server confirmed our observation from experiments on the PC only partially. For select queries, the order is the same as on the PC – Stardog without reasoning being the fastest, Stardog with reasoning being by far the slowest. The only exception in this situation is Q_{S3}, which returns a very large number of results, with which both storages struggle and for the larger datasets the query takes seconds to execute (see Figure 5).

However, the situation is very peculiar for the update queries. For query Q_{D7} Stardog now outperformed GraphDB in both inference settings, while on PC it was the case only for GraphDB with inference enabled. The situation becomes even more complicated for queries Q_{U5} and Q_{I6}, where considerable fluctuations in performance appear in Stardog. Because of these fluctuations, it is very difficult to discover any trends in its performance. We can see from the results, that the differences between Stardog and GraphDB are smaller than on the PC and sometimes Stardog even comes on top of the comparison, but the pattern is not steady. The fluctuations are clearly visible in Figure 6. After computing standard deviation for the Stardog results, it turned out that while for queries Q_{S1}, Q_{S2} and Q_{S3} the standard deviation was around 1 % of the average query execution time, for query Q_{S4} it grows to 27 % in average and for the update queries Q_{U5}, Q_{I6} and Q_{D7} it rises to 46 % in average. The performance of Stardog in these cases appears to be highly unpredictable.

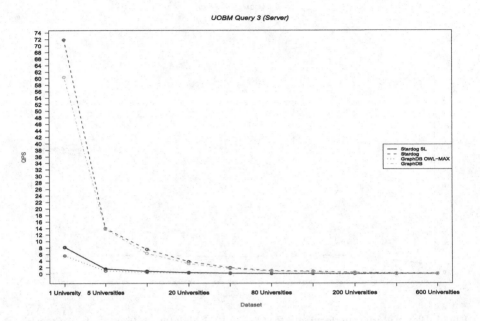

Fig. 5. Plot of storage performance for Q_{S3} on UOBM datasets. Large number of results has a significant impact on performance of the storages.

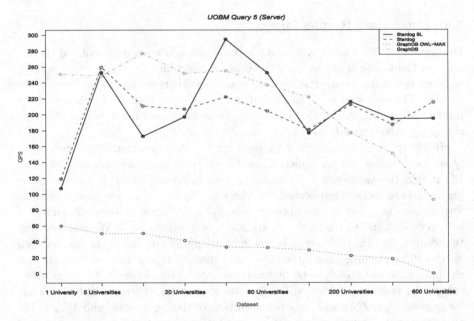

Fig. 6. Plot of storage performance for Q_{U5} on UOBM datasets. Considerable fluctuations appear in performance of Stardog.

It is also worth noting that Stardog was not able to handle the dataset with 800 LUBM universities and kept crashing on queries. GraphDB, on the other hand, failed to work with the UOBM 600 universities dataset (using the OWL-Max ruleset), throwing exceptions when queries were sent to it.

6 Conclusion

We have designed a benchmark for evaluating suitability of ontology storages for object-oriented applications and used it to test two of the most advanced contemporary storage engines. Both storages showed extremely good performance in case of select queries without reasoning. Our theoretical expectations about materialization being slow on bulk insert and real time reasoning at query time were also confirmed. More surprising was the fact that GraphDB, using total materialization, did in most cases outperform Stardog even for update operations, for which Stardog should be theoretically more suitable. Overall, GraphDB appears to be more suitable for the object-oriented application access scenario, in which frequent data updates are expected, because it provides satisfiable performance even for large datasets. Stardog clearly outperforms GraphDB only in case of select queries without reasoning.

However, GraphDB (and storages performing materialization in general) has a major disadvantage in that the user has to specify inference level before actually inserting data into the storages. Real time reasoning, on the other hand, lets the user choose reasoning level for every query he executes.

In the future, we would like to more closely investigate the performance fluctuations of Stardog in the server environment. They appear without any obvious reason and cause the performance of the storage to be extremely unpredictable. Also, based on the benchmark results and the characteristics of the storages, we will research possible optimizations for OntoDriver implementations, for example the results indicate that when loading an entity, it is more favourable to use only bound subject in the queries (Q_{S1}), instead of doing a union of triple patterns based on properties (Q_{S2}). Q_{S2OPT} has worse performance than Q_{S2}, which is not surprising, given that Q_{S2} uses only *UNION* and thus has PTIME complexity, whereas Q_{S2OPT} with *OPTIONAL* is PSPACE-complete [19].

Acknowledgment. This work was supported by grants No. SGS13/204/OHK3/3T/13 Effective solving of engineering problems using semantic technologies of the Czech Technical University in Prague and No. TA04030465 Research and development of progressive methods for measuring aviation organizations safety performance of the Technology Agency of the Czech Republic.

References

1. Bishop, B., Kiryakov, A., Ognyanoff, D., Peikov, I., Tashev, Z., Velkov, R.: OWLIM: A family of scalable semantic repositories. Semantic Web - Interoperability, Usability, Applicability (2010)

2. Bizer, C., Schultz, A.: The Berlin SPARQL benchmark. International Journal On Semantic Web and Information Systems (2009)
3. Broekstra, J., Kampman, A., van Harmelen, F.: Sesame: a generic architecture for storing and querying RDF and RDF schema. In: Horrocks, I., Hendler, J. (eds.) ISWC 2002. LNCS, vol. 2342, pp. 54–68. Springer, Heidelberg (2002)
4. Carroll, J.J., Dickinson, I., Dollin, C., Reynolds, D., Seaborne, A., Wilkinson, K.: Jena: implementing the semantic web recommendations. In: Proceedings of the 13th International World Wide Web conference (Alternate Track Papers & Posters), pp. 74–83 (2004)
5. Garcia-Castro, R.: Benchmarking semantic web technology. Studies on the Semantic Web. IOS Press, Amsterdam (2009)
6. Gearon, P., Passant, A., Polleres, A.: SPARQL 1.1 Update. Tech. rep., W3C (2013)
7. Grove, M.: Empire: RDF & SPARQL Meet JPA. semanticweb.com, April 2010. http://semanticweb.com/empire-rdf-sparql-meet-jpa_b15617
8. Guo, Y., Pan, Z., Heflin, J.: LUBM: A benchmark for OWL knowledge base systems. Journal of Web Semantics 3(2–3), 158–182 (2005). http://dx.doi.org/10.1016/j.websem.2005.06.005, http://www.bibsonomy.org/bibtex/2924e60509d7e1b45c6f38eaef9a5c6bb/gromgull
9. Harris, S., Seaborne, A.: SPARQL 1.1 query language. Tech. rep., W3C (2013)
10. JCP: JSR 317: Java^{TM} Persistence API, Version 2.0 (2009)
11. Křemen, P.: Building Ontology-Based Information Systems. Ph.D. thesis, Czech Technical University, Prague (2012)
12. Křemen, P., Kouba, Z.: Ontology-driven information system design. IEEE Transactions on Systems, Man, and Cybernetics: Part C 42(3), 334–344 (2012). http://ieeexplore.ieee.org/xpl/freeabs_all.jsp?arnumber=6011704
13. Ledvinka, M., Křemen, P.: JOPA: developing ontology-based information systems. In: Proceedings of the 13th Annual Conference Znalosti 2014 (2014)
14. Ledvinka, M., Křemen, P.: JOPA: accessing ontologies in an object-oriented way. In: Proceedings of the 17th International Conference on Enterprise Information Systems (2015)
15. Ledvinka, M., Křemen, P.: Object-UOBM: An Ontological Benchmark for Object-oriented Access. Tech. rep., Czech Technical University in Prague (2015)
16. Ma, L., Yang, Y., Qiu, Z., Xie, G.T., Pan, Y., Liu, S.: Towards a complete OWL ontology benchmark. In: Sure, Y., Domingue, J. (eds.) ESWC 2006. LNCS, vol. 4011, pp. 125–139. Springer, Heidelberg (2006)
17. Motik, B., Parsia, B., Patel-Schneider, P.F.: OWL 2 Web Ontology Language Structural Specification and Functional-Style Syntax. W3C recommendation, W3C, October 2009. http://www.w3.org/TR/2009/REC-owl2-syntax-20091027/
18. Patel-Schneider, P.F., Motik, B., Grau, B.C.: OWL 2 Web Ontology Language Direct Semantics. W3C recommendation, W3C, October 2009. http://www.w3.org/TR/2009/REC-owl2-direct-semantics-20091027/
19. Schmidt, M., Meier, M., Lausen, G.: Foundations of sparql query optimization. In: Proceedings of the 13th International Conference on Database Theory, ICDT 2010, pp. 4–33. ACM, New York (2010)
20. Sirin, E., Parsia, B., Grau, B.C., Kalyanpur, A., Katz, Y.: Pellet: A practical OWL-DL reasoner. Web Semantics: Science, Services and Agents on the World Wide Web 5(2), June 2007
21. Zhou, Y., Grau, B.C., Horrocks, I., Wu, Z., Banerjee, J.: Making the most of your triple store: query answering in OWL 2 using an RL reasoner. In: Proceedings of the 22nd International Conference on World Wide Web (2013)

Semantically Enrichable Research Information System SocioNet

Sergey Parinov[1(✉)], Victor Lyapunov[2], Roman Puzyrev[3], and Mikhail Kogalovsky[4]

[1] Central Economics and Mathematics Institute of RAS, Moscow, Russia
sparinov@gmail.com
[2] Institute of Computational Mathematics and Mathematical Geophysics SB RAS,
Novosibirsk, Russia
vic@socionet.ru
[3] Institute of Economics and Industrial Engineering SB RAS, Novosibirsk, Russia
prl@mail.ru
[4] Market Economy Institute of the RAS, Moscow, Russia
kogalov@gmail.com

Abstract. Our paper presents a semantically enrichable type of research information systems, which differs from the traditional one by allowing users to create semantic linkages between information objects and to enrich by this the initial content. This approach was implemented as a whole ecosystem of tools and services at the SocioNet research information system, which is publicly available for the research community. Making semantic linkages, the SocioNet users create over metadata from its content a semantic layer that visualizes their scientific knowledge or hypothesis about relationships between research outputs. Such facilities, in particular, open new opportunities for authors of research outputs. Authors can essentially enrich metadata of their research outputs after the papers have been published and have become available at the SocioNet content. Authors can provide comments and notes for updating publication abstracts, data about motivations for citing the papers in the reference lists, research association with newer relevant publications, data about their personal roles and contributions into the collective research outputs, etc.

Keywords: Research information system · Semantic enrichment · Semantic linkage · Scientific relationship · Taxonomy · Controlled vocabulary · SocioNet

1 Introduction

We present a new type of a research information system (RIS). It provides for its users facilities to create semantic linkages between its information objects in a decentralised fashion. In this way, researchers can express publically their professional knowledge, hypotheses or opinions about scientific relationships between research outputs. These expressions make for semantic enrichment of the RIS content.

We define the research information system as a system designed according to (or compatible with) recommendations of the Current Research Information System

© Springer International Publishing Switzerland 2015
P. Klinov and D. Mouromtsev (Eds.): KESW 2015, CCIS 518, pp. 147–157, 2015.
DOI: 10.1007/978-3-319-24543-0_11

(CRIS) [2, 3] and based on a CERIF data model [4]. This approach provides a proper and convenient environment for implementing the semantic linkage technique and enrichment facilities for authors. The growing popularity of the CRIS-CERIF approach improves standardization and interoperability among numerous research information systems that are necessary for integrating its contents in a form of common data and information space (DIS). The use of CRIS-CERIF guarantees that enrichment data created at one RIS can be easily moved, visualized and re-used outside the originating information system at other RIS or at an Institutional Repository (IR).

The demonstrated approach to make a research information system semantically enrichable is based on the following background: a) the CERIF Semantics [4]; b) the web annotation and the open annotation specifications[1] from W3C; c) taxonomy of scientific relationships which can exist between research information objects [12, 13, 14]; d) the specification of registered authors with their personal profiles linked with their publications [8].

We implemented our approach as a whole ecosystem of tools and services at the SocioNet research information system. It is publicly available for the research community at https://socionet.ru/.

Our ecosystem opens new opportunities for authors of research outputs. Authors can essentially enrich metadata of their research outputs after the papers have been published and have become available within SocioNet. Authors can provide data about their personal roles and contributions into the collective research outputs, comments and notes for updating publication abstracts, data about motivations for citing the papers in the reference lists, research association with newer relevant publications, etc.

In the next section, we provide a short historic overview of the SocioNet RIS development during the last 15 years. We also discuss its current state. The third section provides details about the recent results in developing semantic enrichment ecosystem within SocioNet RIS. The fourth section concludes the paper.

2   SocioNet Research Information System

The Socionet system development started in 1997 as the RuPEc project. That project built a computer mirror and Russian language interfaces for the RePEc.org data and its basic services. It also added the first in Russia public open archive to submit research papers in Social Sciences for its online presenting at RuPEc in Russian language and at RePEc in English [7]. At that time, RePEc already had become the biggest world metadata aggregator system for research papers in Economics. To assist RuPEc/RePEc users with monitoring the intensive input flow of new research papers we designed in 1999 a concept of researchers' personal information robots including its ecosystem [6]. By the concept such information robot as an active personal researcher's software agent should filter the input flow of new papers according the researcher's interests and interacts with information robots of other researchers to provide its owner an improved information support.

---

[1] http://www.w3.org/community/openannotation/

Using the RuPEc background, the concept of the personal information robot [6] and a concept of the research information space for researchers in Social Sciences [13] we designed a research information system called SocioNet [9].

In 2000, following an award from the Ford Foundation[2] we started to run the SocioNet research information system at http://socionet.ru/. From that time onward SocioNet has run its own aggregator service. It aggregates more research metadata collections and open repositories than RePEc provided. It allowed us to build and update a research data and information space (DIS) on a daily basis. At that time, it served social scientists only. Most of its users came from the Russian language research community. We also presented the SocioNet system to the Russian research community as an open technical platform to develop specific scientific information resources and online services [17].

In 2002, we started an implementation of a concept of a permanent researcher's representation. It should allow researchers to collect and permanently represent their research outputs and personal records regardless of changing institutional affiliation [16]. As a first step, we created the SocioNet Personal Zone as an add-in online workbench and a managing system for academic electronic assets. It allows a scientist to deposit and manage different types of collections of research outputs and materials (e.g. "personal profile", "institutional profile", "paper", "article", "book", etc.). The Personal Zone service also included the software of the "personal information robot" to trace new additions/changes within DIS according personal research interests of users and notify them about relevant findings [18].

In 2004, we implemented at SocioNet some features of a social network. The users got new tools to create and manage semantic linkages between information objects of DIS. At the beginning, it was linkages between personal profiles <-authorship-> publications and organizational profiles <-affiliation-> personal profiles. From that time, personal and organizational profiles at SocioNet can represent in some way the professional social networks of research actors [18].

In 2007, we opened a scientometric section at SocioNet. A special service is monitoring everyday changes of DIS information objects (publications, personal and organizational profiles, etc.) and creates some statistical representation of activities that produced these changes. The SocioNet scientometric database has been accumulating from the start of 2007. The SocioNet statistics section provides a large set of time series indicators. It includes indicators of views/downloads aggregated according linkages between DIS information objects, e.g. a sum of views/downloads for all publications linked with a personal profile, or the next step of aggregation – a sum of personal indicators for all people linked with an organization's profile, and so on [5]. In 2009, a monitoring service at SocioNet started tracing all changes of semantic linkages. We added to the Socionet statistics subsystem some indicators based on the semantic linkages data [15].

In 2011, we used the results of this research to guide social network features development at SocioNet [10]. We proposed a concept of the Semantic Linkages Open Repository (SLOR), which implemented at SocioNet enables scientists to express in a

---

[2] Ford Foundation provided 4 grants for the SocioNet project during 2000 – 2007.

computer-readable form their knowledge, hypothesis or opinions about multiple scientific relationships that can exist between research outputs [11]. Technically it means that we built a multilayer network of semantic linkages over information objects from DIS content.

Researchers typically re-use research objects, thus creating relationships between them by citing. We propose a concept of a research e-infrastructure semantic segment. It allows scientists unlimited re-use of research information systems (RIS) content. The semantic linkage technique implemented at RIS SocioNet provides researchers with tools and services for semantic linking of any pair of research objects, for which metadata are available within SocioNet content. This instrument also allows researchers a decentralized development of semantic vocabularies that guarantee a covering by this technique any new types of relationships.

The conceptual development of SocioNet after 2013 and its new supported use cases are presented in detail at the next section of this paper.

Since 2009, the SocioNet works as a multidiscipline RIS freely available for all researchers. Socionet is a full-functional modern RIS driven by a community of researchers communicating in Russian [10]. Currently, we are also creating the pure English-language version of the system, which will be available for the international research community and RIS developers.

At the beginning of May 2015, the SocioNet system aggregates more than 8000 collections with scientific materials (all types: personal/organizational profiles, publications, theses, etc.). It includes about 7000 collections from RePEc.org and about 1000 collections from Russian providers of research content. The collections in total have about 3.27 million information objects of different types (records). These include about 220.000 personal profiles and about 30.000 organizational profiles. 300 new records arrive on an average day and one or two new collections arrive in a typical week. SocioNet covers 15 scientific disciplines described using 16 data types.

The total number of linkages among the SocioNet information objects is about 9.4 million. On May 10th 2015 after 3 months of testing and experiments with the new facilities for authors to enrich metadata of their publications there are only 211 semantic linkages recently created by registered authors. Among other linkages the biggest groups are: about 7,3 million citation linkages imported from the CitEc database [1]; about 1,3 million "publication" linkages from researchers' personal profiles to their publications and about 60 thousands "person" linkages from organizational profiles to researchers' profiles; and etc.

The semantic linkages data aggregated at Socionet are used in the system to:

- build a visualization of DIS structure in a form of a graph and to provide graphical navigation tool;
- generate scientometric indicators based on accumulated semantic data;
- create reports for notification system; and etc.

Currently SocioNet has following main subsystems that provide for data processing (see Figure 1):

1. The Information Hub (IH) aggregates scientific metadata from different data providers and organizations and gives it back in a standardized form (https://socionet.ru/docs/infohubs.htm).
2. The Research Portal visualizes the interdisciplinary research data and information space (https://socionet.ru/portal.html) using the full SocioNet IH metadata content. It presents aggregated information objects and semantic linkages between them for users' navigation.

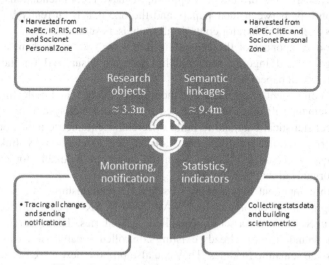

Fig. 1. SocioNet data sources and main services

3. An online workbench called SocioNet Personal Zone (https://spz.socionet.ru/) is there for SocioNet users to create, manage and submit to DIS single materials, whole collections and archives. SocioNet users can create and manage a network of semantic linkages between DIS objects.
4. Monitoring and scientometric services provide researchers useful daily updated scientometric database (https://socionet.ru/stats.xml). All calculated scientometric indexes are public and can be used for research assessments and for scientometric studies.

3   Ecosystem of the SocioNet Tools and Services for Supporting Semantic Enrichment

The first component of the ecosystem is the semantic linkage technique, which allows users to create different types of semantic linkages between papers, personal profiles, etc. This new users' facility is illustrated by the following main use cases:

- Users can annotate text fragments of a paper's abstract to provide readers with additional and/or newer information on the topic. We give details in section 3.1;

- Users can link their papers together, e.g. to provide information about its open access or newest versions; and to show to readers an evolution of ideas or a development of approaches through a set of users' papers. We have more in section 3.2;
- Users can contribute data on how they used the works referenced in their paper. We have more in section 3.3.

Additionally users can specify the roles of their co-authorship in the making of a collective paper, share their professional opinion, or make recommendations, comments about relationships between their papers and the one that is currently browsed by a reader. The system administrator controls all such users submissions.

The second component of the ecosystem is a visualization mechanism. All user-created outgoing and ingoing semantic linkages are visualized on the page that describes a research paper.

The third component is service for monitoring changes and collecting statistics. All created semantic linkages are processed by the SocioNet system on an everyday base to collect statistical data and to build different scientometric indicators. For personal and organizational profiles, the statistics are aggregated by links between Organization <-> Person <-> Paper. Such indicators are available for every paper, personal or organizational profile.

The fourth component is taxonomy of scientific relationships. We built it current version using available ontologies like SPAR, SWAN, SKOS, etc. [15]. Taxonomy is represented in SocioNet by a set of controlled vocabularies. The research community can create new and develop already existing controlled vocabularies, which are used in tools to create semantic linkages. They can also propose new use cases of using this technique over the research outputs dataset.

The fifth component is the notification service. The registered users can switch on the e-mail notification service, which will inform them when someone creates/modifies a semantic linkage with their papers, or when someone is changing papers that the user linked together, and so on.

The sixth component is the interoperability service. Developers of RIS services can take and use the data of all created semantic linkages. The data are freely available by two main ways: 1) by OAI-PMH protocol with CERIF output format; 2) by REST API in XML form.

3.1   Annotating of Papers' Abstract

After logging into the system, one can annotate the abstract (if it is present) of any paper available at SocioNet. A user can, however, not create a new abstract.

The paper's author makes the annotation of the abstract highlighted by a yellow background colour. If a non-author creates an annotation the annotated text, it will be on a pink background. The text of an annotation is a pop-up. It appears if you point your mouse on the annotated text fragment. All annotations on the paper are listed at the right with links to detailed views of the annotation data. See an example of annotated abstract at Fig. 2.

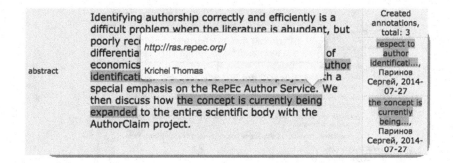

Fig. 2. Example of annotated abstract of a paper

If a user wants to create a new annotation - just select a text fragment within an abstract of a paper. A user will see an icon to open a form to create an annotation.

If a user is an author of the annotated paper, the user will have in the drop-down list "Relationship type" only the blank value "no relationship". It is because the authors cannot evaluate their own paper. But in the other case the user will have in this list a controlled vocabulary called "Professional opinions and evaluation"[3].

From technical point of view all created annotations exist in the SocioNet system as semantic linkages, where the source object of the linkage is the personal profile of the linkage's author, the target object is the annotated paper and the semantic of the linkage is a value from the controlled vocabulary or the "no relationship" value.

3.2   Linking Author's Papers Together

When users are logged into the SocioNet system and browse their papers, they will see to the right of the paper's full-text link the text: "Create a link to a related paper of yours?" Or if the paper's metadata does not have a full text link, there is a text "Create a linkage with appropriate paper?" If the users click on this menu they will get a form for linkage creation as at the Fig. 3.

In this form under the field "Comments", users will see a list of all their claimed publications. A user has to check one of the publications in this list that has a relationship to the paper currently viewed in a browser. Then the users have to select a specific type of the relation between these two papers from the drop-down list the "Relationship type". Optionally they may also enter some comments.

Currently, the system provides two controlled vocabularies for selecting a relationship type between papers belonging to the same author: 1) relationships among versions and components of a research publication; and 2) relationships of development and complement between research outputs.

---

[3] All used controlled vocabularies are available at https://socionet.ru/section.xml?h=metrics_interdisciplinary&l=en

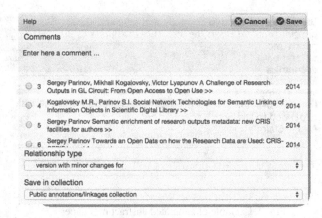

Fig. 3. An example of a form to create a semantic linkage between papers

Once a linkage is created it is visualized on web pages of both linked papers' metadata as additional information. See an example at the Fig. 4.

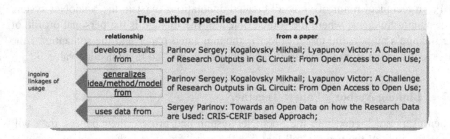

Fig. 4. An example of relationships created by an author of linked papers

3.3   An Author Contributes Motives for Using Papers from their Papers' Reference Lists

The SocioNet system uses the CitEc data about citations and similar internal data. When the citation data for a paper is available, SocioNet displays a reference list for the currently browsed paper. The list is limited to publications that are available at SocioNet. In the list there may be two sections: a) referenced papers claimed as own by author(s) of this paper; b) papers of other authors or unclaimed papers.

When users are logged into the system and browse one of their papers, on the right they will see a link "[+]" for each reference. This link opens the form to specify their motives of using the referenced paper.

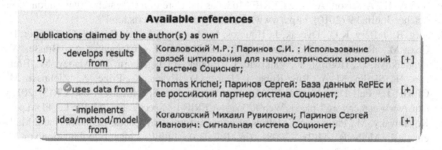

Available references

Publications claimed by the author(s) as own

1)	-develops results from	Когаловский М.Р.; Паринов С.И. : Использование связэй цитирования для наукометрических измерений в системе Соционет; [+]
2)	uses data from	Thomas Krichel; Паринов Сергей: База данных RePEc и ее российский партнер система Соционет; [+]
3)	-implements idea/method/model from	Когаловский Михаил Рувимович; Паринов Сергей Иванович: Сигнальная система Соционет; [+]

Fig. 5. An example of the enriched reference list provided by the paper's author

For this specific use case, a controlled vocabulary defines relationships of development and complement between two papers, which was used in the previous use case and described in section 3.2.

The data added by the author about citation motivations is highlighted by yellow-colour background as seen at the Fig. 5. Pointing a mouse on it, one may see a pop-up comment if it was provided. The link allows viewing detailed data about the linkage.

4 Conclusion

Since semantic enrichment facilities became available for SocioNet users only in March 2015 we have not sufficient usage statistics at the moment.

The current configuration of the SocioNet system demonstrates potential multiple benefits, which the research information systems of the new semantically enrichable type can provide for the research community.

We believe that the approach we demonstrated has good prospects, because the research outputs authors have at least two reasons to enrich ordinary information about their papers typically provided by publishers. First there is something that is not supported by the traditional publication metadata model (e.g. roles/impacts of co-authors in making a paper, motivations why authors used publications listed at their papers references section, etc.). Second something important may have happened after the paper was published (e.g. authors found some important methodological associations and theoretical hierarchical relations, etc. with research outputs published after their papers).

Acknowledgements. We are grateful to Thomas Krichel for his useful comments. The Russian Foundation for Basic Research currently funds this project, grant 15-07-01294-a.

References

1. Barrueco, J.M., Krichel, T.: Building an autonomous citation index for GL: RePEc, the Economics working papers case. The Grey Journal **1**(2), 91–97 (2005)
2. Jeffery, K., Asserson, A.: CERIF-CRIS for the European e-Infrastructure. Data Science Journal **9** (2010). http://www.codata.org/dsj/special-cris.html

3. Jeffery, K., Asserson, A.: The CERIF Model as the Core of a Research Organisation. Data Science Journal **9** (2010). http://www.codata.org/dsj/special-cris.html
4. Jörg, B., Jeffery, K.G., Dvorak, J., Houssos, N., Asserson, A., van Grootel, G., Gartner, R., Cox, M., Rasmussen, H., Vestdam, T., Strijbosch, L., Clements, A., Brasse, V., Zendulkova, D., Höllrigl, T., Valkovic, L., Engfer, A., Jägerhorn, M., Mahey, M., Brennan, N., Sicilia, M.-A., Ruiz-Rube, I., Baker, D., Evans, K., Price, A., Zielinski, M.: CERIF 1.3 Full Data Model (FDM): Introduction and Specification. euroCRIS (2012). http://www.eurocris.org/Uploads/Web%20pages/CERIF-1.3/Specifications/CERIF1.3_FDM.pdf
5. Kogalovsky, M., Parinov, S.: Metrics of online information spaces. Economics and Mathematical Methods **44**(2) (2008) (in Russian). http://socionet.ru/publication.xml?h= repec:rus:mqijxk:17
6. Krichel, T., Levin, D., Parinov, S.: Active information robot as a software agent of a researcher within RePEc/RuPEc research information systems. In: Proceedings of The first Russian Conference on Digital Libraries (1999) (in Russian). https://socionet.ru/ publication.xml?h=RePEc:rus:mqijxk:1
7. Krichel, T., Lyapunov, V., Parinov S.: RePEc and RuPEc: wep-portal of publications in Economics. EL-Pub-99 Conference, Novosibirsk (1999) (in Russian). https://socionet.ru/ publication.xml?h=RePEc:rus:ieiets:1999_6863
8. Krichel, T., Zimmermann, C.: Author identification in economics,… and beyond. Working Paper Series des Rates für Sozial-und Wirtschaftsdaten **222** (2013)
9. Parinov, S.: Socionet.ru as a model of the second generation of a research information space. Information Society (1), 43–45 (2001) (in Russian). https://socionet.ru/ publication.xml?h=RePEc:rus:mqijxk:7
10. Parinov, S.: CRIS driven by research community: benefits and perspectives. In: proceedings of the 10th International Conference on Current Research Information Systems. Aalborg University, Denmark, June 2–5, 2010, pp. 119–130 (2010). http://socionet.ru/ publication.xml?h=repec:rus:mqijxk:23
11. Parinov, S.: Open repository of semantic linkages. In: Proceedings of 11th International Conference on Current Research Information Systems e-Infrastructure for Research and Innovations (CRIS 2012), Prague (2012). http://socionet.ru/publication.xml?h=repec: rus:mqijxk:29
12. Parinov, S.: Towards a Semantic Segment of a Research e-Infrastructure: necessary information objects, tools and services. Journal: Int. J. of Metadata, Semantics and Ontologies **8**(4), 322–331 (2012). doi:10.1504/IJMSO.2013.058415. http://socionet.ru/pub.xml?h= RePEc:rus:mqijxk:30
13. Parinov, S., Bogomolava T.: Creation of the common information space for research communities. In: V International Conference on Digital Publications EL–Pub2000, Novosibirsk, 2000 (2000) (in Russian). https://socionet.ru/publication.xml?h=RePEc:rus: ieiets:2000_6862
14. Parinov, S., Kogalovsky, M.: A technology for semantic structuring of scientific digital library content. In: Proc. of the XIIIth All-Russian Scientific Conference RCDL 2011. Digital Libraries: Advanced Methods and Technologies, Digital Collections, October 19–22, pp. 94–103. Voronezh State University (2011) (in Russian). http://socionet.ru/publication. xml?h=repec:rus:mqijxk:28
15. Parinov, S., Kogalovsky, M.: Semantic Linkages in Research Information Systems as a New Data Source for Scientometric Studies. Scientometrics **98**(2), 927–943 (2013). http://socionet.ru/pub.xml?h=RePEc:rus:mqijxk:31

16. Parinov, S., Lypunov, V., Puzyrev, R.: Socionet System as a platform for developing of research information resources and online services. Digital Libraries **6**, i. 1 (2003). (in Russian). https://socionet.ru/publication.xml?h=RePEc:rus:ieiets:2003_3817
17. Parinov, S., Puzyrev, R., Lyapunov V.: A concept of the permanent online representation of a researcher. In: EL-Pub2003 Conference, Novosibirsk, 2003 (2003) (in Russian). https://socionet.ru/publication.xml?h=RePEc:rus:ieiets:2003_6859
18. Parinov, S., Krichel, T.: RePEc and socionet as partners in a changing digital library environment, 1997 to 2004. In: Proceedings of Russian Conference on Digital Libraries, 29.09 – 01.10 2004, Pushchino, Russia, 2004. https://socionet.ru/publication.xml?h=RePEc:rus:mqijxk:26

Aspect Extraction from Reviews Using Conditional Random Fields

Yuliya Rubtsova[1](✉) and Sergey Koshelnikov[2]

[1] A.P. Ershov Institute of Informatics Systems, Siberian Branch of the Russian
Academy of Sciences, 630090 Novosibirsk, Russia
yu.rubtsova@gmail.com
[2] Independent Developer, Novokuznetsk, Russia
koshelnikovsa@gmail.com

Abstract. This paper describes an information extraction and content
analysis system. The proposed system is based on a conditional random field algorithm and intended to extract aspect terms mentioned in
the text. We use a set of morphological features for machine learning.
The system is used for automatic extraction of explicit aspects and also
to automatic extraction of all aspects (explicit, implicit and sentiment
facts), and tested on two domains: restaurants and automobiles. We show
that our system can produce quite a high level of precision which means
that the system is capable of recognizing aspect terms rather accurately.
The system demonstrates that even a small set of features for conditional random field algorithm can perform competitively and shows good
results.

Keywords: Aspect detection · Aspect extraction · CRF · Information
retrieval · Information extraction · Content analysis

1 Introduction

With the popularity of blogs, social networks and users' reviews sites growing
every year, Web users post more and more reviews. As a result an enormous
pool of reviews, evaluations and recommendations in various domains has been
accumulated. That data attracts attention of both the researchers dealing with
opinion mining, sentiment analysis and trend recognition and the businessmens
who are more interested in the practical application of reputation marketing in
general and sentiment analysis in particular. Automatic sentiment analysis is
mostly used at the following levels:

- Document level [1–3],
- Sentence or phrase level [4],
- Aspect level [5–7].

Generally people express their opinions not on the product or service as a
whole but on some part, feature or characteristic thereof that is the aspect that
shall be extracted from the text and subjected to sentiment analysis. The aspect

© Springer International Publishing Switzerland 2015
P. Klinov and D. Mouromtsev (Eds.): KESW 2015, CCIS 518, pp. 158–167, 2015.
DOI: 10.1007/978-3-319-24543-0_12

in our terms represents the opinion target. Simply aspect means a feature of a product. The aspect-level sentiment analysis can give us much more useful information on the authors opinion on various features of the product or service under analysis than sentiment analysis of the whole text.

System described in this paper took a part into Dialogue Evaluation section – SentiRuEval (Dialogue conference 2015): evaluation of sentiment analysis systems for the Russian language [8]. The participants of the evaluation were required to perform the following 5 subtasks:

A. Extract explicit aspects from the offered review,
B. Extract all the aspects from the offered review,
C. Perform sentiment analysis of the explicit aspects,
D. Categorize the aspects terms by predefined categories,
E. Evaluate the aspects categories as related to the offered review in general.

Statistical information about train and test collections such as a number of reviews or amount of explicit terms in different domains can be find in Table 1. Almost equal size of train and test collections can be explained by the fact that SentiRuEval organizers first provided training collections for develope and train classifiers, later a test collections for participation in evaluation was granted. The collections consists of users reviews of restaurants or automobiles depending on domain.

Table 1. Collections statistics

	Restaurants		Automobiles	
	Train	Test	Train	Test
Number of reviews	201	203	217	201
Number of explicit terms	2822	3506	3152	3109
Number of implicit terms	636	657	638	576
Number of fact terms	523	656	668	685

This paper describes the system that was used to perform Tasks A and B during SentiRuEval evaluation. The rest of the paper is structured as follows. In Section 2 we discuss the current state of the art and different mechanisms of aspects extraction from product reviews. In Section 3 the descriotion of system is given. Section 4 demonstrates the performance of system as compared to the results of systems of other SentiRuEval participants. We discuss errors made by presented system in section 5. Section 6 presents details conclusions and prospects of the future development.

2 Related Work

There are four major approaches to extract aspects from texts. The first one is based on the frequency of nouns and/or noun phrases. Commonly people use similar terms to describe the features and their attitude to the products and another terms used to describe other details (situation, required accompanying information) in their comments. Thus counting frequency of the most common nouns and/or phrases in the texts of the same domain helps to extract explicit aspect terms from a large number of reviews [9]. The precision level of that algorithm later has been improved by 22% with the recall decreasion 3% only [10]. As common words appear frequently in texts and are often defined as aspects, a filtering mechanism was invented to exclude most common non-aspect nouns and/or phrases from the analysis results [11]. The second approach is based on simultaneous extraction of both sentiment words (user opinions) and aspects. As any opinion is expressed in relation to an object, by looking for sentiment words we can find aspects they relate to. Hu and Liu used this approach to find low-frequency aspects [9]. Another approach is supervised machine learning. Generally for the purposes of aspect extraction supervised machine learning is focused on sequence labeling tasks because aspects and opinions on the products are often interrelated and constitute of a sequence of words. The most wide-spread methods of supervised machine learning are hidden Markov modeling (HMM) [12] and conditional random fields (CRF) [13–15]. The fourth approach is unsupervised machine learning or topic modeling. Topic modeling assumes that each document consists of a mixture of topics and each topic has its probability distribution [16,17]. Numerous works on aspect extraction with the use of topic modeling approach are based on the methods of probabilistic latent semantic analysis (pLSA) model [18] and latent Dirichlet allocation (LDA) model [19]. To perform complex tasks such as simultaneous aspect extraction and sentiment analysis or simultaneous aspect extraction and categorization, one can employ combination of different approaches such as maximum entropy and latent Dirichle allocation [20] or semi supervised model with the topic modeling approach when user provides some seed words for a few aspect categories [21].

3   System Description

We participated into two evaluation tasks:

- Extract the explicit aspects, i.e. extract a part of the object under analysis or one of its characteristics such as engine for the domain of automobiles or service for the domain of restaurants,
- Extract all the aspects of the object under analysis that includes extraction of explicit aspects, implicit aspects (an aspect + the authors unambiguous opinion on the aspect) and sentiment facts (when the author uses no opinion expressions but specifies a fact that unambiguously reveals his or her attitude to the object).

To extract opinion targets or aspects from sentences containing opinion expressions, we utilized CRF. CRF shows comparatively good results for the task of aspect extraction from reviews. For instance, for SemEval-2014 shared task

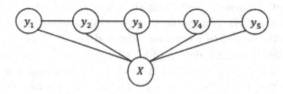

Fig. 1. An example of conditional random field

related to aspect-based Sentiment Analysis, two best results have been obtained by systems that were based on CRF [22].

Conditional Random field is a type of discriminative undirected probabilistic graphical model. It is used to encode known relationships between observations and construct consistent interpretations. Let $X = (x_1, ..., x_n)$ be the sequence of observed data (speaking in terms of our tasks these are tokens of a review). Let $Y = (y_1, ..., y_n)$ be the sequence of random variables associated with the vertices of the graph G (labels we want to learn to predict). Therefore in our case a graphics model looks as it shown in Fig. 1.

CRFs models a conditional probability p(Y|X) over hidden sequence Y given observation sequence X. That is the conditional model is trained to label an unknown observation sequence X by selecting the hidden sequence Y which maximizes p(Y|X) [5]. Than the conditional distribution p(Y|X) can be formalized as Formula 1:

$$P(Y|X) = \frac{1}{Z(X)} exp(\sum_{c \in C} \lambda_c f_c(y_c, X)) \quad , \tag{1}$$

where, C is a set of all graphs cliques, f_c set of all features, λ_c is its corresponding weight. $Z(x)$ is a normalization function (Formula 2):

$$Z(X) = \sum_{y} exp(\sum_{c \in C} \lambda_c f_c(y_c, X)). \tag{2}$$

There are two main advantages of CRFs:

1. their conditional nature, resulting in the relaxation of the independence assumptions of the observed variables,
2. CRFs avoid the label bias problem. As CRF has a single exponential model for the joint probability of the entire sequence of labels given the observation sequence (not only one given state). Hence, even if some data is missing, the observation sequence can still be labeled with less number of features. That is usefull for us as trainig collection is limited.

We utilized the Mallet tool as a software implementation of CRF [23].

3.1 Labeling

Jakob and Gurevych [13] represented the possible labels following the Inside-Outside-Begin (IOB) labelling schema: B-Target, identifying the beginning of an opinion target; I-Target, identifying the continuation of a target, and O for other (non-target) tokens. As we used sequential labeling, we assigned a label to each word in the sentence where s-e indicated the start of an explicit aspect term, c-e indicated the continuation of an explicit aspect term, s-i indicated the start of an implicit aspect term, c-i indicated the continuation of an implicit aspect term (just as for facts-terms: s-f for start fact, c-f for continuation fact) and O indicated a non-aspect term. To extract morphological features (e.g. POS and lemma) described in the next section, we used TreeTagger for the Russian language [24]. We also noticed that automobile brands are often written in the Latin alphabet and/or contain numbers such as "Nissan Micra" or "VAZ 2109". So for the collection of cars we added the rules that made it possible to recognize a full car name (or brand) as a single explicit term. As you can see in Table 4, this had some positive results – the System was ranked 3rd by the exact matching variant of F-measure. We also converted all the capital letters into lowercase as the software tools may take "Engine" and "engine" as two different aspects, which is not true. However we show a drawback of lowercase converting in the section error analysis.

3.2   Features

Word. We used the token itself and its neighboring words in a [-1, +1] window to get more information on the context the word is used in.

POS. The part-of-speech (POS) tag of the current token was used as a feature. Aspect terms are often expressed by nouns. POS tagging adds useful information on the part of speech the word belong to. To determine the part of speech we used TreeTagger – a tool that performs complete morphological analysis. We reduce complete morphologic analysis up to the parts of speech such as N for "engine" and V for "driving".

Lemma. The lemma of the current token was used as a feature. Due to the enormous number of word-forms in Russian language we added the normal form of word as a feature. To extract lemmas we also utilized a TreeTagger.

3.3   Architecture

We built the system which was tested under two conditions:

- **Condition 1:** CRF with all the above-mentioned labels. We used s-e, c-e and O labels for explicit aspect extraction to perform the Task A and s-e, c-e, s-i, c-i, s-f, c-f, O labels to extract all the aspect terms for the Task B.
- **Condition 2:** Combination of the results of two CRFs – CRF for extraction of explicit aspect terms and CRF for extraction of implicit aspect terms + sentiment facts terms (but not explicit). Task A was performed using only condition 1 and Task B – using both conditions.

Further in the paper we would use shortness "system 1" for system under condition 1 and "system 2" for system under condition 2.

4   Results

The results of Tasks A and B were evaluated by F-measure. Two cases of
F-measure were calculated: exact matching and partial matching. Macro F1-
measure in this case means calculating F1-measure for every review and averag-
ing the obtained values. To measure partial matching, the intersection between
gold standard and extracted term was calculated for every term. Tables 2 to
6 demonstrate the System performance of Task A and Tables 7 to 9 refer to
performance of Task B. The results of the System were compared to the baseline
and the two best results of SentiRuEval participants.

Table 2. Task A results, Restaurant
domain, exact matching

System	Precision	Recall	F-measure
baseline	0.5570	0.6903	0.6084
$No1$	0.7237	0.5738	0.6319
$No2$	0,6358	0.6327	0.6266
Word+POS	0.6610	0.5150	0.5704
+Lemma	0.6674	0.5417	0.5899

Table 3. Task A results, Restaurant
domain, partial matching

System	Precision	Recall	F-measure
baseline	0.6580	0.696	0.6651
$No1$	0.8078	0.6165	0.7280
$No2$	0.7458	0.7114	0.7191
Word+POS	0.7380	0.5630	0.6277
+Lemma	0.7485	0.5937	0.6520

Table 4. Task A results, automobile
domain, exact matching

System	Precision	Recall	F-measure
baseline	0.5747	0.6287	0.5941
$No1$	0.7600	0.6218	0.6761
$No2$	0.6619	0.6560	0.6513
Word+POS	0.7109	0.5454	0.6075
+Lemma	0.7040	0.5785	0.6256

Table 5. Task A results, automobile
domain, partial matching

System	Precision	Recall	F-measure
baseline	0.7449	0.6724	0.6966
$No1$	0.7917	0.7272	0.7482
$No2$	0.8561	0.6551	0.7304
Word+POS	0.7970	0.6047	0.6747
+Lemma	0.7908	0.6485	0.6991

As it can be observed from Table 1-4, the System demonstrated high precision
level in both domains (2nd position in Task A for both domains: automobiles
and restaurants by Precision metrics). It shall be noted that in the domain
of cars the results were better when lemma feature was not in useit may be
concerned to pre-processing rules to the automobiles collection. In Task B system
showed rather high precision level (see Table 5-8). In the domain of restaurants
system 1 (condition 1) with word+pos+lemma features ranked 3rd amount all
the participants by the partial matching case of F-measure.

Table 6. Task B results, Restaurant domain, exact matching

System	Precision	Recall	F-measure
baseline	0.5466	0.6477	0.5872
$No1$	0.6094	0.6006	0.6001
$No2$	0.7336	0.5132	0.5962
System 1 Word+POS	0.6393	0.4563	0.5258
+Lemma	0.6398	0.4872	0.5469
System 2 Word+POS	0.6521	0.4585	0.5316
+Lemma	0.6715	0.4916	0.5615

Table 7. Task B results, Restaurant domain, partial matching

System	Precision	Recall	F-measure
baseline	0.6716	0.5931	0.6193
$No1$	0.7562	0.6108	0.6679
$No2$	0.6687	0.6371	0.6452
System 1 Word+POS	0.7104	0.4934	0.5692
+Lemma	0.7099	0.5294	0.5953
System 2 Word+POS	0.7246	0.4579	0.5478
+Lemma	0.7524	0.4936	0.5851

Table 8. Task B results, automobile domain, exact matching

System	Precision	Recall	F-measure
baseline	0.5979	0.5896	0.5886
$No1$	0.7701	0.5535	0.6366
$No2$	0.6563	0.6164	0.6301
System 1 Word+POS	0.6908	0.4763	0.5561
+Lemma	0.6706	0.5187	0.5781
System 2 Word+POS	0.7190	0.4821	0.5683
+Lemma	0.7012	0.5204	0.5893

Table 9. Task B results, automobile domain, partial matching

System	Precision	Recall	F-measure
baseline	0.7833	0.6060	0.6743
$No1$	0.8143	0.6510	0.7148
$No2$	0.7954	0.6470	0.7042
System 1 Word+POS	0.7936	0.532	0.6255
+Lemma	0.7773	0.5848	0.6561
System 2 Word+POS	0.8086	0.5100	0.6130
+Lemma	0.7824	0.5582	0.6389

5   Error Analysis

An analysis of the errors indicated some common mistakes: not recognized and excessively recognized. In general there is one more type of error for the task of aspect extraction – partially recognized aspect terms. Due to provided evaluation scripts we wont be able to observe third type of mistake. From Table 10, we can find that a major bunch of errors is related to not recognized aspect terms. We isolated four types of our systems' errors.

5.1   Technical Errors

Special Symbols. Our system does not perform well when dealing with sequences containing markup characters like ""Caesar" salad" ("Салат "цезарь"").. In such cases the system returns only a part of an aspect: ""Caesar salad" ("Салат "цезарь") without the closing """.

Table 10. Error type distribution for the task A (exact matching).

	Restaurants	Automobiles
Word+POS		
not recognized	65%	68%
excessively recognized	35%	32%
Word+POS+lemma		
not recognized	63%	65%
excessively recognized	37%	35%

Lower Case. As it was mentioned in Section 3.1 all the capital letters were converted into lowercase. But we did not leave out that some of specific terms were lost. For instance "TO" (technical maintenance in the automobile domain) and "то" (the particle).

5.2   No Recognition

Shortcuts. Our system cannot find shotcuts i.e. rubles ⤳ rub ⤳ R. The dictionary of frequently used shortcuts could help to remedy this.

Listings. The system deals with listings quite poorle. It found some listed items but not all of them, i.e "Vegetables, **salads "Caesar"**, salmon" (the item that system has found is shown in bold).

5.3   Partial Recognition

Before Head Word. The system can better deal with nouns and more precisely extract nouns as an aspect term: "Добавляла **вина**" ("pour **wine**"). However we found several non-noun terms which were partly recognized by the system: "Официант **хамил**" ("The waiter **was rude**").

After Head Word. We have also found that not only terms before the head word cause difficulties for the system, but also terms after it i.e. "**местечко** вуглу" ("**a place** in the corner"). It should be noted that there were relatively fewer mistakes than the mistakes of the previous type.

5.4   Excessive Recognition

Our system does not always precisely deal with named entities, i.e. sometimes it extracts names like "Александр" ("Alexander") which are not an aspect term.

It can also be observed from the Table 10 that adding Lemmas as a CRF feature leads to increasing excessively recognized terms. We compared system under two conditions and found out that the second one can better deal with collocations. For instance, it extracted "duck soup" ("суп из утки") instead of just "soup" ("суп") extracted by the system under Condition 1. However collocations can be problematic even under Condition 2 because occasionally the system can extract too many irrelevant terms. For example "sea food pasta to husband" ("пасту с морепродуктами, мужу").

In the future, we would like to experiment with additional statistical and lexical features of CRF. Using additional text collections can also make further improvements.

6   Conclusion

We presented aspect extraction system built on the basis of conditional random field algorithm. Realization of these system demonstrated that preprocessing and using even a small set of features for CRF shows comparatively good results by the overall F-measure. The performance of our system was comparable to the best results of SentiRuEval participants. Subsequently we are going to add statistical informaion as a CRFs' feature. We are also planning to make a research and find a way to improve the recall results without reduce a precision.

References

1. Pang, B., Lee, L., Vaithyanathan, S.: Thumbs up?: sentiment classification using machine learning techniques. In: Proceedings of the ACL-02 Conference on Empirical Methods in Natural Language Processing, vol. 10, pp. 79–86 (2002)
2. Rubtsova, Y.V.: Development and research domain independent sentiment classifier. SPIIRAS Proceedings 5(36), 59–77 (2014)
3. Turney, P.D.: Thumbs up or thumbs down?: semantic orientation applied to unsupervised classification of reviews. In: Proceedings of the 40th Annual Meeting on Association for Computational Linguistics, pp. 417–424. ACL (2002)
4. Wilson, T., Wiebe, J., Hoffmann, P.: Recognizing contextual polarity: An exploration of features for phrase-level sentiment analysis. Computational linguistics 35(3), 399–433 (2009)
5. Zhang, L., Liu, B.: Aspect and entity extraction for opinion mining. In: Data Mining and Knowledge Discovery for Big Data, pp. 1–40 (2014)
6. Liu, B.: Sentiment analysis and opinion mining. Synthesis Lectures on Human Language Technologies 5(1), 1–167 (2012)
7. Marrese-Taylor, E., Velásquez, J.D., Bravo-Marquez, F.: A novel deterministic approach for aspect-based opinion mining in tourism products reviews. Expert Systems with Applications 41(17), 7764–7775 (2014)
8. Loukachevitch, N.V., Blinov, P.D., Kotelnikov, E.V., Rubtsova, Y.V., Ivanov, V.V., Tutubalina, E.: SentiRuEval: testing object-oriented sentiment analysis systems in russian. In: Proceedings of International Conference Dialog (2015)
9. Hu, M., Liu, B.: Mining and summarizing customer reviews. In: Proceedings of the Tenth ACM SIGKDD International Conference on Knowledge Discovery and Data Mining, pp. 168–177 (2004)
10. Popescu, A.M., Etzioni, O.: Extracting product features and opinions from reviews. In: Natural Language Processing and Text Mining, pp. 9–28 (2007)

11. Moghaddam, S., Ester, M.: ILDA: interdependent LDA model for learning latent aspects and their ratings from online product reviews. In: Proceedings of the 34th International ACM SIGIR Conference on Research and Development in Information Retrieval, pp. 665–674 (2011)
12. Jin, W., Ho, H.H., Srihari, R.K.: Opinionminer: a novel machine learning system for web opinion mining and extraction. In: Proceedings of the 15th ACM SIGKDD International Conference on Knowledge Discovery and Data Mining, pp. 1195–1204 (2009)
13. Jakob, N., Gurevych, I.: Extracting opinion targets in a single-and cross-domain setting with conditional random fields. In: Proceedings of the 2010 Conference on Empirical Methods in Natural Language Processing, pp. 1035–1045. ACL (2010)
14. Lafferty, J., McCallum, A., Pereira, F.: Conditional random fields: probabilistic models for segmenting and labeling sequence data. In: Proceedings of International Conference on Machine Learning (ICML-2001) (2001)
15. Sutton, C., McCallum, A.: An introduction to conditional random fields for relational learning. In: Introduction to Statistical Relational Learning. MIT Press (2006)
16. Brody, S., Elhadad, N.: An unsupervised aspect-sentiment model for online reviews. In: Human Language Technologies: The 2010 Annual Conference of the North American Chapter of the Association for Computational Linguistics, pp. 804–812 (2010)
17. Titov, I., McDonald, R.: Modeling online reviews with multi-grain topic models. In: Proceedings of the 17th International Conference on World Wide Web, pp. 111–120. ACM (2008)
18. Hofmann, T.: Unsupervised learning by probabilistic latent semantic analysis. Machine learning **42**(1–2), 177–196 (2001)
19. Blei, D.M., Ng, A.Y., Jordan, M.I.: Latent dirichlet allocation. The Journal of Machine Learning Research **3**, 993–1022 (2003)
20. Zhao, W.X., Jiang, J., Yan, H., Li, X.: Jointly modeling aspects and opinions with a MaxEnt-LDA hybrid. In: Proceedings of the 2010 Conference on Empirical Methods in Natural Language Processing, pp. 56–65. ACL (2010)
21. Mukherjee, A., Liu, B.: Aspect extraction through semi-supervised modeling. In: Proceedings of the 50th Annual Meeting of the Association for Computational Linguistics: Long Papers, vol. 1, pp. 339–348 (2012)
22. Pontiki, M., Papageorgiou, H., Galanis, D., Androutsopoulos, I., Pavlopoulos, J., Manandhar, S.: Semeval-2014 task 4: aspect based sentiment analysis. In: Proceedings of the 8th International Workshop on Semantic Evaluation, SemEval 2014, pp. 27–35 (2014)
23. McCallum, A.K.: MALLET: A Machine Learning for Language Toolkit (2002)
24. Sharoff, S., Kopotev, M., Erjavec, T., Feldman, A., Divjak, D.: Designing and evaluating russian tagsets. In: LREC (2008)

A Low Effort Approach to Quantitative Content Analysis

Maria Saburova[(⊠)] and Archil Maysuradze

Faculty of Computational Mathematics and Cybernetics,
Lomonosov Moscow State University, 2nd Educational Building, CMC Faculty,
MSU, Leninskie Gory, GSP-1, Moscow 119991, Russia
saburova.mi@yandex.ru, maysuradze@cs.msu.su

Abstract. We propose a workflow for an individual sociologist to be able to use quantitative content analysis in small-scale short-term research projects. The key idea of the approach is to generate a domain-oriented dictionary for researchers with limited resources. The workflow starts like a typical one and then deviates to include content analysis. First, the researcher performs deductive analysis which results in an interview guide. Second, the researcher conducts the small number of interviews to collect a domain-oriented labelled text corpus. Third, a domain-oriented dictionary is generated for the following content analysis. We propose and compare a number of methods to automatically extract a domain-oriented dictionary from a labelled corpus. Some properties of the proposed workflow are empirically studied based on a sociological research on volunteering in Russia.

Keywords: Domain-oriented dictionary · Quantitative content analysis · Term extraction · Low effort sociological workflow

1 Introduction

1.1 Traditional Content Analysis

Content analysis is a research technique for systematic analysis of written communication. Its basic idea is that the large number of words (text units) contained in a piece of text are classified into content categories of interest [6].

Traditional workflow of quantitative content analysis comprises many steps. One of the main concepts of content analysis is a coding scheme — a list of content categories and a procedure which classifies text units into the content categories. Our research focuses on the workflow steps where the coding scheme is developed and utilized.

1. To create a coding scheme, researchers may follow a "deductive" or "inductive" approach. The inductive approach involves automatic derivation of categories based on unlabelled data. The deductive approach is based on comprehensive theoretical considerations. The researchers begin with analytical, or content, categories. These main categories can be further divided

© Springer International Publishing Switzerland 2015
P. Klinov and D. Mouromtsev (Eds.): KESW 2015, CCIS 518, pp. 168–181, 2015.
DOI: 10.1007/978-3-319-24543-0_13

into sub-categories at various levels of hierarchy. It can be said that the coding scheme is the result of the operationalization of the theoretical considerations [8].

In this paper, we are going to address the problem of text unit assignment to categories. That means that sociological projects with predefined categories are easier to adapt to our workflow. The researcher is free to use any approach to develop a list of content categories, and the deductive approach seems to require less effort and less data.

2. Then the researchers define the basic text units to be classified (e.g. individual words, phrases, or paragraphs). Typically researchers tend to classify individual terms in text windows around the objects under study.

3. After that, it is required to develop a code guide. The code guide is essentially a set of categorization rules. Typically the code guide is intended for human coders — experts who perform categorization. A type of the code guide which is convenient for automated processing is a domain-oriented dictionary. The dictionary contains a collection of text units, each unit being exclusively associated with one content category. This dictionary becomes a part of the coding scheme. In the paper we reduce the problem of collecting the dictionary to the problem of text unit assignment to categories based on labelled text units (supervised scenario).

4. When the coding scheme is made, it can be applied to a text corpus by the coders. To apply the coding scheme to the texts in the coherent way the coders follow coding instructions and consult coding examples.

5. The last step of quantitative content analysis is called *quantification*. The occurrences of categorized text units are totalled over the text corpus. There are different software solutions for the step. Automation of the previous steps constitutes a pressing problem.

These steps reveal the complexity of content analysis utilization. It is difficult to develop a coding scheme, especially a dictionary for a code guide. A lot of people are required to analyse large text collections, such as books, essays, news articles, speeches and other written material. For coding step it is also required to teach people to asses text units coherently. In order to secure a good quality of the data a coding workshop should be held, where the coders are familiarized with the coding scheme and made aware of potential pitfalls. And many assessors should be included in this process because of the requirement of quality.

Manual development of the coding scheme often results in a list of questions that should be answered by assessors for each text. Usually the questions are subtle and require the understanding of implicit topics and sentiments, so they cannot be answered automatically using machine learning or natural language processing techniques. On the other hand, this is also an advantage of this method, because it enables researchers to identify implicit concepts and their properties. In contrast, coding using dictionary can be automated. There are many software for quantitative content analysis: Concordance 2.0, Diction 5.0, General Inquirer, TextAnalyst, WordStat v5.0 and so on [14]. Most of the programs use a standard large dictionary (which is inappropriate for domain-specific projects) or demand the dictionary from users. Therefore the main complexity in this type of research is to obtain the domain-oriented dictionary. Our research aims to automate the domain-specific dictionary creation by means of machine learning. To perform it, we had to recognize and solve nonstandard type of machine learning problem — feature distribution among content categories.

1.2 Low Effort Workflow for Individuals

There are many individual researchers who want to use content analysis in their studies. These researchers have little resources and cannot afford many assessors. Their researches are limited in time and conducted in specific field. Therefore individual researchers want to use traditional content analysis, but they have no enough resources or time.

The goal of our work is to provide individual researchers with a low effort content analysis workflow. At present, a typical workflow of an individual researcher includes interviewing of a small number of respondents. We claim that the data collected during the interview design and the interviewing may be used to develop a domain-specific dictionary.

The complete interviewing process includes the following steps [12]:

1. Thematizing: Clarifying the purpose of the interviews and the concepts to be explored.
2. Designing: Laying out the process through which youll accomplish your purpose. This should also include ethical considerations.
3. Interviewing: Doing the actual interviews.
4. Transcribing: Creating a written text of the interviews.
5. Analyzing: Determining the meaning of the information gathered in the interviews in relation to the purpose of the study.
6. Verifying: Examining the reliability and validity of the information gathered.
7. Reporting: Telling others what you have learned or discovered.

Let us compare the two workflows. On one hand, there is a labour-intensive content analysis method and computer programs developed specifically for this process. However, such programs require a domain-oriented dictionary. On the other hand, there are low effort sociological researches that collect interviews. We are going to use the collected interview data as a labelled text corpus.

These workflows have steps analogous with each other. Interview design corresponds to the deductive step of the coding scheme creation in content analysis. Another similarity between the semi-structured interview analysis and the content analysis is that main categories and particular questions are selected during coding scheme development. A question list is composed as a result of coding scheme analysis and can be used for the interviewing process. However, in small sociological researches it is common to summarize materials obtained from a small number of respondents only. If the researches were given a tool to process large data timely, they would study large text corpora.

To easily use content analysis algorithms in low-effort researches, we propose a workflow when an individual researcher proceeds to automatic quantitative content analysis after interviewing and transcribing steps. To make it possible, we propose a method of automatic construction of a domain-specific dictionary that only uses data collected during the interviewing. The method can be performed on a regular personal computer.

The rest of the paper is organized as follows. In Section 2 we formalize the notion of dictionary. In Section 3 we review related work. Section 4 describes particular qualities of the problem. Section 5 introduces a tripartite data model which underlies our formal constructions. The mathematical description of proposed methods resides in Section 6. In Section 7 we describe experimental setup and discuss the results. Section 8 concludes the paper.

2 Dictionary: The Lexical Core of Categories

In our research, a dictionary is a list of the units that should be unambiguously assigned to one of the categories. A part of dictionary, which related to one category, we perceive as lexical core of category. This idea is formalized by the following statements:

1. The presence of units is the text marker. Then marker is a binary feature.
2. Dictionary unit presence is a category reference indicator. Some markers are assigned to a class and each of them are assigned directly to one class.
3. We consider the problem of creating a dictionary as the problem of distributing the features, which occurs in data mining.

The problem of feature distribution by classes consists in the follows. Given a training set in which each object has a feature description and a class label from a finite set of predefined classes. Requires every feature assigned uniquely to either one of the predefined classes or special additional class. Interpretation of additional class depends on the subject area.

Note that in this formulation there is no initial marking of features relating to classes. Such markings can be used for quality evaluation of the solution.

In the texts categorization area [17] and the content analysis [7,18] the considered problem can be interpreted as the problem of lexical (semantic) core of category separation. In this case, the objects are text fragments, classes are text collections categories, features show the presence of lexical markers in texts (e.g., single words, phrases, specific terms). Such descriptions are typical for the bag-of-words and vector space models [13]. The additional class are sometimes referred to a common vocabulary class.

3 Related Work

3.1 Lexical Core Definition

Lexical core of a category is defined as a set of such lexical markers (words, phrases, terms) that their presence in the text clearly assigns the text to this category. In that way, the markers from the lexical core of category are significant for this category and at the same time are not significant for the text assignment to other categories. In this work we do not consider the case where a lexical marker is significant for multiple categories. As well, "negative" markers are not considered too. Negative marker is a marker such that its presence or absence prohibits to assign the text to a certain category. If the word presence forbids a class, these negative markers are called negative keywords. Excluding negative markers from the study are due to the fact that they are not well-established in data mining cases because of reducing the generalization ability.

To better describe the concept of lexical core, it is useful to compare it with the semantic core, which is used in the subject area of search engine optimisation. Semantic core of object is the set of markers that describes the object and which reference in the search request leads to object selection in the search results. For example, site position in search engine results depends on the completeness and accuracy of the semantic core development [3]. Notice the following differences between lexical and semantic kernels. First, in our work we talk about class cores while in the field of search engine optimisation focuses on the object cores. Secondly, we work with markers that are determined by the objects creators (e.g. author keywords), and in the field of search engine optimisation we work with markers used by potential object users. The differences between the lexical and semantic core are concerned with input data, but the prospective outcomes (i.e. markers sets) are similar. Therefore, it is rational to consider both formulations.

3.2   Lexical Core vs. Semantic Core

In the literature the term "lexical core" is used in various other senses that are not relevant to this work. To avoid displacement of concepts, we list these alternative meanings. *Lexical language core* is often mentioned in linguistics and is defined as the set of core lexical units that are opposed to the peripheral lexical units [11]. *Semantic kernel* is used in machine learning as a *meaningful* measure of closeness in the documents space [4][9]. In the information retrieval area, the term *semantic core* is defined as a special data structure, that describes the contents of the document. This semantic core is a semantic network with vertices (keywords and phrases selected from the document), and the weight between connection nodes is calculated based on some similarity measure [5].

3.3   Quality Measures for Lexical Cores

In the above mentioned papers on lexical/semantical kernels the quality scores are usually specified for the main problem and not for the lexical kernel itself.

Involving assessors is another method to control the quality of the dictionaries. Assessors evaluate words that were selected to the dictionaries. There are two kinds of this evaluation process.

In first method assessors receive a list of all units and a list of all categories. They should choose one category for every unit. The second method is devoted to the quality assessment of the words marked by the algorithm.

3.4   Learning Topic Models

Topic modeling area is quite close to out research. Although basic problem statements have important differences: topic modeling is concerned with clustering of words and documents by topics that are unknown in advance. The topic model of text documents collection determines how topics are distributed in each document and which words (terms) determine every topic [20]. An important difference between our problem statements and topic modeling statements is that the number of topics (and especially their list) is not known in advance in most applications and is one of the most important parameters for setting up a topic model. Also, unlike the studied problem, in the topic modeling statement it is required to find the distribution of each word on all topics. That is, the probabilities of belonging to each cluster are determined for every feature. However, there are methods, that add the requirement of unambiguity the word-topic relation, for example, methods of regularization. The combination of regularizers usually requires structural adjustment of model [10], although more efficient approaches were proposed recently [19].

There are topic quality measures that are used in topic modeling and can be used to evaluate dictionary quality. Such measures are usually internal or external evaluations of topic coherence (interpretability) [16]. Topic interpretability is estimated subjectively. Topic quality measure should be well correlated with *interpretability by experts* measure. The pointwise mutual information method is recommended in [15]. The general idea is that the topic is called coherent if the most frequent topic words appear close to each other nonrandomly in the collection. In the current research we can consider dictionary coherence. If the words in the dictionary are ranked, then we can consider the coherence of the dictionary top part (for example, top-10, top-100). Also a part of words assigned to the common vocabulary can be considered as a quality measure.

Anchor words idea was suggested [2] in topic modeling recently. Anchor word has non-zero probability only in one topic. If a document contains this anchor word, then it is guaranteed that the corresponding topic is among the set of topics used to generate the document [1]. Therefore the set of anchor words can be interpreted as topic dictionary.

4   Motivation

Let us describe the properties of considered problem.

1. In our problem statements the results will obtain their own interpretation and value. In similar research considered in literature features are assigned to classes only to increase classification quality.
2. We are required to make a decision on each feature, i.e. it is necessary to distribute all features among categories. This condition is not required in most of publications. Usually most of features are rejected.

3. In our research each feature should be labelled uniquely. As opposed, in all publications each feature can be labelled with a few classes.
4. The ratio of the number of features to the number of precedents is much greater than in traditional classification problems.
5. We interpret each feature as a positive assessment of the corresponding properties existence. In particular, the marker is interpreted as the presence of some object properties.
6. In our problem statement features have a Boolean type or can be naturally reduced to this type.

Consequently, the problem of feature distribution among classes in the described form has not been investigated previously in the literature. Addressing this gap and proposing methods for solving the problem is the goal of this paper.

Note that our assignment of every feature to exactly one class has no semantic basis; we perform such assigment based on purely statistical properties of the feature. This approach can result in markers that can fit several categories according to common sense. However, our experiments show that most of markers are very reasonable and accepted by experts.

5   Tripartite Data Model

In this study we focus on the problems where features are markers or measures of some properties. Data in such problems can be naturally represented by the relational model using a set of binary relations. We call such model *tripartite* and specified its three components: objects, markers and classes. We also define three binary heterogeneous relations between the units of analysis. The relation is called heterogeneous if it connects different units of analysis.

This model is convenient for formalizing and solving many applied analytical tasks, in particular in sociology, scientometrics, text processing and other fields. Different problems can be formalized according to this model: object classification, class definition of the new object and many others, including markers distribution to the classes. Many problems are defined according to the scheme where two relations are given, and the third should be restored.

The tripartite model formalization can be clarified for the problem of marker distribution among the classes. In this case the relation between markers ans classes becomes functional – it partially maps markers to the original classes. A model where some binary relations are partial mappings, will be called the *tripartite semihard model*.

In the problem of assignment classes to features the binary relation between objects and classes is a (total) mapping, and the relation between objects and markers is arbitrary (many to many). Degenerate situation where the object is not associated with any marker or the marker is not associated with any object, will not be considered. In other words, the relation between documents and markers should be left-full and right-full.

6 Dictionary Construction Methods

6.1 Function as a Classifier Argument

In the studied problem statement, the markup is given for objects rather than features. Therefore, we cannot immediately state the problem of markers classification and should start with reducing the problem of feature classification to the task of object classification. For this reason we propose an information model where partial function from attributes to the classes is included explicitly as a parameter. In other words, the classifier assigns the feature to the class. Required partial function will be obtained automatically after fitting classifier of this model to the data.

We introduce the following notation:

1. T — the number of features, t — feature number from 1 till T,
2. I — the number of labeled objects, i — object number from 1 till I,
3. J — the number of classes, j — class number from 1 till J,
4. a_t — class number, which is mapped with feature t, required function,
5. f_{it} — value of feature t for object i, in particular, 0 or 1 for binary relation object-feature,
6. c_i — real object label i.

We use linear information model as one of the simplest. We introduce non-negative feature's weight, which is marked as w_t. It is required to classify the object with features $f_1, \ldots, f_T$. The estimate of object belonging to the class k is calculated as the sum of the weights products and values of those features t, which is assigned to this class:

$$\Gamma_k = \sum_{t=1}^{T} w_t f_t [a_t = k].$$

We interpret the feature values here as positive measures of some properties. Decision rule assigns the object to the class with the highest rating:

$$A = argmax_k \Gamma_k.$$

6.2 Multiclass SVM Analogue Method

We describe now learning method for algorithm from the information model. Parameters $\{a_t\}$ and $\{w_t\}$ will be configured by solving margin maximizing problem. Introduced method has lots of similarities with multiclass SVM. Margin is defined as the difference between the score for the real class and the maximum estimation among the other classes.

$$\frac{1}{2}||w||^2 + C \sum_{i,j} \xi_{ij} \to \min_{w, \{\xi_{ij}\}_{i,j}} \tag{1}$$

$$\sum_t w_t f_{it}([a_t = c_i] - [a_t = j]) \geq 1 - \xi_{ij}, \ \forall i, \ \forall j \neq c_i \tag{2}$$

$$w_t \geq 0, \ \forall t \tag{3}$$

$$\xi_{ij} \geq 0, \ \forall i, \ \forall j \neq c_i \tag{4}$$

Slack variables ξ_{ij} are introduced here to deal with the case when classes are not linearly separable. When sample is linearly separable, problem can be simplified:

$$\frac{1}{2}||w||^2 \rightarrow \min$$
$$\sum_t w_t f_{it}([a_t = c_i] - [a_t = j]) \geq 1, \ \forall i, \ \forall j \neq c_i \tag{5}$$
$$w_t \geq 0, \ \forall t$$

Dual problem is defined for solving this problem.

$$\sum_{i,j} \alpha_{ij} - \frac{1}{2}||\beta_t + X_{ijt}^T \alpha_{ij}||^2 \rightarrow \max$$
$$0 \leq \alpha_{i,j} \leq C, \tag{6}$$
$$\beta_t \geq 0, \ \forall t$$

Here α_{ij} и β_t is dual variables, X_{ijt} is defined as

$$X_{ijt} = f_{it}([a_t = c_i] - [a_t = j]). \tag{7}$$

After dual problem solving, it is needed to return to initial features.

$$\beta_t = 0, where X_{ijt}^T \alpha_{ij} \geq 0$$
$$\beta_t = -X_{ijt}^T \alpha_{ij}, where X_{ijt}^T \alpha_{ij} < 0. \tag{8}$$

Initial features can be find from formula:

$$w_t = \beta_t + X_{ijt}^T \alpha_{ij}. \tag{9}$$

The dual problem is a linear programming problem, when a_i are fixed. Interior-point method can be used to solution this problem.

Coordinate descent method is used to train a_i:

1. The algorithm starts from initial point: every feature is assigned to the class in which it often occurs.
2. On each iteration random feature s is selected. For this feature look over all classes for which this feature vote.
3. Weights w_t are optimized for each of these classes, when a_t are held.
4. Class a_s with the maximal value of the dual problem functional is assigned to the feature.
5. The procedure is repeated until convergence or until the specified number of iterations will be reached.

6.3   One-vs.-one SVM in Relation to the Multiclass Problem

Here we propose another dictionary development algorithm. This algorithm based on the same idea of feature distribution during object classification. We consider SVM algorithm for binary classification problem:

$$
\begin{aligned}
&\|w\|^2 + C\sum_{i=1}^{\ell}\xi_i \to \min_{w,\xi}; \\
&y_i\langle w, x_i \rangle \geq 1 - \xi_i, \quad \forall i = 1,\ldots,\ell; \\
&\xi_i \geq 0, \quad \forall i = 1,\ldots,\ell.
\end{aligned} \tag{10}
$$

The problem of multiclass classification can be reduced to the set of binary classification problems. We use one-vs.-one scheme:

1. We train binary classifiers a_{sk} for all classes pairs $s \neq k$;
2. Each of them distinguishes documents of class s from documents of class k;
3. Weights w_t^{sk} is considering to each classifier;
4. If $w_t^{sk} > 0$, then feature t vote for class s, else k;
5. Feature t is assigned to class s, if $w_t^{sk} > 0$ for more than a half pairs $k \neq s$.

7   Experiments

7.1   Data Description

We chose responses to interview questions for our experiments. The data was obtained from the project "Resource of avantgarde groups volunteerism for Russian modernization", which was implemented by the Fund "Public opinion" in collaboration with researchers with the use of state support funds allocated by the Institute for public planning grant in accordance with the decree of the President of the Russian Federation from 02 March 2011 No. 127rp[1].

The data consists of 20 interviews with leaders of volunteering organizations. Interview categories are: "Supervisor portrait", "Objectives and content of the organization's activities", "The Concept of volunteerism", "Working with volunteers", "Volunteers portrait", "Incentives and barriers to volunteering activities".

Each document was divided into 6 sections in accordance with the categories. Each section was considered as one object, for a total of 120 objects. Each interview category represents one class. We have normalized each word in the text (note that different Russian words can have similar English translation, which is the result of language specifics and not because of normalization problems). Stop-words were not excluded for two reasons: (1) methods were designed in such way that stop-words should be assigned to special additional class and (2) presence of stop-words in our domain-specific texts may have some signal. After text normalization and duplicates filtering the corpus consists of 7241 word.

Assessor labeling was used for dictionary quality evaluation. Experts reviewed each word in the dictionary and evaluated a relation between the word and

---

[1] The data can be provided by the Fund "Public Opinion" on request: fom@fom.ru

Table 1. Dictionary produced by "Multiclass SVM analogue" method. There are 6 categories. For each category the first 18 words are shown. Words are ordered by their score (not shown). For each word experts assessed whether the word belongs to the category. The columns display Russian transliteration, English translation, and precision at corresponding level. Note that different Russian words may have equal English translations. Russian words are normalized.

Supervisor portrait			Objectives and content of the organization's activities			The Concept of volunteerism		
special'nost'	specialty	100%	finansirovanie	financing	100%	nazyvaju	call	100%
uchus'	learn	100%	itog	summary	100%	nazvat'	call	100%
skol'ko	how much	67%	reshenie	solution	100%	razovyj	one	100%
nemnogo	a little	50%	budushhee	future	100%	ponjatie	the concept	100%
sozdanie	creation	60%	istochnik	source	100%	obshhestvennik	public man	100%
gde	where	67%	voznikaju	arise	83%	bezvozmezdnyj	free	100%
ozhidanie	waiting	71%	zasluga	merit	86%	aktivist	activist	100%
universitet	University	75%	poslednij	last	75%	inogda	sometimes	100%
okonchanie	the end	78%	naibolee	the most	67%	znachimyj	significant	100%
god	year	70%	reshit'	to solve	70%	sistematicheskij	systematic	100%
reshil	decided	73%	cel'	goal	73%	dobrovol'chestvo	volunteering	100%
davno	long	75%	trudnost'	the difficulty	75%	social'no	social	100%
lichno	personally	77%	vlast'	power	77%	jepizodicheskij	episodic	100%
opravdalsja	justified	79%	vtoroj	second	71%	darit'	to give	100%
objazannost'	duty	80%	sposob	method	73%	schitaju	think	100%
rasskazal	told	81%	postavit'	to put	75%	besplatnyj	free	100%
institut	Institute	82%	stavlju	put	71%	mezhdu	between	94%
posle	after	78%	reshat'	to solve	72%	opredelenie	definition	94%
Working with volunteers			Volunteers portrait			Incentives and barriers to volunteering activities		
shtatnyj	staffing	100%	chashhe	more often	0%	meshaju	disturb	100%
dovolen	happy	100%	muzhchina	man	50%	otnoshus'	am	50%
navyk	skill	100%	zhenshhina	woman	67%	municipal'nyj	municipal	67%
special'nyj	special	100%	stanovljus'	become	75%	gosudarstvennyj	state	75%
proishozhu	happen	80%	molodoj	young	80%	prestizhen	prestigious	80%
internet	Internet	83%	dumaju	think	67%	naselenie	population	83%
pishu	write	86%	dobryj	good	71%	bol'shinstvo	most	86%
vazhno	important	88%	starshe	older	75%	modno	fashionable	88%
obojtis'	do	89%	sluchaj	case	67%	struktura	structure	89%
obraz	the way	90%	edinyj	single	60%	strana	country	90%
lichnyj	personal	91%	portret	portrait	64%	kazhetsja	it seems	82%
privlekat'	to attract	92%	procent	percentage	67%	doverie	trust	83%
meroprijatie	the event	92%	narisovat'	draw	69%	gorod	the city	85%
dorog	roads	86%	zhena	wife	64%	resurs	resource	86%
jetap	stage	87%	duh	the spirit	60%	ispol'zujushhij	using	87%
bez	without	81%	politicheskij	political	63%	dobrozhelatelen	friendly	88%
professional'nyj	professional	82%	religioznyj	religious	65%	doverjaju	trust	88%
sovmestnyj	joint	83%	blagopoluchnyj	safe	67%	biznes	business	89%

obtained category as 0 or 1. The main difficulty here is that it is hard to evaluate a category for the word without any context. We say that the word belongs to a category if there is a context in which the word is consistent with category name, questions, and comments of this category from interview guide.

7.2 Experimental Results and Discussion

Experimental results represented in 1 are obtained from the first method, which was called "Multiclass SVM analogue" method. Experiment results represented in 2 are obtained from the second method — One-v.s.-one SVM. In these tables the first 18 words of obtained dictionaries are represented. Experts reviewed each word in the dictionary and evaluated a relation between the word and obtained category as 0 or 1; the votes were aggregated by majority vote. Each method allows to calculate an importance of the word:

1. The "Multiclass SVM analogue" method infers a weight for each feature, and we take this weights as feature importances.
2. The "One-v.s.-one SVM" method infers feature weights for each pair (s, k) of classes. We average this weights over all class pairs with $w_t^{sk} > 0$ for each feature, and use this average as an importance value.

The exact value of feature importance has no significant interpretation; we use it only to define the order of words inside each class. Based on this evaluation we

Table 2. Dictionary produced by "One-v.s.-one SVM" method. There are 6 categories. For each category the first 18 words are shown. Words are ordered by their score (not shown). For each word experts assessed whether the word belongs to the category. The columns display Russian transliteration, English translation, and precision at corresponding level. Note that different Russian words may have equal English translations. Russian words are normalized.

Supervisor portrait			Objectives and content of the organization's activities			The Concept of volunteerism		
special'nost'	specialty	100%	itog	summary	100%	aktivist	activist	100%
uchit'sja	to learn	100%	reshenie	solution	100%	nazyvat'	call	100%
skol'ko	how much	100%	finansirovanie	financing	100%	razovyj	one	100%
gde	where	100%	istochnik	source	100%	obshhestvennik	public man	100%
rasskazat'	to tell	100%	budushhee	future	100%	inogda	sometimes	100%
nemnogo	a little	83%	naibolee	the most	83%	social'no	social	100%
posle	after	71%	cel'	goal	86%	znachimyj	significant	100%
sozdanie	creation	75%	trudnost'	the difficulty	88%	ponjatie	the concept	100%
ozhidanie	waiting	78%	zasluga	merit	89%	vozmezdnyj	reimbursable	100%
zanjat'sja	to do	80%	postavit'	to put	90%	jepizodicheskij	episodic	100%
okonchanie	the end	82%	poslednij	last	82%	schitat'	take	100%
universitet	University	83%	sposob	method	83%	sistematicheskij	systematic	100%
potom	then	77%	zametnyj	noticeable	77%	dobrovol'chestvo	volunteering	100%
opravdat'sja	excuses	79%	vlast'	power	79%	platnyj	paid	93%
lichno	personally	80%	voznikat'	to occur	73%	ljuboj	any	87%
god	year	75%	reshat'	to solve	75%	dobrovolec	volunteer	88%
nachat'	to start	76%	novyj	new	71%	mezhdu	between	82%
zakonchit'	finish	78%	vtoroj	second	67%	volontjor	volunteer	83%
Working with volunteers			Volunteers portrait			Incentives and barriers to volunteering activities		
shtatnyj	staffing	100%	chastyj	frequent	0%	meshat'	disturb	100%
navyk	skill	100%	muzhchina	man	50%	otnosit'sja	apply	50%
dovol'nyj	happy	100%	zhenshhina	woman	67%	dobrozhelatel'nyj	friendly	67%
special'nyj	special	100%	portret	portrait	75%	bol'shinstvo	most	75%
internet	Internet	100%	molodoj	young	80%	municipal'nyj	municipal	80%
obojtis'	do	100%	duh	the spirit	67%	gosudarstvennyj	state	83%
jetap	stage	100%	edinyj	single	57%	prestizhnyj	prestigious	86%
kontrolirovat'	control	100%	stanovit'sja	to become	63%	naselenie	population	88%
zatrata	cost	100%	blagopoluchnyj	safe	67%	doverie	trust	89%
stimulirovat'	to stimulate	100%	aktivnyj	active	70%	modno	fashionable	90%
privlekat'	to attract	100%	cennost'	value	73%	razvitie	development	91%
dorogoj	dear	92%	starshij	senior	75%	strana	country	92%
bez	without	85%	jekonomicheski	economically	77%	struktura	structure	92%
privlech'	to attract	86%	apolitichnyj	apolitical	79%	kollega	colleague	93%
vazhno	important	87%	princip	the principle	73%	biznes	business	93%
sotrudnik	employee	88%	gruppa	group	75%	doverjat'	trust	94%
pisat'	write	82%	iskat'	search	71%	kazhetsja	it seems	88%
proishodit'	to happen	78%	vozrast	age	72%	soobshhestvo	community	89%

count the precision at each level. Recall value could also be of interest, but its estimation is too expensive in our setting (the full ground truth domain-oriented dictionary should be build by experts). Dictionaries from two methods are quite similar but not the same. Both of them are consistent with expert's opinion and can be used as a domain-oriented dictionary in low effort sociological workflow.

The first method is very memory-intensive and requires to solve a non-trivial quadratic programming problems which can be time consuming. From that perspective the second method appears to be more suitable in practice.

8   Conclusion

We proposed and implemented a low effort sociological workflow that allows individual researchers to use the quantitative content analysis. The main challenge in this type of research is to obtain the domain-specific dictionary. At present, it is common for an individual researcher to interview respondents. Our technique makes it possible to collect the dictionary from interview data. So, after the interviewing the individual researcher can proceed to qualitative content analysis. The technique may be run on a regular personal computer. The problem of dictionary construction is formalized in terms of feature distribution and two original solutions are proposed. Proposed methods were implemented and tested on real data. Experiment results were consistent with the expert opinion. Future work will shift the focus to user interaction.

Acknowledgments. This work is partially supported by the Russian Foundation for Basic Research projects No. 13-01-00751a and No. 15-07-09214a.

References

1. Arora, S., Ge, R., Halpern, Y., Mimno, D., Moitra, A., Sontag, D., Wu, Y., Zhu, M.: A practical algorithm for topic modeling with provable guarantees. arXiv preprint arXiv:1212.4777 (2012)
2. Arora, S., Ge, R., Moitra, A.: Learning topic models-going beyond svd. In: 2012 IEEE 53rd Annual Symposium on Foundations of Computer Science (FOCS), pp. 1–10. IEEE (2012)
3. Arsirij, E., Antoshhuk, S., Ignatenko, O., Trofimov, B.: Avtomatizacija razrabotki i obnovlenija semanticheskogo jadra sajta s dinamicheskim kontentom. Shtuchni-jintelekt (2012)
4. Basili, R., Cammisa, M., Moschitti, A.: A Semantic Kernel to Classify Texts with Very Few Training Examples. Informatica (Slovenia) **30**, 163–172 (2006)
5. Baziz, M., Boughanem, M., Aussenac-Gilles, N.: Conceptual indexing based on document content representation. In: Crestani, F., Ruthven, I. (eds.) CoLIS 2005. LNCS, vol. 3507, pp. 171–186. Springer, Heidelberg (2005)
6. Bengston, D.N., Xu, Z.: Changing national forest values: a content analysis. Research Paper NC-323. St. Paul, MN: US Dept. of Agriculture, Forest Service, North Central Forest Experiment Station (2006)
7. Berelson, B.: Content analysis in communication research (1952)

8. von dem Berge, B., Poguntke, T., Obert, P., Tipei, D.: Measuring intra-party democracy
9. Cristianini, N., Shawe-Taylor, J., Lodhi, H.: Latent semantic kernels. Journal of Intelligent Information Systems **18**(2–3), 127–152 (2002)
10. Khalifa, O., Corne, D.W., Chantler, M., Halley, F.: Multi-objective topic modeling. In: Purshouse, R.C., Fleming, P.J., Fonseca, C.M., Greco, S., Shaw, J. (eds.) EMO 2013. LNCS, vol. 7811, pp. 51–65. Springer, Heidelberg (2013)
11. Kuznecov, A.M.: Strukturno-semanticheskie parametry v leksike: na materiale anglijskogo jazyka. Nauka (1980)
12. Kvale, S., Brinkmann, S.: Interviews: Learning the craft of qualitative research interviewing. Sage (2009)
13. Manning, C.D., Raghavan, P., Schütze, H., et al.: Introduction to information retrieval, vol. 1. Cambridge university press Cambridge (2008)
14. Neuendorf, K.: Computer content analysis programs (2015). http://academic.csuohio.edu/kneuendorf/content/cpuca/ccap.html (Accessed July 13, 2015])
15. Newman, D., Karimi, S., Cavedon, L.: External evaluation of topic models. In: Australasian Doc. Comp. Symp., 2009. Citeseer (2009)
16. Newman, D., Lau, J.H., Grieser, K., Baldwin, T.: Automatic evaluation of topic coherence. In: Human Language Technologies: The 2010 Annual Conference of the North American Chapter of the Association for Computational Linguistics, pp. 100–108. Association for Computational Linguistics (2010)
17. Sebastiani, F.: Machine learning in automated text categorization. ACM Computing Surveys **34**(1), 1–47 (2002)
18. Stemler, S.: An overview of content analysis. Practical Assessment, Research & Evaluation **7**(17), 137–146 (2001)
19. Voroncov, K.V., Potapenko, A.A.: Reguljarizacija verojatnostnyh tematicheskih modelej dlja povyshenija interpretiruemosti i opredelenija chisla tem. Mezhdunarodnaja konferencija po komp'juternoj lingvistike "Dialog", pp. 676–687 (2014)
20. Vorontsov, K., Potapenko, A.: Pregularization, robustness and sparsity of probabilistic topic models. Computer Research and Modeling **4**(4), 693–706 (2012)

Semantic Clustering of Website Based on Its Hypertext Structure

Vladimir Salin[1]([✉]), Maria Slastihina[1], Ivan Ermilov[2], René Speck[2],
Sören Auer[3], and Sergey Papshev[1]

[1] Saratov State Technical University, 410054 Saratov, Russia
salinvs@gmail.com, masha-fat@yandex.ru, spapshev@list.ru
[2] Universität Leipzig, AKSW/BIS, PO BOX 100920, 04009 Leipzig, Germany
{ivan.ermilov,speck}@informatik.uni-leipzig.de
[3] Universität Bonn, CS/EIS, Römerstraße 164, 53117 Bonn, Germany
auer@cs.uni-bonn.de

Abstract. The volume of unstructured information presented on the
Internet is constantly increasing, together with the total amount of websites and their contents. To process this vast amount of information it
is important to distinguish different clusters of related webpages. Such
clusters are used, for example, for knowledge extraction, named entity
recognition, and recommendation algorithms. A variety of applications
(such as semantic analysis systems, crawlers and search engines) utilizes
semantic clustering algorithms to recognize thematically connected webpages. The majority of them relies on text analysis of the web documents
content, and this leads to certain limitations, such as long processing
time, need of representative text content, or vagueness of natural language. In this article, we present a framework for unsupervised domain
and language independent semantic clustering of the website, which utilizes its internal hypertext structure and does not require text analysis.
As a basis, we represent the hypertext structure as a graph and apply
known flow simulation clustering algorithms to the graph to produce a
set of webpage clusters. We assume these clusters contain thematically
connected webpages. We evaluate our clustering approach with a corpus
of real-world webpages and compare the approach with well-known text
document clustering algorithms.

1 Introduction

The volume of unstructured information presented on the Internet in
human-readable form is constantly increasing, together with the total amount
of websites and their contents. Technologies for extracting, analyzing, automatic accessing and processing data become increasingly more important in
Web with its continuous growth. However, finding and analyzing information
relevant to a problem at hand from such a vast amount of information is still
a major challenge in the Web. With processing such information volumes, it is
important to distinguish collections of thematically connected webpages. Webpage clustering is used widely in a variety of web data extraction applications,

© Springer International Publishing Switzerland 2015
P. Klinov and D. Mouromtsev (Eds.): KESW 2015, CCIS 518, pp. 182–194, 2015.
DOI: 10.1007/978-3-319-24543-0_14

for example, for knowledge extraction, search results representation or recommendation algorithms (i.e. [5,10,11,13]).

The majority of such applications use clustering methods based on text analysis, treating webpages as common text documents, pushing aside their hypertext attributes. This leads to well-known limitations of text analysis techniques (varies for different algorithms), i.e. polysemy-capturing problem, limitations of bag of words model or at least requirement to have a representative amount of text content in the document. In addition, text clustering usually requires a preliminary step of documents indexing, which should be performed for every document in a target collection (thus, requiring full text scan of every webpage). As for treating webpages as text documents, this also implies extracting target text content from the HTML structure of the webpage, excluding template wrapping or other insufficient information. Overall, it becomes reasonable to take into consideration not only text contents of website pages, but also their hypertext features. Search engines usually do this for page ranking to improve search results representation, by analyzing their indexes of incoming external hyperlinks from other websites to the current one and thus indirectly determining its topic. Obviously, it requires a global index of the websites in the Internet, which is unfeasible for the majority of applications.

To tackle the problem of website semantic clustering, we designed and implemented an approach, which clusters webpages using inner hypertext structure of the website. The rationale of our approach is that if we group webpages with a number of hyperlinks inside group higher than hyperlinks to webpages outside the group, we can consider webpages in the group as thematically connected. With partitioning a whole website in these groups, we form a set of semantic clusters of webpages. To perform this partition, we create a link graph of the corresponding hypertext structure as a basis and apply graph-clustering algorithms based on the flow simulation principle (e.g. MCL, BorderFlow)

In particular our contributions are:

- We describe website clustering approach based on the analysis of hypertext structure of the website.
- We design and implement software system, which can construct website model and apply clustering algorithms to provide collections of thematically connected webpages.
- With help of this system, we evaluate our approach and compare it with existing text-based clustering techniques on the corpus of real-world data.
- We provide the source code of the whole framework for further reuse[1].

The paper is structured as follows: In section 2, we outline existing web data extraction systems, clustering techniques utilized in those systems as well as related work on web data extraction for ontology learning and various clustering algorithms. In section 3, we discuss the crawling approach used in our framework we present. In section 4, we present the architecture of our keyword extraction framework and describe its general workflow. We evaluate our framework in section 5 and conclude as well as outline future work in section 6.

---

[1] https://github.com/sainnr/website-graph-cluster

2   Related Work

The research field Web Data Extraction (WDE) is dealing with Information Extraction (IE) on the Web. An outline of existing WDE systems and their application domains is given in [9]. In particular, the authors distinguish enterprise and social web applications. The survey provides insights on the techniques for WDE as well as it gives examples for possible applications. However, it does not delve into the inner workings of WDE systems and thus lacks information on clustering approaches and their usage inside WDE systems. Another WDE work is [8], concentrated solely on an overview of WDE techniques. The authors differentiate two main types of techniques, one is based on wrapper/template induction and an another is automatic extraction.

Another related field of research is IE for Ontology Learning (OL). In [12] Suchanek describes IE from well-formed sources, that are projects like DBpedia [2], YAGO [18] and KOG [21]. All three projects aim to extract information from Wikipedia and to construct an ontology, which supports querying (e.g. SPARQL queries) and question answering. In the same paper Suchanek reports about systems, which are designed to extract information from any web page on the Web: OntoUSP [17], NELL [4] and SOFIE [19]. These systems are centered around NLP processing of web documents using different approaches, but do not perform webpage clustering.

Web clustering has an important role in WDE and Semantic Web areas. The survey [5] explains and compares various clustering techniques applied to web documents. Most of them are text-clustering algorithms, including an efficient Suffix-Tree Clustering (STC) [22]. STC has been improved and become a basis for Lingo [15], both used in Carrot^2 framework[2] [16] and its commercial successor Carrot Search[3]. While these algorithms show good results on corpus of data of average size, they have certain limitations common for all of them: required full-text analysis for every webpage, polysemy-capturing problem, limitations of bag of words model and other.

In contrast to text-based clustering, various systems employ clustering of webpages based on their HTML features. This usually includes webpage's internal document object model (DOM) tree analysis, or mixed approach, where hypertext markup combined with text content during analysis. For instance, EXALG – an information extraction approach described in [1] – clusters webpages into "equivalence classes" by sets of tokens, found in the hypertext markup. As for another example, in [6] the authors utilize clustering based on paths in the DOM trees. Authors also list other DOM structure based clustering approaches. Generally, for these approaches the similarity of webpages to be grouped in one cluster is determined by similarity of various hierarchies in internal HTML structure of each webpage.

Hyperlinks between pages are also playing important role in Web Information Retrieval. Thus, search engines utilize incoming hyperlinks data for website's

---

[2] http://project.carrot2.org
[3] www.carrot-search.com

pages not only to rank webpages in search results [3], but also to determine their topic and similarity with other pages [7]. But for effective analysis with incoming hyperlinks, such approach requires a large corpus of indexed websites and webpages, which is commonly available only for search engines.

3   Graph-Based Clustering Approach

In this paper, we propose the website clustering approach underlined by the following hypothesis: websites have groups of pages with a higher level of connectivity inside the group than with pages outside. We suppose, that in general, links are specified between webpages with crossing topics. A higher level of connectivity in group of webpages display that topics are intensively shared between pages in a group. Such groups of webpages are forming sections of websites referring to certain topics.

An approach is applicable to any hypertext structure in general, while a website is a particular case of such hypertext model. Formally, we represent a hypertext structure $H = (P, L)$ with directed graph $G = (V, E)$, where:

- $V = P$ is a set of vertices $v_1, v_2, \ldots, v_n \in V$, which correspond to hypertext documents.
- $E = L$ is a set of edges between vertices: $e(v, u) \in E, v, u \in V$, which are hyperlinks between documents.

To find communities in the graph, we employ existing graph clustering algorithms, based on flow simulation principle. This can be, for instance, Markov Chain Clustering (MCL) [20] or BorderFlow [14] algorithm. Results include collections of clustered vertices of the graph.

Mentioned graph clustering algorithms assume that provided as input directed graph is a weighted graph. Although weights are not required for the most of the clustering algorithms, the usage of weights can drastically improve the clustering results. This can be used as extension point of the approach. In example, weights can be pre-calculated with another clustering algorithm (e.g. text-based clustering).

We also suppose that our approach will be able to include into clusters webpages without textual content. By analysing incoming hyperlinks to such pages from others, we can discover semantics of these pages without necessity to analyse media or binary data contained in them.

Finally, we presume that performance of graph-based website clustering will be higher than common text-based clustering (which includes indexing and further index analysis). For both types of approaches, in this test we will assume that required data has been already extracted from the website, to exclude crawling and transporting costs. Required data includes connectivity structure (*"webpage A has a link to webpage B"*) and text contents from the webpages for graph-based and text-based clustering, correspondingly.

To examine our approach, in section 5 we compare the results of graph-based clustering with credible text-based algorithm Carrot[2] on the corpus of webpages

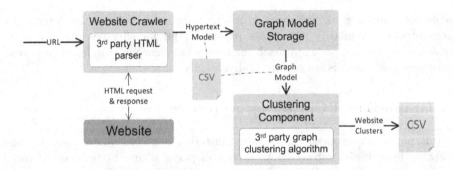

Fig. 1. The architecture of the keyword extraction process

of a real-world website. We also prove the ability to determine clusters for web-pages with no text content, and estimate a performance of the approach, in comparison with existing one.

4 Architecture and Workflow

In this section, we explain the architecture and the workflow of the framework that we have designed to perform graph-based clustering of the website.

The framework consists of three major components, highlighted on the figure above (see Figure 1):

1. The *website crawler* parses the hypertext structure of the website by provided URL;
2. The *graph model storage* constructs a graph model of the hypertext from the data obtained by website crawler, and stores it for further analysis;
3. The *website clustering component* clusters the graph from graph model storage with one of supported algorithms.

As for software platform, we use Java 7 web application, running on Apache Tomcat application server. It also uses additional libraries for HTML data extraction and graph clustering. The following subsections describe Design and Workflow of each component in detail.

4.1 Parsing the Hypertext Structure of Web Sites

To extract required information from the webiste, we use straightforward HTML parser – JSOUP[4]. So far, we assume that every webpage has no asynchronous content and fully loaded at a time JSOUP connects to the host. We understand, that various modern websites intensively employ JavaScript and interactive content on the webpages, but the crawling of this sort of data is not in scope of this paper, as well as extracting data from media. This limitation can be eliminated

---

[4] http://jsoup.org

by using modern state of the art crawlers which are able to extract information from media and interactive contents (e.g. OXPath crawler[5]).

We have built our crawler around JSOUP and provided interface to crawl a whole website by its URL. As the result, the website crawler component parses a selected website and extracts the following types of information: (1) each webpage URL, (2) links between webpages, (3) webpage text content (not required for graph clustering).

The component outputs its crawling data into CSV file, where every row looks like the following:

[ID, URL from, URL to]

The file represents a connectivity of the website and can be used for further purposes.

4.2 Constructing the Web Site Graph

With crawling results provided from the previous component, we can easily build a graph model of the hypertext structure. As it was mentioned in section 3, we treat webpages as vertices and hyperlinks as edges. The order of pages in hyperlinks matters, because we need a directed graph to use as an input for clustering algorithm.

Regarding weights, we have no additional information extracted from the website by default, which can be treated as weight and meet our clustering approach. So we use the same weight for all edges equal to 1.

The component converts constructed graph model to the specific CSV format, expected by clustering component:

[URL from, URL to, Weight]

4.3 Graph Model Clustering

We use existing implementations of flow simulation algorithms in correspondence with the approach presented in section 3. The CUGAR Graph Clustering and Visualization Framework[6] serves well in this case. It written in Java and includes implementations of the following five algorithms: Affinity Propagation, Border-Flow, Chinese Whispers, k-Nearest Neighbors and MCL algorithm. We use BorderFlow and MCL in our approach as graph clustering algorithms. This library also allows using these algorithms through an API without heavy interfaces and visualizations.

We provide graph model data obtained from the previous component to CUGAR and execute BorderFlow and MCL for it. An API of CUGAR supports various parameters of the clustering, on which clustering results depend. We show specific values of these parameters along with clustering results in section 5.

---

[5] http://www.oxpath.org
[6] https://github.com/renespeck/Cugar

When clustering complete, CUGAR produces output file, in which every row contains a collection of vertices corresponding to a certain cluster. In section 5, we examine these clusters and conclude about efficiency.

5   Evaluation

To evaluate the clustering approach, described above, we have used the following techniques. At first, we showcase clustering results: a number of clusters, produced by applying chosen algorithms, average size of each cluster, standard deviation and time consumed. Then, we compare execution time and measure performance of these algorithms. After that, we estimate precision of different clustering approaches: one provided in this paper and others based on text clustering. To perform this, we compare results in semantic clustering problem, where website clustering needs to produce a number of webpage groups related to a certain topic. There are two basic requirements for clusters: 1) Defined topics should not be too broad and common, e.g. related to the whole website, 2) Each cluster should include at least three webpages. Finally, we examine how the proposed approach deals with webpages without text content, e.g. media or other specific formats.

5.1   Experimental Setup

To perform evaluation, we use a real-world website as data source. The website of Agile Knowledge and Semantic Web (AKSW) Research Group[7] provides information about AKSW research group, their projects, team members, events, etc. It has about 500 hypertext documents available on the main domain. Also, there is a set of OntoWiki webpages, which mostly contains technical and administrative information and so were not analyzed.

From the technical point of view, we use an implementation of our framework, written in Java. We use BorderFlow and MCL algorithms as graph-based clustering, provided by CUGAR library. To compare with, we use Carrot^2 workbench for text-based clustering, which provides implementations of two industry-proven clustering algorithms: STC and Lingo. Overall, we compare four different algorithms of clustering.

The processes of website crawling, clustering and keywords analyzing were performed on dualcore Intel Core i5 CPU M460 with 2.53GHz and 4Gb RAM. It runs under Windows 8.1 with Java(TM) SE Runtime Environment (build 1.8.0 45−b15), used for Java applications.

5.2   Experimental Results

As it was described in evaluation approach, we have performed website clustering using four different algorithms. Beforehand we were required to extract data from

---

[7] http://aksw.org

the website with help of the crawler: hypertext structure required for graph model construction and text contents for text-based clustering.

From 498 hypertext documents, found on the main domain of aksw.org, only 343 of them were unique, while others had similar URLs with duplicate content.

Table 1. Data extraction results from http://aksw.org.

	.html	.rdf	.ttl	.csv	Others
Num. of documents (%)	343 (26.6%)	479 (37.1%)	451 (34.9%)	9 (0.7%)	9 (0.7%)

In addition, there were found almost 950 non-hypertext documents of different format, linked from these pages (see Table 1).

Table 2. Clustering characteristics of chosen algorithms applied to aksw.org.

	MCL	BorderFlow	Lingo	STC
Number of Clusters	77	108	51	58
Avg. Docs per Cluster	12.54	9.05	31.90	97.88
Standard Deviation	77.16	21.54	19.51	47.38
Time Spent, sec.	8.9	27.8	1.9	0.2

A brief overview of cluster contents is given in Table 2.

To measure a performance of the approach using BorderFlow and MCL, we have measured 20 test clustering runs of these algorithms. Using default implementations with no additional performance improvements, we have received average 27.8 sec for clustering with BorderFlow and 8.9 sec for MCL for their better input parameters. We also used benchmark results provided by Carrot[2] workbench. Lingo and STC are tuned better and show 1.9 sec and 0.2 sec in average, correspondingly. BorderFlow and MCL computed a graph with whole 1290 documents found on aksw.org, while Lingo and STC operated only HTML documents, which are only 343. Due to technical reasons, we were unable to complete clustering with *Inflation* higher then 1.46.

There were not enough clusters with $Inflation = 1.46$ for uniform coverage of all webpages, and cluster dispersion was too high. In our expectations, the best results in matter of precision and time are provided with *Inflation* close to 2.0 (see Figure 2). We suppose that in further experiments it will produce results similar to BorderFlow clustering.

We have examined precision of the approach in our semantic clustering task. To do that, we manually checked all clusters provided by clustering algorithms and made conclusion regarding 1) the semantic similarity of pages in the cluster, 2) how cluster meets our requirements of topic broadness and minimum size.

Thus, for graph-based algorithms, we have computed a precision for every cluster and than got average from all clusters. Rather common example of precise cluster produced by BorderFlow is described below.

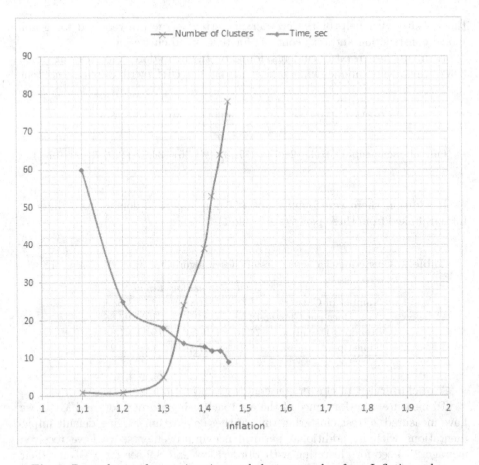

Fig. 2. Dependency of execution time and clusters number from Inflation value.

As shown on Figure 3, the sample cluster contains such URLs as http://aksw. org/DiegoEsteves, http://aksw.org/BettinaKlimek, http://aksw.org/Groups/ NLP2RDF, etc. All of them relate to personal pages of the *NLP2RDF* group members. We can make sure of this after looking on the real Web page with URL (see Figure 4).

For text-based clustering, we assumed that precision equals 100% for all clusters because of the approach specifics. Nevertheless, clusters itself are often broader than needed, so STC proposed clusters under such topics as *Open, Systems, Current* and others.

So far, BorderFlow showed unpredictably good results and came with almost 95% of precision (see Table 3). MCL has failed due to technical reasons, and we are going to eliminate this issue in further experiments. Lingo solved the problem very well, producing only few clusters with broad topic with resulting precision of 96%. In comparison to Lingo, STC did not so well, returning lots of wide and uncertain topics defined by common keywords. Additionally, Lingo and STC produced a set of documents related to *Others* cluster, in other words, not related to any other

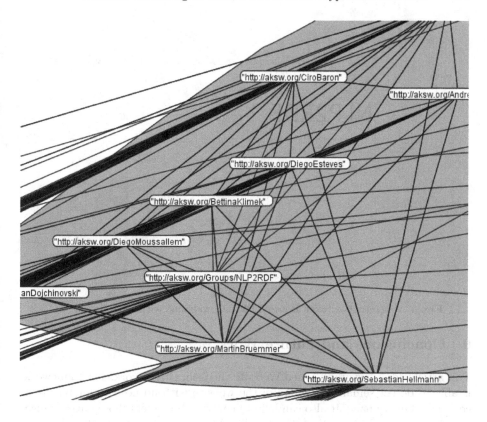

Fig. 3. Sample cluster visualization with CUGAR framework.

cluster. While for STC such "cluster" included only 2 documents, a corresponding cluster of Lingo consists of 51 document. Graph-based algorithms have no such non-clustered documents.

Finally, we have assessed how clustering approach deals with non-text documents. As it was mentioned above, text-based clustering is inapplicable here. While graph-based algorithms correctly detected clusters for such pages. They have found exact clusters with .ttl and .rdf documents related to original Web pages with no need to analyze file contents. For other formats, like CSV or PDF, they also did well and covered such documents with clusters of well-known pages.

Table 3. Average precision of clusters & number of non-clustered documents produced by different algorithms.

	MCL	BorderFlow	Lingo	STC
Average Precision	15.1%	94.9%	96.1%	84.5%
Num. of Non-clustered Docs	–	–	51	2

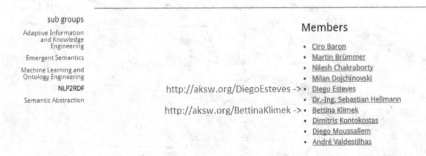

Fig. 4. A screenshot taken from NLP2RDF webpage with URL highlights.

6   Conclusions and Future Work

This article describes graph-based Web site clustering framework. The framework is able to detect semantic clusters in the website with no need to analyze text contents of every page. It also can help to cover with clusters those pages, which contents are hard to analyze directly, like binary documents, media files and others. Framework shows medium performance in comparison with industry-proven and well-tuned clustering algorithms (e.g. Lingo or STC), but has wide capabilities to be improved in this direction.

Our clustering-based keyword extraction framework still has the following limitations. Most obvious is the crawling limitation i.e. the lack of interactive content support. This is an implementation-specific limit which can be bypassed by using more complex crawling tools (e.g. OXPath). As it was mentioned in section 5, we have experienced a technical issue with MCL implementation. We are going to solve it in further experiments and expect results similar to BorderFlow algorithm. Another way to improve the approach is to add weights.

Graph-based clustering algorithms support weighted graphs, so we can use an external source of weights to improve clustering precision. For instance, we can combine them with text-based clustering algorithms and use such mixed approach to reduce limitations from of approaches.

Quality measurement techniques also require further improvements. Currently used evaluation approach with manual assessment of clusters has certain limitations. This includes poor scalability to apply the approach for large websites of different knowledge domains. To verify experimental results on additional websites, new evaluation techniques will be used.

We plan extend the framework in two directions: mitigate limitations and apply the framework as a backend for existing applications (e.g. conTEXT[8]).

References

1. Arasu, A., Garcia-Molina, H.: Extracting structured data from web pages. In: Proceedings of the 2003 ACM SIGMOD international conference on Management of data, pp. 337–348. ACM (2003)
2. Auer, S., Bizer, C., Kobilarov, G., Lehmann, J., Cyganiak, R., Ives, Z.G.: DBpedia: a nucleus for a web of open data. In: Aberer, K., Choi, K.-S., Noy, N., Allemang, D., Lee, K.-I., Nixon, L.J.B., Golbeck, J., Mika, P., Maynard, D., Mizoguchi, R., Schreiber, G., Cudré-Mauroux, P. (eds.) ASWC 2007 and ISWC 2007. LNCS, vol. 4825, pp. 722–735. Springer, Heidelberg (2007)
3. Brin, S., Page, L.: The anatomy of a large-scale hypertextual web search engine. Computer Networks and ISDN Systems 30(1–7), 107–117 (1998). Proceedings of the Seventh International World Wide Web Conference. http://www.sciencedirect.com/science/article/pii/S016975529800110X
4. Carlson, A., Betteridge, J., Wang, R.C., Hruschka, Jr., E.R., Mitchell, T.M.: Toward an architecture for never-ending language learning. In: Proceedings of the Conference on Artificial Intelligence (AAAI) (2010)
5. Carpineto, C., Osinski, S., Romano, G., Weiss, D.: A survey of web clustering engines. ACM Computing Surveys 41(3), July 2009. http://doi.acm.org/10.1145/1541880.1541884
6. Chakrabarti, D., Mehta, R.: The paths more taken: matching dom trees to search logs for accurate webpage clustering. In: Proceedings of the 19th International Conference on World Wide Web, pp. 211–220. ACM (2010)
7. Croft, W.B., Metzler, D., Strohman, T.: Search engines: Information retrieval in practice, chap. 4.5. Addison-Wesley Reading (2010)
8. Devika, K., Surendran, S.: An overview of web data extraction techniques. International Journal of Scientific Engineering and Technology 2(4) (2013)
9. Ferrara, E., Meo, P.D., Fiumara, G., Baumgartner, R.: Web data extraction, applications and techniques: A survey. CoRR abs/1207.0246 (2012)
10. Hollink, V., van Someren, M., Wielinga, B.J.: Navigation behavior models for link structure optimization. User Modeling and User-Adapted Interaction 17(4), 339–377 (2007)
11. Kosala, R., Blockeel, H.: Web mining research: A survey. ACM Sigkdd Explorations Newsletter 2(1), 1–15 (2000)
12. Lehmann, J., Völker, J. (eds.): Studies on the Semantic Web, chap. Information Extraction for Ontology Learning. Akademische Verlagsgesellschaft - AKA GmbH, P.O. Box 41 07 05, 12117 Berlin, Germany (2014)
13. Ngomo, A.C.N., Lyko, K., Christen, V.: Coala-correlation-aware active learning of link specifications. In: The Semantic Web: Semantics and Big Data, pp. 442–456. Springer (2013)
14. Ngonga Ngomo, A.-C., Schumacher, F.: Borderflow: a local graph clustering algorithm for natural language processing. In: Gelbukh, A. (ed.) CICLing 2009. LNCS, vol. 5449, pp. 547–558. Springer, Heidelberg (2009)

---

[8] http://context.aksw.org/app/

15. Osinski, S., Stefanowski, J., Weiss, D.: Lingo: search results clustering algorithm based on singular value decomposition. In: Proceedings of the International Conference on Intelligent Information Systems (IIPWM 2004), Zakopane, Poland, pp. 359–368 (2004)

16. Osiński, S., Weiss, D.: Carrot^2: design of a flexible and efficient web information retrieval framework. In: Szczepaniak, P.S., Kacprzyk, J., Niewiadomski, A. (eds.) AWIC 2005. LNCS (LNAI), vol. 3528, pp. 439–444. Springer, Heidelberg (2005)

17. Poon, H., Domingos, P.: Unsupervised ontology induction from text. In: Proceedings of the 48th Annual Meeting of the Association for Computational Linguistics, pp. 296–305. ACL 2010, Association for Computational Linguistics, Stroudsburg (2010). http://dl.acm.org/citation.cfm?id=1858681.1858712

18. Suchanek, F.M., Kasneci, G., Weikum, G.: Yago: a core of semantic knowledge. In: Proceedings of the 16th International Conference on World Wide Web, pp. 697–706. ACM (2007)

19. Suchanek, F.M., Sozio, M., Weikum, G.: Sofie: a self-organizing framework for information extraction. In: Proceedings of the 18th International Conference on World Wide Web, pp. 631–640. ACM (2009)

20. Van Dongen, S.M.: Graph clustering by flow simulation (2001)

21. Wu, F., Weld, D.S.: Automatically refining the wikipedia infobox ontology. In: Proceedings of the 17th International Conference on World Wide Web, pp. 635–644. ACM (2008)

22. Zamir, O., Etzioni, O.: Web document clustering: a feasibility demonstration. In: SIGIR 1998: Proceedings of the 21st Annual International ACM SIGIR Conference on Research and Development in Information Retrieval, Melbourne, Australia, August 24–28 1998, pp. 46–54 (1998). http://doi.acm.org/10.1145/290941.290956

Interactive Coding of Responses to Open-Ended Questions in Russian

Nikita Senderovich[✉] and Archil Maysuradze

Faculty of Computational Mathematics and Cybernetics,
Lomonosov Moscow State University, 2nd Educational Building,
CMC Faculty, MSU, Leninskie Gory, GSP-1, Moscow 119991, Russia
senderovich.nikita@yandex.ru, maysuradze@cs.msu.su

Abstract. We propose an interactive technique to categorize the responses to open-ended questions. The open-ended question requires a response which is a natural language phrase. A typical analysis of the phrases starts with their 'coding', that is, identifying themes of the responses and tagging the responses with the themes they represent. The proposed coding technique is based on interactive cluster analysis. We study theoretically and empirically the hierarchical (agglomerative, divisive) and partitional clustering algorithms to pick the best one for short Russian responses. We address the problem of the short phrase sparseness with thesaurus smoothing. We introduce an iterative process where users can provide some feedback to a clustering result. A domain-oriented system of statements is developed for users' feedback. The system is proved to be able to provide any clusters the user desires. The technique is implemented as a web service for responses in Russian.

Keywords: Open-ended questions · Short text categorization · Interactive clustering · Russian thesaurus

1 Introduction

In last decades qualitative analysis in sociology has become a widely used instrument. Compared to classical quantitative approach, qualitative research is based on unstructured source data. Both approaches are applied in survey analysis, which is commonly used to gather opinion on a wide variety of subjects: governmental agencies conduct surveys to communicate view of different social groups on political, social and economic conditions; commercial structures use survey results to enhance product quality and achieve gain in sales. Two main types of survey questions can be identified by degree of freedom given to the respondent:

1. *closed-ended questions* — questions with a predefined set of answers, respondent has to choose one or more variants
2. *open-ended questions* — questions, where respondent has to write a short textual response in his own words

© Springer International Publishing Switzerland 2015
P. Klinov and D. Mouromtsev (Eds.): KESW 2015, CCIS 518, pp. 195–209, 2015.
DOI: 10.1007/978-3-319-24543-0_15

Opposed to closed-ended questions, open-ended questions cannot be directly analyzed using quantitative methods, their analysis requires more complex approach.

For manual analysis of open-ended responses the following process is commonly used [1,3]:

1. every response is read and a list of main ideas represented in the texts is created
2. the structure of the list created on the previous step is reviewed and refined, short labels (*codes*) are assigned to each item on the list
3. each response is marked with one or several codes according to the contents

This process is called *coding of open-ended question*, it is aimed at converting qualitative information provided by respondents into quantitative form for subsequent analysis. The result of the first two steps is called the *codebook*. The example of coding results can be observed on figure 1 (only a part of result is presented). The question was taken from Sociological Bulletin of Public Opinion Foundation, dated 26 May 2011. The respondents were asked the following question: "Which statements made by Dmitry Medvedev at the press-conference did you memorize and like most?" We see that the set of responses contains the groups "youth policy", "cancellation of vehicle inspection", "innovation, modernization" and "the fight against corruption". For each group the most typical answers are presented.

Что из того, о чём говорил Д. Медведев на пресс-конференции, Вам больше всего запомнилось и понравилось?

Молодёжная политика	«наша молодёжь будет жить лучше»; «о школьниках, студентах»; «Медведев болеет за молодёжь, даёт им работу»; «уделял внимание молодёжи»
Отмена техосмотра	«про техосмотр»; «упрощение системы прохождения осмотров автомобилей»; «он и сказал, что техосмотр теперь будут оформлять не в ГАИ, а при ОСАГО»
Инновации, модернизация	«усовершенствование производства, инновации»; «модернизация»; «надо продолжать процессы модернизации в экономике и политике»; «развитие науки»
Борьба с коррупцией	«о коррупции в рядах чиновников»; «о борьбе с коррупцией»; «реформы надо продолжать и жёстче бороться с коррупцией»; «коррупция»

Fig. 1. Example of open-ended question analysis result. The text on the top is the wording of the question. In the left column of the table the names of the groups discovered (in red) are situated. In the right column several typical answers are presented for each group.

On the one hand, methodology of sociological research lists many cases, when open-ended questions are more appropriate than close-ended [2]. In these cases usage of open-ended questions allows the researcher to approach the inner world of respondent, deeply understand his point of view without imposing boundaries by the strict format of the response. Open-ended questions are known to provide unbiased results, which is especially important when the objects of sociological research are vague and unsystematic views on complex phenomena of social reality. In addition, open-ended questions stimulate respondents to analyze the subject of the questions thoroughly and give more complete answers [1].

On the other hand, the described coding technique induces several serious problems. First, this technique is extremely laborious. Therefore, manual coding is performed by a group of analysts. The following workflow is commonly used:

1. a codebook is compiled according to a subset of answers (this step is usually done by a senior analyst)
2. a full set of responses is divided into parts and categorized by a group of analysts according to the codebook

One problem of this process is that codebook can be incomplete after the first step, so coders have to spend effort to modify it consistently on the second step. Another problem is that both of those steps are prone to subjectivity, which is often used as an argument against the qualitative techniques [2]. Unification of analysis results requires additional time-consuming procedures. The examples of intercoder agreement methods can be found in [4].

To sum up, the cost of manual analysis of open-ended questions is prohibitively high and no proven industry standard for efficient automated analysis is developed by now. That is why open-ended questions are rarely included into the questionnaires, and even if included, then for large volumes of collected data the answers do not get adequate analysis. In these circumstances, efficient automation of coding is a topical problem.

In this paper, we propose a new low-effort workflow for coding open-ended questions based on interaction of analysts with automated system. The rest of the paper is organized as follows. In section 2 related work is considered. In section 3 the system overview is given and proposed workflow is described and discussed in detail. Section 4 contains detailed description of mathematical procedures chosen for each step of data processing in the proposed system. Validation of the system is discussed in section 5. Section 6 concludes the paper.

2 Related Work

Many general-purpose automated systems were proposed to analyze textual information. However, only a few systems take into account specific character of the task considered and can be used to work with open-ended questions.

In the work [5] Japanese authors suggest an automatic method for dividing open-ended responses into 3 classes: positive, negative or request. The method is based on the use of classification, information provided by analyst is used to build training set.

More general analysis can be performed using IBM SPSS Text Analytics for Surveys. It is a proprietary system, based on a wide variety of prepared domain-oriented linguistic resources: thesauri, lists of synonyms and lists of stop-words. Key feature of the product is work with groups of answers. User can operate with keywords for each group, create subgroups, merge groups and move responses from one group into another. The accent in this product is made on receiving reproducible results and gathering expert opinion to achieve optimal coding. The main problem of the product is that it does not support Russian language.

Several attempts have been made to automatize open-ended response coding in Russian. Systems DISKANT [2] and VEGA [3] were proposed to tackle the challenges of traditional coding methods. Methodologically both of the systems follow the manual process of coding described above, automatizing both codebook creation and codes assignment.

In DISKANT, the representative phrases are chosen by the analyst at the first step of analysis. These phrases define a classifier which is applied on the second step to categorize the responses according to similarities to representative phrases. DISKANT implies an iterative workflow, in which user adds portions of responses and updates classifier until all the data is classified.

VEGA is a newer system based on DISKANT. It provides an automatic procedure that builds groups of responses via comparison of phrases. A dictionary-based semantic analyzer is used to form the groups of relevant responses.

In this paper we present an interactive web-based system for analysis of open-ended questions, which supports a novel workflow oriented on cooperative analysis. The proposed workflow allows for efficient automation at all steps. For each step we selected and implemented appropriate data processing techniques. Analysts perform coding by gradually refining the results proposed by the system rather than grouping the responses manually. The "intellectual core" of the system is text clustering algorithm, which takes into account the opinion of the users. For typical number of responses in a survey the algorithm gives out the result instantly, so the system provides a continuous process of analysis. The system is based on linguistic resources for Russian language.

3   System Overview

As we have discussed above, the key problems of open-ended response coding are laboriousness and subjectivity. In this section we present system which is designed to solve both of the problems simultaneously.

3.1   Interactive Clustering

To deal with the laboriousness we explicitly formulate open-ended coding task as *short texts clustering task with disjoint clusters*. Generally, clustering methods are aimed at building groups of objects (clusters), so that objects in one cluster are closer to each other than objects in different clusters. In case of text collection it is assumed that the clustering result represents semantic partition of the collection. If open-ended questions are analyzed, we can associate each cluster with a code in a codebook. It should be noted that the result of clustering often can be considered as a classifier, which can be used to process new observations. Similarly, the codebook compiled for one set of responses can be later used to code new portion of data. In this sense all the processes considered above imply solution of clustering problem using specific methods.

In our research we assume that clusters are disjoint, which means that every response contains only one idea. Observation of real data from surveys confirm validity of this assumption: the answers for clearly posed question rarely consist of more than one thought, and even if such responses occur, analyst can always divide them into homogeneous parts on the stage of data preparation.

Many efficient clustering techniques were recently developed by machine learning and information retrieval communities. In section 4.4 the methods most appropriate for text clustering are considered. Important issue we concentrate on is sparseness of source data. Due to brevity of text in vast majority of responses, additional effort must be made to measure similarity between texts adequately.

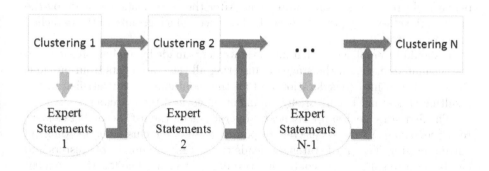

Fig. 2. Interactive clustering process

Usage of clustering procedure is expected to provide efficient automation of basic steps of coding process — creation of the codebook and assigning codes to responses. However, the result of the automatic clustering provided by system can be unsatisfactory. That is why we allow the user to modify the result. We provide analyst with set of instruments, which can be used to express feedback. The statements made by analyst are taken into account by the clustering algorithm. The process is continued until the desired clustering is achieved. The process of gathering analyst's opinion in interactive fashion is shown on figure 2. In the following subsection the set of statements available to user is listed and it is proved, that any clustering can be built with their help. In section 4.4 the statements are formalized for usage in clustering algorithm.

3.2   User Statements

On each step of iterative process the user can alter the clustering using instruments provided by the system. Careful consideration of the situations that can be
encountered in analysis of real-world open-ended responses allowed us to develop
the interface. The set of statements available to the analyst is the following:

1. select the subset of responses
2. attach selected subset to existing cluster
3. attach selected subset to new cluster
4. detach responses of selected subset from clusters they are attached to
5. withdraw selected subset from consideration
6. complete the formation of cluster
7. continue the formation of cluster
8. remove the cluster

In the beginning of the process all the responses are "free" (*detached*) — they
are not attached to any cluster, so on the first step of interactive process the
clustering procedure groups responses automatically and provides initial set of
clusters. On the next step analyst can fix responses in clusters or move them
between clusters using attach statement. After the statements are made by the
analyst, the clustering procedure can be launched, which groups all the detached
responses automatically.

It should be emphasized that all the statements made by analyst on each step
are accumulated, i.e. on the stage of clustering all the statements from previous
steps are taken into consideration and all the requirements are satisfied in the
resulting clustering. Let us briefly comment on each of the statements.

The first statement supports next 4 operations on the list. Second statement
tells the system to move selected responses to another cluster or fix them in
current cluster. The third statement leads to increase in number of clusters and
can be used to split cluster containing two different ideas. The fourth statement
is opposite to the second and the third and makes the responses "free", they can
be attached to any cluster by automatic clustering procedure. This operation
is necessary if user made a mistake or changed his opinion. The fifth statement
is required to remove insignificant responses from the analysis. In most surveys
there are respondents, who answer with cliche or off-topic sentences. Statement
5 proposes a way to eliminate such responses. It is important that this statement
can be applied to each response only once, that is, it is irreversible.

Last three statements manipulate with clusters. Statement 6 tells the system
that the cluster is ready, and automated clustering procedure must not add
or remove any responses from it. Statement 7 is opposite to statement 6. The
last statement decreases number of clusters and withdraws all the responses of
deleted cluster from consideration.

Also an operation of renaming of the clusters is available. This operation
does not affect the result and is needed for convenience of analyst.

For proposed system of statements the following theorem can be formulated.

Theorem 1. *Statements 1, 3, 5, 8 allow to achieve arbitrary clustering.*

Proof. We are going to demonstrate, how to achieve any predefined clustering $C_1, \ldots, C_k$. First, using statements 1 and 5 all the insignificant responses are removed. Next, for $i = 1, \ldots, k$ with statements 1 and 3 the desired cluster C_i is built. Finally, all the initial clusters (which are empty by now) are removed using statement 8.

This proof demonstrates an algorithm, in which number of user actions required to build arbitrary clustering depends linearly on the number of analyzed responses, i.e. the complexity of the process is comparable with reading all the responses. However, in average case implemented automatic clustering method allows to reduce amount of user input substantially, which is demonstrated in Section 5.

3.3   Presentation of the Current State

After the primary clustering and every clustering performed in accordance with expert's wishes the data is organized in the following way.

There are two types of clusters:

– *fully formed clusters*: these clusters are stable, their contents cannot be changed by automatic clustering procedure
– *candidate clusters*: these clusters contain both attached and detached responses and can be modified by automatic clustering procedure

Every cluster has a name or a code, representing its main idea.

Also, three types of responses can be identified:

– *attached responses*: these responses were fixed in their clusters by expert, their cluster cannot be changed by automatic clustering procedure
– *detached responses*: cluster of these responses are determined by automatic clustering procedure
– *withdrawn responses*: these responses were considered insignificant by the user and removed from the rest of data set

Every attached and detached response belongs to exactly one cluster. The described structure is presented to analyst on each iteration of coding, he estimates the quality and takes measures to enhance the results.

The coding process is finished, when there are no detached responses left, that is, all the responses are either fixed in a cluster or withdrawn.

3.4   Cooperative Workflow

Interactive system increases productivity of the analyst dramatically and allows to build the desired clustering without tedious procedures of manual codebook compilation. Obviously, single analyst can perform the coding himself, but in this case the issue of subjectivity arises. To speed up the refining of automatically built clustering and deal with the problem of subjectivity we propose the following cooperative workflow. Several analysts work on open-ended response coding via web interface simultaneously in real time. Each expert can make statements from the list given in section 3.2 and run automatic clustering procedure. All the statements form a growing pool of expertise to be considered by the clustering method at each iteration of the proposed interactive process.

Main advantage of the workflow is that no preliminary intercoder agreement is required. All the experts observe the presentation of current state all the time, and control the coding process. In case if matters of opinion arise during the process, experts are notified by the system, they can discuss the problem, reach an agreement and continue the work. Opposed to traditional approach to coding, the result of the analysis in this case is guaranteed to be consistent and there is no need to spend additional effort to compile the results of individual analysts after they finished their work. Also, participation of several experts guarantees the increase of objectivity of the coding result compared to research performed by an individual analyst, because all the expert decisions are reviewed by other experts, the mistakes can be discovered, discussed and corrected.

It is important to emphasize that the proposed workflow in combination with web-interface of the system provides an opportunity for crowdsourcing, that is, achieving result through feedback given by volunteers. However, we believe that in most cases more adequate coding will be performed by ones of qualified researches working in a group and not by hundreds of people unfamiliar with the subject of research.

4   Data Processing Steps

In course of analyst's work with answers for one open-ended question the data comes through many stages, which must be supported in the system. In following subsections the opportunities and solutions for each step are discussed.

4.1   Data Import

Overview of survey industry standards showed that the raw data received from respondents, is commonly represented on the computer in one (and often for the convenience of researchers in more than one) of the following formats: SPSS, SAS, CSV, Microsoft Excel. Due to the widespread use of the Microsoft Excel format, data import in our system is currently implemented for this format. The proposed web-interface allows to operate with surveys containing multiple questions, and start multiple analyses for each question. For each entity standard CRUD interface is supported and additional text information can be provided by the user.

4.2   Natural Language Processing

The raw data given on the input is a collection of short texts in Russian. Before the responses can be analyzed using clustering techniques, each text undergoes the following processing stages:

- *segmentation*: division of the text into separate sentences
- *tokenization*: division of the text into separate words (terms)
- *normalization*: finding special normal form for each term

The first two stages are technical tasks, they are carried out using regular expressions. However, the normalization stage is a non-trivial and extensively studied recognition problem. Normalization allows to consider forms of the same word as one term, which is especially important for sparse source data. Normalization task can be formulated as a task of building equivalence relation in the set of all terms. One approach widely used for normalization of texts is stemming (see the review [6]). However, for Russian language it is known to show inferior results. In our system we use an approach based on usage of OpenCorpora: open corpus of Russian language, which provides grouping of word forms. Another problem, which requires solution, is the problem of disambiguation. We addressed this issue via part-of-speech tagging.

4.3   Text Model

When natural language processing is finished, the model of each text is built. On this step several models are available: models, based on representing texts as term sequences [7] or usage of frequent itemsets [8]. For our system we chose standard Vector Space Model with binary features. If D — set of responses, W — dictionary of all terms, which occurred in texts of responses, n_{dw} — number of occurrences of term w in document d, then every document d is represented as a vector of length $|W|$ (cardinality of set W):

$$d = [f_1^d, \ldots, f_{|W|}^d]^T, \text{ where } f_w^d = [n_{dw} > 0], \quad d \in \mathbb{R}_+^{|W|} \tag{1}$$

We use binary features instead of commonly used frequencies and TF-IDF values because short responses rarely contain repeating words.

The main issue complicating further processing is the problem of *sparseness*. Collections of short texts are characterized by the lack of statistical information on the occurrence of words and lack of common context information. It makes difficult the selection of adequate similarity measure and building of clustering algorithm. To overcome this difficulty, different approaches are used to enrich the model with additional information. To take into account semantic similarities between terms two sources of additional information are commonly used: set of auxiliary relevant texts and semantic graphs and nets.

In studies [11] and [12], the first approach was successfully used to build thematic models for short texts using Twitter and Wikipedia respectively. In work [9] the output of search engines was used to expand the context of short texts.

In [13], the second approach is applied, lexical database for the English language Word Net is used and proximity matrix P that reflects semantic relations between the terms is built. $P_{ij} \in [0, 1]$ and the bigger value P_{ij} is, the closer in sense the terms i and j are. The ontology was considered as an undirected graph of semantic connections with terms as vertices and relations hyponym-hyperonym and synonym-synonym as edges. To estimate value P_{ij}, the shortest distance between corresponding vertices in the graph was calculated and inverted.

For our project we used a similar approach and used RuThes — thesaurus of Russian language [10]. Matrix P is obtained using the same idea. In the work [14], links in Wikipedia are used to estimate the proximity between terms, but we believe that general-purpose thesaurus is more appropriate for the task of analyzing open-ended responses, which mainly consist of general vocabulary. In the following subsection the use of matrix P for solving clustering problem is described in detail.

4.4   Text Clustering

Generally, clustering algorithms can produce *partitional* (or flat) clustering or *hierarchical* clustering. Hierarchical clustering implies a tree of nested clusters. The construction of such a tree is also called the task of taxonomy. Unlike hierarchical clustering, flat clustering does not form nested clusters, they are all are on the same level.

Text clustering is a specific clustering task. In this subsection we are going to make a brief overview and analysis of several classical text clustering algorithms and address the issue of source data sparsity for each of them.

Traditional Hierarchical Approaches. The classical approaches to the construction of hierarchical clustering are *agglomerative* and *divisive* clustering algorithms. When building a hierarchical clustering using agglomerative algorithms, objects are gradually merged into bigger clusters. Thus, a partition evolves from the configuration where each object is a separate cluster to the configuration with single cluster containing all objects. When using divisive algorithms, on the contrary, configuration evolves from larger to smaller clusters.

If the distance between each pair of objects is chosen and a formula to recalculate intercluster distances after two clusters are merged is given, then an agglomerative clustering algorithm is fully defined. Indeed, on each step, two closest clusters can be merged, and all the distances from new cluster to other clusters can be recalculated for use on the following steps.

A widely used family of agglomerative clustering is defined by the formula from the famous work of Lance and Williams [15]:

$$d(U \cup V, S) = \alpha_U d(U, S) + \alpha_V d(V, S) + \beta d(U, V) + \gamma |d(U, S) - d(V, S)|. \quad (2)$$

After choosing the values α, β and γ, this formula can be used to recalculate the intercluster distances on the steps of agglomerative algorithm. Examples of widely used special cases of formula (2) are single linkage distance:

$$d(C_i, C_j) = \min_{x \in C_i, y \in C_j} d(x, y) \quad (3)$$

and unweighted average distance:

$$d(C_i, C_j) = \frac{1}{|C_i||C_j|} \sum_{x \in C_i} \sum_{y \in C_j} d(x, y). \tag{4}$$

To measure the similarity between texts represented as vectors in euclidean space, the vectors are normalized and the cosine measure is used:

$$s(u, v) = (u, v), \qquad ||u|| = ||v|| = 1. \tag{5}$$

Studies [16], [17] analyze a number of agglomerative and divisive algorithms for text clustering (the texts considered are long enough). In these studies clustering with unweighted average distance (UPGMA) shows best results among agglomerative algorithms.

The formula (5) does not take sparsity into account, however, we solve this problem using proximity matrix P:

$$s'(u, v) = \frac{(Lu, Lv)}{||Lu||||Lv||}, \qquad L^T L = P. \tag{6}$$

Here text responses u and v are not necessary of unit length, because the formula provides normalization. The matrix L can be obtained using Cholesky decomposition, because matrix P can always be made positively definite by increasing the numbers on the main diagonal. This addition can be interpreted as increase in significance of term coincidence in responses. It is important to emphasize that similarity (5) is a special case of (6), when $P = I$.

After this modification any hierarchical algorithm that takes distances between objects on the input can be used for short text clustering.

Spherical k-Means. Among partitional clustering algorithms the spherical k-means algorithm [18] is successfully used for text clustering.

Generally, formulation of the problem is the following. We want to partition a sample of n objects $x_1, x_2, \ldots, x_n$ into k clusters. Let us denote with $r_1, r_2, \ldots, r_n$ labels of clusters for each object ($r_j \in \{1, 2, \ldots, k\}$), and with $C_i = \{x_j | r_j = i\}$, $i = 1, 2, \ldots, k$ — sets of objects in clusters. The clusters must be disjoint and contain all the objects:

$$C_i \cap C_j = \varnothing, \ i \neq j, \quad \bigcup_i C_i = \{x_1, x_2, \ldots, x_n\}. \tag{7}$$

The algorithm finds cluster centroids and minimizes the intracluster distances by maximizing the similarity between objects and these centroids and determining values of labels r_j.

Spherical k-means assumes that all the objects belong to unit sphere $x_i \in \mathbb{S}_+$, $\forall i = 1, 2, \ldots, n$, and the following functional with constraints is maximized:

$$\sum_{i=1}^{k} \sum_{x_j \in C_i} (x_j, c_i) \longrightarrow \max_{c, r}, \ ||c_i|| = 1 \tag{8}$$

Formulas for the steps of optimization process are the following:

$$\mu_i = \frac{1}{|C_i|} \sum_{x_j \in C_i} x_j, \qquad c_i = \frac{\mu_i}{||\mu_i||}, \qquad r_j = \underset{i}{\operatorname{argmax}}(x_j, c_i) \qquad (9)$$

where c_i — unit vectors, in case of text clustering they are believed to correspond to "central notions" of text collection.

To use semantic smoothing provided by matrix P in spherical k-means the following modification is proposed. Let us use P in optimization problem (8) by changing x_j to y_j, where y_j is defined by formula:

$$y_j = \frac{Px_j}{||Px_j||}. \qquad (10)$$

As formula (10) touches only input and guarantees that $||y_j|| = 1$, this change allows to use standard spherical k-means without any modification. Such change can be interpreted as expansion of response texts by adding semantically related terms. Indeed, the construction of matrix P guarantees that vector y_j will have additional positive components, which correspond to the terms that are close in sense to the original terms of the response x_j.

Experimental Evaluation. In this section the experimental evaluation of 4 different short text clustering methods discussed above is performed. UPGMA and single linkage clustering represent agglomerative clustering, DIANA (DIvisive ANAlysis clustering) represents divisive algorithms, spherical k-means represents partitional methods.

Model data sets M1–M4 of increasing complexity simulating real-world data were prepared. Our data generation procedure allows to control size and structure of the sample: number of responses N, number of clusters k, number of keywords in each cluster (real-world clusters are usually formed around 1-10 keywords), number of general vocabulary words common for all clusters. We also control different levels of noise, which make the sample more complex: amount of general vocabulary in responses, amount of keywords of other clusters in responses. Along with the responses, corresponding proximity matrix P is generated. The noise level for matrix P—amount of semantically related words appearing in different clusters—is chosen as well.

The characteristics of data sets and clustering algorithms performance can be found in table 1. For model data the sample sizes were chosen as common numbers of respondents participating in the survey (several hundreds). The quality is measured using standard F-measure, which we can calculate because we know the true classification of objects. If we denote by n number of objects clustered, by n_i size of i-th ground true class, by n_j size of j-th found cluster, by n_{ij} number of objects of class i in cluster j, then the precision, recall and F-measure of correspondence of cluster j for class i can be calculated according to following formulas:

$$P(i,j) = \frac{n_{ij}}{n_j}, \quad R(i,j) = \frac{n_{ij}}{n_i}, \quad F(i,j) = \frac{2R(i,j)P(i,j)}{R(i,j) + P(i,j)}. \qquad (11)$$

Table 1. Text clustering algorithms performance on model data sets of increasing complexity, F-measure

N	k	Complexity factors	Method Smoothing	UPGMA no	yes	SL no	yes	DIANA no	yes	SKM no	yes
300	5	none	M1	1.00	**1.00**	1.00	**1.00**	1.00	**1.00**	1.00	**1.00**
500	10	+general vocab.	M2	0.89	0.90	0.78	0.87	0.66	0.93	1.00	**1.00**
1000	15	+common keywords	M3	0.61	0.75	0.35	0.53	0.48	0.56	0.79	**0.81**
1000	15	+proximity noise	M4	0.61	0.67	0.35	0.47	0.48	0.57	0.79	**0.80**

The F-measure of overall correspondence between classes and clusters for partitional algorithm:

$$F_p = \sum_i \frac{n_i}{n} \max_j F(i,j) \tag{12}$$

For hierarchical clustering we follow [16] and for each class calculate correspondence to each cluster in the cluster tree T and select maximum:

$$F_h = \sum_i \frac{n_i}{n} \max_{j \in T} F(i,j) \tag{13}$$

As we can see from Table 1, as expected, the quality decreases with the increase of data set complexity and noise levels (addition of proximity noise in experiments without smoothing does not decrease the quality as no proximity matrix is used). In all cases the proposed methods of smoothing allowed to achieve significant gain in quality. Spherical k-means demonstrated the best results among clustering methods compared. This algorithm was chosen for the system and adapted for interactive clustering, as shown below.

Formalization of User Statements. In our system for open-ended responses coding we use spherical k-means as a basic clustering algorithm. Below we show, how user statements announced in 3.2 are taken into account by the automated clustering algorithm.

Let us denote detached responses with $x_1, x_2, \ldots, x_l$, and attached responses with $x_{l+1}, x_{l+2}, \ldots, x_{l+q}$. All the statements made by experts modify the contents of these two sets, labels r_j for each attached response and number of candidate clusters. To take these modifications into account we use a semi-supervised approach. If we have k candidate clusters in the response, then formulas (9) take the form:

$$\mu_i = \frac{1}{|C_i|} \sum_{x_j \in C_i} x_j, \ c_i = \frac{\mu_i}{||\mu_i||}, \ i \in \{1, \ldots, k\} \tag{14}$$

$$r_j = \underset{i}{\operatorname{argmax}}(x_j, c_i), \ j \in \{l+1, \ldots, l+q\} \tag{15}$$

These formulas show, how to assign detached responses to candidate clusters taking into account the information about attached objects provided by experts.

5   System Validation

In this section the results of experiments with real-world survey data are presented. Performance evaluation was conducted in order to ensure that implemented system meets the requirements of the domain and provides efficient reduction of analyst's effort in the process of coding.

Responses to three open-ended survey questions (Q1–Q3) were coded by an expert using the implemented web service. In course of the work the information about user's interaction with the system was gathered. In particular, we were interested in amount of effort required to achieve the clustering that satisfied the expert. To measure laboriousness of the process we use total number of mouse clicks and total number of iterations of the interactive process described in section 3.1, i.e. number of automatically built clusterings. The clicks were counted only in the process of analysis, the clicks made for authorization in the system and data import were not included. The data sets contain different number of responses and different number of topics touched by respondents. The latter number can be estimated as number of clusters in the final data partition. Table 2 contains information about data sets and results of the experiments.

Table 2. Metrics of open-ended questions coding in the system

Data Set	Responses	Clicks	Iterations	Clusters
Q1	43	17	4	3
Q2	125	49	15	10
Q3	727	130	27	17

As we can see from the results, the number of clicks is significantly less than the number of responses, which indicates the utility of the proposed system compared to manual coding.

6   Conclusion

In this paper we have reviewed the domain of open-ended response coding and identified problems researchers face in course of their work. We proposed a novel workflow based on interactive computer-aided process which aims to increase the objectivity and reduce the laboriousness of research. For each step of data processing possible variants were analyzed and appropriate solutions were developed based on empirical results and needs of the domain considered. Although much more research must be carried out before the state-of-the-art system for open-ended response coding for Russian language is developed, we are optimistic that our contribution will serve as a basis for further studies.

Acknowledgments. The reported study was partially supported by the Russian Foundation for Basic Research (RFBR), research projects No. 13-01-00751a and No. 15-07-09214a.

References

1. Geger, A. E.: The use of open-ended questions in the measurement of value orientations. In: Sociology Yesterday, Today, Tomorrow: 2-nd Sociological Readings in Memory of V.Golofast, pp. 48–60. SPb (2008)
2. Saganenko, G.I.: A comparison of non-comparable: study of comparative research on the basis of open-ended questions. Sociological Journal **3-4**, 144–156 (1998)
3. Boyarsky, K.K., Kanevsky, E.A., Saganenko, G.I.: On the issue of automatic text classification. Economic-mathematical studies: mathematical models and information technology, 253–273(2009)
4. Carey, J.W., Morgan, M., Oxtoby, M.J.: Intercoder agreement in analysis of responses to open-ended interview questions: Examples from tuberculosis research. Cultural anthropology methods **8**(3), 1–5 (1996)
5. Sakurai, S., Orihara, R.: Analysis of Textual Data based on multiple 2-class Classification Models. International Journal of Computational Intelligence **4**(4) (2008)
6. Jivani, A.G.: A comparative study of stemming algorithms. Int. J. Comp. Tech. Appl. **2**(6), 1930–1938 (2011)
7. Zamir, O., Etzioni, O.: Web document clustering: a feasibility demonstration. In: Proceedings of the 21st Annual International ACM SIGIR Conference on Research and Development in Information Retrieval, pp. 46–54. ACM (1998)
8. Fung, B.C., Wang, K., Ester, M.: Hierarchical document clustering using frequent itemsets. SDM **3**, 59–70 (2003)
9. Sahami, M., Heilman, T.D.: A web-based kernel function for measuring the similarity of short text snippets. In: Proceedings of the 15th International Conference on World Wide Web, 377–386. ACM (2006)
10. Loukashevich, N.V.: Thesauri in problems of information retrieval. Moscow University Printing House (2011)
11. Hong, L., Davison, B.D.: Empirical study of topic modeling in twitter. In: Proceedings of the First Workshop on Social Media Analytics, pp. 80–88. ACM (2010)
12. Jin, O., Liu, N.N., Zhao, K., Yu, Y., Yang, Q.: Transferring topical knowledge from auxiliary long texts for short text clustering. In: Proceedings of the 20th ACM International Conference on Information and Knowledge Management, pp. 775–784. ACM (2011)
13. Siolas, G., d'Alché-Buc, F.: Support vector machines based on a semantic kernel for text categorization. In: Proceedings of the IEEE-INNS-ENNS International Joint Conference on Neural Networks, IJCNN 2000, vol. 5, pp. 205–209. IEEE (2000)
14. Varlamov, M. I., Korshunov A. V.: Computing semantic similarity of concepts using shortest paths in Wikipedia link graph. JMLDA, 1107–1125 (2014)
15. Lance, G.N., Williams, W.T.: A general theory of classificatory sorting strategies 1 Hierarchical systems. The Computer Journal **9**(4), 373–380 (1967)
16. Zhao, Y., Karypis, G.: Evaluation of hierarchical clustering algorithms for document datasets. In: Proceedings of the Eleventh International Conference on Information and Knowledge Management, pp. 515–524. ACM (2002)
17. Steinbach, M., Karypis, G., Kumar, V.: A comparison of document clustering techniques. KDD workshop on text mining **400**(1), 525–526 (2000)
18. Buchta, C., Kober, M., Feinerer, I., Hornik, K.: Spherical k-means clustering. Journal of Statistical Software **50**(10), 1–22 (2012)

Measuring the Quality of Relational-to-RDF Mappings

Darya Tarasowa[✉], Christoph Lange, and Sören Auer

Institute of Computer Science, University of Bonn & Fraunhofer IAIS,
Bonn, Germany
{darya.tarasowa,math.semantic.web}@gmail.com, auer@cs.uni-bonn.de

Abstract. Mapping from relational data to Linked Data (RDB2RDF) is an essential prerequisite for evolving the World Wide Web into the Web of Data. We propose a methodology to evaluate the quality of such mappings against a set of objective metrics. Our methodology, whose key principles have been approved by a survey among RDB2RDF experts, can be applied to evaluate both automatically and manually performed mappings regardless of their representation. The main contributions of the paper are: (1) assessing the quality requirements for mappings between relational databases and RDF, and (2) proposing methods for measuring how well a given mapping meets the requirements. We showcase the usage of the individual metrics with illustrative examples from a real-life application. Additionally, we provide guidelines to improve a given mapping with regard to the specific metrics.

Keywords: Data quality · Quality assessment · Quality metrics · RDB2RDF

1 Introduction

Translating the data stored in relational databases (RDB) to the linked data format is an essential prerequisite for evolving the current Web of documents into a Web of Data. In order to be effectively and efficiently reusable, linked data should meet certain data quality requirements [21]. Assessing the quality of a linked dataset created from RDB may be a laborious, repetitive task if the dataset is frequently recreated from its RDB source, e.g. after any update to the RDB. We therefore claim that it is possible to positively influence the quality of a linked dataset created from RDB by improving the quality of the RDB2RDF *mapping* that produces the linked data.[1] To the best of our knowledge there has not been prior research towards collecting and describing quality requirements

---

[1] Here, we use the term "mapping" to refer to the function that maps relational database columns to RDF properties, but not to materialisations of such mappings in concrete languages or representations, nor to tools that would execute such a function.

© Springer International Publishing Switzerland 2015
P. Klinov and D. Mouromtsev (Eds.): KESW 2015, CCIS 518, pp. 210–224, 2015.
DOI: 10.1007/978-3-319-24543-0_16

for RDB2RDF mappings. Thus, this paper aims to fill the gap by providing a system of metrics to measure the quality of RDB2RDF mappings.

A large number of tools for mapping relational data to RDF exist already[2]; they implement different mapping approaches, often allowing to customize the mapping. To standardize the description of mappings, the W3C RDB2RDF Working Group has released two recommendations in 2012 (more details in Section 3.1): Direct Mapping [1], which produces RDF graph representations directly from a relational database (data and schema) and the Relational Database to RDF Mapping Language (R2RML) [5] for expressing customized mappings.

In this paper, we aim at developing a system of quality metrics that can be applied both to direct and customized mappings that works with different representations of mappings (R2RML or proprietary formats, visual diagrams, tables, etc.). Any of these representations are suitable for being evaluated with the proposed system as long as one can derive a list of database columns (including unmapped ones) and their corresponding RDF properties (for mapped ones).

To determine the scope of requirements that can be posed to RDB2RDF mappings, we studied the state of the art in related research fields such as ontology matching, linked data quality assessment and RDB2XML mappings. However, as Sect. 2 shows, these metrics collected from the scientific community do not solve the given problem entirely. In order to fulfil the list, we followed the Direct and R2RML Mapping recommendations. Some of the RDB2RDF features standardized in the documents are connected with the output data quality dimension, while others influence the quality of the mapping itself. For example, the ability to define R2RML views allows to incorporate domain semantics into the mapping an opportunity that we consider to increase the quality of mapping. We propose not only a system of metrics but also define means of measuring them, along with guidelines to improve the rating of a dataset w.r.t. each metric.

The paper is structured as follows: in Sect. 2 we discuss the existing approaches, in Sect. 3 we summarize the quality requirements for mappings and the metrics for measuring the quality. Section 4 presents the results of the survey conducted in order to collect the community feedback. In Sect. 5, we conclude and propose future research directions.

2   Related Work

RDB2RDF Mapping Approaches. Although previous research has not explicitly focused on collecting requirements for RDB2RDF mappings, many such requirements can be found in best practice and mapping approach descriptions. For instance, in [10], the importance of reusing existing vocabularies to enhance the interoperability of the output dataset is explained. We extend this statement to a set of requirements combined in the *interoperability* dimension, taking into account not only quantitative, but also qualitative metrics.

---

[2] One listing is available at https://github.com/timrdf/csv2rdf4lod-automation/wiki/Alternative-Tabular-to-RDF-converters.

We notice that existing literature on the topic uses incoherent terminology. Often, the term *mapping* is used instead of mapping *language*, e.g. in [2,7]. Discussing the requirements for mapping *language*, both articles mention the following requirements for RDB2RDF *mapping* as well:

- presence of both ETL and on-demand implementation
- incorporating domain semantics that is often implicit or not captured at all in the RDB schema
- indication of time metadata about the dataset during the mapping creation process to control the dataset currency (we subsume this metric under "data quality")
- intensive reuse of the existing ontologies

Requirements for Mappings Between Relational Data and XML. The topic of mapping relational data to *XML* is related to RDB2RDF mapping due to the similarity between the XML and RDF data models. The earliest articles on the quality of RDB2XML mappings (e.g. [16,17]) only take into account the performance of the mapping algorithms. This is because RDB2XML mappings are mostly produced automatically and do not allow customization. Only few authors (e.g. [15]) propose metrics for evaluating the quality of the output data. However, the proposed metrics evaluate only the syntactic correctness of the output XML and therefore cannot be applied to documents in RDF (except for *presence of syntax errors*).

Other approaches (e.g. [18]) prove the need for customizable techniques of mapping due to the wide gap between these two formats. As their major evaluation criterion, they use the *efficiency of query processing*. We adopt this approach and base our *simplicity* metric on it. Liu et al. [13] describe an approach to design a high-quality XML Schema from ER diagrams. The authors define a list of requirements for the design; the most relevant one for our purposes is *information preservation*. However, the metrics for *measuring* such requirements are not discussed. We study the information preservation requirement in detail and provide objective metrics in the *Faithfulness of Output* dimension.

Requirements for Ontology Matching. Mapping between a database schema and an RDF vocabulary can also be viewed as a special case of ontology matching. Several studies propose requirements for measuring the quality of an ontology matching. According to [8], all proposed measures can be distinguished between compliance measures, measures concerned with system usability and performance measures focusing on runtime or memory usage. As our study focuses on evaluating the quality of mapping itself, we do not take the system usability or performance dimensions into account.

In the evaluation of ontology matching, compliance measures are based on the two classical information retrieval measures of *precision* and *recall* [20]. We adapt these metrics to the evaluation of RDB2RDF mappings and include them in the *faithfulness of output* dimension as *coverage* and *accuracy of data presentation* metrics.

Measuring Linked Data Quality. The quality of mapping correlates with the quality of output linked data produced by the mapping. Poor design decisions made at the stage of defining a mapping, such as using deprecated classes, redundant attributes or badly formed URIs, decreases the quality of the output data. Therefore, metrics for the quality of the output data can be viewed as metrics for quality of the mapping.

The field of assessing the quality of linked data is still in its infancy, but several articles have addressed it already. Our recent survey [21] collects and compares the existing papers, the most complete and detailed ones being Bizer's PhD thesis [4], Flemming's master's thesis [9] and empirical evaluations by Hogan et al. [11,12]. The survey provides formal definitions of data quality dimensions and metrics as well as evaluates existing tools for (semi-)automatic measurement of linked data quality.

The current paper assumes that the quality of a linked dataset is influenced by the mapping that produces it and thus categorizes the metrics from the survey from the perspective of the RDB2RDF mapping. We select those metrics that are related to the mapping process and adapt them to the RDB2RDF domain.

3   Quality Requirements

This section gives a detailed overview of the proposed quality requirements for RDB2RDF mappings, ways of measuring them (metrics) and guidelines for improving mappings w.r.t. these metrics. Our proposed system incorporates four quality dimensions with 14 objective metrics overall. For assessing the overall quality of a mapping, one would, in practice, assign *weights* to the metrics. Their choice depends on the goal of the mapping process. For example, when the goal of the mapping is to accurately represent the relational data, the metrics in the "faithfulness of the output" dimension should be assigned the highest weight.

3.1   Quality of the Mapping Implementation and Representation

The requirement of mapping quality implementation and representation combines the requirements for resultant data accessibility and standard compliance of the mapping representation.

Data Accessibility. Data accessibility describes how the result of the mapping is accessed. This metric is also known in the literature as "access paradigm", "mapping implementation" or "data exposition" [19]. There are two possibilities: (i) Extract Transform Load (ETL) and (ii) on-demand mapping. According to [7], ETL means physically storing triples produced from relational data in an RDF store. The disadvantage of ETL is that that, whenever the RDB is updated, you have to re-run the entire ETL process, even if just one RDB record has changed, carrying out an often redundant synchronization process. However, in the ETL case nothing more than the RDF store is needed to answer a query.

Table 1. Summary table of proposed metrics system

Requirement	Description	Measure
Quality of the mapping implementation and representation		
Data accessibility	Describes how the mapping result can be accessed.	ETL/on-demand/both
Standard compliance	Characterizes if the mapping representation is standard compliant.	boolean
Faithfulness of the output		
Coverage	Characterizes the mapping completeness	percentage of DB columns mapped
Accuracy of data representation	Characterizes the mapping correctness	percentage of correctly mapped DB columns
Incorporation of domain semantics	Shows level of domain semantics incorporation	percentage of properties that link to the results of SQL queries
Quality of the output		
Simplicity	Shows the simplicity of SPARQL queries returning the frequently demanded values	percentage of complex SQL queries results integrated into the mapping
Data quality	Characterizes the quality of output data	aggregation of linked data quality metrics ($\rightarrow$ Table 2)
Data integration	Characterizes the interlinking degree of the output data	percentage of external instances integrated into the resultant dataset
Interoperability		
Reuse of existing ontologies	Shows the amount of reused vocabulary elements	percentage of reused properties and classes
Quality of reused vocabulary elements	Characterizes the quality of chosen for reuse properties and classes	accumulated quality and popularity of reused vocabulary elements
Accuracy of reused properties	Characterizes the accuracy of properties reuse	percentage of accurately reused properties
Accuracy of reused classes	Characterizes the accuracy of classes reuse	percentage of accurately reused classes
Quality of declared classes/properties	Shows the quality of ontology documentation	accumulated quality of declared classes/properties

On-demand mapping is realized by translating a SPARQL query into one or more SQL queries at query-time, evaluating these against (a set of) unmodified relational database(s) and constructing a SPARQL result set from the result sets of such SQL queries. In contrast to the ETL implementation, on-demand mapping requires more resources for processing each query. However, the on-demand implementation does not face the synchronization issue and does not replicate the data. In the light of these advantages and disadvantages, we claim that the best solution is to implement a mapping with both data access approaches. Thus, the index of implementation takes a value equal to 1, if both implementations are present and 0.5 otherwise.

Standard Compliance. An RDB2RDF mapping can either be represented as a set of customized rules or through a generic set of rules (as defined by the W3C Direct Mapping standard [1,3]). Often, the output of a Direct Mapping may not be useful, that is, it may not adequately take the structural/semantic complexity of the database schema into account. Thus, while the applicability of a Direct Mapping satisfies the requirements for the "standard representation" metric, not using the customized rules will lead to a loss of points w.r.t. other metrics.

Languages for representing customized mappings have been surveyed in [19]. Until recently, no standard representation language for RDB2RDF mappings existed, however, as of 2012, R2RML [5] has been released as a W3C recommendation. As it is the only mapping language that has been standardized to date, we do not consider other (proprietary) formats reasonable.

Thus, we propose that if there is no material representation of a mapping available, it should be assumed that a Direct Mapping is carried out. We define the "standard representation" metric to be one if the mapping is represented in *R2RML* or if there is no representation (and therefore a Direct Mapping is applicable), and zero otherwise.

3.2 Faithfulness of the Output

In terms of RDB2RDF mapping we define the faithfulness of output as an abstract measure of similarity between the source data and resultant dataset.

Coverage. This metric indicates the ratio of the database columns mapped to the RDF. In general, a high coverage increases the faithfulness of the output data. However, reaching the highest level of coverage may conflict with privacy restrictions. Therefore, great care should be taken when mapping any kind of personal (sensitive) data that might be linked with other data sources or ontologies. It may even be illegal to create or to process such linked information in countries with data protection laws without having a valid legal reason for such processing [6].

Moreover, application-specific data such as statistics of usage or service tables often are not included into the mapping due to its application-related nature. Thus, in real-world applications, the coverage metric never reaches one.

Accuracy of Data Representation. When mapping relational data to RDF, the accuracy of data representation is tightly connected to data formatting issues. For example, differences in the representation of numeric values between the database and RDF can cause inaccuracies in the output data. Inaccurate dealing with not-Latin characters leads to loss of data meaning. We propose the following algorithm to evaluate the accuracy index of the mapping:

1. for each mapped database column containing numeric data, compute the average value of the numbers in this column;
2. find an average value for the corresponding property in the RDF output, and compare it to the average computed in step 1;
3. add a point for each coinciding average (considering the statistical error)
4. for each mapped database column containing literal data, analyze the readability of the corresponding properties; add a point for each completely readable property;
5. calculate a sum of the points obtained in steps 3 and 4 and divide the sum on the total number of columns mapped.

Incorporating Domain Semantics. The incorporation of domain semantics is one of the crucial aspects that indicate the quality difference between direct and customized mappings. Measuring this requirement helps to estimate the direct benefit of mapping customization. Generally, a direct mapping does not incorporate domain semantics; in this case the metric takes a value of zero. The extent of domain semantics incorporation can be measured by counting number of *class properties* which take values from any database table *other than* the table that corresponds to a class. The metric is then calculated as the ratio between this number and the count of properties summed up over all classes in the mapping.

To improve the mapping w.r.t. this metric, implicit relations between the data in the database should be explicitly modelled in the mapping. This process also increases the simplicity of the mapping, as it requires integration of the SQL query results into the mapping, thereby simplifying (future) SPARQL queries for obtaining these values.

3.3 Quality of the Output

Quality of the output combines requirements of the output data quality in aspects of simplicity of usage, level of interlinking and objective data quality metrics.

Simplicity. One often has the task of mapping highly complex data models to RDF. In that case, Direct Mapping produces an RDF output that may be difficult to use, especially when considering the limitations of the SPARQL query language. Thus, useful information from the source database may lose its value in the RDF dataset that results from mapping. Metrics for the quality of the output should therefore take the simplicity of the RDF dataset into account. By simplicity of RDF data, we mean the simplicity of *operating* on it. In other words, the simplicity of data determines the simplicity (or length in terms of abstract syntax) of the SPARQL queries returning frequently demanded values. To increase the simplicity, the mapping should aim to produce a dataset, that can be queried for frequently demanded values by relatively simple SPARQL constructions. To do this, the *frequently demanded values returning by the complex SQL queries* should be integrated into the mapping. Such preparations not only increase the simplicity of the output, but also *incorporate domain semantics* not presented in the relational database explicitly (cf. Section 3.2).

To calculate the index of simplicity, first a list of complex SQL queries should be assembled. We propose to consider a query "complex" in the following cases:

- a query joins at least two tables or views,
- a query supposes recursive computations over one table or view.

After the list is assembled, frequently demanded values, returned by the queries should be selected. This selection is subjective and should be carried out by a group of developers and administrators of the project. The simplicity metric is then calculated as the percentage of *frequently demanded values returned by complicated SQL queries* that have been integrated into the mapping.

Table 2. Data quality metrics divided into four groups according to the stage of mapping creation, on which they can be influenced.

Requirements for linked data quality and their metrics	
1. Influenced by mapping	*3. Depend on relational data*

1. Influenced by mapping

- **Completeness:** influenced by coverage
- **Validity-of-documents:** influenced by quality and accuracy of reused and newly determined classes
- **Interlinking:** influenced by data integration
- **Availability:** influenced by dereferenceability of reused and newly defined classes
- **Consistency:** influenced by reuse

2. Depend on mapping

- *Provenance: indication of metadata about a dataset*
- *Verifiability: verifying publisher information, authenticity of the dataset, usage of digital signatures*
- *Licensing: machine-readable/human-readable license, permissions to use the dataset, attribution, Copyleft or ShareAlike*
- *Validity-of-documents: no syntax errors*
- *Consistency: entities as members of disjoint classes, usage of homogeneous datatypes, misplaced classes or properties, misuse of owl:datatypeProperty or owl:objectProperty, bogus owl:InverseFunctionalProperty values, ontology hijacking*
- *Conciseness: redundant properties/instances, not-unique values for functional properties, not-unique annotations*
- *Performance: no usage of slash-URIs, no use of prolix RDF features*
- *Understandability: human-readable labelling of classes, properties and entities by providing rdfs:label, human readable metadata*
- *Interpretability: misinterpretation of missing values, atypical use of collections, containers and reification Currency: currency of data source*
- *Volatility: no timestamp associated with the source*

3. Depend on relational data

- *Completeness: values for a property are not missing*
- *Amount-of-data: see [21]*
- *Provenance: trustworthiness of RDF statements, trust of an entity, trust between two entities, trust from users, assigning trust values to data/-sources/rules, trust value for data*
- *Believability: see [21]*
- *Accuracy: see [21]*
- *Consistency: no stating of inconsistent property values for entities, literals incompatible with datatype range*
- *Interpretability: interpretability of data*
- *Versatility: provision of the data in various languages*

4. Depend on publishing

- *Availability: accessibility of the server, accessibility of the SPARQL end-point, accessibility of the RDF dumps, no structured data available, no dereferenced back-links*
- *Performance: see [21]*
- *Security: see [21]*
- *Response-time: see [21]*
- *Conciseness: keeping URIs short*
- *Understandibility: indication of one or more exemplary URIs, indication of a regular expression that matches the URIs of a dataset, indication of an exemplary SPARQL query, indication of the vocabularies used in the dataset, provision of message boards and mailing lists*
- *Versatility: provision of the data in different serialization formats, application of content negotiation*
- *Currency: see [21]*
- *Timeliness: see [21]*

Data Quality. The quality of a mapping can partly be assessed by evaluating the quality of the output RDF data. Section 2 points to approaches for assessing data quality. However, when evaluating the quality of a mapping, not all aspects of output data quality need to be taken into account. This is due to the fact that not all aspects of linked data quality are affected by the mapping stage.

We confine ourselves to the objective requirements discussed in [21] and divide them into four groups (cf. Table 2):

- Requirements that are influenced by mapping quality implicitly. Increasing the quality of the mapping in turn increases the quality of data.

- Requirements that are influenced by mapping explicitly. The proposed data quality index discussed below aggregates these metrics.
- Requirements that depend on the quality of data stored in the database. We consider these metrics to be out of the scope of this paper.
- Requirements that depend on the quality of linked data publishing. We do consider these metrics to be out of the scope of this paper.

The metrics and methods of measuring them are discussed in detail in [21]. To evaluate the quality of mapping with regard to output data quality we propose to aggregate only the metrics explicitly depending on the mapping. There are two possible strategies for calculating our overall data quality metric based on the individual metrics: assigning the same weight to all individual metrics, or assigning different weights to different dimensions or even to individual metrics.

Data Integration. The key advantage of Linked Data is its ability to effectively integrate data from disparate, heterogeneous data sources. In most cases, the output dataset resulting from a mapping can be linked to existing datasets via explicitly modelled relationships between entities. As mentioned in [14], the use of domain ontologies along with user defined inference rules for reconciling heterogeneity between multiple RDB sources, is an effective integration approach for creating an RDF. A simple metric for data integration can be defined as the number of external datasets linked to the one evaluated. However, this metric cannot be mapped to a value in the interval $[0, 1]$ in an obvious way, as needed for computing the overall mapping quality from the values of the individual metrics. Thus, we propose an alternative measure to evaluate the data integration level: index of data integration. It can be calculated as the ratio between the number of external instances integrated in the resulting RDF dataset and the total number of instances.

3.4   Interoperability

The interoperability requirement tackles the aspect of a mapping to produce interoperable data, which can be easily linked to and integrated with other ontologies and datasets.

Reuse of Existing Ontologies. The reuse of existing ontology elements (i.e. classes and properties), increases the interoperability of the output dataset. Additionally, this reuse prevents one from having to introduce new elements. This requirement can be measured using two metrics: the ratio of reused properties and the ratio of reused classes. However, not only the quantity, but also the *quality* of reused properties and classes is important. This aspect is covered by the next metric.

Quality of Reused Vocabulary Elements. Measuring the quality of reused properties or classes is not trivial. As a large number of vocabularies has been published on the Web, many vocabulary elements are repeatedly declared instead of being reused.

We claim that the best choice of a class or property to reuse depends on two parameters: (i) the quality of the class or property itself and (ii) the frequency of its usage in LOD in comparison with semantically similar alternatives. Thus, to measure the quality of each individual property or class we propose the following workflow:

1. Measure the quality of the chosen vocabulary element (class/property)
2. Find alternatives to the chosen element and measure their quality
3. Compare the quality metrics of the chosen element and the best alternatives

We propose to compute the quality index (i_{qual}) of the chosen vocabulary element as the product of the following two indexes: the index of documentation quality (i_{doc}) and the index of popularity (i_{pop}). The proposed index of documentation quality is computed differently for classes and properties. Both for classes and properties, the index of documentation quality takes into account dereferenceability as well as documentation by `rdfs:label` and `rdfs:comment` (preferably in multiple languages). If the class or property is explicitly deprecated, i.e. its `owl:deprecated` annotation property equals `true`, we define its quality index as zero. Additionally, for classes, their relation to other classes should be indicated (rdfs:subClassOf or owl:equivalentClass).

For properties, `rdfs:range` and `rdfs:domain` should be defined. Based on the presence of the properties definitions mentioned above, a decision about quality of the documentation for a vocabulary element (possibly automated) should be made. The index of popularity aims to measure the frequency of usage of the class or property on the Web in comparison with semantically similar alternatives. This index can be taken from services such as Linked Open Vocabularies.[3]

As an example, we evaluate the property `agrelon:hasChief`[4] that links an *organization* to its *chief*. The property is dereferenceable, it has labels available in four languages; however, no `rdfs:range`, `rdfs:domain` or `rdfs:comment` is specified. Based on this, we define its i_{doc} as 0.5. For measuring the frequency of usage we type the term 'chief' into the search field of the Linked Open Vocabularies service. Looking through the results, we can conclude that on the Web of Data the term 'chief' is most commonly used to model a military commander and the chosen property `agrelon:hasChief` has a low popularity metric value of 0.271. Thus, the quality index for this evaluated property is $i_{pop} * i_{doc} = 0.271 \cdot 0.5 = 0.1355$.

The next task is to find the most commonly used term for the evaluated property. The list of possible substitutes will include properties matching 'chief', 'leader', 'head', or 'boss'. For each item on the list the property with the highest i_{pop} and satisfying the following requirements, should be found:

- `rdfs:comment`, `rdfs:domain` and `rdfs:range` statements should correspond to the domain model

---

[3] http://lov.okfn.org.
[4] fullURI:http://d-nb.info/standards/elementset/agrelon.owl#hasChief.

– depending on the application settings, special requirements such as presence
of an inverse property in the same vocabulary may need to be satisfied.

In our case, the metrics for the best candidates are represented in Sect. 3.
Due to space limitations, we only take into account the first two synonyms from
that list, as the two other ones do not have matches that satisfy the requirements
given above. According to the investigation, the `agrelon:hasChief` property is
not the best possible alternative for linking an organization to its chief. The
`swpo:hasLeader` property should be used instead, as its quality index is i_{pop} ·
$i_{doc} = 0.682 \cdot 0.8 = 0.5456$.

Table 3. Metrics for semantically identical properties to link an organization and its
chief

	'chief'	'leader'
best candidate	agrelon:hasChief	swpo:hasLeader
i_{pop}	0.271	0.682
i_{doc}	0.5	0.8
i_{qual}	**0.1355**	**0.5456**

The last step is to compare the quality of the chosen property and the best
possible alternatives. The resultant score for the chosen property is calculated
as the ratio between its quality index and the quality index of the best possible
alternative: $i_{qual_{chosen}}/i_{qual_{best}}$ where $i_{qual_{best}}$ is the quality index of the best alternative and $i_{qual_{chosen}}$ is the quality index of the evaluated property. In our case,
choosing the `agrelon:hasChief` property adds $0.1355/0.5456 = 0.248$ points
to the interoperability metric. Thus, the overall value of the *quality of reused
vocabulary elements* metric is defined as the ratio between the sum of the quality
indexes of all reused vocabulary elements and the number of reused vocabulary
elements.

Accuracy of Reused Properties. We determine two requirements for accurate
reuse of existing properties: (i) respecting the property definition and (ii) unambiguous meaning of the property. Respecting the property definition means that
the domain model must be consistent with the definition of the property, namely
its `rdfs:range`, `rdfs:domain` and `rdfs:comment` relations. Unambiguous meaning is important when similar relations are presented in the domain model. For
example, consider the domain model of our SlideWiki OpenCourseWare authoring platform[5] and the following relations between decks (collections of slides):

```
– Deck1  sw:isTranslationOf  Deck2
– Deck2  sw:isRevisionOf     Deck3
– Deck3  sw:isVersionOf      Deck4
```

---

[5] http://www.slidewiki.org.

Here, Deck2 results from *translating* Deck1 into a different language, Deck3 is a result of *editing* Deck2, and Deck4 results from *moving* Deck3 into another e-learning platform (for example, Moodle[6]). If we decide to reuse the property dcterms:isVersionOf instead of one of these three properties from SlideWiki's domain-specific vocabulary, the meaning of the property will be ambiguous. A better solution in this case is to declare all three new properties to be sub-properties of dcterms:isVersionOf.

The index of accuracy of reused properties can be calculated as the number of accurately reused properties (i.e. the properties, that satisfy both requirements) in relation to the total number of reused properties in the dataset.

Accuracy of Reused Classes. An important aspect of reusing classes is the semantic *compatibility*. By this we mean the compatibility of the meaning of a reused class and a domain object declared to be an instance of the class. The index of accuracy of reused classes is defined as the ratio between semantically compatible reused classes and the total number of reused classes. We illustrate the issue with an example below.

Let us assume that we need to link a deck of slides to its CSS style. The property oa:styledBy from the *Open Annotation Data Model ontology*[7] could be chosen to model the link. However, its domain is oa:Annotation, which is not compatible with the sw:Deck class in terms of its intended semantic. If such a statement occurs within the mapping, the reused class oa:Annotation should be considered as incompatible for reuse.

To measure the requirement we propose to calculate the index of the accuracy of reused classes. It can be calculated as the number of reused classes semantically compatible with domain objects in relation to the total number of reused classes.

Quality of Declared Classes/Properties. In order to obtain high quality, the classes/properties whose *definition* is *introduced* by the mapping should meet the requirements of documentation quality analogically to reused vocabulary elements (see Sect. 3.4). Thus, the proposed index of quality of declared vocabulary elements is computed separately for class and properties and accumulates the documentation quality score in relation to the total number of properties/classes declared.

4   Evaluation

In order to evaluate how well the proposed methodology agrees with real-life common practices, we conducted a survey using a questionnaire.[8] The survey was formed of statements, one per requirement from Sect. 3. Each requirement was phrased in the style of a practical guideline, in that complying with this

---

[6] http://moodle.org.

[7] http://www.w3.org/ns/oa.

[8] http://slidewiki.org/application/questionnaire.php.

guideline when designing a mapping would help the mapping to obtain the highest possible score for the corresponding metric. For example, the requirement "accuracy of reused properties" (Sect. 3.4), evaluated by combination of two metrics, was divided into two statements: "The properties chosen for reuse should be available, dereferenceable and have unambiguous meaning in the application domain." and "When choosing the properties for reuse, *rdfs:domain*, *rdfs:range* and *rdfs:comment* must be taken into account." For each statement the experts had to express to what extent they agreed with it. Thus, the agreement of a majority of experts with a statement would prove the relevancy of both the requirement and the proposed way of its measuring. We did not include requirements for *output data quality*, *coverage* and *accuracy of data* in the survey, as their metrics had been proposed by prior research. In addition to the opinions about the statements we collected open feedback.

Table 4. Results of survey on degree of agreement with the key concepts of the proposed methodology. Numbers represent the degree of agreement from *absolutely agree* (5) to *absolutely disagree* (1). The colors indicate the self-estimated level of expertise in the RDB2RDF domain from *expert* (darkest) to *experienced* (lightest).

Requirement	P1	P2	P3	P4	P5	P6	P7	P8	P9	P10	P11	P12	P13	Mode
Data accessibility	4	2	5	5	4	5	5	4	4	2	4	2	5	5, 4
Representation	2	2	4	5	1	5	4	4	3	4	3	2	5	4
Incorporation of domain semantics	4	3	3	4	3	3	3	4	2	5	5	3	5	3
Simplicity	3	3	3	4	3	3	4	4	5	2	1	4	4	4, 3
Data integration	4	3	4	3	5	2	5	4	3	4	2	4	3	4
Reuse of existing ontologies	5	3	4	3	5	4	5	4	5	2	2	4	2	5
Quality of reused properties (frequency)	4	4	4	3	4	3	4	4	3	2	2	4	2	4
Quality of reused properties (dereferenceability)	5	1	3	4	5	3	5	4	5	4	4	4	4	4
Accuracy of reused properties	4	4	3	4	5	4	5	4	4	4	3	4	5	4
Accuracy of reused classes	5	4	4	3	4	4	4	3	4	4	3	4	5	4
Quality of declared classes/properties	4	3	3	4	2	4	5	4	5	2	2	4	4	4

The survey was announced to the RDB2RDF community via mailing lists and personal e-mails. We received 13 individual responses. All participants assessed their level of RDB2RDF expertise as either *experienced* or *expert* (the two highest out of four possible levels). They could decide either to stay incognito or to fill in their name, affiliation and institution. Section 4 shows the results.

Due to the high level of participants' experience in the domain, we chose not to leverage the individual opinions by calculating their means or medians. Instead, we base our analysis on the *mode value*. We did not calculate separate mode values for responses from participants with different experience levels ("experienced" vs. "expert"), as we do not consider the difference between these two groups sufficiently significant to influence the responses (however, we indicate the level of experience in the result table).

As Sect. 4 shows, the experts approved most of the requirements. The ones that the experts were doubtful about were the *incorporation of domain semantics* and *simplicity* requirements. This outcome can, however, be explained by the circumstance that these two requirements are difficult to explain in a short statement. On the other hand, there were experts who accepted both these requirements, even with a value of *absolutely agree*. Thus, we consider the low overall agreement with these two requirements to result from incomplete understanding of the statements, as the requirements and their metrics are not trivial. Finally, within the open feedback no participant suggested further objective requirements (besides ones aggregated in the data quality requirement), which provides evidence of the completeness of our system, at least in view of today's state-of-the-art.

5 Conclusion

In this paper, we proposed a methodology to evaluate the quality of mappings between relational and linked data. In particular, we proposed a set of 14 requirements for mapping quality and described ways of measuring them. We believe that the most of the measures can be done (semi-)automatically and will attempt to prove that in our future work. As we show in the paper, the proposed system can not only be used to evaluate the mappings, but also as a guideline to increase the quality of the mapping. Additionally, we evaluated the relevance of our proposed set of requirements by conducting a survey. A total of 13 experienced individuals, mainly from the RDB2RDF community, participated in our survey. The analysis of their responses allows us to claim that the community accepts our requirements and their metrics.

Acknowledgments. We would like to thank the anonymous experts as well as Richard Cyganiak (INSIGHT@NUI Galway), Ravi Kumar (TCS), Mr. Spenser Kao (Bureau of Meteorology, Australia), Dr. Nikolaos Konstantinou (National Technical University of Athens), Freddy Priyatna (Ontology Engineering Group), Juan Sequeda (University of Texas at Austin), Tim Lebo (Tetherless World/RPI), Oscar Corcho (UPM), Dr. Pedro Szekely and Jose Luis Ambite (University of Southern California). We are grateful to Mr. Nicolas Van Peteghem for providing us with one of the test databases.

References

1. Arenas, M., et al.: A Direct Mapping of Relational Data to RDF. Working Draft. W3C (2012). http://www.w3.org/TR/rdb-direct-mapping/
2. Auer, S., et al.: Use Cases and Requirements for Mapping Relational Databases to RDF (2010). http://www.w3.org/2001/sw/rdb2rdf/use-cases/reqscore (visited on June 12, 2013)
3. Bertails, A., Prud'hommeaux, E.G.: Interpreting relational databases in the RDF domain. In: K-CAP, pp. 129–136 (2011)

4. Bizer, C.: Quality Driven Information Filtering: In the Context ofWeb Based Information Systems. PhD thesis. Free University of Berlin (2007)
5. Das, S., Sundara, S., Cyganiak, R.: R2RML: RDB to RDF Mapping Language. Recommendation. W3C (2012). http://www.w3.org/TR/rdb-direct-mapping/
6. Dean, M. et al.: OWL Web Ontology Language Reference. Recommendation. W3C (2004)
7. Erling, O.: Requirements for Relational to RDF Mapping (2008). http://www.w3.org/wiki/Rdb2RdfXG/ReqForMappingByOErling (visited on June 12, 2013)
8. Euzenat, J., Shvaiko, P.: Ontology alignment. Springer (2007)
9. Flemming, A.: Quality Characteristics of Linked Data Publishing Datasources. MA thesis. Humboldt-Universität of Berlin (2010)
10. Hillairet, G., Bertrand, F., Lafaye, J.-Y.: MDE for publishing data on the semantic web. In: TWOMDE, pp. 32–46. http://ceur-ws.org/Vol-395/
11. Hogan, A., et al.: An empirical survey of linked data conformance. Web Semantics **14**, 14–44 (2012)
12. Hogan, A., et al.: Weaving the pedanticweb. In: LDOW (2010). http://ceurws.org/Vol-628/
13. Liu, C., Li, J.: Designing quality XML schemas from E-R diagrams. In: Yu, J.X., Kitsuregawa, M., Leong, H.-V. (eds.) WAIM 2006. LNCS, vol. 4016, pp. 508–519. Springer, Heidelberg (2006)
14. Sahoo, S.S., et al.: A Survey of Current Approaches for Mapping of Relational Databases to RDF. RDB2RDF Incubator Group Report. W3C (2009)
15. Sahuguet, A.: Everything you ever wanted to know about DTDs, but were afraid to ask (extended abstract). In: Suciu, D., Vossen, G. (eds.) WebDB 2000. LNCS, vol. 1997, pp. 171–183. Springer, Heidelberg (2001)
16. Schmidt, A., et al.: XMark: a benchmark for XML data management. In: VLDB, pp. 974–985 (2002)
17. Shanmugasundaram, J., et al.: Efficiently publishing relational data as XML documents. The VLDB Journal **10**(2–3), 133–154 (2001)
18. Shanmugasundaram, J., et al.: Relational databases for querying xml documents: limitations and opportunities. In: VLDB, pp. 302–314. Morgan Kaufmann (1999)
19. Spanos, D.-E., Stavrou, P., Mitrou, N.: Bringing relational databases into the semantic web: A survey. Semantic Web **3**(2), 169–209 (2012)
20. Van Rijsbergen, C.: Information Retrieval (1979)
21. Zaveri, A., et al.: Quality Assessment Methodologies for Linked Open Data. Semantic Web Journal, major revision (2013). http://www.semantic-web-journal.net/content/quality-assessment-linked-open-datasurvey

Pattern Mining and Machine Learning
for Demographic Sequences

Dmitry I. Ignatov[✉], Ekaterina Mitrofanova, Anna Muratova,
and Danil Gizdatullin

National Research University Higher School of Economics, Moscow, Russia
dignatov@hse.ru
http://www.hse.ru

Abstract. In this paper, we present the results of our first studies in
application of pattern mining and machine learning techniques to analysis of demographic sequences in Russia based on data of 11 generations
from 1930 to 1984. The main goal is not prediction and data mining
methods themselves but rather extraction of interesting patterns and
knowledge acquisition from substantial datasets of demographic data.
We use decision trees as techniques for demographic events prediction
and emergent patterns for searching significant and potentially useful
sequences.

Keywords: Demographic sequences · Sequence mining · Emergent
patterns · Emergent sequences · Decision trees · Machine learning

1 Introduction and Related Work

The analysis of demographic sequences is a very popular and promising direction of study in demography[1,2]. The life courses of people consist of the chains
of events in different spheres of life. Scientists are interested in the transition
from the analysis of separate events and their interrelation to the analysis of the
whole sequences of the events. However, this transition is slowing by the technical
peculiarity of working with sequences. As of today, demographers and sociolo-
gists do not have an available and simple instrument of such analysis. Some
demographers possessing programming skills are successfully making sequence
analysis [3–5] and developing statistical methods [6–10], but the majority of
the social scientists have the only option to cooperate with other scientists to
extract knowledge from demographic data. Commonly, demographers rely on
statistics, but sophisticated sequence analysis techniques only start to emerge
in this field [11]. Since traditional statistical methods cannot face the emerging
needs of demography, demographers start showing a great interest in techniques
of computer science [12].

Human demographic behaviour can be very different varying over different generations, gender, education level, religious views etc., however, hidden similarities
can be found and generalised by specially designed techniques. Even though there

© Springer International Publishing Switzerland 2015
P. Klinov and D. Mouromtsev (Eds.): KESW 2015, CCIS 518, pp. 225–239, 2015.
DOI: 10.1007/978-3-319-24543-0_17

are many methods developed so far, the field is far from convergence with traditional sequence mining techniques that studied in Data Mining. Machine Learning (ML) and Data Mining (DM) are rather young and rapidly developing fields that require professional knowledge of computer science, which is usually missing in social sciences.

Another positive tendency is the availability of easy to use tools from ML & DM community like Weka, Orange, SPMF etc. that do not presume expertise in programming. For those social scientists who are able to program, Python (and R as well) and many its packages as scikitlearn are ready to use.

So, one of the goals of this study is to find possible ties between areas and try to use Machine Learning and Pattern Mining to this end.

We essentially rely on two previous works [8,12] and strive to obtain similar results by means of decision tree learning implemented in Orange. However, those papers demonstrate only classification techniques as a tool of choice. The main goal of the authors was to find rules (patterns) that discern demographic behaviour of Italian and Austrian people. The classification itself was rather the mean but not a goal. Good classification results only assured us that the classifier is suitable, but the if-then rules from an obtained decision tree give us the patterns to interpret from demography viewpoint. From this point, blackbox approaches like SVM and artificial neural networks do not match the task; they can be better in prediction but do not produce interpretable patterns.

Thus, the next natural avenue is pattern mining and sequence mining in particular, so we use SPMF [13] and its sequence mining techniques as a tool. To make these methods more suitable for finding significant patterns in demographic setting we adapt so called emergent patterns approach from [14].

The paper is organized as follows. In Section 2, we describe our demographic data. In section 3, we propose how to use decision trees and find interesting patterns in demographic sequences. Section 4 introduces sequence mining and emergent patterns that we combined. Experimental results are reported in two subsections of Section 5. Section 6 concludes the paper.

2   Data Description and Problem Statement

The dataset for the study is obtained from the Research and educational group for Fertility, Family formation and dissolution of HSE[1]. We use the panel of three waves of the Russian part of Generation and Gender Survey (GGS), which took place in 2004, 2007 and 2011[2]. The dataset contains records of 4857 respondents (1545 men and 3312 women). The gender imbalance of the dataset is caused by the panel nature of the data: the leaving of the survey by the respondents is an uncontrollable process. That is why the representative waves combined in a panel with the structure less close to the general sample.

---

[1] http://www.hse.ru/en/demo/family/

[2] This part of GGS "Parents and Children, Men and Women in Family and in Society" is an all Russia representative panel sample survey: http://www.ggp-i.org/

In the database, for each person the following information is indicated: date of birth, gender (male, female), generation, type of education (general, higher, professional), locality (city, town, village), religion (yes, no), frequency of church attendance (once a week, several times in a week, minimum once a month, several times in a year or never) and the date of significant events in their lives such as: first job experience, completion of education of the highest level, leaving the parental house, first partnership, first marriage, birth of the first child. There are eleven generations: first (those who was born in 1930–34), second (1935–39), third (1940–44), fourth (1945–49), fifth (1950–54), sixth (1955–59), seventh (1960–64), eighth (1965–69), ninth (1970–74), tenth (1975–79) and eleventh (1980–84).

There is a variety of questions that demographers would like to answer:

– What are the most typical first life-course events for different generations?
– What is the difference between men and women in terms of demographic behaviour?
– What are the non-trivial but robust patterns in life-course events which are not evident from the first glance?
– What are the prospective starting event and next (after the last surveyed) event for an individual of a certain type (e.g. youngest generations)?

There are many different variations of similar questions and all they in fact need proper means of pattern mining.

3   Why Decision Tree Learning?

First, to instantiate more focused questions from Section 2 we answer those requests that can be formulated in classification setting:

– What is the first life course event given the general person's descriptions?
– What is the next course event given the general person's descriptions and previous demographic behaviour?
– What are the typical patterns that discern men and women?

We decided to use decision trees (DT) [15,16] to fulfill these queries since DT provide us with not only predictions but with classification if-then rules. In fact, we cannot only predict the first life course event of a given individual but must to say which features in his/her profile is the reason. These if-then rules are also good discriminative patterns in analysing men and women behaviour.

There is a peculiarity of the method. Consider two if-then rules from a decision tree T in binary classification task with two classes $\{+, -\}$:

$$r_1 : a_1 = value_1, a_2 = value_2, \ldots, a_n = value_n \rightarrow class = +$$

$$r_2 : a_1 = value_1, a_2 = value_2, \ldots, a_n = value_n^* \rightarrow class = -$$

On the one hand $a_1, a_2, \ldots,$ and a_n are the most discriminative attributes w.r.t. to attribute selection function for branching, but on the other hand r_1 and r_2 differ only in the value of the last node. This form of rules seems to be a restriction since objects of different classes share a majority of similar attribute values. Hence, treatment of other types of patterns is necessary as well.

4   Sequence Mining and Emergent Patterns

4.1   Frequent Sequence Mining

The frequent sequence mining problem was first introduced by Agrawal and Srikant [17] for analysis of customer purchase sequences: "Given a set of sequences, where each sequence consists of a list of events (or elements) and each event consists of a set of items, and given a user-specified minimum support threshold of *minsup*, sequential pattern mining finds all frequent subsequences, that is, the subsequences whose occurrence frequency in the set of sequences is no less than *minsup*."

We reproduce the more formal definitions from [18]. Let $I = \{i_1, i_2, \ldots, i_n\}$ be the set of all items (or atomic events). An *itemset* is a nonempty set of items. A *sequence* is an ordered list of events (itemsets). A sequence s is denoted $\langle e_1 e_2 e_3 \ldots e_l \rangle$, where event e_1 happens before e_2, which happens before e_3, etc. Event e_i is also called an element of s. The itemset (or event) is denoted $\{a_1, a_2, \ldots, a_q\}$, where a_i is an item. The brackets are omitted if an element has only one item, that is, element $\{a\}$ is written as a (an atomic event).

A particular item can occur at most once in an event of a sequence, but can occur multiple times in different events of a sequence. In case of first life-course events an item cannot occur more than once, since e.g. the event "first child birth" cannot happen again in the lifecourse of a particular person. The number of occurrences of items in a sequence is called the *length of the sequence*, i.e. an l-sequence has length l. A sequence $\alpha = \langle a_1 a_2 \ldots a_n \rangle$ is called a *subsequence* of another sequence $\beta = \langle b_1 b_2 \ldots b_m \rangle$, and β is a *supersequence* of α, denoted as $\alpha \sqsubseteq \beta$, if there exist integers $1 \leq j_1 < j_2 < \ldots < j_n \leq m$ such that $a_1 \subseteq b_{j1}, a_2 \subseteq a_{j2}, \ldots, a_n \subseteq b_{jn}$.

A *sequence database*, D, is a set of sequences. For the discussed domain, D contains sequences for all individuals in the demographic survey. A sequence s is said to contain a sequence α, if α is a subsequence of s. The *support of a sequence* α in a sequence database D is the number of sequences in the database containing α: $sup_D(\alpha) = \#\{s | s \in D \ \& \ \alpha \sqsubseteq s\}$. When the sequence database is clear from the context, it can be denoted as $sup(\alpha)$. Given a positive integer *minsup* (or relative $rminsup \in [0, 1]$) as the minimum support threshold, a sequence α is called *frequent* in sequence database D if $sup_D(\alpha) \geq minsup$. Sometimes a frequent sequence is called a *sequential pattern*.

A frequent sequence s is called *closed* for given $minsup = \theta$ and sequence set D iff there is no its supersequence with the same support. Mining closed sequential patterns results in a significantly less number of sequences than in case of the full set of sequential patterns. Moreover, the full set of frequent subsequences (with their supports) can be recovered from the closed subsequences.

4.2   Emergent Sequences

Emergent patterns [14] in data mining is simply another instantiation of John Stuart Mill's ideas on formalisation of inductive reasoning (for example, cf. the difference method in [19]). To find a hypothesis for classification of an object to be positive or negative (one can consider several classes as well), one can compare all positive examples and use their common descriptions to this end. If such a common positive description does not occur in the descriptions of negative examples, it can be called a hypothesis [20,21].

We define *emergent sequences* as frequent subsequences of sequences of a particular class, which less frequent in the sequences of the rest classes. Thus, one can find such sequences for classes men and women to reveal discriminative patterns.

Let D_1 and D_2 be two datasets and s be a sequence. For $i \in \{1, 2\}$ denote support of s in dataset D_i as $sup_i(s)$. The *growth rate* of s is defined as follows:

$$GrowthRate(s) = \begin{cases} 0, & \text{if } sup_1(s) = 0 \text{ and } sup_2(s) = 0 \\ \infty, & \text{if } sup_1(s) = 0 \text{ and } sup_2(s) \neq 0 \\ \frac{sup_2(s)}{sup_1(s)}, & \text{otherwise} \end{cases} \qquad (1)$$

A sequence s is called *emergent* (for class 2) if its GrowthRate exceeds a predefined threshold. The *sequence contribution* to class C_i is defined as follows:

$$score(s, C_i) = \sum_{e \sqsubseteq s} \frac{GrowthRate(e)}{GrowthRate(e) + 1} \cdot sup_i(e), \qquad (2)$$

where $e \sqsubseteq s$. In case of unbalanced classes the contribution values need to be normalised e.g. by arithmetic mean or median.

Note that in DM community there are alternative definitions of statistically significant and unexpected patterns [22].

5   Experiments and Results

5.1   Machine Learning Experiments

To perform classification experiments[3] we mainly use Orange [23] and WEKA [24] environments and adhoc scripts in Python.

Prediction of First Life-Course Events. QUESTION: *What is the first life course event given the general person's descriptions?*

In the first task the class attribute is "First event". In fact it can be a conjunction of several atomic events that happened together w.r.t to the time granularity, e.g. within the same month (see Table 1).

However, such events are rather rare and will impose low prediction quality. So, we untangle these events to be atomic keeping their feature description the same. That is, for an individual with class value $\{work, separation\}$ we produce two new rows with the class values *work* and *separation* respectively 2.

---

[3] The anonymised datasets for each experiment are freely available in CSV files: http://bit.ly/KESW2015seqdem.

gender	education type	locality	religion	how_often	generation	1_event
f	general	town	yes	sev_a_year	9	marriage, sep_par
f	professional	town	yes	sev_a_year	10	work
f	higher	town	yes	sev_a_year	3	work
m	professional	town	yes	never	9	education
f	professional	town	yes	min_once_a_month	3	work, education
m	higher	town	yes	never	7	sep
m	general	town	yes	never	2	work, education
m	higher	town	yes	never	8	sep
f	general	town	yes	min_once_a_month	1	education
m	professional	town	yes	never	8	education
f	professional	town	yes	never	7	education
f	professional	town	yes	sev_a_year	6	education
m	professional	town	yes	never	8	education
m	professional	town	yes	never	4	education
f	general	town	yes	once_a_week	3	education
f	general	town	yes	min_once_a_month	4	education
f	higher	town	yes	sev_a_year	3	work

Fig. 1. Excerpt of data for the first event prediction task

The classification accuracy on this dataset for complex events and atomic is 0.37 and 0.41 respectively. Usually, such low value is unacceptable for machine learning task. One of the reasons is the data unbalance, i.e. $\frac{\#women}{\#men} \approx 2$. To overcome the difficulty we use SMOTE oversampling technique from WEKA package. After oversampling the number of men has risen from 1680 to 3360. However, the classification accuracy has not gained dramatically: $CA = 0.43$.

From the obtained decision tree 3 one can see that with probability 46.9 % if a person obtained higher education, then his/her first event is separation from parents.

If a person has general education and lives in a countryside or a town, then the first event is finishing of education in 46.5 % and 42.0 % cases respectively. However, if a person lives in a city, this is "first job" in 47.3 % cases.

If a man has professional education and lives in a town or in a countryside, then his first event will be "first job" in 41.0 % and 39.6 % respectively; for a man living in a city, he will complete education in 36.5 % cases. However, if a woman has professional education, her first events are different. Thus, if a woman lives in a countryside or a town, then the first event is separation from parents in 38.5 % and 36.6 % cases respectively. If she is living in a city being not a religious person, then in 32.1 % cases her first even is "first job" but, in case she is religious, she will separate from parents first in 33.3 % cases.

All the first events have not that high frequencies which means that there is no strong dependencies between individuals' descriptions and their first event outcome. However, in case we suppose that all the events are uniformly distributed, we obtain that each event has probability $100/6 \approx 16.6\%$. So, even 30 % of cases observed in the tree leaf is a rather high result.

Note that we have chosen kNN and SVM just to see whether decision trees (DT) are not much worse than the other popular ML methods based on

gender	education type	locality	religion	how_often	generation	1_event
f	general	town	yes	sev_a_year	9	marriage
f	professional	town	yes	sev_a_year	10	work
f	higher	town	yes	sev_a_year	3	work
m	professional	town	yes	never	9	education
f	professional	town	yes	min_once_a_month	3	work
m	higher	town	yes	never	7	sep
m	general	town	yes	never	2	work
m	higher	town	yes	never	8	sep
f	general	town	yes	min_once_a_month	1	education
m	professional	town	yes	never	8	education
f	professional	town	yes	never	7	education
f	professional	town	yes	sev_a_year	6	education
m	professional	town	yes	never	8	education
m	professional	town	yes	never	4	education
f	general	town	yes	once_a_week	3	education
f	general	town	yes	min_once_a_month	4	education
f	higher	town	yes	sev_a_year	3	work
f	general	town	yes	min_once_a_month	4	work

Fig. 2. The dataset for the first event prediction task with untangled events in the class attribute

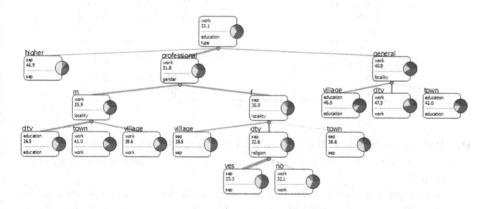

Fig. 3. The decision tree diagram for the first event prediction task

different approaches. Thus, in all our ML experiments we use 15-fold cross-validation with parameter tuning, C-SVM with RBF kernel and starting cost parameter 1.0, DT with Information Gain splitting criterion and no less 70 objects in leaves without binarisation. From the result summary one can conclude that decision trees (DT) classifier demonstrates comparable quality (Brier score 0.68) as kNN and SVM (Brier score 0.686). Moreover, this set of methods has the same events of low prediction quality: first child, first marriage, and first partner are rather unpredictable as first events at all. So, separation from parents, first job, and completion of first education are the typical first events.

Table 1. Classification performance for the first life-course event prediction

Classifier	Classification Accuracy	F_1	Precision	Recall
First child				
Classification Tree	0.42	n/a	n/a	0.0
kNN	0.39	n/a	0.0	0.0
SVM	0.42	n/a	n/a	0.0
First education				
Classification Tree	–	0.42	0.44	0.39
kNN	–	0.4	0.40	0.40
SVM	–	0.42	0.45	0.39
First marriage				
Classification Tree	–	n/a	0.0	0.0
kNN	–	0.08	0.12	0.06
SVM	–	n/a	n/a	0.0
First partner				
Classification Tree	–	n/a	0.0	0.0
kNN	–	0.10	0.16	0.07
SVM	–	n/a	n/a	0.0
Separation from parents				
Classification Tree	–	0.47	0.41	0.53
kNN	–	0.42	0.41	0.44
SVM	–	0.50	0.40	0.64
First job				
Classification Tree	–	0.45	0.44	0.47
kNN	–	0.42	0.41	0.43
SVM	–	0.40	0.45	0.36

Prediction of Next Life-Course Events. QUESTION: *What is the next course event given the general person's descriptions and previous demographic behaviour?*

As an input for the next life-course event prediction we take the same individuals with all their general descriptors like gender, education, living place, religion, visiting frequency of religious events, generation and important demographic events with the indication of time they happened in months starting from the person's birth. The current last event that happened in the life-course of a particular person is a target attribute (class).

Here we deal with the same problem of multiple atomic events in the target variable. Therefore, we use the same untangling transformation.

We encode the events as features in three different ways:

1. BE or binary encoding (value 1 means that event has happened for a given person and 0 otherwise),
2. TE or time encoding (the age when the event happened in months),
3. PE or pairwise encoding.

There are 7 possible combinations of these encoding schemes.

For pairwise encoding of two events a and b as values: "$<$" means that either a precedes b or b has not happened yet, "$>$" means that either a follows b or a has not occurred yet, "$=$" designates that a and b has happened simultaneously w.r.t. time granularity, "n/a" denotes that neither a or b has happened.

Table 2. Comparison of classification accuracy of different encoding schemes for next life-course event prediction. Bold font means the best result for given encoding, sign ($\sim$) means very close results, and (*) means the best result in the column.

Encoding scheme	Unbalanced data Classification Accuracy	Balanced data Classification Accuracy
Binary	0.8498(*)	**0.8780(*)**
Time-based	0.3516	**0.3591**
Pairwise	**0.7161**	0.7013
Binary and time-based	0.7293($\sim$)	**0.7459**
Binary and pairwise	0.8407	**0.8438**
Time-based and pairwise	**0.5465**	0.4959
BE, TE, and PE	0.7295($\sim$)	**0.7503**

From the resulting Table 2 it is easy to see that the best classification accuracy is attained via binary encoding scheme on the balanced data, 0.88, but for the unbalanced dataset the best value does not differ dramatically, 0.85. Pure time-based encoding scheme is the worst in both cases. Pairwise encoding usually helps to improve the results of other encoding schemes, but in combination with binary one it may slightly worsen the accuracy.

	br	child	div	education	marriage	partner	sep	work	
br	583	63	0	1	17	0	7	2	**673**
child	11	2371	0	7	0	6	42	3	**2440**
div	142	53	397	0	0	0	8	1	**601**
education	0	0	0	1041	0	0	0	10	**1051**
marriage	59	79	0	2	177	1	36	1	**355**
partner	0	42	101	0	26	142	14	2	**327**
sep	0	28	0	8	0	0	975	5	**1016**
work	0	19	0	34	0	0	12	375	**440**
	795	**2655**	**498**	**1093**	**220**	**149**	**1094**	**399**	**6903**

Fig. 4. The confusion matrix for the next event prediction ("br" means "break up" and "div" means "divorce" events) in case of binary encoding and the balanced dataset

In Fig. 4 the confusion matrix (true class vs predicted) is shown. We can see that there are more zeros outside of the main diagonal in comparison to the first event prediction task. The most confusing classes are "first divorce" ("break-up" predicted in 142 cases and "child birth" in 53 cases), first partner ("child birth" and "divorce" in 42 and 101 cases respectively) and first marriage ("break-up" and "child birth" predicted in 59 and 79 cases respectively). Since the tree does not have a domain knowledge, divorce may be very similar to the break-up outcome ceteris paribus without taking into account marriage event. The hypothesis that in some cases a father will rather prefer divorce than to care about his child being married need to be separately tested.

Since the tree is rather humongous to be put as a figure we provide several examples of the obtained rules below (Table 3).

Table 3. Several rules from the obtained decision tree for the next events' prediction task

Premise (path in the tree)	Conclusion (leaf)	Confidence
Education and child birth	Separation from parents	93.9%
Education, separation from parents, child birth	First job	98.9%
Male, child birth, education, partner, separation from parents, and first job	Marriage	83.2%
Female, child birth, education, partner, separation from parents, and first job	Break-up	54.6%
Child birth, education, marriage, partner, separation from parents, and first job	Break-up	78.1%
First job, separation from parents, education, marriage, and child birth	Divorce	72.9%
Female, education, separation from parents, and first job	Child birth	78.1%
Education, separation from parents, marriage	Child birth	95.7%
Education (general or professional), partner, separation from parents, and first job	Child birth	60.5% or 54.5% resp.
Education	First job	90.3%
Education and First job	Separation from parents	76.7%

So, the obtained rules is food for thoughts to demographers, however even an ordinary data analyst may be curious why 3rd and 4th rules in Table 3 differ only by gender but result in marriage for men and break-up for women.

The obtained rules may include attribute "generation" in the premise as well. For example, if generation is 10th (1975-1979) a person has religious beliefs and professional education, then 40.9% the last event is child birth, but in case the person is atheistic then it will most likely result in break up.

Gender Prediction Rules. QUESTION: *What are the typical patterns that discern men and women?*

To find discriminative patterns from men and women, we perform similar data transformations, namely balancing and combinations of three encoding schemes. We use both general descriptions and demographic events as object attributes.

Table 4. Comparison of classification accuracy of different encoding schemes for gender prediction

Encoding scheme	Unbalanced data Classification Accuracy	Balanced data Classification Accuracy
Binary	0.6838(*)	0.5824
Time-based	0.6827	0.6758
Pairwise	0.6817	0.5896
Binary and time-based	0.6842($\sim$)	0.6647
Binary and pairwise	0.6815	0.5923
Time-based and pairwise	0.6827	0.6743
BE, TE, and PE	0.6842($\sim$)	0.6915(*)

For this task balancing does not improve predictive accuracy but rather makes it lower; however, the slightly better result than in case of binary encoding (0.69 vs 0.68) is obtained via using balanced data and all three encoding schemes (see Table 4).

However, for the best unbalanced and balanced data we have different values of precision and recall. Thus for the unbalanced data and binary encoding scheme we have $F_1 = 0.17$, Precision=0.25, and Recall=0.16 for men class and $F_1 = 0.8$, Precision=0.7, and Recall=0.93 for women. The situation is quite better for the balanced data and the full combination of encoding schemes: $F_1 = 0.7$, Precision=0.68, and Recall=0.73 for male and $F_1 = 0.68$, Precision=0.71, and Recall=0.65 for female.

Let us present several found patterns.

The predicted target class value is Men:

- First job after 19.9 years, marriage in 20.6-22.4, education before 20.7, break up after 27.6, divorce before 30.5 (confidence is 65.9%)
- First job after 19.9, marriage in 20.6-22.4, break-up before 27.6 (conf. 61.1%)
- First job before 17.2, marriage in 20.6-22.4, break-up before 27.6 (confidence 61.3%)
- First job after 21, marriage after 29.5 (confidence 70.2%)
- Child after 22.9, marriage in 23.9-29.5 (confidence 69.3%)
- Marriage in 22.4-23.3 (confidence 65.4%)
- Marriage in 23.3-23.9, child after 24.7 (confidence 67%)

The predicted target class value is Women:

- First job in 18.2-19.9, marriage in 20.6-22.4, break-up after 27.6, divorce after 30.5 (confidence 71.9%)

- First job in 18.2-19.9, marriage in 20.6-22.4, break-up after 27.6, divorce before 30.5 (confidence 70.9%)
- First job in 17.2-19.9, marriage in 20.6-22.4, break-up before 27.6 (conf. 62.8%)
- First job in 17.7-21, marriage after 29.5 (confidence 62.8%)
- Child before 22.9, marriage in 23.8-29.5 (confidence 61.2%)

Note that the patterns are rather specific; it causes low predictive ability.

5.2   Pattern Mining Experiments

Mining Frequent Closed Sequences. To find frequent closed sequences we can use any efficiently implemented algorithm; thus, we used BIDE [25] from SPMF and set the minimal support threshold to $minsup = 0.1$.

The most frequent 1-event sequence is education with $sup = 4857$, the most frequent 2-event sequence is first job, and then child birth with $sup = 3828$, the most frequent 3-event sequence is first job, then marriage, then child birth with $sup = 2762$, and the most frequent 4-event sequence is education, then first job, marriage, and child birth with support equals to 1091.

Event "Child birth" happened for 4399 out of 4857 respondents: The longest closed sequential pattern starting with "Child birth" is $\langle child\ birth, education \rangle$ with support 1154.

The longest closed sequential pattern starting with "Education" is $\langle education, first\ job, marriage, child\ birth \rangle$ with $sup = 1091$. "Marriage" event took place for 4201 out of 4857. The longest closed sequential pattern starting with "Marriage" is $\langle marriage, child\ birth, education \rangle$, $sup = 941$.

Event "First partner" happened for 1839 out of 4857 respondents. The longest closed sequential pattern starting with "First partner" is $\langle\ partner, marriage, child\ birth \rangle$, $sup = 676$. The longest closed sequential pattern starting with "First job" is $\langle first\ job, education, marriage, child\ birth \rangle$ with support 687.

The longest closed sequential pattern starting with "Separation from parents" ($sup = 4723$) is $\langle\ separation, first\ job, marriage, child \rangle$, $sup = 822$.

It is interesting that events "separation from parents" and "marriage" happened for 833 out of 4857 respondents. Here, the longest closed sequential pattern is $\langle \{separation\ from\ parents, marriage\}, child\ birth \rangle$, $sup = 777$.

Emergent Sequences. For experiments with emergent sequences we use PrefixSpan [26] from SPMF. Since we have two classes, men and women, we has obtained two sets of emergent sequences for relative $minsup = 0.005$; for each class we use 3312 sequences after oversampling. The best classification accuracy (0.936) has been reached via 80:20 cross-validation at minimal growth rate 1.0, with 577 rules for men and 1164 for women and 3 non-covered objects.

List of emergent sequences for women (with their class contribution):

$\langle \{partner, education\}, \{children\}, \{break\text{-}up\} \rangle$, 0.0147

⟨{*separation*}, {*children*}, {*work*}, {*education*}⟩, 0.0121

⟨{*separation, partner*}, {*marriage*}, {*education*}⟩, 0.0106

⟨{*work, education, marriage*}, {*separation*}⟩, 0.0102

⟨{*work, partner, education*}, {*break-up*}⟩, 0.0098

⟨{*separation, partner*}, {*children*}, {*work*}⟩, 0.0092

⟨{*partner, education*}, {*marriage*}, {*break-up*}⟩, 0.008

⟨{*work*}, {*partner, education*}, {*break-up*}⟩, 0.008

⟨{*work, partner, education*}, {*children*}, {*break-up*}⟩, 0.008

⟨{*work, partner*}, {*children*}, {*divorce*}⟩, 0.008

⟨{*separation, partner, education*}, {*break-up*}⟩, 0.0072

List of emergent sequences for men:

⟨{*education*}, {*separation*}, {*work*}, {*marriage*}⟩, 0.0124

⟨{*separation, education*}, {*work*}, {*partner*}, {*children*}⟩, 0.0079

⟨{*education*}, {*separation*}, {*work*}, {*marriage*}, {*children*}⟩, 0.0074

⟨{*education*}, {*separation*}, {*partner*}, {*marriage*}, {*children*}⟩, 0.0065

⟨{*work*}, {*education*}, {*marriage, partner*}, {*divorce, break-up*}⟩, 0.0057

⟨{*divorce, break-up*}, {*children*}⟩, 0.0055

⟨{*work*}, {*divorce, break-up*}, {*children*}⟩, 0.0055

⟨{*education*}, {*marriage*}, {*work, children*}⟩, 0.005

⟨{*partner*}, {*divorce, break-up*}, {*children*}⟩, 0.005

⟨{*marriage*}, {*divorce, break-up*}, {*children*}⟩, 0.005

⟨{*education*}, {*partner*}, {*divorce*}, {*children*}⟩, 0.005

6   Conclusion and Future Work

We have shown that decision trees and sequence mining could become the tools of choice for demographers. To this end we have found various patterns hoping that some of them are of interest to demographers and this is really the case for our second co-author, a professional demographer, and her colleagues.

Machine learning and data mining tools can help in finding regularities and dependencies that are hidden in voluminous demographic datasets. However, these methods need to be properly tuned and adapted to the domain needs. For example, in frequent subsequences between their two subsequent events in a corresponding sequence from dataset D may happen several other events. Thus, our domain experts require us to use "sequences of starting events without gaps" which are just prefix strings in computer science terms. In the near future we are planning to implement emergent prefix-string mining to bridge the gap. As for decision trees, we mentioned the problem of high similarity of decision rules as paths with different terminal nodes and preceding leaves but sharing the same starting subpath. It may be a restriction for interpretation matters and we need to try different rule-based techniques as well. Thus, we need rule-based techniques that are able to cope with unbalanced multi-class data [27]. Another interesting venue is usage of Pattern Structures to sequence mining [28].

Acknowledgments. We would like to thank Jaume Baixeries, Mehdi Kaytoue, and anonymous reviewers. This study (grant no. 14-05-0054 "Studying of the dynamics of formation and development of families and fertility using data of selective surveys") was supported by the Academic Fund Program of National Research University Higher School of Economics in 2014. The first author has been supported by the Russian Foundation for Basic Research grants no. 13-07-00504 and 14-01-93960 and made a contribution within the project "Data mining based on applied ontologies and lattices of closed descriptions" supported by the Basic Research Program of the same university.

References

1. Aisenbrey, S., Fasang, A.E.: New life for old ideas: The second wave of sequence analysis bringing the course back into the life course. Sociological Methods & Research **38**(3), 420–462 (2010)
2. Billari, F.C.: Sequence analysis in demographic research. Canadian Studies in Population **28**(2), 439–458 (2001)
3. Aassve, A., Billari, F.C., Piccarreta, R.: Strings of adulthood: A sequence analysis of young british womens work-family trajectories. European Journal of Population **23**(3/4), 369–388 (2007)
4. Jackson, P.B., Berkowitz, A.: The structure of the life course: Gender and racioethnic variation in the occurrence and sequencing of role transitions. Advances in Life Course Research **9**, 55–90 (2005)
5. Worts, D., Sacker, A., McMunn, A., McDonough, P.: Individualization, opportunity and jeopardy in american womens work and family lives: A multi-state sequence analysis. Advances in Life Course Research **18**(4), 296–318 (2013)
6. Abbott, A., Tsay, A.: Sequence analysis and optimal matching methods in sociology: Review and prospect. Sociological Methods & Research (2000)
7. Billari, F., Piccarreta, R.: Analyzing demographic life courses through sequence analysis. Mathematical Population Studies **12**(2), 81–106 (2005)
8. Billari, F.C., Frnkranz, J., Prskawetz, A.: Timing, Sequencing, and Quantum of Life Course Events: A Machine Learning Approach. European Journal of Population **22**(1), 37–65 (2006)
9. Gauthier, J.A., Widmer, E.D., Bucher, P., Notredame, C.: How Much Does It Cost? Optimization of Costs in Sequence Analysis of Social Science Data. Sociological Methods & Research **38**(1), 197–231 (2009)
10. Ritschard, G., Oris, M.: Life course data in demography and social sciences: Statistical and data-mining approaches. Advances in Life Course Research **10**, 283–314 (2005)
11. Gabadinho, A., Ritschard, G., Mller, N.S., Studer, M.: Analyzing and Visualizing State Sequences in R with TraMineR. J. of Statistical Software **40**(4), 1–37 (2011)
12. Blockeel, H., Fürnkranz, J., Prskawetz, A., Billari, F.C.: Detecting temporal change in event sequences: an application to demographic data. In: Siebes, A., De Raedt, L. (eds.) PKDD 2001. LNCS (LNAI), vol. 2168, pp. 29–41. Springer, Heidelberg (2001)
13. Fournier-Viger, P., Gomariz, A., Gueniche, T., Soltani, A., Wu, C.W., Tseng, V.S.: SPMF: A Java Open-Source Pattern Mining Library. Journal of Machine Learning Research **15**, 3389–3393 (2014)
14. Dong, G., Li, J.: Efficient mining of emerging patterns: discovering trends and differences. In: Proc. of the Fifth ACM SIGKDD Int. Conf. on Knowledge Discovery and Data Mining, KDD 1999, pp. 43–52. ACM (1999)

15. Breiman, L., Friedman, J.H., Olshen, R.A., Stone, C.J.: Classification and Regression Trees. Wadsworth (1984)
16. Quinlan, J.R.: Induction of decision trees. Machine Learning **1**(1), 81–106 (1986)
17. Agrawal, R., Srikant, R.: Mining sequential patterns. In: Proceedings of the Eleventh International Conference on Data Engineering, pp. 3–14 (1995)
18. Han, J., Kamber, M.: Data Mining: Concepts and Techniques, 2nd edn. Morgan Kaufmann (2006)
19. Mill, J.S.: A system of logic, ratonative and inductive, vol. 1. J. W. Parker, London (1843)
20. Finn, V.K.: On Machine-Oriented Formalization of Plausible Reasoning in the Style of F. BackonJ. S. Mill. Semiotika i Informatika **20**, 35–101 (1983)
21. Kuznetsov, S.O.: Learning of simple conceptual graphs from positive and negative examples. In: Żytkow, J.M., Rauch, J. (eds.) PKDD 1999. LNCS (LNAI), vol. 1704, pp. 384–391. Springer, Heidelberg (1999)
22. Low-Kam, C., Raissi, C., Kaytoue, M., Pei, J.: Mining statistically significant sequential patterns. In: IEEE 13th Int. Conf. on Data Mining, pp. 488–496 (2013)
23. Demšar, J., Curk, T., Erjavec, A., Gorup, Č., Hočevar, T., Milutinovič, M., Možina, M., Polajnar, M., Toplak, M., Starič, A., Štajdohar, M., Umek, L., Žagar, L., Žbontar, J., Žitnik, M., Zupan, B.: Orange: Data Mining Toolbox in Python. Journal of Machine Learning Research **14**, 2349–2353 (2013)
24. Bouckaert, R.R., Frank, E., Hall, M.A., Holmes, G., Pfahringer, B., Reutemann, P., Witten, I.H.: WEKA - Experiences with a Java Open-Source Project. Journal of Machine Learning Research **11**, 2533–2541 (2010)
25. Wang, J., Han, J.: BIDE: efficient mining of frequent closed sequences. In: Özsoyoglu, Z.M., Zdonik, S.B. (eds.) Proceedings of the 20th International Conference on Data Engineering, ICDE 2004, pp. 79–90. IEEE Computer Society (2004)
26. Pei, J., Han, J., Mortazavi-Asl, B., Pinto, H., Chen, Q., Dayal, U., Hsu, M.: PrefixSpan: mining sequential patterns by prefix-projected growth. In: Proceedings of the 17th International Conference on Data Engineering, pp. 215–224 (2001)
27. Cerf, L., Gay, D., Selmaoui-Folcher, N., Crmilleux, B., Boulicaut, J.F.: Parameter-free classification in multi-class imbalanced data sets. Data & Knowledge Engineering **87**, 109–129 (2013)
28. Buzmakov, A., Egho, E., Jay, N., Kuznetsov, S.O., Napoli, A., Raïssi, C.: On projections of sequential pattern structures (with an application on care trajectories). In: 10th Int. Conf. on Concept Lattices and Their Applications, pp. 199–208 (2013)

System Description Papers

Extracting Metadata from Multimedia Content on Facebook as Media Annotations

Miguel B. Alves[1,2]([✉]) , Carlos Viegas Damásio[1], and Nuno Correia[3]

[1] CENTRIA, Universidade Nova de Lisboa, 2829-516 Caparica, Portugal
mba@estg.ipvc.pt, {cd,nmc}@fct.unl.pt
[2] ESTG - IPVC, 4900-348 Viana do Castelo, Portugal
[3] CITI, Universidade Nova de Lisboa, 2829-516 Caparica, Portugal

Abstract. This paper presents two ways to extract metadata from Facebook's multimedia content, such as photos and videos, as descriptors of Ontology For Media Resources. We develop an ontology to map metadata in Facebook's multimedia content to the descriptors of Ontology For Media Resources and we develop a SPARQL endpoint that enables reasoning over Facebook multimedia content using Ontology For Media Resources.

1 Introduction

With the spread of the social networks as well as the proliferation of digital cameras and smartphones, we are witnessing an explosively growing number of shared multimedia contents. Facebook, in particular, has more than 900 million users, and can be considered one of the biggest multimedia repository.

A major problem is to make these contents searchable to machines since they constitute complex objects, with low and high level semantics, in order to give support to an efficient multimedia retrieval. This problem has led to many efforts to define a common lingua franca for the retrieval of Web-based multimedia resources, describing the syntactic and semantic features. However, these efforts carried to a proliferation of multimedia metadata formats. To overcome this problem, World Wide Web Consortium (W3C) Media Annotation Working Group (MAWG) proposed the Ontology for Media Resources (OMR) [6], or Media Annotations, an ontology to describe multimedia resources which addresses the interoperability problem between different metadata formats.

In this work our purpose is to extract Facebook multimedia contents metadata as descriptors of Ontology for Media Resources. With the appearance of a standardised Ontology that addresses the multimedia resources interoperability problem between different metadata formats, we believe that, in the future, practitioners will produce reasoning tools mainly based on OMR. In this way, all reasoning produced will consider the different formats. Our work allows an easy link of Facebook multimedia contents to ontologies, sharing the vast knowledge contained therein.

We supply two ways to extract Facebook multimedia contents metadata as descriptors from Ontology for Media Resources. In the first one, Section 4, we create an ontology that maps the Facebook multimedia content descriptors with the

P. Klinov and D. Mouromtsev (Eds.): KESW 2015, CCIS 518, pp. 243–252, 2015.
DOI: 10.1007/978-3-319-24543-0_18

Ontology for Media Resources. Including this ontology in our dataset allows to return the metadata of a Facebook multimedia content as descriptors of OMR. In the second one, Section 5, we develop a SPARQL Endpoint that allows reasoning with OMR descriptors. Before explaining the details of our work, we will start with an introduction of Facebook in Semantic Web, in Section 2, and we introduce the Ontology for Media resources in Section 3, finishing with conclusions in Section 6.

2   Facebook on the Semantic Web

Facebook provides an Graph API[1], a simple HTTP-based API that gives access to the Facebook social graph, uniformly representing objects (people, photos, events and pages) in the graph and the connections between them (e.g., friend relationships, shared content, and photo tags). This social network also has a query language, FQL, Facebook query language[2], SQL look-alike. The Graph API returns the data in JSON format, which can be translated to RDF, and in RDF format, containing Linked Data (HTTP(S)) URIs that dereference in accordance with httpRange-14 [7] [10]. Hence, the data provided by the Facebook Graph API can be obtained utilising the RDFS [9] and OWL [2] vocabularies. The RDF data is returned in Turtle format.

3   Ontology for Media Resources

The aim of Ontology for Media Resources [6], or Media Annotations, is to link various media resources descriptions together, bridging the different descriptions of media resources, providing a core set of properties that can be used to transparently express them. The metadata of multimedia content is represented in different formats which hardly interoperate although they partially overlap. The Ontology for Media Resources has the goal of improving the interoperability between media metadata schemas, providing an interlingua ontology and an API designed to facilitate cross-community data integration of information related to media resources in the web, such as video, audio, and multimedia contents [8].

4   Mapping Between Facebook Descriptors and Ontology for Media Resources

There exists an ontology[3] in OWL (with some declarations in OWL 2 [4] that we will explain later) which defines the mapping between Facebook descriptors and the Ontology for Media Resources (OMR). Considering that we add this file to our dataset, that also contains the data of Facebook multimedia contents, we can obtain all the information with OMR descriptors. We remind that we can

---

[1] https://developers.Facebook.com/docs/graph-api/

[2] https://developers.Facebook.com/docs/reference/fql/

[3] http://www.estg.ipvc.pt/mbentoalves/fb_omr_map.owl

add to our dataset directly the data obtained through the Graph API since we can get data in RDF/Turtle. Therefore, if we have the following statements in our dataset that represents metadata defined using Facebook descriptors:

```
@prefix fb_schema: <https://graph.facebook.com/schema/~/> .
</1526310794319806#>
    fb_schema:id "1526310794319806" ;
    fb_schema:created_time "2014-12-19T11:29:30+00:00"^^xsd:dateTime .
```

we can get the same data mapped to OMR.

```
@prefix ma: <http://www.w3.org/ns/ma-ont#>
</1526310794319806#>
    rdf:type ma:Image ;
    ma:creationDate "2014-12-19T11:29:30+00:00"^^xsd:dateTime .
```

To simplify the reading in the previous statements and in the rest of the document, besides the well known prefixes *rdf, rdfs, owl, xsd*, consider the following prefixes:

```
page: <https://graph.Facebook.com/schema/page#>
fb_schema: <https://graph.Facebook.com/schema/~/>
geo: <http://www.w3.org/2003/01/geo/wgs84_pos#>
swrlb: <http://www.w3.org/2003/11/swrlb#>
swrl: <http://www.w3.org/2003/11/swrl#>
map: <http://www.estg.ipvc.pt/mbentoalves/map_fb_omr#>
ma: <http://www.w3.org/ns/ma-ont#>
api: <tag:graph.Facebook.com,2011:/>
```

In our ontology, we map the Facebook photos as images' classes in OMR and Facebook videos as videos' classes. Both of those classes are sub-classes of multimedia resources. To distinguish both, as is not clear in the properties of Facebook descriptors, we resort to properties that one of the classes have and the other not. The next statements defines what is a photo and what is a video. The definition of Facebook multimedia contents as OMR is given by the next statements.

```
map:Image
    owl:equivalentClass [
        rdf:type owl:Restriction ;
        owl:minCardinality "1"^^xsd:nonNegativeInteger ;
        owl:onProperty fb_schema:images ] ;
    owl:equivalentClass ma:Image .
map:Video
    owl:equivalentClass [
        rdf:type owl:Restriction ;
        owl:minCardinality "1"^^xsd:nonNegativeInteger ;
        owl:onProperty fb_schema:length ] ;
    owl:equivalentClass ma:VideoTrack .
```

Table 1 defines direct mappings of object properties and datatype properties between Facebook and OMR.

Table 1. Mappings of object and data properties between Facebook and OMR

Facebook	OMR
fb_schema:created_time	ma:creationDate
fb_schema:place	ma:createdIn
fb_schema:link	ma:hasSource
fb_schema:source	ma:hasSource
fb_schema:picture	ma:hasSource
fb_schema:name	ma:title
page:location	ma:hasLocationCoordinateSystem
fb_schema:height	ma:frameHeight
fb_schema:width	ma:frameWidth
fb_schema:latitude	geo:lat
fb_schema:longitude	geo:long
fb_schema:length	ma:duration

The property **ma:hasCreator** identifies the author of the resource. As the identification of the creator in Facebook is defined as an internal *id*, we need to define a transitive relationship between **fb_schema:from** and **fb_schema:link** to identify the creator by an URL. OWL2 allows *Property Chain Inclusion*, which consists in a property defined as the composition of several properties. We make use of this requirement to map the authors of the resources between Facebook and OMR.

```
map:hasCreator
    rdf:type owl:ObjectProperty ;
    owl:propertyChainAxiom (fb_schema:from fb_schema:link);
    owl:equivalentProperty ma:hasCreator .
```

We map the tags of the Facebook multimedia contents to OMR keywords. An issue is this mapping is that in the documentation of OMR is recommended to be an URI as best practice. However, also can be used plain text. In OMR ontology, **ma:hasKeyword** is an object property. Only in DL full object properties and datatype properties are not disjoint. Therefore, we create an object property **map:hasKeyword** to be equivalent to **ma:hasKeyword** in OMR. The mapping of the tags of the Facebook multimedia contents to OMR keywords is also a transitive relationship, implemented as a *Property Chain Inclusion*, between **fb_schema:tags**, **fb_schema:data** and **api:has**. As the descriptions should be an URI, we created a class *map:Description* which defines all the descriptions of the Facebook data. This class is the range of **map:hasKeyword** object property.

```
map:hasKeyword
    rdf:type owl:ObjectProperty ;
    owl:propertyChainAxiom (fb_schema:tags fb_schema:data api:has);
    rdfs:range map:Description ;
    owl:equivalentProperty ma:hasKeyword .
```

```
map:Description
    owl:equivalentClass [
        rdf:type owl:Restriction ;
        owl:minCardinality "1"^^xsd:nonNegativeInteger ;
        owl:onProperty fb_schema:name
    ] .
```

To get the tag in plain text, we need to resort to *fb_schema:name* data type property as we show in the next SPARQL command:

```
Select ?i ?l
where {
    ?i ma:hasKeyword ?k .
    ?k fb_schema:name ?l .
}
```

In Facebook, the upload of an image can trigger the creation of several images with different dimensions. These images created can be considered also as an image resource. Therefore, the mapping between these created resources is also done. Once, is a transitive relationship between the object properties **fb_schema:images** and **api:has**.

```
map:hasRelatedImage
    rdf:type owl:ObjectProperty ;
    owl:propertyChainAxiom (fb_schema:images api:has);
    owl:equivalentProperty ma:hasRelatedImage .
```

4.1   SWRL Reasoning

The properties **ma:locationLatitude** and **ma:locationLongitude** identify the GPS coordinates where a multimedia content was taken. To get this information in Facebook we need to define a transitive relationship between **page:location** and **fb_schema:latitude** or **fb_schema:longitude**. We cannot use property chains of OWL 2 because **fb_schema:latitude** and **fb_schema:longitude** are not object properties but datatype properties. So, we resort to SWRL rules [5], which also implies OWL2 reasoning. The follow SWRL rule defines both latitude and longitude where a multimedia content was taken.

```
page:location(?x, ?y), fb_schema:latitude(?y, ?z)
    -> map:locationLatitude(?x, ?z)

page:location(?x, ?y), fb_schema:longitude(?y, ?z)
    -> map:locationLongitude(?x, ?z)

map:locationLatitude owl:equivalentProperty ma:locationLatitude
map:locationLongitude owl:equivalentProperty ma:locationLongitude
```

To get the location name where a multimedia content was taken, we also need a SWRL rule. The location name can be retrieved with the property **page:name**. However, this property is too generic, so, to make sure that is a location, first we define what is a location, through the class **map:Location**. We define the locations as all resources with the property *ma:isCreationLocationOf*. In turn, *ma:isCreationLocationOf* is an inverse property of *ma:createdIn* that is mapped with *fb_schema:place*. Our SWRL rule defines a datatype property, *map:locationName*, that defines the location name of a given location, in text plain. This datatype property is mapped with *ma:locationName*.

```
map:Location
    owl:equivalentClass [
        rdf:type owl:Restriction ;
        owl:minCardinality "1"^^xsd:nonNegativeInteger ;
        owl:onProperty ma:isCreationLocationOf
    ] .


map:Location(?x), page:name(?x, ?y)
    -> map:locationName(?x, ?y)
map:locationName owl:equivalentProperty ma:locationName
```

4.2   A Practical Example

Next, we list Semantic data extracted from Facebook (List 1) and the equivalent data in OMR (List 2). We removed some data without importance so that the list would not be too large. Links very large were also cut.

```
prefix : <https://graph.Facebook.com/schema/~/>
</1526310794319806#>
    :id "1526310794319806" ;
    :created_time "2014-12-19T11:29:30+00:00"^^xsd:dateTime ;
    :from </1526312517652967#> ;
    :height 720 ;
    :images [
        api:has [
            :height 960 ; :width 720 ;
            :source <https://scontent.xx.fbcdn.net/...&oe=56076F28> ] ;
        api:has [
            :height 800 ; :width 600 ;
            :source <https://scontent.xx.fbcdn.net/...&oe=55BEE636> ] ] ;
    :link <https://www.facebook.com/photo.php?fbid=1526310794319806...&type=1> ;
    :name "photo 1" ;
    :picture <https://scontent.xx.fbcdn.net...&oe=55C669F0> ;
    :place </106268452745904#> ;
    :source <https://scontent.xx.fbcdn.net/...&oe=55FAE94A> ;
    :updated_time "2014-12-23T10:58:30+00:00"^^xsd:dateTime ;
    :width 540 ;
```

```
    :tags [
      :data [
        api:has [
          :name "surface 1" ;
          :created_time "2014-12-23T10:58:30+00:00"^^xsd:dateTime ;
      ] ] ] .
</1526312517652967#>
  :id "1526312517652967" ;
  :link <https://www.facebook.com/app_scoped_user_id/1526312517652967/> .
</106268452745904#>
  :id "106268452745904" ;
  :name "Brie-Comte-Robert, France" ;
  :location [
    :latitude 48.6833 ;
    :longitude 2.61667 ] .
```

Listing 1 - Semantic data extracted from Facebook

```
<file:///1526310794319806#>
  ma:createdIn <file:///106268452745904#> ;
  ma:creationDate "2014-12-19T11:29:30+00:00"^^xsd:dateTime ;
  ma:date "2014-12-19T11:29:30+00:00"^^xsd:dateTime ;
  ma:frameHeight 720 ;
  ma:frameWidth 540 ;
  ma:hasContributor<https://www.facebook.com/app_scoped_user_id/1526312517652967/>;
  ma:hasCreator <https://www.facebook.com/app_scoped_user_id/1526312517652967/> ;
  ma:hasKeyword <file:///56095229859#> ;
  ma:hasRelatedImage [
    ma:frameHeight 960 ;
    ma:frameWidht 720 ;
    ma:RelatedResource <https://scontent.xx.fbcdn.net/...&oe=56076F28> ;
    ma:hasSource <https://scontent.xx.fbcdn.net/...&oe=56076F28> ;
    ma:isImageRelatedTo <file:///1526310794319806#> ],
    [
    ma:frameHeight 800 ;
    ma:frameWidht 600 ;
    ma:RelatedResource <https://scontent.xx.fbcdn.net/...&oe=55BEE636> ;
    ma:hasSource <https://scontent.xx.fbcdn.net/...&oe=55BEE636> ;
    ma:isImageRelatedTo <file:///1526310794319806#> ] ;
  ma:hasRelatedLocation <file:///106268452745904#> ;
  ma:hasRelatedResource
      <https://scontent.xx.fbcdn.net/...&oe=55FAE94A> ;
  ma:hasSource
      <https://scontent.xx.fbcdn.net/...&oe=55FAE94A> ;
  ma:title "photo 1" .
```

```
<file:///106268452745904#>
    ma:isCreationLocationOf <file:///1526310794319806#> ;
    ma:isLocationRelatedTo <file:///1526310794319806#> ;
    ma:locationLatitude 48.6833 ;
    ma:locationLongitude 2.61667 ;
    ma:locationName "Brie-Comte-Robert, France" .
<https://www.facebook.com/app_scoped_user_id/1526312517652967/>
    ma:hasContributedTo <file:///1526310794319806#> ;
    ma:hasCreated <file:///1526310794319806#> .
```

Listing 2 - OMR representation of data extracted from Facebook

5   SPARQL Endpoint for Querying Multimedia Content on Facebook

In this work, we also created a SPARQL endpoint to get information from Facebook multimedia contents. In this way, we do not need to have the information of a given Facebook multimedia content in our dataset. The SPARQL endpoint is available at http://www.estg.ipvc.pt/mbentoalves/fb_omr_map. Due to of privacy checks, the majority of API calls on Facebook need to include an access token. This access token provides temporary, secure access to Facebook APIs, and should be provided to the SPARQL endpoint. The *id* of the multimedia content (object id) also must be provided to the SPARQL endpoint. Thus, we can select information using OMR ontology as SPARQL endpoints are normally used. Next, we present an example of a SPARQL command using the SPARQL endpoint.

```
prefix ma: <http://www.w3.org/ns/ma-ont#>
Select ?i ?ln {
    SERVICE <http://www.estg.ipvc.pt/mbentoalves/fb_omr_map
    ?access_token=<ACCESS_TOKEN>&object_id=<OBJECT_ID>>
    {
        ?i ma:createdIn ?l .
        ?l ma:locationName ?ln .
    }
}
```

The SPARQL endpoint developed also allows retrieve semantic data of all photos or videos of a Facebook profile. For that, we have a parameter in our endpoint service, called *param*. Assigning the value *getPhotos* to this parameter, we get all photos and its semantic data whereas assigning the value *getVideos* we get all videos and its semantic data.

```
prefix ma: <http://www.w3.org/ns/ma-ont#>
Select ?i ?ln {
    SERVICE <http://www.estg.ipvc.pt/mbentoalves/fb_omr_map
    ?access_token=<ACCESS_TOKEN>&param=getPhotos>
    {
```

```
        ?i ma:createdIn ?l .
        ?l ma:locationName ?ln .
    }
}
```

It was referred before that one of the main contributions of our work is link the Facebook multimedia contents to ontologies, sharing the knowledge therein. Next, we give an example using the SPARQL endpoint developed in this work that illustrates how to connect the photos of Facebook to Linked Open Data, namely with DBpedia [1,11]. The aim of Linking Open Data Project [3] is using the web to create typed links between data from different sources via mapping of ontologies. In this way, instead of having isolated islands we have global interlinked datasets. Linked Data refers to data published on the Web in such a way that it is machine-readable, its meaning is explicitly defined, it is linked to other external data sets and can be accessed by them. Linked Data principles provide a basic recipe for publishing and connecting data using the infrastructure of the Web while adhering to its architecture and standards. In this example, the link to DBpedia is done through the FactForge SPARQL endpoint[4] and we get the DBpedia uri of the photo location. As DBpedia is the central ontology of Linked Open Data, we are able to perform an unlimited number of reasoning over Facebook multimedia contents, with connections to more than one thousand datasets.

```
PREFIX omgeo: <http://www.ontotext.com/owlim/geo#>
PREFIX dbp-ont: <http://dbpedia.org/ontology/>
PREFIX om: <http://www.ontotext.com/owlim/>
prefix ma-ont: <http://www.w3.org/ns/ma-ont#>
Select ?p ?RR {
    SERVICE <http://www.estg.ipvc.pt/mbentoalves/fb_omr_map?access_token=
<ACCESS_TOKEN>&object_id=<OBJECT_ID>> {
        ?i ma-ont:createdIn ?l .
        ?l ma-ont:locationLatitude ?la ;
            ma-ont:locationLongitude ?lo .
    }
    SERVICE<http://factforge.net/sparql> {
        ?p omgeo:nearby(?la ?lo "1mi");
            a dbp-ont:Settlement ;
            om:hasRDFRank ?RR .
    }
} ORDER BY DESC(?RR)
```

6   Conclusion

Ontology for Media Resources addresses the multimedia resources interoperability problem between different metadata formats. Reasoning over multimedia contents will have a wide range if is based on OMR. Therefore, we propose to

---

[4] http://factforge.net/

extract Facebook multimedia contents metadata as descriptors of Ontology for Media Resources. We supplied two ways to do this task. One way was the development of an ontology that maps the metadata obtained by the Facebook Graph API with the descriptors of OMR. The other way was the implementation of a SPARQL endpoint that receives the identification of a Facebook multimedia content as parameter (as well as an access token for privacy purposes), and allows reasoning using OMR descriptors. Our work links the Facebook multimedia contents to ontologies, sharing the knowledge therein.

References

1. Auer, S., Bizer, C., Kobilarov, G., Lehmann, J., Cyganiak, R., Ives, Z.: Dbpedia: A nucleus for a web of open data. The Semantic Web, 722–735, November 2008
2. Bechhofer, S., van Harmelen, F., Hendler, J., Horrocks, I., McGuinness, D., Patel-Schneijder, P., Stein, L.A.: OWL web ontology language reference, February 10, 2004
3. Bizer, C., Heath, T., Berners-Lee, T.: Linked data - the story so far. International Journal on Semantic Web and Information Systems 5(3), 1–22 (2009)
4. Cuenca, B., Horrocks, I., Motik, B., Parsia, B., Patel-Schneider, P., Sattler, U.: OWL 2: The next step for OWL. Web Semantics 6(4), 309–322 (2008)
5. Horrocks, I., Patel-Schneider, P.F., Boley, H., Tabet, S., Grosof, B., Dean, M.: SWRL: A semantic web rule language combining OWL and RuleML. W3c member submission, World Wide Web Consortium (2004). http://www.w3.org/Submission/SWRL
6. Lee, W., Bailer, W., Burger, T., Champin, P.A., Evain, J.P., Malaise, V., Michel, T., Sasaki, F., Soderberg, J., Stegmaier, F., Strassner, J.: Ontology for Media Resources 1.0, February 2012. http://liris.cnrs.fr/publis/?id=5453, w3C Recommendation. http://www.w3.org/TR/mediaont-10/
7. Mendelsohn, T.B.L.N.: What is the range of the http dereference function? (14), May 2012. http://www.w3.org/TR/2011/WD-turtle-20110809/
8. Stegmaier, F., Bailer, W., Bürger, T., Döller, M., Höffernig, M., Lee, W., Malaisé, V., Poppe, C., Troncy, R., Kosch, H., Van de Walle, R.: How to align media metadata schemas? Design and implementation of the media ontology. In: Workshop on Semantic Multimedia Database Technologies (SeMuDaTe 2009), SAMT 2009, Graz, Austria, December 2, 2009. Also published as CEUR Workshop Proceedings, Graz, Austria, vol. 539, December 2009. http://www.eurecom.fr/publication/2978
9. W3C: Rdfs (2014). http://www.w3.org/TR/rdf-schema/
10. Weaver, J., Tarjan, P.: Facebook linked data via the graph api. Semantic Web 4(3), 245–250 (2013). http://dblp.uni-trier.de/db/journals/semweb/semweb4.html#WeaverT13
11. Yu, L.: A Developer's Guide to the Semantic Web. Springer (2011)

SPARQL Commands in Jena Rules

M.B. Alves[1,2]([✉]), C.V. Damásio[1], and N. Correia[3]

[1] CENTRIA, Universidade Nova de Lisboa, 2829-516 Caparica, Portugal
mba@estg.ipvc.pt, {cd,nmc}@fct.unl.pt
[2] ESTG - IPVC, 4900-348 Viana Do Castelo, Portugal
[3] CITI, Universidade Nova de Lisboa, 2829-516 Caparica, Portugal

Abstract. SPARQL is a powerful query language to manipule RDF data. Rule-based inference over RDF, as Jena reasoner supports, allows storing and manipulation of knowledge. Furthermore, a RDF rule-based inference engine allows to overcome some of OWL expressiveness limitations. Combining SPARQL with rules brings a more powerful way to represent knowledge and increase the expressiveness in Jena.

1 Introduction

Jena framework[1] is a free and open source Java framework for building Semantic Web applications. It provides a programmatic environment for RDF, RDFS, OWL, a query engine for SPARQL and it includes a rule-based inference engine. Jena is wide used in Semantic Web applications because it offers an "all-in-one" solution for Java.

SPARQL [10] is the standard language for querying RDF[13][12] data, and is for RDF data that SQL is to relational databases. SPARQL is an existing W3C standard with well-formed query semantics across RDF data, it has a widespread use amongst most RDF query engines and graph stores, and provides sufficient expressivity for both queries and general computation of data.

Jena includes a general purpose rule-based reasoner which is used to implement both the RDFS and OWL [1][7][2] reasoners, but is also available for general use (in fact, Jena OWL reasoner is a sound implementation of a subset of OWL). A rule language is needed for several reasons [8]. A rule language allows the reusing of existing rulesets, implementations and expertise. Furthermore, OWL has expressiveness limitations [8] and a rule language adds expressivity to it. Jena reasoner supports rule-based inference over RDF graphs and provides forward chaining, backward chaining and a hybrid execution model.

The goal of this project is to allow the use of SPARQL commands in Jena rules. Thus, we increase the expressiveness of Jena resulted from the combination of the rules with SPARQL commands. This document is organised as follows. In Section 2 we introduce to the SPARQL-based rules, in Section 3 we show several examples of SPARQL-based rules, with both purpose of to show demonstrative examples and to show different ways of declaring SPARQL-based rules in Jena.

---

[1] https://jena.apache.org

© Springer International Publishing Switzerland 2015
P. Klinov and D. Mouromtsev (Eds.): KESW 2015, CCIS 518, pp. 253–262, 2015.
DOI: 10.1007/978-3-319-24543-0_19

Section 4 details some aspects of the implementation, while in Section 5 we present some results of the performance of the SPARQL-based rules in Jena. Section 6 presents related works with our work and we finish with our conclusions in Section 7.

2   SPARQL Inferencing

This project was inspired in SPIN Rules [4][11][6]. SPARQL Inferencing Notation (SPIN), a W3C Member Submission, is a SPARQL-based rule and constraint language for the Semantic Web. SPIN supplies a mechanism to represent reusable SPARQL queries as templates. Despite this, the purpose of our work is not to implement SPIN in Jena. However, we share the main motivations [11], providing Jena with the mechanisms to take the same expressiveness as the spin frameworks, namely:

- combines concepts from object oriented languages, query languages, and rule-based systems to describe object behavior on the web of data;
- links class definitions with SPARQL queries to capture constraints and rules that formalize the expected behavior of those classes;
- SPARQL is used because it is an existing W3C standard with well-formed query semantics across RDF data;
- has existing widespread use amongst most RDF query engines and graph stores, and provides sufficient expressivity for both queries and general computation of data;

The main expressiveness differences between SPARQL and a rule language have been described in [9]. Both have limitations and one can complement the other. Furthermore, empirically, we know that there is knowledge that we can better represent by SPARQL and there is knowledge that can be better represented by rules. This project lets Jena developers represent their knowledge with the approach that they think it is more appropriate.

Example 1 shows a rule that cannot be captured neither by OWL 2 role inclusion chain axioms or by original Jena rules. In this example, a given student is diligent in a given course if he doesn't fail more than two times.

```
(?s ex:isDiligent ?c) <-
    (\\\SPARQL
        (select ?s ?c
        where {
            ?s exa:enroledAt ?c .
            MINUS {
                select ?s ?c
                where {
                    ?s exa:failsTo ?l .
                    ?l exa:isLessonOf ?c .
                }
                group by ?s ?c
                having (count(1) > 2)
            }
        }
    \\\SPARQL).
```

Example 1

3   SPARQL in Jena Rules

Summary, we allow the use of SPARQL in the bodies of Jena rules to define classes, object properties, which link individuals to individuals, and datatype properties to link individuals to literals. Without much rigour and in a free way, we can compare to SQL views in relational databases. In a Jena rule, a SPARQL command must be enclosed by (\\\ SPARQL ... \\\ SPARQL). Next, we will give some examples of the syntax of SPARQL commands in Jena rules. In example 2 the class *ex:Square* is defined based on a SPARQL command, which states that a rectangle is square if the width is equal to the height. In example 3 we calculate the value of a property based on other properties, namely, the area of a rectangle is the product between the width and the height. This is also an example how business rules can be represented.

```
(?r rdf:type ex:Square) <-
    (\\\SPARQL
        select ?r
        where {
            ?r ex:width ?width .
            ?r ex:height ?height .
            FILTER(?width = ?height) .
        }
    \\\SPARQL) .
```

```
(?r ex:area ?area) <-
    (\\\SPARQL
        select ?r ?area
        where {
            ?r ex:width ?width .
            ?r ex:height ?height .
            bind( ?width * ?height as
?area ) .
        }
    \\\SPARQL) .
```

Example 2   Example 3

Examples 4 and 5 also represents business rules. In Example 4, is defined the last time when a product was ordered. In example 5, where is defined a business rule that states that each product must have an unique identifier, shows that this approach also can be used in projects of data quality management, by the definition of rules that can capture data inconsistency.

```
(?p ex:lastOrderDate ?d) <-
    (\\\SPARQL
        select ?p (max(?dt) AS ?d)
        where {
            . . .
        }
    \\\SPARQL) .
```

```
(?p_id ex:violationRule ex:ViolationUnique)
<-
    (\\\SPARQL
        (Select ?p_id
        where {
            ?p rdf:type ex:Product .
            ?p ex:productCode ?p_id .
        }
        group by ?p_id
        having count(1) > 1).
    \\\SPARQL) .
```

Example 4   Example 5

In our approach, we can make reference to an external variable in a SPARQL command, i.e., a variable shared with another rule condition. For that, we use the symbol "&" in the SPARQL command as is shown in Example 6. In this way, a SPARQL command is not an isolated body term in the antecedent of a rule but can be combined with other body terms. Therefore, we can have body terms to infer data to be used in a SPARQL command, limiting the output data to be returned to the inferring task. All the variables of a SPARQL command that makes reference to external variables, must be instantiated by a previous body term. In the forward mode of Jena rules we can have more than one consequence for a given set of antecedents. In the same manner, we can deduce more than one conclusion from a SPARQL command, as we show in Example 7.

```
(?x rdf:type ex:IronMan) <-
    ex:ironMan ex:numberOfSports ?n .
    (\\\SPARQL
      (Select ?x
      Where {
        ?x ex:playSport ?y .
      }
      group by ?x
      having (count(1) >=&n)
    \\\SPARQL) .
```

```
(ex:ironMan ex:numberOfSports ?n),
(\\\SPARQL
  (Select ?x (count(1) as ?z)
  Where {
    ?x ex:playSport ?y .
  }
  group by ?x
  having (count(1) >=&n)
\\\SPARQL) ->
(?x rdf:type ex:IronMan),
(?x ex:numberOfSportsPlayed ?z).
```

Example 6   Example 7

In our system it is possible for a SPARQL command to call a rule, as is shown in Example 8. In this way, we do not use only asserted but also inferred data.

```
(?x ex:sportPartner ?z) <-
  (?x ex:playSport ?y),
  (?z ex:playSport ?y),
  notEqual(?x, ?z).
```

```
(?x rdf:type ex:sportPal) <-
  (\\\SPARQL
    (Select ?x
    Where {
        ?x ex:sportPartner ?y .
    }
    group by ?x
    having (count(1) >= 10)
  \\\SPARQL) .
```

Example 8

Jena includes a general purpose rule-based reasoner which is used to implement both the RDFS and OWL reasoners but is also available for general use. This reasoner supports rule-based inference over RDF graphs and provides forward chaining, backward chaining and a hybrid execution model[5]. Combining this general purpose rule-based reasoner with our implementation, it is possible to develop templates for OWL2 reasoning. This is useful when we do not have an OWL2 reasoner or we only want to guarantee some of OWL2 constraints. In this way, it is also possible to have an OWL2 reasoning in both inference modes of Jena rules, backward and forward, whereas most of OWL2 reasoners work only in forward mode. In Example 9 it is shown an excerpt of a template to OWL2, with an *owl:Restriction* on *owl:minQualifiedCardinality*.

```
(?bn rdf:type owl:Restriction),              (\\\SPARQL
(?bn owl:onProperty ?p)                         (Select ?x
(?bn owl:onClass ?c)                            Where {
(?bn owl:minQualifiedCardinality ?n) ->           ?x &p &c .
                                                }
                                                group by ?x
                                                having (count(1) >=&n)
                                             \\\SPARQL).
```

Example 9

Example 8 is also a direct implementation of the OWL2 inference $>=$ 10 *sportPartner* $\sqsubseteq$ *sportPal*. We can implement specific restrictions when we do not have an OWL2 reasoner or even inconsistency rules that we cannot represent in OWL2.

4   System Details

The system presented in this work is available at https://github.com/mbentoalves/jena/tree/trunk/jena-core and works with Apache Jena 2.12.0. In the folder *doc* there is a document that explains how to prepare the Jena framework to use SPARQL commands in Jena rules. This system works in all rules engines modes foreseen by Jena, namely, forward, forwardRETE, backward and hybrid[5]. The implementation was done directly in Jena engine modes, except for the case where a rule combines SPARQL commands with rules terms. In this last case, it was developed a specific engine to evaluate this kind of rules, that we detail below in sub-section 4.1. In Jena, a rule file is parsed at reading time. We changed the rule parse of Jena to recognise and parse SPARQL declarations as body terms. To guarantee that the SPARQL command is well-constructed in its syntax we call the SPARQL parser of Jena. The SPARQL parser of Jena is also used to decompose the SPARQL command in its elementary constructs. Some processing models need this information, namely the forward engines, to fire rules. All the rules engines were changed to allow rules based in SPARQL commands in its processing model. Our purpose was to include in the rules engines rules based on SPARQL commands, we didn't perform any changes in the processing model. However, we discuss later, in Section 5, that in the future, we could make changes to the processing model because of performance issues. To execute a SPARQL command, we also make use of the Jena SPARQL engine.

4.1 Combining SPARQL Commands with Body Terms in a Specific Query Engine

Discussions with the Jena community concluded that was very difficult to incorporate SPARQL commands in Jena rules combined with other body terms. All the design of all inference engines assumes triples and not terms with an undetermined number of variables. So, it was concluded that every time the system requires an evaluation of a rule that combines triples with SPARQL commands, that evaluation should be done by a proper engine instead of the engines available in Jena. So, it was necessary to developed an engine for that purpose. The engine developed uses a tabling approach. Tabling[14] is a technique for goal-oriented evaluation of logic programs by storing computed answers in tables, combining the characteristics of the traditional top-down strategy with those of the bottom-up evaluation. A tabling algorithm produces a forest of proof-trees, one for each goal executed in the system. Each tree will have an associated table, where the answers produced by that proof-tree are stored. In the engine developed, triples and SPARQL commands are both tabled. This engine works eiher in forward mode or in backward mode.

5 Benchmark Tests

We performed some bechmark tests to evaluate the performance of SPARQL commands in rules. We made use of the data generated by *the Lehigh University Benchmark* [3], consisting in 14 datasets. The data generated is about an University system and the OWL schema can be consulted in http://swat.cse.lehigh.edu/onto/univ-bench.owl. This benchmark also defines (SPARQL) queries, but we didn't use them because they could not be transformed directly into rules (at least, with sense). We define our own rules that are described below and we execute each one in each dataset, in backward mode and in forward mode (*forwardRETE*). The purpose of these rules is to return the same data using a rule with (jena) body terms and a rule based on SPARQL command.

```
(?u ub:hasProfUniv ?p) <-
    (?p rdf:type ub:Professor),
    (?u rdf:type ub:University),
    (?d rdf:type ub:Department),
    (?p ub:worksFor ?d),
    (?d ub:subOrganizationOf ?u) .
```

Rule 1 - Jena original rules

```
(?u ub:hasProfUniv ?p) <-
    (\\\SPARQL SELECT ?u ?p
     WHERE {
        ?p rdf:type ub:Professor .
        ?u rdf:type ub:University .
        ?d rdf:type ub:Department .
        ?p ub:worksFor ?d .
        ?d ub:subOrganizationOf ?u .
     } \\\SPARQL) .
```

Rule 1 - SPARQL rule

```
(?u ub:hasStudent ?s) <-
    (?s rdf:type ub:Student),
    (?u rdf:type ub:University),
    (?d rdf:type ub:Department),
    (?s ub:memberOf ?d),
    (?d ub:subOrganizationOf ?university).
```

Rule 2 - Jena original rules

```
(?u ub:hasStudent ?s) <-
    (\\\SPARQL SELECT ?u ?s
        WHERE {
            ?s rdf:type ub:Student .
            ?u rdf:type ub:University .
            ?d rdf:type ub:Department .
            ?s ub:memberOf ?d .
            ?d ub:subOrganizationOf
    ?university .
        } \\\SPARQL) .
```

Rule 2 - SPARQL rule

```
(?s ub:hasProfessor ?p) <-
    (?p rdf:type ub:Professor),
    (?s rdf:type ub:Student),
    (?p ub:teacherOf ?c),
    (?s ub:takesCourse ?c) .
```

Rule 3 - Jena original rules

```
(?s ub:hasProfessor ?p) <-
    (\\\SPARQL SELECT ?s ?p
        WHERE {
            ?p rdf:type ub:Professor .
            ?s rdf:type ub:Student .
            ?p ub:teacherOf ?c .
            ?s ub:takesCourse ?c .
        } \\\SPARQL) .
```

Rule 3 - SPARQL rule

```
(?u ub:hasPublication ?p) <-
    (?p rdf:type ub:Publication),
    (?p ub:publicationAuthor ?Author),
    (?a rdf:type ub:Professor),
    (?u rdf:type ub:University),
    (?d rdf:type ub:Department),
    (?a ub:worksFor ?d),
    (?d ub:subOrganizationOf ?u) .
```

Rule 4 - Jena original rules

```
(?u ub:hasPublication ?p) <-
    (\\\SPARQL SELECT ?u ?p
        WHERE {
            ?o rdf:type ub:Publication .
            ?o ub:publicationAuthor ?a .
            ?a rdf:type ub:Professor .
            ?u rdf:type ub:University .
            ?d rdf:type ub:Department .
            ?a ub:worksFor ?d .
            ?d ub:subOrganizationOf ?u .
        } \\\SPARQL) .
```

Rule 4 - SPARQL rule

Our results show that in backward mode, rules based on SPARQL commands are, in average, 80% faster than the original jena rules. We argue that SPARQL engine of Jena is faster than the backward engine. Our tests also show that the performance rate increases with the size of the dataset. We created another dataset where we merge the 14 datasets generated by the bechmark tests tool.

The execution of rules based on SPARQL commands was, in average, almost 100 times faster.

In forward mode, the execution of the rules with SPARQL commands was, in average, 100 times slower than the execution of the original jena rules. We argue that this happens because the forward engine fires the SPARQL command every time that a triple is inserted in the dataset and there are a match triple pattern with the constructs of the SPARQL command in the rule, and therefore a lot of recomputations occurs. Our intention is to deal with the problem of the performance as a future work. In a first sight to problem, we cannot consider a SPARQL command as a regular jena body term, as we did in our implementation. We should try to postpone the evaluation of the rules that contains SPARQL commands to avoid repeated evaluations of these kind of rules.

We also evaluate the engine developed on rules that combines SPARQL commands with body terms. The commands listed above were changed to put some terms outside the SPARQL command, in one of the versions before the SPARQL and in the another one after the SPARQL command. Next, we list the changes done in the first command listed above (we did the same for all commands but we do not list because of lack of space).

```
(?u ub:hasProfUniv1 ?p) <-              (?u ub:hasProfUniv2 ?p) <-
    (?p rdf:type ub:Professor),             (\\\SPARQL SELECT ?u ?p ?d
    (?u rdf:type ub:University),            WHERE {
    (\\\SPARQL ASK                              ?p rdf:type ub:Professor .
        WHERE {                                 ?u rdf:type ub:University .
            ?d rdf:type ub:Department .         ?p ub:worksFor ?d .
            &p ub:worksFor ?d .             } \\\SPARQL),
            ?d ub:subOrganizationOf &u .    (?d rdf:type ub:Department),
        } \\\SPARQL) .                      (?d ub:subOrganizationOf ?university)
```

                  Rule 5   Rule 6

Our results show that the engine which evaluates rules that combines SPARQL commands with body terms is, in average, 20 times slower than the backward mode. However, the distribution is not linear. The rules where the terms appear before than the SPARQL commands are about 40 times slower whereas the rules where the terms appear after than the SPARQL command are about 50% slower. As we referred before, working on performance is in our minds to the next step.

6   Related Work

It was already referred in Section 2 that this work was inspired in SPIN rules. A SPIN API built on Jena is available, released by TopQuadrant[2]. Comparing with the implementation of SPIN rules referred, our implementation has advantages.

---

[2] http://www.topquadrant.com/

With the TopQuadrant implementation, and in a Jena application, we cannot resort to the rule-based inference engine of Jena. In our implementation, a SPARQL command can resort to a rule of the ruleset (cf. Example 8 in Section 3).

Our implementation can run in all Jena engine modes, while TopQuadrant implementation does the inference as the forward mode does. Furthermore, in our implementation we can combine body terms with SPARQL commands. Analysing the examples supplied by TopQuadrant, we cannot define directly a class based on a SPARQL command. In Figure 1 we show the definition of the class *Square* in TopQuadrant implementation, where we can see that the class is defined as a constraint, ie, what is a *Square*. In Section 3, Example 2, we showed how we could define this class in our implementation.

Fig. 1. The definition of the class *Square* in TopQuadrant implementation

7   Conclusion

In this work, we presented our implementation to allow the definition of SPARQL commands on Jena rules. With our work, Jena developers can combine SPARQL commands and rules to describe objects on the web of data, define object properties to link individuals to individuals, define datatype properties to link individuals to literals. Our implementation works in all engine modes of Jena, while others external reasoners, like TopQuadrant implementation, do reasoning only as forward mode does. Analysing the results presented in 5, the system has a good performance in backward mode but we have a problem of performance in forward mode and in the engine that evaluate rules that combine terms with SPARQL commands that we should resolve as future work. The project is on *GitHub* (https://github.com/mbentoalves/jena/tree/trunk/jena-core) as well as the instructions to prepare the Jena environment to allow SPARQL commands in Jena rules.

References

1. Bechhofer, S., van Harmelen, F., Hendler, J., Horrocks, I., McGuinness, D.L., Patel-Schneider, P.F., Stein, L.A.: OWL Web Ontology Language Reference. Tech. rep., W3C. http://www.w3.org/TR/owl-ref/ (February 2004)
2. Bechhofer, S., van Harmelen, F., Hendler, J., Horrocks, I., McGuinness, D., Patel-Schneijder, P., Stein, L.A.: OWL web ontology language reference (February 10, 2004)

3. Guo, Y., Pan, Z., Heflin, J.: Lubm: A benchmark for owl knowledge base systems. Web Semant. 3(2–3), 158–182 (2005). http://dx.doi.org/10.1016/j.websem.2005. 06.005
4. Knublauch, H., Hendler, J.A., Idehen, K.: Spin - overview and motivation (2011). http://www.w3.org/Submission/2011/SUBM-spin-overview-20110222/
5. Jena Documentation: Reasoners and rule engines: Jena inference support. http:// jena.apache.org/documentation/inference/
6. Knublauch, H.: Spin - sparql syntax (2011). http://www.w3.org/Submission/2011/ SUBM-spin-overview-20110222/
7. McGuinness, D.L., van Harmelen, F.: Owl web ontology language overview (REC-owl-features-20040210) (2004)
8. Parsia, B., Sirin, E., Grau, B.C., Ruckhaus, E., Hewlett., D.: Cautiously approaching swrl. Preprint submitted to Elsevier Science (2005). http://www.mindswap. org/papers/CautiousSWRL.pdf
9. Polleres, A.: From sparql to rules (and back) (2007)
10. Prud'hommeaux, E., Seaborne, A.: Sparql query language for RDF. Latest version available as http://www.w3.org/TR/rdf-sparql-query/ (January 2008). http://www.w3.org/TR/2008/REC-rdf-sparql-query-20080115/
11. Spinrdf: Spin - sparql inference notation. http://spinrdf.org/
12. Tauberer, J.: What is RDF and what is it good for? (January 2008). http://www. rdfabout.com/intro/?section=contents
13. W3C: Resource description framework (RDF): Concepts and abstract syntax (February 2004)
14. Warren, D.S.: Memoing for logic programs. Commun. ACM 35(3), 93–111 (1992). http://doi.acm.org/10.1145/131295.131299

Gathering Photos from Social Networks Using Semantic Technologies

M.B. Alves[1,2]($\boxtimes$), C.V. Damásio[1], and N. Correia[3]

[1] ESTG, Instituto Politécnico de Viana do Castelo,
4900-348 Viana do Castelo, Portugal
mba@estg.ipvc.pt, cd@fct.unl.pt
[2] CENTRIA, Universidade Nova de Lisboa, 2829-516 Caparica, Portugal
[3] CITI, Universidade Nova de Lisboa, 2829-516 Caparica, Portugal
nmc@fct.unl.pt

Abstract. We present a system based on a Semantic Web approach to retrieve photos from events, organizations or even related to semantic concepts using context and social information, without require extra annotation work by the publishers. We make use of the knowledge of the system, represented in ontologies and semantic rules, to allow users search using its own terminology.

1 Introduction

The motivation of our work is moving towards an easy searching and browsing of photos collections as is required by the huge amount of digital photo collections made available on the web by the photographers in different repositories, like Facebook, Picasa or Flickr. The gap between the photo information and the users desire is addressed by us through a Semantic Web approach, namely by a) associating photo metadata with precisely defined semantics, represented through ontologies [7], and b) through reasoning over this information. In this work, we describe a system that searches for photos on the web, that can be tailored to events, organisations, or in general with some domain specific concept. We combine information that we have in ontologies with the information about the photos, either photo metadata or contextual information, to retrieve photos of a given event, from a given person, or in a given place. The tool presented in this work is tailored to a specific domain. This system acts as a semantic mashup of photos collection, in other words, as a personal collection, but in reality these photos are spread in the web, social networks and photo databases. Our system requires a knowledge model of the domain, represented by a domain ontology and by rules. This information model gives to the system knowledge about the domain, allowing queries in a terminology recognised by the user. As a result, we are dealing with the semantic gap that exists in multimedia content [16], the lack of coincidence between the information that can be extracted from the photo and the meaning of that photo to the human.

This document is organised as follows. In Section 2 we present our approach and we explain how a semantic web approach can meet our purposes in photo

© Springer International Publishing Switzerland 2015
P. Klinov and D. Mouromtsev (Eds.): KESW 2015, CCIS 518, pp. 263–272, 2015.
DOI: 10.1007/978-3-319-24543-0_20

retrieval. In Section 3 we detail our system architecture and we explain each component of the architecture. In Section 4 we analyze our work and, finally we finish with the conclusions in Section 6.

2   Semantic Web Approach to Multimedia Retrieval

In our Semantic Web approach we use ontologies to formally describe the domain. Upper-level ontologies, describing very general concepts that are the same across all domains, are used to modelling concepts such as Events, Photos, Time, etc. In this work we have used: Ontology for Media Resources [8], to describe media resources; LODE [14], ontology for Linking Open Descriptions of Events; Time ontology [6], FOAF [3] for describing persons; SUMO [12] for generic concepts; and we map some concepts to Wordnet [10] according to the linked open data principles [1,2]. Each domain, for which we want to implement a photo retrieval engine with the approach described in this work, requires a particular domain ontology, also known as lower-level ontology, to represent the domain-specificities, the "leaf level" knowledge. We will model the domain ontology using OWL2[5]. To overcome some of the OWL limitations [11], we also use semantic rules to add expressivity and expertise to our model. To extract information from ontologies, we resort to SPARQL [13].

Now, we will illustrate how our Semantic Web approach is used to support photo retrieval, giving meaning to the content. In subsection 2.1 we will show some demonstrative examples how object properties, which link individuals to individuals, are supported by rules. In subsection 2.2 we will present an example of a specific domain knowledge. To simplify reading of the OWL and rules statements presented in the rest of the document, besides the well known prefixes *rdf*, *rdfs*, *owl*, *xsd*, consider the following prefixes, corresponding to the ontologies presented previously:

```
lode: <http://linkedevents.org/ontology/>
foaf: <http://xmlns.com/foaf/0.1/>
ma: <http://www.w3.org/ns/ma-ont#>
sumo: <http://www.ontologyportal.org/SUMO.owl#>
don: <http://www.example.org/don#>
```

The ontology *don* is our domain ontology where is represented the knowledge of the system domain.

2.1   Semantic Model and Rules

In any photo retrieve system it is important to define if a given photo may belong to a given event or not. In our domain ontology, we define an object property *happenedIn* having as domain *ma:Image* and as range *lode:Event* to make the relationship between photos and events instances. We define some rules to deduce, in our system, when a given *Photo* can belong to a given *Event*. These are general rules independent of the specific domain. We present our rules using the syntax `Conclusion <- Premises(body atoms)`.

Rule 1:

```
(?Photo don:happenedIn ?Event) <-
    (?Photo don:wasTakenAtTimeOf ?Event), (?Person don:isTaggedIn ?Photo),
    (?Person don:participates ?Event).
```

Accordingly, by **Rule 1**, we declare that a given *Photo* belongs to a given *Event* if: *s1*) the *Photo* was taken at the same time of the *Event*; *s2*) there is at least one *Person* that was tagged in the *Photo*; *s3*) who participated in the *Event*. The first statement, *s1*, makes use of the object property *wasTakenAtTimeOf* which is supported by rules to define if a given photo was taken while the event occurred. The *isTaggedIn* and *participates* are also object properties that define if a *Person* is tagged in a *Photo* and if a *Person* participates in a *Event*. In Section 3 we explain how our knowledge base is fed. Notice that **Rule 1** cannot be captured by OWL2 role inclusion chain axioms.

Rule 2:

```
(?Photo don:happenedIn ?Event) <-
    (?Photo don:wasTakenAtTimeOf ?Event), (?Photo don:wasTakenInSamePlace ?Event).
```

Rule 2 declares that a given *Photo* belongs to a given *Event* also if *s1*) The *Photo* was taken at the same time of the *Event*; and *s2*) that *Photo* was taken in the same place of the *Event*. The object property *wasTakenInSamePlace* is defined by a rule that defines if a *Photo* was taken in the same place of a *Event*. This rules encompasses several possible cases, captured by other rules in the system or by custom *built-in* functions, such as:

- Using GPS coordinates to determine if a location is in the radius of another;
- Compare Facebook id locations;
- Use the GPS coordinates and Facebook id locations to determine if a given place is in the radius of another;
- compare the different locations where an event can occur. An event can also take place in different locations;

A complex situation is captured by **Rule 3**: if we have a photo of a given event, all the photos of the same publisher that were taken at the same time are also photos of the event.

Rule 3:

```
(?Photo don:happenedIn ?Event) <-
    (?Photo1 don:happenedIn ?Event), (?Photo don:wasTakenAtTimeOf ?Event),
    notEqual(?Photo1, ?Photo),
    (?Photo1 ma:hasCreator ?Publisher), (?Photo ma:hasCreator ?Publisher).
```

2.2   Specific Domain Knowledge

To discuss some parts of the domain ontology and to focus on the significance of this domain ontology on the photo retrieval tool, we will use swimming competitions as Use Case. Swimming competitions are organised by genre and age groups, such as 10 and under, 11-12, 13-14, and so on, or J10, J11, J12, etc.

In a given season, 2013-2014 for example, the age group 11-12 is for all swimmers that were born in 2002 and 2003. So, we have created a class for age groups in a generic way and age groups in a given season. In Figure 1, we show an extract of the referred classes, beyond *Swimmer, Season* and *Competition*. The purpose is point that our system makes use of domain knowledge both to reason over the domain information and to recognise terminology and concepts understood by the users, as well as align concepts with the ontologies.

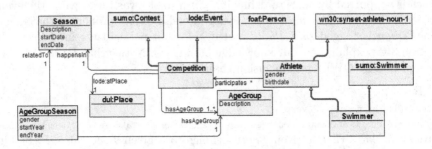

Fig. 1. Sub-model of the classes of the Use Case

2.3   Queries with Confidence

Our approach allows the introduction of a confidence value to ranking the images. This is done trough a confidence value (real number between 0.0 and 1.0) of inferred triples. The RDF reification vocabulary is extended to associate a confidence to each inferred triple used in search dimensions/values, according to the following pattern stating that a given *Relation* between a *Subject* and an *Object* has a given *Confidence*:

```
?bn rdf:subject Subject .
?bn rdf:predicate Relation .
?bn rdf:object Object .
?bn don:confidence Confidence .
```

If the same triple is obtained with different confidence values, then their maximum is used. The same maximum operation is used for combining confidence in search group expressions (OR), while minimum is used for combining the search expressions (AND). For instance, let's consider that the user wants photos from the swimmer *Taylor Moore* in season *2013/2014*. Let's also consider that the photo *IMG_2436* was retrieved as photo of *Taylor Moore* with a confidence of 0.9 in one rule and with a confidence 0.8 in other rule. The given photo also belongs to the season *2013 2014* with a confidence of 1. The final score of the photo *IMG_2436* is 0.9. This corresponds to the use of gödel fuzzy logic t-norm and t-conorm operators for conjunction and disjunction, respectively. Our system approach is different from DL-Media [17] since fuzzy reasoning is not used inside in the reasoner, but only at the interface level to rank results (even though, the above construct rules can be seen as fuzzy rules).

Next, we show an example how a confidence can be associated to inferred triples. For that, let's consider a more specific situation in our Use Case. There is a good possibility to find photos of a given *Swimmer* if we search for the photos of the competition in his age group. Even if we do not have access to the list of competitors in the competitions, we can assume that a given athlete participates in most of the competitions of his age group. Therefore, we have an object property *mightHaveParticipated* whose domain is the *Athlete* and the range is the *Competition*, which defines that an *Athlete* could have participated in a *Competition*. A rule defines this relation. So, **Rule 4** defines the photos where the athletes may appear:

```
Construct {
    ?bn rdf:subject ?Athlete .
    ?bn rdf:predicate exa:appear .
    ?bn rdf:object ?Photo .
    ?bn exa:confidence "0.7"^^xsd:decimal .
}
where {
    bind (afn:uuid() as ?bn) .
    ?Photo don:happenedIn ?Competition .
    ?Competition don:hasAgeGroup ?AgeGroup .
    ?Athlete don:hasAgeGroup ?AgeGroup .
}
```

In this example, we used the SPARQL clause *Construct* to produce new data with ranking information to be added to our model. However, in our system we make use of a work developed by us that allows to combine SPARQL commands in rules. In this work[1], SPARQL commands can be combined with rules both in forward mode and in backward mode.

3   System Architecture

In Figure 2 is represented the architecture of our tool. Our system uses the APIs of Facebook, Flickr and Picasa to retrieve the photos, the information associated with the photo and the context information. We simply use the information that we can obtain with the photo and the normal operations that the users usually perform: tagging photos, with text tags or people, indicate the place where the photos were taken, or give a name to an album. The information is extracted from the multimedia databases and is kept in a knowledge base to support the inference engine. The inference engine, besides the knowledge base, makes use of the semantic model of the domain and the rules defined. Some data can be materialised in the knowledge base either to obtain a better performance at query time or because of reasoner limitations, such as OWL reasoning over dynamic data. The photos are available to the users through a web interface that retrieve the photos that answer to the users queries.

---

[1] https://github.com/mbentoalves/jena/blob/trunk/jena-core/docs/
SPARQLCommandsInRules.md

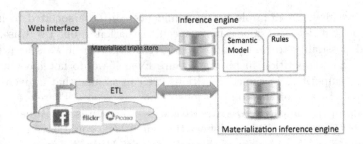

Fig. 2. System architecture of the photo retrieval engine

3.1 ETL Process

The Extract, Transform and Load process (ETL), acts like a web crawler. ETL is configured to periodically look into the photo collections that we consider relevant such as Facebook, Flickr or Picasa accounts, looking for new photos. The metadata that we can get from these new photos is extracted and saved using the vocabulary specified by the Ontology for Media Resources. One aspect that is important to a good performance of the system is what can be deduced at runtime and what can be pre-processed. Therefore, the transform task can make use of the semantic model and the rules to do inference and materialize some of the consequences in the pre-processing task.

3.2 Semantic Model and Rules

A domain ontology must be developed to represent the application domain. We make use of the domain ontology to provide the knowledge of the domain that allows us to achieve a higher precision in the retrieval process. Each domain has its own vocabulary, the terms that are recognised by the users. Our system makes use of domain knowledge both to reason over the domain information and to recognise terminology and concepts understood by the users, as well as align concepts with the ontologies. Without a domain ontology, we couldn't use these terms as a search dimension/facet. Our knowledge about the domain allows us to address the problem of the semantic gap between the photos and the meaning of those photos to the users. Rules must also be implemented to overcome the limitations of OWL, enriching the knowledge representation of our system, such as defining how a photo can be associated with an event, as we listed in Section 2.

3.3 Multimedia Content Sources

Our system uses the APIs of Facebook[2], Flickr[3] and Picasa[4] to retrieve the photos. Regarding Facebook, starting from the webpage of the club or the organisation, we search for photos on friends or on users that put a "Like" in a given page.

---

[2] https://developers.facebook.com/docs/reference/apis/
[3] http://www.flickr.com/services/api/
[4] https://developers.google.com/picasa-web/

For instance, in our use case, the swimming club have a Facebook page which accepts friends or can be target of a "Like". Facebook provides an Graph API[5], a simple HTTP-based API that gives access to Facebook social graph, uniformly representing objects in the graph and the connections between them. The data is returned in JSON format, which can be translated to RDF [9]. In Flickr or Picasa, we must define the users that publish photos that are interesting to us. Alternatively, we can search for tags or album names that we believe that will often occur, or that can be used to distinguish them from other photo albums. However, this way requires publishers to annotate their albums or photos with these specific tags. This tagging operation is necessary to focus the search of external collections of photos, otherwise it would not be possible to find them in the Web because of the amount of photos available, besides of resource limitations imposed by the APIs. This is the only requirement that users should be aware of when publishing their photos in these social networks, otherwise recall could be very low. Our system tries to use the information associated with the photo and the context information in the retrieval task, trying to not impose any extra work to the users. Considering that the users do not spend much time in photo classification or tagging, we simply use the information that we can obtain with the photo and the normal operations that the users usually performing: tagging photos, text tags or people, indicate the place where the photos were taken, give a name to an album, etc. Therefore, the system collects the information about the photos on the web, and with the support of an information model of the domain, represented by a domain ontology and by rules, allowing the users to query and retrieve photos through a web application.

3.4   The Query Process and the Interface

The users make queries through a Web interface that returns the links to the photos that are related to the queries. These queries are answered using the information kept in the knowledge base, making inferences from the semantic model and the rules. The inference engine collects all the expressions that we consider that can be used as search expression such as the athletes, the competitions, the age groups and the seasons. This list is available to the web interface grouped by search dimensions. The user selects the expressions to support his search between the available expressions. An in-string filter is supplied to support the task of search expressions. If the user chooses more than one expression to search, the result is conjunction of all search expressions. Moreover, the user can group search expressions and the result is the disjunction of these grouped search expressions. We have a semantic model to support the querying. This semantic model is a meta-model within which the classes of search dimensions are defined in the web interface. Furthermore, is also defined which descriptions should be used as search expressions. For instance, in Use Case we can search for a *Athlete* by *foaf:name* or by *foaf:nick*. This meta-model, that must be tailored to each different domain, allows the system to know what must be searched.

---

[5] https://developers.facebook.com/docs/graph-api/

With this approach, we do not need any change in code in a new system. Everything is knowledge provided to the system and everything is kept outside in simple configuration files. Next, we provide an excerpt of the meta-model for our Use Case:

```
:LabelSwimmer rdf:type :LabelsDim ;      :SwimmerDim rdf:type :SearchDim ;
    :belongsToDim :SwimmerDim ;               :isAssociatedTo :Swimmer .
    :labelDim     foaf:name ,          :isPhotoOfAthlete rdf:type :PropertyDim ;
                  foaf:nick .              :belongsToDim :SwimmerDim .
```

The class *SearchableEntity* defines the classes that may have meaning to the user and that can be used as a search dimension in the web interface. In the implementation for Use Case are used:

$$SearchableEntity \equiv$$
$$AgeGroup \sqcup Competition \sqcup dul{:}Place \sqcup Season \sqcup Swimmer$$

3.5   System Details

Our implementation is based on Jena framework[6], a free and open source Java framework for building Semantic Web applications. One of the main reasons for choosing Jena is because using it offers an "all-in-one" solution for Java, OWL reasoning, inference and rule engine. We use Pellet[7][15] together with Jena to make OWL 2 inference. The TDB component of Jena is used for RDF storage and query.

4   Discussion

The system presented in this work was tailored to be enhanced at production time. The semantic model and the rules are kept in configuration files. Any change to these files only requires an re-initialisation of the system. Thus, we can readily improve our semantic model or our rules, adding new knowledge to our system or refining the existing one. There are no relevant privacy concerns since we make use of the APIs (Flickr, Picassa, Facebook) that only return publicly available information.

We performed some benchmarking with a small example based on Use Case described and by only using Facebook as source, using a Facebook account of a swimming club. As Facebook does not provide the list of friends since version 2.0 of Graph API, we searched for photos in Facebook of all people that already interacted with the account of the club, with a like, with a comment or by being tagged in a photo of the club. In a universe of 3599 friends, the system focused on 172 friends, 49 albums and 1148 photos. In the ETL process was defined that the object property *happenedIn* should be materialised. It were retrieved 431 photos, 425 of which were distributed over 9 albums. We had 100% precision

---

[6] https://jena.apache.org
[7] http://clarkparsia.com/pellet/

in the retrieved photos. We inspected the photos that were published in the window time of the event but that were not retrieved, achieving a recall of 95,5%. We didn't analyse the precision by search dimension because in our system it is an open question, and depends of each new implemented domain. If we want to give relevance to the precision, we define rules that represent exactly one relationship or, at most, with a high probability of occurrence. If we want to give relevance to the recall, we define rules to represent how relationships may happen, even if those rules bring some fake positive results. As we can introduce a confidence factor in our rules, we can give relevance to the recall but improving the F1-Score, also referred F-score or F-measure, a measure that combines precision and recall, being the harmonic mean of precision and recall. An implementation in a real situation is on-going work that can be tried at http://www.estg.ipvc.pt/~mba/SemanticPhotosSearch/.

5 Related Work

To the best of our knowledge, there are no works with the capabilities of our approach which employ a knowledge-base approach, specified with OWL 2 ontologies and rules, to retrieve photos. In subsection 2.3 we have already referred to the DL-Media [17], an ontology multimedia information retrieval system, which combines logic-based retrieval with multimedia feature-based similarity retrieval. An ontology layer is used to define (in terms of a fuzzy extension of a DLR-Lite like description logic [4]) the relevant abstract concepts and relations of the application domain, while a content-based multimedia retrieval system is used for feature-based retrieval. Compared to our approach, it is not possible to define rules like **Rule 1** in Section 2 (or even any king of role inclusion axioms). Moreover, the underlying fuzzy-logic system used is the same as in our approach to attach confidence values to inferred triples, but DL-media is more expressive regarding the fuzzy reasoning component since ontological axioms have themselves a fuzzy semantics.

6 Conclusion and Future Work

In this work, we presented a system to retrieve photos using a Semantic Web approach. Our system uses the context information of the photo or annotations done by the user and other metadata that can be retrieved from social networks to combine with the knowledge of the system, represented by a domain ontology and by rules, to classify the photos. The system acts like a mashup repository of collections of photos even if these photos are distributed along the web. The user can search for photos using its own terminology, since it is related with the domain. In this way, we try to overcome the problem of the semantic gap between the photos information and the means of that photo to the user. The user can create personal collections dynamically like "Photos of the national championship", "Photos of Richard at 10 years old". We can perform this because we have knowledge of the domain. Our system makes use of the normal interaction of the users with Web repositories and social sites, and does not require extra work from them. As future work, we want to allow the inclusion of external tools, giving us the possibility to combine a Semantic Web approach with other methodologies. This is mainly important to make use of the best techniques used in content-based information retrieval (face recognition, for example).

References

1. Berners-Lee, T.: Linked data - design issues (2006). http://www.w3.org/DesignIssues/LinkedData.html
2. Bizer, C., Heath, T., Berners-Lee, T.: Linked data - the story so far. International Journal on Semantic Web and Information Systems 5(3), 1–22 (2009)
3. Brickley, D., Miller, L.: FOAF Vocabulary Specification 0.97. Namespace document (January 2010). http://xmlns.com/foaf/spec/20100101.html
4. Calvanese, D., Lembo, D., Lenzerini, M., Rosati, R.: Data complexity of query answering in description logics. In: Proc. of KR 2006, pp. 260–270. AAAI Press (2006)
5. Cuenca, B., Horrocks, I., Motik, B., Parsia, B., Patel-Schneider, P., Sattler, U.: OWL 2: The next step for OWL. Web Semantics 6(4), 309–322 (2008)
6. Hobbs, J.R., Pan, F.: Time ontology in OWL (September 2006). http://www.w3.org/TR/owl-time
7. Hofweber, T.: Logic and ontology. In: Zalta, E.N. (ed.) The Stanford Encyclopedia of Philosophy. Spring 2013 edn. (2013)
8. Lee, W., Bailer, W., Burger, T., Champin, P.A., Evain, J.P., Malaise, V., Michel, T., Sasaki, F., Soderberg, J., Stegmaier, F., Strassner, J.: Ontology for Media Resources 1.0 (February 2012). http://liris.cnrs.fr/publis/?id=5453, w3C Recommendation, http://www.w3.org/TR/mediaont-10/
9. Manola, F., Miller, E.: RDF primer. W3C Recommendation 10, 1–107 (2004). http://www.w3.org/TR/rdf-primer/
10. Miller, G.A.: Wordnet: a lexical database for english. Commun. ACM 38(11), 39–41 (1995)
11. Parsia, B., Sirin, E., Grau, B.C., Ruckhaus, E., Hewlett., D.: Cautiously approaching swrl. Preprint submitted to Elsevier Science (2005). http://www.mindswap.org/papers/CautiousSWRL.pdf
12. Pease, A., Niles, I., Li, J.: The suggested upper merged ontology: A large ontology for the semantic web and its applications. In: Working Notes of the AAAI-2002 Workshop on Ontologies and the Semantic Web (2002)
13. Prud'hommeaux, E., Seaborne, A.: Sparql query language for RDF. Latest version available as http://www.w3.org/TR/rdf-sparql-query/ (January 2008). http://www.w3.org/TR/2008/REC-rdf-sparql-query-20080115/
14. Shaw, R., Troncy, R., Hardman, L.: LODE: Linking open descriptions of events. In: Gómez-Pérez, A., Yu, Y., Ding, Y. (eds.) ASWC 2009. LNCS, vol. 5926, pp. 153–167. Springer, Heidelberg (2009)
15. Sirin, E., Parsia, B., Grau, B., Kalyanpur, A., Katz, Y.: Pellet: A practical OWL-DL reasoner. Web Semantics: Science, Services and Agents on the World Wide Web 5(2), 51–53 (2007)
16. Smeulders, A.W.M., Worring, M., Santini, S., Gupta, A., Jain, R.: Content-based image retrieval at the end of the early years (2000)
17. Straccia, U., Visco, G.: Dl-media: an ontology mediated multimedia information retrieval system. In: Proceedings of the International Workshop on Description Logics (DL-07), vol. 250. CEUR, Insbruck (2007)

Ontology-Based Approach to Scheduling of Jobs Processed by Applications Running in Virtual Environments

Maksim Khegai, Dmitrii Zubok$^{(\boxtimes)}$, and Alexandr Maiatin

ITMO University, St. Petersburg, Russia
MaxHegai@rambler.ru, zubok@mail.ifmo.ru, mavr.mkk@gmail.com
http://www.ifmo.ru/

Abstract. This paper presents an ontology-based approach to the problem of jobs scheduling in case where jobs are processed by applications running in virtual environments and number of applications and their performance varies over time. Using ontology-based framework brings benefits when system has a varying number of components and their performing properties are also non-constant. The work is focused on ontology model needed to organize information exchange for intelligent agents embedded into virtual machines and gathering information about applications performance. In cases when jobs of one type can be processed by several applications having different performance, the existence of optimal threshold queuing policy has been proven earlier. It can reduce the average job processing time. In order to calculate thresholds we need relevant information about active applications and their current performance, the rate of jobs stream, the number of jobs in the queues, etc. The presented approach solves the problem of effective gathering of relevant information about the system state based on intelligent agents interaction where each intelligent agent uses ontology to publish only information about changes that are relevant to decision making. This reduces the system's overhead for monitoring of ongoing parameters.

Keywords: Ontology · Scheduling · Performance · Virtualization · Intelligent agents

1 Introduction and Motivation

Scheduling and resources allocation are two the most important problems when it comes to controlling cloud computing systems. Even though there are a lot of methods for solving each of these tasks, in practice a cloud system control model is required. It must include solutions for both problems. A typical architecture of modern cloud computing systems is based on virtualization technologies.

Applications run in virtual machines that are located on physical servers which allows to provide a balance between performance and reliability, especially in cases when the intensities of incoming jobs streams are random and cannot be

© Springer International Publishing Switzerland 2015
P. Klinov and D. Mouromtsev (Eds.): KESW 2015, CCIS 518, pp. 273–282, 2015.
DOI: 10.1007/978-3-319-24543-0_21

predicted. Technologies of live migrations and dynamic resources reallocation for virtual machines allow to keep high reliability by isolating applications while at the same time providing effective resources utilization [5] [2]. An incoming jobs stream arrives with different types of jobs. In the system different applications are located in virtual machines and each of them can process only one single type of jobs. Applications can process a number of jobs which provides an effective utilization of resources while processing several jobs at the same time. Such a technique is usual to distributed web-applications.

For an efficient resources utilization of some software nodes that host several virtual machines, live migration methods and technologies are commonly used. All this leads to the situation when parameters such as number of applications that process jobs and their performance change with time.

One of the primary methods of scheduling in cloud computing systems is utilization of service policies for queues of incoming jobs. This was researched for cases when jobs of different types are being distributed on one single server [12] and on several servers with the same performance [1]. There, however, are no practical results in solving the problem of scheduling for several servers with different performance.

An optimal threshold queuing policy for jobs with the same type on a set number of devices (applications) with a set ratio of performance was theoretically [8] and experimentally [13] proven. The queuing policy is characterized by ratio of devices' performance and should be changed if number of devices or their performance was changed. Also, for each intensity of incoming jobs stream there is a range of ratios when the threshold policy is better than the conservative one but outside of this range there is almost no difference between those two service policies and the overhead is higher when using the threshold one. The effects of the described policy and achievement of adequate jobs processing performance are possible only when the intensity of the incoming jobs stream with considered average time of their processing is matched to the overall performance of applications that process them. Either resources reallocation or changing the number of virtual machines is required. Those control methods were properly researched in [9] [3]. The current architecture includes appropriate controlling components. However they also need actual information about system's parameters.

As a result the control of a cloud system becomes two-leveled. On the higher level the problem of providing a required overall performance basing on incoming jobs stream intensity is solved by changing the number of virtual machines and resources allocating. On the lower level more precise and fast distribution of jobs to applications with straightened overall performance is performed.

On the high level control is implemented in a control service, hosted in a separate virtual machine. Low-level control is implemented in controllers that contain components for queuing, based on some queuing management tool, for example RabbitMQ.

Thus, a problem of providing controllers, that define optimal service policies on both levels, with actual information about system's state appears. To benefit from using a service policy we need to have actual information about number and performance of appropriate applications and intensity of incoming jobs flows of each type. The information about significant changes in those parameters must be available to controller in time comparable to a single job's processing time. The usage of an active centralized monitoring with common data storage is inappropriate in this case because a high intensity of polling of virtual machines and a frequent update of data storage will lead to a high overhead.

Because every type of jobs has its own controller, a necessity in service of big number of intense data exchange flows will appear. As a result a monitoring tool with common data storage will be a bottleneck. On the other hand to use service policies mentioned earlier the system doesn't need to have history of changes and only needs actual information, so an appropriate controller needs to get only the information about significant changes in parameters.

Systems where only parameters needed to calculate an optimal service policy change are well researched, for example in [6] and usually have a recalculation of controlling parameters in definite periods of time. Those periods are based on system's unchanging parameters. In our case a configuration of the system is changed instead of separate parameters; a set of virtual machines with application changes as well as an incoming jobs type. Thus, as the system works sources of jobs and consumers of information are changed. In this case a solution may be found in a multi-agent approach with a common ontology. Every application will be polled by an agent that has a certain evaluation algorithm and that sends information only when parameters exceeded a threshold value. Threshold values may change in time as well, for example at different working mode or at different jobs type priorities; if such a change occurred agents need to receive the new values. Incoming jobs flows and resources management are polled by other agents with their own evaluation algorithms. That allows the system to be flexible in case of appearance of new jobs types and applications that process them. As a result the monitoring overhead will be reduced.

Hence, a way to provide an information exchange between agents is required. One of the ways is usage of ontologies. This approach was presented in [4] however only the problem of monitoring of parameters is solved; the problem of scheduling and processing time evaluation is left unsolved. In [10] and [11] ontologies are used to solve the resources matching problem. Proposed models are aimed at finding a node with sufficient resources for each job but don't define applications' performance nor provide queues management. Our goal is to build a multi-agent system's architecture, intellectual agents' ontologies and a common ontology for a knowledge base, integrated in the presented two-leveled system.

2   Ontology-Based Multi-agent System Architecture

Developed ontology must have a module structure. Agents' ontologies will be integrated into agents that perform their own tasks and the whole ontology must be stored in a knowledge base. The knowledge base must contain actual information and its synchronization between agents according to established set of rules. Thus, agents' ontologies must be compatible with each other. For that a model of interactions between agents must be built and their purpose must be described. The model of interactions supposes that three kinds of intelligent agents exist and is presented on the figure 1.

1. Performance monitoring agents. They work in virtual machines with applications and perform an evaluation of their performance. As a parameter for evaluation a time needed to process one request of the same type is taken. Since this time is random an intelligent agent must have a decision making algorithm that will decide if information about changes in performance should be published in the knowledge base.
2. Incoming jobs stream monitoring agents. They work in every controller and evaluate incoming jobs stream intensity. Random nature of the stream also determines the need of an algorithm for intelligent agents that will evaluate changes and decide if the information about them should be published.
3. Resources monitoring agents. They work on hosts and interact with virtual machines monitors to get actual info about changes in resources quotas that the monitor provides. Need of this agent is defined by the fact that the decision to change quotas may not only be made by the controlling subsystem but also by an administrator coming from their own needs. This agent is required to evaluate overall performance of applications.

Every physical server has Xen-hypervizor virtualization environment installed. In one of the environment at least one virtual machine exists: the control node. This node stores ontologies, exchanges information about ontologies, creates, deletes and starts virtual machines with applications. Each virtual machine has an intelligent agent and an application that processes jobs. Virtual machines that process jobs of the same type have one common controller. Every controller handles queuing and sends jobs to virtual machines. All virtual machines and controllers are connected into one virtual local network via

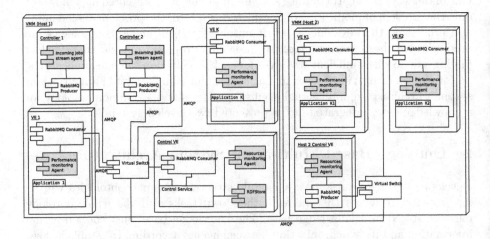

Fig. 1. Multi-agent system architecture

virtual router. To exchange messages RabbitMQ framework and AMQP protocol are used. Every other physical server has only virtual machines with their
controllers, controlled by the main control node in the main physical server.

To build agents ontologies we will look at the information they require and
the information we expect to get from them. Presented ontologies were visualized
using VOWL plugin for Protege ontologies editor.

2.1 Performance Monitoring Agent

Entity, that this agent works with, are "virtual machine" (VM), "application"
(Application) and "job" (Job). The ontology is presented at Figure 2.

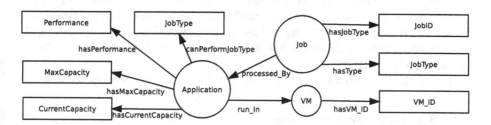

Fig. 2. Performance monitoring agent ontology

Entity "virtual machine" for this agent is characterized by only one parameter: an identification number of an instance. It also identifies the agent itself.

Entity "job" is characterized by two parameters: its identification number
and type.

Entity "application" is characterized by many parameters. Monitoring of
those parameters is the task of this agent. CurrentCapacity is the current number of jobs, simultaneously processed by this application. MaxCapacity is the
maximal number of simultaneously processed jobs. The parameter is calculated
in the virtual machines controller basing on provided to the virtual machine
RAM. Performance is the current performance as an average time of job processing for this application. If the changes in performance exceeds a threshold
value the information about it is published in the knowledge base.

2.2 Incoming Job Stream Monitoring Agent

Entities this agent works with: "controller" (Controller), "queue" (Queue), "job
stream" (Job_Stream), "job" (Job). The ontology is presented on Figure 3.

Entity "controller" is characterized by a single parameter: type of jobs this
agent distributes. This value is also an identification number of a controller.

Entity "queue" is characterized by next parameters. "Jobs type" is defined by
a controller that controls the queue. "Queue size" is number of jobs of the same
type that are waiting to be processed. "Thresholds vector" is a set of threshold

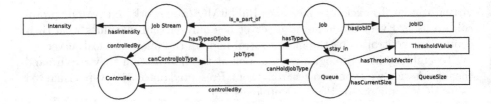

Fig. 3. Incoming jobs stream monitoring agent ontology

values. Exceeding them will result in usage of another machine. Those values are calculated by a controller and are published there if they changed.

Entity "job stream" is characterized by two parameters. Parameter "jobs type" connects the stream and the controller that distributes its jobs. Parameter "intensity" is evaluated by the agent basing on control of new jobs. If changes in the intensity exceed a defined value the agent publishes the information about this in the knowledge base.

Entity "job" is equivalent to the entity "job" in previously described ontology.

2.3   Resource Monitoring Agent

Entities this agent works with: "host", "virtual machine", "resource", "resource types". The ontology is presented on Figure 4.

Entity "virtual machine" is equivalent to the entity "virtual machine" in the agents ontology of the performance monitoring agent.

Entity "host" is characterized by a single parameter: host identification number. It identifies resources monitoring agent's instance for this host.

Entity "resource" is a class that derives other entities that define resources types. In most cases those entities are CPU, RAM, I/O resources, and network resources. But this list is not final and, depending on virtual machines monitor and applications, may be expanded. Resource monitoring agent's ontology contains every resource type entity that was allocated to each virtual machine on the current host. Every resource type is characterized by a single parameter: allocated resource type value. The common ontology is presented on Figure 5.

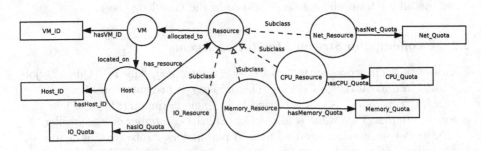

Fig. 4. Resources monitoring agent ontology

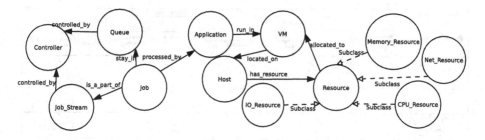

Fig. 5. Common ontology

Each agent's ontology has at least one entity common with other agents' ontologies. That allows consolidating them in a one single ontology that provides storage of actual information on every object in the system.

3   Agents Behavior

The algorithms of agents are based on the principle of independent decision making about publication of information about changes in an object it polls. The criteria of evaluation depends on the fact that changes are not random but instead have stable tendency. Information exchange occurs as a publication of the agent's current ontology into knowledge base. Life cycle of each agent includes: initialization, information gathering, deciding if it needs to publish the information, finalizing the work.

3.1   Performance Monitoring Agent

This agent is initialized when a new virtual machine with application is created. When initializing it subscribes to changes in knowledge base via agents interactions with the knowledge base. As a result agent gets an unchangeable information for its ontology: its virtual machine's identification number and jobs type that its application processes identification number.

During its activity the intelligent agent evaluates the current performance by using moving average method [7]. This method allows to smooth up fluctuations and find changes in performance that will not change for some time. In case when the average value exceeded a threshold value agent publishes its ontology with changed values in the knowledge base and continues evaluation, setting new basic value for its performance. Figure 6 presents the algorithm for this agent.

While using this method the agent gets information about time when job was received from the queue manager and about the time when the job was finished and the result was sent by RabbitMQ producer and calculates the processing time of the job. The resulting value is used in calculating average change. When a signal to stop a virtual machine is received the agent unsubscribes from changes and all the information about this agent is deleted from the knowledge base.

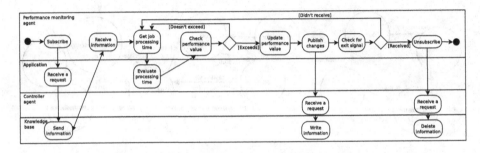

Fig. 6. Performance monitoring agent's algorithm

3.2 Incoming Lob Stream Monitoring Agent

This agent is started when a new type of jobs appear. It leads to creation of a virtual machine with controller inside that will manage scheduling for this type of jobs. When the agent is initialized it gets unchangeable information about this stream's jobs type (identification number) and publishes information about this jobs type existence into knowledge base. Agent concludes if there are applications that are able to process its type of jobs and if there are none waits for their appearance. This agent's algorithm is presented at the figure 7.

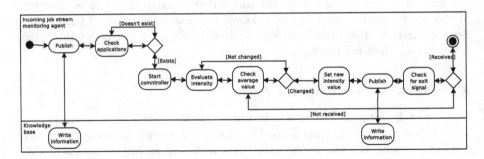

Fig. 7. Incoming jobs stream monitoring agent's algorithm

If such applications exist the agent initiates start of a controller and creating of queues for this type of jobs. After start of a controller agent evaluates intensity of the incoming stream, gathering information about incoming jobs from controller. If the average number of jobs in a set period of time changed for a set value, agent publishes its ontology with changed values in the knowledge base and continues evaluation after setting a new value for stream's intensity.

3.3 Resource Monitoring Agent

This agent is initialized when a new physical server is started and subscribes to changes in knowledge base, receiving unchangeable information about host's identification number. After initialization the agent constantly gathers information from the virtual machines monitor about active virtual machines and their resources quotas. If any quota has been changed the agent publishes its ontology to the knowledge base. If a new virtual machine was started, the agent publishes information about it in the knowledge base, getting its identification number.

3.4 Agents Implementation

Since the built architecture is supposed to be used for web-based applications it has PHP5 and MySQL server installed. Agents and controllers were also created with PHP5 and ARC2 RDF system was used to manage ontologies. ARC2 provides a wide variety of parsers for ontologies structures and supports SPARQL to query them. Ontologies themselves are stored as RDF triples in a MySQL database. Since AMQP is already used to send requests to applications it is also used to exchange information between agents and a controller.

4 Conclusion and Future Work

The effective control of a complex system with changing configuration, for example a modern cloud computing system, demands providing actual information about many parameters to control components. A described method allows to organize monitoring of the changes in the parameters to minimize overheads cost by using intelligent agents that independently poll system's parameters and publish only changed information. The key element is the common context knowledge base, shared among applications and contributed by agents.

The use of ontology-based approach also allows to make information sharing between agents flexible and independent from technologies and agents algorithms. The paper demonstrates that this method can be used to build a certain architecture, implemented with current modern technologies. Examples of agents ontologies, knowledge base and agents algorithms are presented.

Future work will expand the architecture, make it more flexible and add the ability to support more advanced scheduling and resource allocation algorithms that require information sharing. More system's objects will be presented and more virtualization techniques will be used, for example paravirtualization and os-level virtualization at the same time. The ontology and algorithms of the intelligent agents will also be improved to provide a flexible way to control threshold values. That will reduce overhead costs, increase system response time and increase overall performance of the system.

Acknowledgments. This work was partially financially supported by the Government of Russian Federation, Grant 074-U01. The presented result is also a part of the research carried out within the project funded by grant #15-07-09229 A of the Russian Foundation for Basic Research.

References

1. Abdullah, M., Othman, M.: Cost-Based Multi-QoS job scheduling using divisible load theory in cloud computing. In: Dell'Olmo, P., Pesenti, R., Speranza, M.G. (eds.) Computers & Operations Research, vol. 34, pp. 928–935. Elsevier (2007)
2. Arzuaga, E., Kaeli, D.R.: Quantifying load imbalance on virtualized enterprise servers. In: Proceedings of the First Joint WOSP/SIPEW International Conference on Performance Engineering, pp. 235–242 (2010)
3. Saraswathia, A.T., Kalaashrib, Y.R.A., Padmavathi, S.: Dynamic resource allocation scheme in cloud computing. In: Procedia Computer Science, vol. 47, pp. 30–36. Elsevier (2015)
4. Funika, W., Janczykowski, M., Jopek, K., Grzegorczyk, M.: An ontology-based approach to performance monitoring of MUSCULE-bound multi-scale applications. In: Procedia Computer Science, vol. 18, pp. 1126–1135. Elsevier (2013)
5. Hu, W., Hicks, A., Zhang, L., Dow, E.M., Soni, V., Jiang, H., Bull, R., Matthews, J.N.: A quantitative study of virtual machine live migration. In: Proceedings of the 2013 ACM Cloud and Autonomic Computing Conference (2013)
6. Jina, H., Linga, X., Ibrahimb, S., Caoa, W., Wua, S., Antoniub, G.: Flubber: Two-level disk scheduling in virtualized environment. In: Future Generation Computer Systems, vol. 29, pp. 2222–2238. Elsevier (2013)
7. Mivule, K., Turner, C.: Applying moving average filtering for non-interactive differential privacy settings. In: Procedia Computer Science, vol. 36, pp. 409–415. Elsevier (2014)
8. Rykov, V., Efrosinin, D.: Numerical analysis of optimal control policies for queueing systems with heterogeneous servers (2002)
9. Tanga, R., Yuea, Y., Dinga, X., Qiua, Y.: Credibility-based cloud media resource allocation algorithm. Journal of Network and Computer Applications 46, 315–321 (2014)
10. Tangmunarunkit, H., Decker, S., Kesselman, C.: Ontology-Based resource matching in the grid – the grid meets the semantic web. In: Fensel, D., Sycara, K., Mylopoulos, J. (eds.) ISWC 2003. LNCS, vol. 2870, pp. 706–721. Springer, Heidelberg (2003)
11. Yoo, H., Hur, C., Kim, S., Kim, Y.: An ontology-based resource selection service on science cloud. In: Slezak, D., Kim, T., Yau, S.S., Gervasi, O., Kang, B.-H. (eds.) GDC 2009. CCIS, vol. 63, pp. 221–228. Springer, Heidelberg (2009)
12. Zhang, Z.G., Love, E., Song, Y.: The optimal service time allocation of a versatile server to queue jobs and stochastically available non-queue jobs of different typess. In: Dell'Olmo, P., Pesenti, R., Speranza, M.G. (eds.) Procedia Computer Science, vol. 18, pp. 1857–1870 (2013)
13. Zubok, D., Maiatin, A., Kiryushkina, V., Khegai, M.: Functional model of a software system with random time horizon. In: 2015 17TH Conference of Open Innovations Association (FRUCT), pp. 259–266 (2015)

Aigents: Adaptive Personal Agents for Social Intelligence

Anton Kolonin[✉]

Aigents Group, Pravdy 6/12, 630090 Novosibirsk, Russian Federation
akolonin@gmail.com
http://aigents.com/

Abstract. The paper reports on the implementation of adaptive personal software agents for collaborative computational intelligence. It outlines the main goals of the project, the basic implemented features, and describes the prospective depelopment plan.

Keywords: Adaptive intelligence · Distributed intelligence · Experiential learning · Ontology · Peer-to-peer · Social collaboration · Software agents · Subsymbolic intelligence · Symbolic intelligence · Ubiquitous computing

1 Introduction

The objective of the Aigents project[1] [1] is creating personal software agents capable of adaptive learning upon user input and feedback as well as collaborative communications across social connections of the users. In the end, it is expected that a network of such agents will provide a backbone for global computational intelligence.

The basic idea of building an agent is ensuring it is more than just a psychologically attractive toy like Tamagotchi [2] or a personal assistant with a pre-defined set of functions of narrow artificial intelligence [3], having an agent able to develop new knowledge and skills during ongoing self-development in the course of interaction with its human master.

The suggested work takes its ideological origin from the Webmind project led by Ben Goertzel [4] at the turn of the XXI century and is intended to create technical infrastructure for the emergence of global internet intelligence (and the author of this paper was one of the contributors to that project). Since then, the latest advance in creating really distributed intelligent systems was described in the work of Sebastian Tramp and others [5].

The latest approach [5] targets to build up a dynamic and world-wide distributed semantic network with meanings valued by social connections established according to the existing standards of Semantic Web and Linked Data. The purpose of our project is complementary yet different we are focusing on creating intelligent agents capable to extract meanings (i.e. semantics) from the raw

---

[1] http://aigents.com/

© Springer International Publishing Switzerland 2015
P. Klinov and D. Mouromtsev (Eds.): KESW 2015, CCIS 518, pp. 283–290, 2015.
DOI: 10.1007/978-3-319-24543-0_22

web data and communication logs, interacting to humans and one-to-another via conventional linguistic or graphical interface, and using sort of human-computer "interlingua" extensible in the course of interaction.

2   Principal Goals

Along the roadmap of the Aigents project, there are short-term, mid-term and long-term milestones with complexity and practical usability gradually increasing over time as discussed below.

First what our agents learn is *autonomous exploration and watching of web pages and sites*, timely extracting information required by their masters and immediate delivery of the news, based on the masters' preferences and feedback.

Also, agents belonging to different users are getting the ability to *communicate to with each other relying on social connections* of their masters, creating communities based on their interests and growing their knowledge assets incrementally.

Further, agents are getting the ability to *manage computational devices that they populate - autonomously*, following explicit commands that they learn and implicit intents of the users that they guess, following users' voices and gestures.

Finally, agents acquire capability to *control the surrounding Internet of Things* getting the ability to learn about new things and their properties and capabilities autonomously without explicit or implicit commands from a human master or help from other agents.

Moreover, once agents learn enough about the preferences, beliefs and ways of thinking specific to their human masters, they would get the ability to serve as *intelligent proxies of their users*, performing redundant presentation operations in social networks for them in everyday life or even providing the ability to create an intelligent death-mask for after-life presence online.

In the world that we are approaching and anticipating, each human will manage its environment and get exposed to it with help of such an agent. This self-learning friend and servant would be capable to deliver information of the world and functions of the surrounding things and to act upon them - *serving each user, communities of people and entire humanity.*

3   Major Features

There are several key features, design decisions and implementation options that are assumed being critical for reaching the goals posed above.

Adaptive experiential learning [4], with different reinforcement techniques such as self-reinforced (unsupervised learning), explicit user feedback (supervised learning) and implicit user feedback (self-reinforced on the basis of goals posed by a user or user profile captured to anticipate imagery feedback from them).

Ubiquitous availability, having agent software available for all computational platforms and being able to communicate across any communication channels, as displayed on Fig.1. We achieve this with 100.

Ontological extensibility, having very little footprint of the foundation ontology hardcoded at the system initiation level, so that most of the knowledge and capabilities of an agent are learned in the course of interactions with the environment including the user (acting as a teacher). That is, the ultimate end goal for the project is to make it possible to pass the baby Turing test [7] eventually. The idea is to either enable the user to construct extensions to agent's ontology manually, or let the agent build it on its own as part of experiential learning with possibility to correct the emerged agent's belief from the user side, if needed.

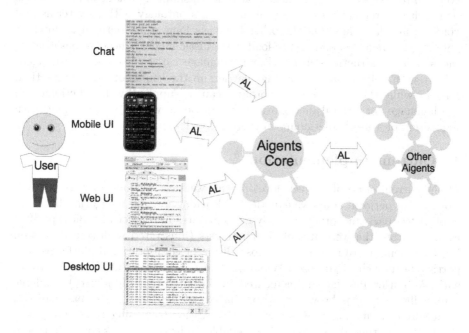

Fig. 1. Overall architecture of Aigents software platform with different kinds of Aigents User Interface (UI) interacting with the Aigents Core in the same way as different Aigents interact one with another.

Unified symbolic and subsymbolic reasoning [6], incorporating classic symbolic approaches (for instance, when text patterns are being detected in the text) and associative subsymbolic techniques (say to assign of a fact or an object to some category [8]). This is being done so that while the backbone ontology data is symbolic, the rational truth value of each portion of the data could be evaluated based on statistical evidence of the data in a given context.

Distributed intelligence, having all basic intelligent functions either implemented locally within the agent itself, or accessible within the peer-to-peer community of agents sharing knowledge and functional abilities within the community. Having an option for local execution of such intelligent tasks as processing natural language text, speech and imagery information may be critical for many geographical markets without reliable high-bandwidth Internet coverage.

Social collaboration is assumed to be the way to evaluate statistically confident and context-specific truth values for subsymbolic reasoning within a social evidence-based knowledge representation model [9] with account to information experienced by different users and agents. This is also critical for rapidly spreading the acquired knowledge and skills within distributed communities of users who own such agents and let them get connected to one another.

Linguistic unification is based on simplification of the linguistic model down to the "foundation ontology" of a "newborn" agent [1]. On the one hand, it is expected to give users enough flexibility to learn simple textual communications along with incremental extension of an agent's ontology with new terms and words in any language. On the other hand, as long as no permanent internet connection is required and no pre-loaded linguistic model is needed, basic words and simple constructions in any Earth language can be learned by the agent quickly with help of native language carriers in the course of their interaction. That is, while the original agent ontology can be supplied with a dictionary in one language (or several dictionaries), it can be grown up further along with acquisition of a user's dictionary in their native language.

4   Current Implementation

At the current state of project development, we have Aigents software created. Now, it can perform adaptive experiential learning for web navigation based on implicit feedback and provide timely news updates in respect to topics specified by users, from the web sites of their interests (illustrated with screenshots on Fig.1). Aigents Core is available across all major computational platforms supporting Java (such as Microsoft Windows, Linux, Macintosh/OSX and Android), with Web user interface implemented in JavaScript (with jQuery) available across different Web browsers. Also, chat-style interface to Aigents core can be accessed by email as well as raw TCP/IP session (say using Telnet program). While the existing Web version is accessible at http://aigents.com/, it is also publicly available for hosting under any other domain with a similar or altered user interface.

The agent architecture (Fig. 2) could be described as a set of processes reflecting communications with the external world and agent's modes plus dedicated components for handling AL messages, web sites, session contexts and data persistence.

There are processes bound to the agent's self, extending the basic Selfer process, implementing respective self modes (Fig.3). Further, there are processes to run in the context of Selfer, implementing user modes, extending the basic Conversationer process. Finally, there are processes in the context of Selfer, to deal with communications, extending the basic Communicator process, such as Cmdliner, Emailer, SMSer, TCPer and HTTPer implementing respective communication channels and protocols. There is also Siter component holding a cache of the page data indexed by site URLs and their time stamps.

In order to parse AL inputs and generate AL outputs there are respective Reader and Writer components translating data flow from Communicator to

Conversationer and back. To perform proper contextual disambiguation these components are referring to Storager component providing the content to get the actual belief ontology data and to Sessioner component to adjust communication to the context of a specific agent's user.

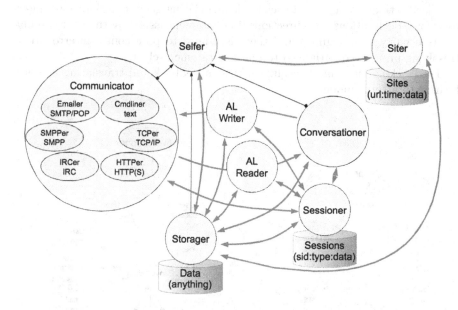

Fig. 2. Internal architecture of Aigents software platform.

In the current implementation, Storager keeps all information in proprietary in-memory database structure efficient enough to deal with personal-wide data assets without input-output overhead associated with conventional databases (as discussed in [8]). The internal Java design, however, enables to plug scalable graph databases in order to support deployments dealing with corporation-wide amounts of data.

The basic Selfer and Conversationer processes are extended with modes performing more specific operations described below:

Interrogation, Confirmation, Declaration, Direction these user modes correspond to handling one of the four Agent Languages statements respectively.

Login, Registration, Verification, Logout user modes implementing authentication functionality, so that an authenticated context of further conversation can be established by completing either Login or Registration procedure (where Verification is used to confirm Registration) and then the context can be cleaned up by Logout at the end. Authentication workflow can potentially be executed on both sides of each communication peers establishing mutual authentication so that not only the server is certain that it serves the correct client, but the client is also certain that it is connected to the correct server. The purpose is to isolate the properties belonging to a user in an agent's belief and also assure the communication is established to the correct peer agent.

Email Change, Verification Change these user modes are specific forms of Declaration augmented with extra confirmations via email or SMS with special confirmation codes.

Clarification it is a special user mode associating generic declarations, interrogations, declarations and directions if a statement issued by the peer communication party is ambiguous and there is a need to pose contra-interrogations (resolving unresolved variables) to make a statement clear.

Feedback is a user mode evaluating user's feedback and translating it to self Learning Patterns mode.

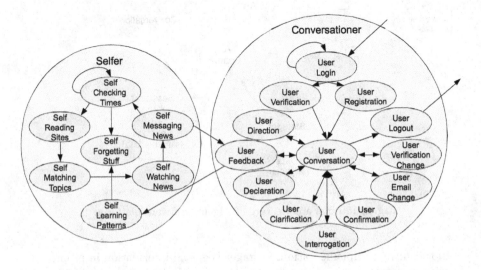

Fig. 3. Processes implementing modes specific to operations of Aigents self and users connected to it or associated with it.

Conversation is a centric user mode recognizing conversational text patterns from the perspective of a current user context, dispatching the control flow to the appropriate mode and then getting the control back with an updated context. In a simple form is it a matter of recognizing respective AL statements but in reality it is also a matter of using special patterns indicative to other modes. The patterns are expected to be the same textual patterns discussed earlier as part of agent belief associated with things and sites, and they also can be expressed in AL syntax as an expression or a set (disjunctive, conjunctive or successive) of expressions. It is also possible to apply fuzzy pattern matching in the cases when no applicable straight matches are found to handle the conversational context.

Checking Times is a basic self mode periodically checking time for performing updates of sites as specified by users, and initiating a news update cycle starting with the Reading Sites mode.

Reading Sites is a self mode reading structured texts (pages, blocks, columns, paragraphs, utterances) from the sites specified as news origins by a user, and passing the read data further to the Matching Topics mode.

Matching Topics is a self mode matching users patterns from texts read from sites, and passing the found topics of user's interest to the Watching News mode.

Watching News is a self mode tracking historical backlog of the topics matched on sites and catching any novel and salient information appeared, passing the news to the Messaging News mode.

Messaging News is a self mode dispatching news to the users watching corresponding topics (indicating the time, site, actual thing indicated by topic and respective text pattern framing it) and then returning the execution control back to the Checking Times mode.

Learning Patterns is a self mode triggered by user's Feedback mode so topics with a positive or negative feedback can be used to learn or dismiss the patterns associated with them on the origin sites.

Forgetting Stuff this self mode is triggered periodically by Checking Times or occasionally by Learning Patterns in order to compress the belief data operated by an agent. Primarily, this would involve keeping a restricted subset of the data representing the agent's "attention focus" in the local cache (i.e. "short term memory" or STM), given the amount of the available operating memory and pushing currently unnecessary data to persistent storage (i.e. long term memory or LTM). Further, this would deal with getting rid of irrelevant data or data of low importance and confidence ("garbage collection") moving it out of the persistent LTM.

5   Conclusion and Future Work

At the moment, based on the results of ongoing usability testing for the last 9 months, Web and Android versions of Aigents provide timely and reliable updates on the topics of users' interests, not requiring users to actually visit the target web sites (unless there is a need to drill into the topic details). Importantly, it works well even on mobile devices consuming reasonable amount of computational resources so it does not noticeably affect device energy consumption.

Our current and immediate future work is directed towards getting more intelligent implicit feedback from users inferring their needs from their search and browse histories as well as enabling peer-to-peer communications between agents owned by users with established social connections.

Further research is to be conducted to apply experiential learning techniques to the user's intent and sentiment in respect to agent's actions relying on user voice and gestures. The other direction of development would include building or incorporating domain ontologies for particular segments of Internet of Things so that either a personal agent would interact, for example, with home and other appliances or such appliances would rather get the agent core incorporated to enable intelligent communication with the home owner.

At the same time, further development of the discussed technology implies increased importance of security and privacy in respect to personal features of a user learned and captured of an intelligent agents, which requires implementations of peer-to-peer mutual trust policies manageable by users and mechanisms for protecting users' profiles and intellectual property within a distributed system.

References

1. Kolonin, A.: Intelligent Agent for Web Watching: Language and Belief System. Aigents Group (2014). http://aigents.com/papers/2014AgentBeliefKolonin.pdf
2. Griffiths, M.D., Gray, F.: The rise of the Tamagotchi: An issue for educational psychology? BPS Division of Educational and Child Psychology Newsletter **82**, 37–40 (1998)
3. Maheswaran, R.T., Tambe, M., Varakantham, P., Myers, K.: Adjustable autonomy challenges in personal assistant agents: a position paper. In: Nickles, M., Rovatsos, M., Weiss, G. (eds.) AUTONOMY 2003. LNCS (LNAI), vol. 2969, pp. 187–194. Springer, Heidelberg (2004)
4. Goertzel, B.: Creating Internet Intelligence: Wild Computing, Distributed Digital Consciousnes, and the Emerging Global Brain, p. 330. Springer Science & Business Media, Computers (2002)
5. Tramp, S., Frischmuth, P., Ermilov, T., Shekarpour, S., Auer, S.: An architecture of a distributed semantic social network. Semantic Web, 77–95 (2014)
6. Goertzel, B.: Perception processing for general intelligence: bridging the symbolic/subsymbolic gap. In: Bach, J., Goertzel, B., Iklé, M. (eds.) AGI 2012. LNCS, vol. 7716, pp. 79–88. Springer, Heidelberg (2012)
7. Partee, B., et al.: Report of Workshop on Information and Representation, Washington, DC (1985). http://files.eric.ed.gov/fulltext/ED261533.pdf
8. Kolonin, A.: High-performance automatic categorization and attribution of inventory catalogs. In: Proceedings of All-Russia conference Knowledge Ontology Theories (KONT-2013), Novosibirsk, Russia (2013). http://www.webstructor.net/papers/Kolonin-HP-ACA-IC-text.pdf
9. Kolonin, A.: Distributed knowledge engineering. Siberian Forum of the industry of information systems, Novosibirsk (2013). http://www.webstructor.net/news/20130510

Distributed Knowledge Engineering and Evidence-Based Knowledge Representation in Multi-agent Systems

Anton Kolonin[✉]

Aigents Group, Pravdy 6/12, 630090 Novosibirsk, Russia Federation
akolonin@gmail.com
http://aigents.com/

Abstract. The paper describes an architecture of multi-agent distributed knowledge management, its prototype implementation using semantic technologies, and presents a model of structured knowledge representation in such a system. The cognitive aspects of the architecture enables collaborative knowledge engineering in social environments.

Keywords: Cognitive architecture · Belief · Knowledge engineering · Knowledge graph · Knowledge management · Multi-agent system · Ontology · Peer-to-peer · Semantic web · Social collaboration · Software agents

1 Introduction: From Centralized Knowledge Engineering to Distributed Model

Nowadays, the most representative implementations of the Semantic Web vision [1] are supplied by the top Internet content providers such as Google with its Knowledge Graph (Knowledge Vault) [2]. From the perspective of our earlier work [3], it can be classified as *centralized knowledge globalization*, with all semantic information physically contained within a proprietary semantic database owned by a *knowledge aggregator*. In such a model, an access to it can be granted by means of non-intelligent clients connected to an "intelligent" server. The vast majority of internal *knowledge* and hence cognitive capabilities of a system reside inside the perimeter of a corporate data center, even if some tiny fraction of it can be offloaded to a public domain (such as Wikidata) or a particular user (in respect to their personal data). It is also implicit that the knowledge aggregator takes responsibility to maintain the truth value of any piece of knowledge in respect to any event or fact in the outer world.

The alternative model is denoted as *decentralized (distributed) knowledge globalization* [3,4], which assumes the knowledge is semi-evenly distributed across the entire global computational network. This also implies possibility of dynamic redistribution (and possible redundancy) of the knowledge itself, as well as distribution of the points of it processing across a peer-to-peer network, where

© Springer International Publishing Switzerland 2015
P. Klinov and D. Mouromtsev (Eds.): KESW 2015, CCIS 518, pp. 291–300, 2015.
DOI: 10.1007/978-3-319-24543-0_23

different nodes may belong to different owners. The *truth value* of a piece of knowledge turns to be *dynamic* and rather *subjective* specific to agents holding a particular segment of the entire knowledge network, as it was originally invented [1] and fits ideally the emerging "Internet of Things" (IoT) [5]. Motivation and argumentation for developing this model was properly covered earlier, along with description of a distributed semantic version of a social network [4]; herein we discuss a more generic approach to maintenance of distributed semantic knowledge in general and describe our development of a system serving this purpose.

2   Principal Goals: Distributed Knowledge Engineering

For a distributed knowledge engineering environment to emerge in multi-agent software systems, we anticipate it should follow the patterns of social self-organization in human societies. Evolution of distributed computational intelligence is possible as co-evolution with collaborative intelligence of human society. That calls for emergence of a society of computational agents with the following requirements.

There is a need for rich *historical memory* shared by communicating computer agents (e.g. accessible public banks of information available for mutual sharing). It is needed to maintain an open space of semantic graphs which can be formed by means of sharing (donating) the personal semantic graphs by private agents, when each sharing or donation act contains information authored by an agent itself or delegated to an agent for re-distribution and it is considered non-confidential.

Each computer agent should have an *ability to explicitly expose its own knowledge* indicating confidence, proprietary rights and privacy (share-ability in respect to other agents) of it. They also have a right to retain intellectual property on the knowledge they contribute and specify the privacy levels of it so it can be either accessible by peer agent only or forwarded to another agent.

There is a requirement for rich *sensory environment* and accessible *means of gathering novel information*, driving the communication end and enabling development of adaptive intelligent behavior (e.g. search, browsing and messaging against peer computer agents). In order to benefit human users, agents should be capable of adaptive intelligent behaviors finding new patterns and creating new knowledge in multi-factor and dynamically changing environments.

Fertility of diverse behavioral patterns (i.e. computational algorithms) exposed by agents (capable of evolving upon feedback from peer agents) is expected. This is not that much a requirement but more an expected beneficial outcome from the other requirements, assuming agents are equipped with adaptive learning algorithms.

To enable *peer-to-peer communication* in the environment involving multiple agents as well as people, we need a *unified language* based on the common basic ontology. That means not just syntax of declarative descriptions for data sets or imperative programmatic instructions but a whole range of means to convey the meaning of states, intents and inquiries of communicating agents, based on a common "belief system", in syntax, easily parsable by software and comprehensible to humans at the same time. Semantic architecture of a language, regardless of its syntactical representation, be it RDF, Turtle, SPARQL, JSON-LD, Lisp or ORL [6–9] or a combination of these, should support a wide range of communication paradigms.

The latter language should also provide capabilities such as *fuzzy-ness, subjectivity and partial comprehension*. *Fuzzy-ness* implies the need to maintain both truth value and confidence level of an assertion, being able to calculate dynamic truth value of an assertion in different inference contexts (with the process of merging congruent assertions supplied with evidence from different communication subjects and amount of confidence specific to the context). *Subjectivity* means that certain assertions can be treated useful only in the context of a particular belief system but not in others (say Google Knowledge Graph's belief may be somewhat different from same of someone else's). It signifies that there is a need to express this belief-owner-specific knowledge in the communication. *Partial comprehension* requirement suggests that any complex message from one agent to another may be only partially comprehended, to the extent the mental models and ontological beliefs of a sender and a receiver overlap, while the remainder of the message can be ignored.

3   Architectural Approach: Multiple Agent Roles and Configurations

Overall architecture implementing the above-suggested environment can be drawn with the following scheme, involving various agents playing a typical role or a combination of several such roles.

Within the suggested architecture, *storage agents* provide distributed (and likely redundant) storage of structured information while *collector agents* perform information gathering from unstructured media (such as text files, web pages, raw video, audio, scanned paper hardcopy materials, etc.) as well as getting input signals from the outer world (using input devices such as thermometers, motion sensors, microphones, camcorders, etc.). *User agents* establish forward and backward communications with users and operators while *broker agents* serve routing of the messages between all other agents (e.g. implementing topologies such as *cloud storage* and *federated search*). Finally, actor agents can direct actions towards the surrounding social and physical environments (publishing web pages, sending emails and messages, authoring files or activating devices in the physical world).

Different types of agents (Fig. 1) are typical roles rather than narrow specializations, i.e. the same physical instance of an agent can play different roles simultaneously. At the same time, given specific storage and performance capabilities and connectivity graphs, various topologies can be formed (either by manual configuration or adaptive emergence). For instance, a broker agent plus a set of storage agents implement cloud storage. A broker agent with sets of collector agents and user agents managed by user agents form a *search engine* with *crawler service*. In turn, a set of user agents associated with broker agents form *social network*. Finally, all systems mentioned above can be integrated into a meta-system (such as *federated search* or *distributed crowdsourcing* platform) with help of broker agents with a broad specialization.

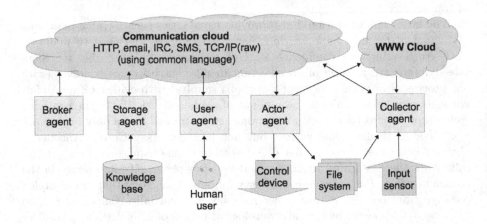

Fig. 1. Roles of distributed intelligence agents.

In order to actualize the possibility described above, there seems to be a demand to agree on an *open communication standard* for agents of emerging computational intelligence, adopted by the involved players. That standard would include specification of interfaces the intelligent agents would support as well as the language to be used for communication among them with the two basic functions: 1) *Output*: Return requested (by search or browse) knowledge primarily to be implemented by public agents (such as semantic search engines) or adapters to them, but also may be supported by any other large and small, corporate and personal agents which could want to contribute to the semantic search space; 2) *Input*: Accept a piece of knowledge distributed by a peer agent with an option to either reject the input (if does not fit an agent's preferences, i.e. its internal belief system) or incorporate it into the belief system with account to the appropriate copyright and privacy constraints. Both interfaces would have synchronous as well as asynchronous versions so that the *Output* may be either given in respect to a synchronous query, or it may be provided asynchronously upon prior subscription. Respectively, the *Input* can take the form of a channel to accepts the data feed as well as a place to subscribe for content to be delivered to a subscriber.

4   Knowledge Representation: Evidence-Based Social Model

Given any agent talk to any other using the same communication language, internal design, the implemented algorithms and programming language of an agent do not matter that much. In order to communicate, however, agents are implied to have some jointly shared system of fundamental knowledge (some belief system) regarding the surrounding world and themselves. They should also have a mechanism for either accepting the knowledge coming to an agent from its outer world (if it is compatible with the agent's belief system), or rejecting it (in the opposite case). Further, for different sorts of accepted knowledge, an agent should be able to make judgments on reliability of different facts, which can be done based on the amount of evidence associated with these facts. Each evidence is considered in terms of trust towards its source. Here we come to the *social evidence-based knowledge representation model.*

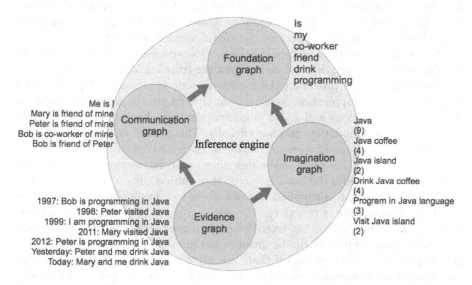

Fig. 2. Specialized subgraphs of the agent knowledge base and the dynamic truth value calculation in the social evidence-based knowledge representation model.

With massively distributed data processing and many-to-many style replication, synchronization of concurrent changes (especially, such as updates and deletes) become a big problem. For instance, if agent A communicates fact P to agent B while B communicates fact Q to A, there is just a counter addition of information to each of the agent's knowledge bases. However, there is a typical scenario where agents argue about something, making conflicting changes to the same data. For instance, agent A tells there are relationships X and Y between P and Q, while agent B argues there is Y and Z but not X who is to be trusted in such case Obviously, both can agree on presence of Y, while X remains as a personal belief of A and B keeps believing in Z. That is, assuming part of the message can be accepted and the reminder can be declined, it can be possible to make each of the agents more knowledgeable in the course of communication, yet not having to destroy the belief system of each of them.

Within the social evidence-based knowledge representation model, *truth value* of any piece of information can be calculated as a sum truth value of its evidence records communicated by peer agents multiplied by the trust levels for each of these peer agents. To achieve this, the entire semantic hyper-graph representing knowledge of an agent can be split in four major sub-graphs (Fig. 2).

The *foundation graph* layer is the cognitive cornerstone for each of the agents. Without that, two agents speaking the same language syntactically would not understand each other if their foundation graphs differ significantly. It is assumed that a foundation graph does not need any fuzzy inference applied to it and there may be some special rules (specific to each agent design) as to how that part of the knowledge is formed. The most favorable approach is to have portions of the imagination graph (discussed further) exceeding the given thresholds of evidence to be hardwired to the foundation graph. Reasoning on this part of knowledge might be called *orthodox*, *stereotypic* or *closed-minded* thinking.

The *imagination graph* is a pool of novel evidence-based knowledge coming to an agent via communication channels. Given the trust levels specific to particular communication peers providing the inputs, as well as amounts of positive and negative evidence supplied for assertions in this graph, the agent is capable to draw its own assertions and either communicate them back to the outer world or upload to the foundation graph eventually. This part of an agent's brain can be considered as *dynamic*, *non-stereotypic* or *open-minded* core.

The *communication graph* layer describes social interaction channels of an agent and also provides the basis for account of subjectivity, so that each fact in the imagination graph is supplied by trust given to a particular communication agent at a time. This is effectively the *social core*, or *personal social network* of an agent, maintaining trust levels for each of peer agents in two dimensions. First how much confidence can be given to incoming information communicated by the peer, in general. Second if there are any confidential restrictions implied for information communicated to the peer for instance, for private knowledge only, or for public share, etc.

The *evidence graph* effectively records temporal facts of evidence exposed by peer agents from communication graph to draw cumulative assertions in imagination graph on that basis. This pool of facts serves as an evidence base for the inference engine calculating the *truth values* with account to subjective grounds as well as with temporal analysis capabilities. Each piece of information here is timestamped and labeled by a peer communicating it. Data stored here can be subject of *evidence compression* with either clustering of fractional time slices into larger time intervals or aggregating evidences from individual peers into larger groups of peers. Further, *evidence can be forgotten*, with either transition of knowledge (derived from the evidence) from the imagination graph to the foundation graph or its complete removal if no supporting evidence was found for a long time (*evidential garbage collection*). The major drives for the forgetting process are physical resources constrains (so the system assures the amounts of all data fit the existing memory) and the basic goal to maintain the most reliable knowledge fitting the system's internal belief to a greater extent.

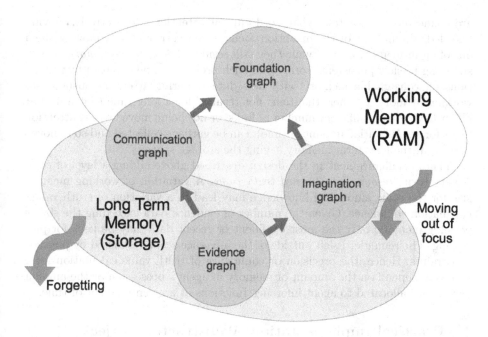

Fig. 3. Specifics of implementing the agent's subgraphs residing in different kinds of memory within the cognitive architecture.

The knowledge representation outlined above leads to possible technical implementation architecture, to a certain extent inspired by OpenCog [10]. The major specific feature of the architecture is support for the social evidence-based knowledge representation model, taking on board practical considerations of physical memory capacity in modern computing devices and the requirements for reasonable response times and energy consumption for end-user devices such as personal computers, tablets and smartphones.

The architecture needs to address the following problem. On the one hand, the graph-based operations are very sensitive to input/output performance if executed with traditional relational or object-oriented databases especially with highly-connected graphs. So the optimal implementation would rely on in-memory operations on graphs, as proved earlier by experiments and implementation of a trainable text classification and attribution system [11]. However, the call for the evidence-based knowledge representation model implies the need for a tremendous amount of linked data to get involved which makes the problem harder.

The trade-off described above would get solved with mechanisms of moving knowledge items in-focus and out-of-focus and forgetting the irrelevant and outdated knowledge aligned with the existing hardware constraints (Fig. 3). That is, we assume that the foundation graph as well as most of (if not all) communication graphs and imagination graphs reside in RAM corresponding to *"working memory"* of human brain at least, as long as parts of the entire graph are connected to any items that need current attention. Respectively, moving knowledge items out of the attention focus would correspond to moving them out of an in-memory cache (while they still reside in *"long term memory"* corresponding to slow persistent storage), or such process can be enforced by restrictions on consumable memory with new data requiring attention pushed into working memory. Further, the items not recalled for a long time (not linked at all, or having an insufficient number of links, or not being moved to the attention focus for a substantial amount of time), can be garbage collected and so removed even from the long term memory saving the storage space.

There is enhancement to the design described above adding a level of complexity to it: *resource-constrained truth value*. A variation of working memory size for the same amount of knowledge may lead to a variation of truth values calculation confidence. Given the number of evidence data exceeding the size of working memory, only the most confident or recent data may be kept for processing. The reminder is left outside of the inference scope restricted by physical constraints. Hence, the precision or confidence of truth value calculation for a fact may depend on the amount of memory in agent's possession or the amount of memory allocated to agent inference functions at a given moment of time.

5   Practical Implementation: Webstructor Project

Based on the requirements, Webstructor project[1] has been under ongoing development since 1995. In 1995–1996, *semantic graph* was employed to describe domain ontologies and operational spaces of systems carrying out data management, inter-personal interactions, interactive form processing, report generation and action script development. On this basis, a respective software platform was created and used to draw wide range of applications including personal diary, time management, business accounting, inventory/sales automation, customer relationship management and others. A system drawback was poor run-time performance, given full normalization of any data and executable code down to nodes and links of a semantic graph stored in a relational database.

In 1997–1999, based on a similar semantic graph model, *object-relational language* (ORL) [9] for inter-agent communication was developed to enable creating a corporate business automation system for the stock exchange domain. It was used to describe the whole application domain including data model, entry forms, reports and all business rules and functions, and create an operable business application.

In 2001, the *agent software for peer-to-peer* knowledge creation and interchange was created as part of the Webstructor project. The computational agents were developed to operate as web server-side Servlets, browser-side Applets or standalone Applications, exchanging the knowledge in many-to-many fashion encoded in ORL statements, with user interfaces capable to browse, search and maintain the knowledge visually in forms of graphs or an interactive ORL console (so the same language was made usable by humans).The gateway between

---

[1] http://www.webstructor.net/

ORL and Lisp was developed and the entire Open Cyc ontology was uploaded to the Webstructor agent system.

In 2006, the Webstructor semantic engine was employed to build a system for 3D visualization, navigation and sharing of complex scientific data. Within the distributed agent system, it enabled visualization, navigation and amendment of virtual object properties in a hyperspace in a collaborative peer-to-peer network.

The existing Webstructor implementation model is simplified, so that only the fundamental graph and the communication graph are present. It implies a *full trust* for agent's interactions assuming any data involved in exchange are an *absolute truth*. There are three different types of agents present in Webstructor. Servlet agent runs on the Web server and performs the broker and storage roles. It serves multiple Applets and Servers over HTTP protocol passing information through between agents and providing intermediate storage at the same time. Applet agent runs in the web browser and provides user access to the whole system. Server agent simultaneously plays the roles of storage, broker and user, so it can be employed to create full-blown distributed peer-to-peer networks.

Two practical applications are present: a visual ontology editor and a spatial data visualization system, both enabling peer-to-peer knowledge sharing. The visual ontology editor provides capabilities to edit various graphs with options to associate vertices with web resources, colors, shapes and image information. This can be used to edit hierarchical graphs as well as recurrent networks. There is also a possibility to create higher-order networks suitable to express logical formulae, for instance. Besides handling input and output data in ORL format, the same content can be imported from CycL language. In addition to graphical editing capabilities, the application provides an interactive console which can be used to manipulate knowledge by means of ORL language.

6 Conclusion: Opportunities and Challenges

On the practical side, assuming industry agreement on an *open cross-platform multi-agent communication protocol (language)*, there is a possibility for a *distributed computational intelligence agent software* to run on every smartphone and personal computer. The software would look like a personal knowledge management assistant, capable to create knowledge content (i.e. authoring things and their properties), establish communications with other agents (as a "knowledge consumer" or as a "knowledge provider" or in both roles) and implement a "distributed knowledge storage cell" role for the entire agent system.

Within the same inter-agent communication infrastructure, application patterns such as a *distributed storage, social network, federated search* and others can be constructed by users upon the need dynamically or emerged on run-time in the course of operations. The topology of the communication graph can be an emergent structure and a part of the entire distributed system knowledge rather than a rigid pre-defined schema.

There are two major problems to be addressed. Primarily, it is essential to develop efficient *technology for dynamic truth value determination* based on context-specific knowledge sets (contextual subgraphs), incorporating multiple contextual restrictions such as participants of the conversation or temporal interval of the problem being explored. Secondarily, it is necessary to come up with a well-understood and accepted procedure (bound to an open protocol employed by community) which would enable *merging knowledge sets* of one agent conveyed to another, accounting for fuzziness, preserving subjectivity, with possibility of partial comprehension.

References

1. Berners-Lee, T., Fischetti, M.: Weaving the Web : The Original Design and Ultimate Destiny of the World Wide Web by its Inventor. Harper San Francisco (1999)
2. Dong, X., Gabrilovich, E., Heitz, G., Horn, W., Lao, N., Murphy, K., Strohmann, T., Sun, S., Zhang, W.: Knowledge vault: a web-scale approach to probabilistic knowledge fusion. In: SIGKDD (2014)
3. Kolonin, A.: The emerging world wide mind. In: Artificial General Intelligence Conference, Beijing (2013). http://www.webstructor.net/news/20130801/
4. Tramp, S., Frischmuth, P., Ermilov, T., Shekarpour, S., Auer, S.: An architecture of a distributed semantic social network. Semantic Web, 77–95 (2014)
5. Gubbi, J., Buyya, R., Marusic, S., Palaniswami, M.: Internet of Things (IoT): A vision, architectural elements, and future directions. Future Generation Computer Systems **29** (2013)
6. Decker, S., Melnik, S., Van Harmelen, F., Fensel, D., Klein, M., Broekstra, J., Erdmann, M., Horrocks, I.: The Semantic Web: The roles of XML and RDF. IEEE Internet Computing **15**(3), 63–74 (2000)
7. World Wide Web Consortium: Turtle Terse RDF Triple Language (2012)
8. Lanthaler, M., Gtl, C.: On using JSON-LD to create evolvable RESTful services. In: Proceedings of the 3rd International Workshop on RESTful Design (WS-REST 2012) at WWW 2012 (2012)
9. Kolonin, A.: Object-relational language and modern tradeoffs in software technology. In: International Andrei Ershov Memorial Conference, PSI 2006, Program Understanding Workshop, Russia (2006). http://webstructor.net/docs/orl/
10. Goertzel, B., Duong, D.: OpenCog NS: A deeply-interactive hybrid neural-symbolic cognitive architecture designed for global/local memory synergy. In: Biologically Inspired Cognitive Architectures II: Papers from the AAAI Fall Symposium (FS-09-01) (2009)
11. Kolonin, A.: High-performance automatic categorization and attribution of inventory catalogs. In: Proceedings of All-Russia Conference Knowledge Ontology Theories (KONT-2013), Novosibirsk, Russia (2013). http://www.webstructor.net/papers/Kolonin-HP-ACA-IC-text.pdf

Author Index

Alves, Miguel B.   243, 253, 263
Andreev, Alexey   102
Andronikou, Vassiliki   32
Artemova, Galina   3
Auer, Sören   48, 182, 210
Avdeeva, Natalia   3

Boyarsky, Kirill   3
Bretschneider, Claudia   16

Chondrogiannis, Efthymios   32
Correia, Nuno   243, 253, 263

Damásio, Carlos Viegas   243, 253, 263
Decker, Stefan   72
Dobrenko, Natalia V.   3, 63

Ermilov, Ivan   182

Galkin, Mikhail   48
Garayzuev, Daniil   102
Gizdatullin, Danil   225
Grozin, Vladislav A.   63
Gusarova, Natalia F.   3, 63

Hasnain, Ali   72

Ignatov, Dmitry I.   225

Kanevsky, Eugeny   3
Karanastasis, Efstathios   32
Kashevnik, Alexey   117
Khegai, Maksim   273
Klimov, Nikolay   102
Kogalovsky, M.R.   87
Kogalovsky, Mikhail   147
Kolchin, Maxim   102
Kolonin, Anton   283, 291
Koshelnikov, Sergey   158
Křemen, Petr   132

Lange, Christoph   210
Lashkov, Igor   117
Ledvinka, Martin   132
Lyapunov, Victor   147

Maiatin, Alexandr   273
Maysuradze, Archil   168, 195
Mehmood, Qaiser   72
Mitrofanova, Ekaterina   225
Mouromtsev, Dmitry   48, 102
Muratova, Anna   225

Oberkampf, Heiner   16

Papshev, Sergey   182
Parfenov, Vladimir   117
Parinov, S.I.   87
Parinov, Sergey   147
Puzyrev, Roman   147

Rubtsova, Yuliya   158

Saburova, Maria   168
Salin, Vladimir   182
Sana e Zainab, Syeda   72
Senderovich, Nikita   195
Shilin, Ivan   102
Slastihina, Maria   182
Smirnov, Alexander   117
Speck, René   182

Tarasowa, Darya   210

Varvarigou, Theodora   32

Zakoldaev, Danil   102
Zillner, Sonja   16
Zubok, Dmitrii   273

Printed in the United States
by Bookmasters

Printed in the United States
By Bookmasters